Reading and politics in early modern England

MANCHESTER 1824

Manchester University Press

Politics, culture and society in early modern Britain

General Editors

PROFESSOR ANN HUGHES
PROFESSOR ANTHONY MILTON
PROFESSOR PETER LAKE

This important series publishes monographs that take a fresh and challenging look at the interactions between politics, culture and society in Britain between 1500 and the mid-eighteenth century. It counteracts the fragmentation of current historiography through encouraging a variety of approaches which attempt to redefine the political, social and cultural worlds, and to explore their interconnection in a flexible and creative fashion. All the volumes in the series question and transcend traditional interdisciplinary boundaries, such as those between political history and literary studies, social history and divinity, urban history and anthropology. They thus contribute to a broader understanding of crucial developments in early modern Britain.

Reading and politics in early modern England

The mental world of a seventeenth-century Catholic gentleman

GEOFF BAKER

Manchester
University Press
Manchester and New York

distributed exclusively in the USA by Palgrave Macmillan

Published by Manchester University Press
Oxford Road, Manchester M13 9NR, UK
and Room 400, 175 Fifth Avenue, New York, NY 10010, USA
www.manchesteruniversitypress.co.uk

Distributed in the United States exclusively by
Palgrave Macmillan, 175 Fifth Avenue,
New York, NY 10010, USA

Distributed in Canada exclusively by
UBC Press, University of British Columbia, 2029 West Mall,
Vancouver, BC, Canada V6T 1Z2

British Library Cataloguing-in-Publication Data is available

Library of Congress Cataloging-in-Publication Data is available

ISBN 978 0 7190 9124 7 paperback

First published by Manchester University Press in hardback 2010

This paperback edition first published 2013

Printed by Lightning Source

For Clare

Contents

Acknowledgements

Completion of this book has been made possible by an AHRC doctoral award, as well as support for research trips from Keele University and short-term research fellowships from the Folger Shakespeare Institute and the Henry E. Huntington Library.

My greatest debt is to Ann Hughes. This project began life as a PhD thesis that Ann supervised, following which, as one of the editors of the monograph series in which this volume appears, she continued to provide insightful comments. Working with Ann has been a thoroughly positive experience (at least for me) and what material of value appears in these pages could not have been completed were it not for her expert guidance. The time and effort Ann has put into developing this project and the writer has gone far beyond the call of duty and I am for ever indebted to her.

While working on this book I have been fortunate to have illuminating discussions and/or been given access to vital materials by the following: Susannah Abbott, David Appleby, Bill Bulman, Richard Cust, Alan Ford, Gabriel Glickman, Andrew Gritt, Christopher Harrison, John Langton, Ann McGruer, Gary Mills, Philip Morgan, Geoffrey Scott, Jonathan Scott, and Maurice Whitehead. Peter Lake first suggested late seventeenth-century Catholicism as a research topic and invited me to present a paper on the subject at Princeton University. Kevin Sharpe and Jim McLaverty examined the thesis upon which this book is based and offered valuable comments about developing it for publication. Ian Atherton has fielded countless questions about early modern religious history with characteristic good humour and provided vital support. Throughout the completion of this project Michael Questier has been unfailingly generous, offering discussion and access to unpublished material, which has informed many of the arguments developed here. Finally, the Centre for Integrative Learning in the University of Nottingham has been a refuge during much of my work on this project, and I am particularly grateful for the support of the senior leadership team: Maggie Ambrose, Martin Binks, Alan Booth and Angela Smallwood.

The staff at all of the Record Offices that I have used have been very helpful, with specific individuals thanked in the footnotes. Staff at Lancashire County Record Office in Preston deserve particular mention. Neil Sayer, Mark Walmsley, Anna Watson, Marie Moss and Ann Hickey were both generous with their support and knowledgeable about the archives. Mark Blundell and Brian Whitlock-Blundell have been enthusiastic about my work and generously provided access to the Blundell archives used in this study.

Sections of the first part of this book appeared in an earlier form in 'William Blundell and late seventeenth century English Catholicism', *Northern History*, 45

(2008), pp. 259–77. I am grateful to Maney Press for permission to republish this material.

I am fortunate to have a supportive family and I must thank my mum Demelza, my dad David, my grandma Sylvia, my sister Ruth and her partner Gareth, my mother-in-law Maureen and my sister-in-law Sally for listening to me moan about William Blundell. The arrival of my nephews Rhys and Little Geoff provided light relief from my studies, and while too young to appreciate the subtle nuances of early modern Catholic history they have hours of such discussion awaiting them.

This book is, of course, dedicated to my partner Clare. She has listened to countless drafts and offered companionship throughout a trying time. The first two questions she is always asked when people find out how long we have been together is 'how?' and 'why?' – I am equally perplexed, but as I am the one reaping the benefits I try not to ask too many questions.

List of abbreviations

Titles of books, articles and chapters have been cited in full in the first instance and abbreviated thereafter. For the main manuscript sources on which this study is based, as well as institutions regularly referred to, the following abbreviations apply. Note that descriptions of Blundell's papers are those used by Lancashire County Record Office.

Account of Jacobite Trial Lancashire County Record Office, DDBl acc. 6121, Box 3, Account of the Jacobite Trial, 1694, copied by Nicholas Blundell
Adversaria Lancashire County Record Office, DDBl acc. 6121, Box 4, Adversaria
Blue Book Lancashire County Record Office, DDBl acc. 6121, Box 2, Blue Book
Blundell (ed.), *Cavalier: Letters* M. Blundell (ed.), *Cavalier: Letters of William Blundell to his Friends, 1620–1698* (London: Longman & Co., 1933)
Bodl. Bodleian Library, Oxford
CAA Cheshire and Chester Archives, Chester
DAA Douai Abbey Archives, Woolhampton
Draft Letter Book Lancashire County Record Office, DDBl acc. 6121, Box 2, 1672–1693 letter book
EEBO *Early English Books Online*
ESTC *English Short Title Catalogue*. Online Edition
FSL Folger Shakespeare Library, Washington DC
Gibson (ed.), *Cavalier's Note Book* T. E. Gibson (ed.), *Crosby Records: A Cavalier's Note Book* (London: Longmans, Green & Co., 1880)
Great Hodge Podge Lancashire County Record Office, DDBl acc. 6121, Box 4, Great Hodge Podge
Harkirk Burial Register Lancashire County Record Office, DDBl acc. 6121, Box 1, Harkirk burial register
Harrison (ed.), *Isle of Man* W. Harrison (ed.), *A History of the Isle of Man. Written by William Blundell, Esq. of Crosby, Co. Lancaster 1648–1656*, 2 vols, Publications of the Manx Society, 25, 27 (1876, 1877)
Historica Lancashire County Record Office, DDBl acc. 6121, Box 4, Historica
HL Huntington Library, California
HMC Historical Manuscripts Commission
Hodge Podge the Third Lancashire County Record Office, DDBl acc. 6121, Box 2, Hodge Podge the Third
LCRO Lancashire County Record Office
Letter Book One Lancashire County Record Office, DDBl acc. 6121, Box 3, William Blundell the Cavalier's letter book 1681–90
Letter Book Two Lancashire County Record Office, DDBl acc. 6121, Box 2, Copies of letters to William Blundell the Cavalier 1665–1679

Letters of Blundell Junior   Lancashire County Record Office, DDBl acc. 6121, Box 6, Letters and accounts of William Blundell the son of the Cavalier
MCL   Manchester Central Library
MNHL   Manx National Heritage Library, Douglas, Isle of Man
NLS   National Library of Scotland, Edinburgh
NRO   Northamptonshire Record Office
NUL   Nottingham University Library
ODNB   *Oxford Dictionary of National Biography* (Oxford: Oxford University Press, 2004). Online Edition
PCRA   Poor Clares of Rouen Archives, Darlington
SA   Sheffield Archives
Small Account Book   Lancashire County Record Office, DDBl acc. 6121, Box 3, Cavalier's Small Account Book 1646–1675
SRO   Staffordshire Record Office
TNA   The National Archives, Surrey
Tyrer, 'Recusancy'   F. Tyrer, 'An Account of the Recusancy of the Blundell of Crosby Family and the Inhabitants of the Township of Little Crosby in Lancashire', 3 vols (Unpublished work held at Lancashire County Record Office, 1955)
WRO   Wigan Record Office

Note on dates and style

Dates are given according to the old-style calendar, though the start of the year is taken as 1 January rather than 25 March. Abbreviations are expanded, but spelling is kept as in original documents; *u*/*v*, *i*/*j* and *vv* have been modernised. Short titles of early works are given throughout and place of publication for early printed works is London unless otherwise stated. References to folios in Blundell's papers follow his own designations, wherein he referred to the recto with the folio number alone and the verso with the folio number followed by 'b'. Not all of Blundell's letters include full dates (i.e. either one or more of the day, month or year is missing), or in some cases there is no date at all. For the purposes of this book, the references for correspondence give as much information about date of authorship as survives.

Introduction

On Friday 25 May 1660 William Blundell, a Catholic gentleman from Lancashire, joined Charles II's entourage on his return from exile. During the trip across the Channel, which Blundell recorded with glee in his commonplace books, he noted that the occupants of the ship measured themselves against each other, notching their heights on a beam. On examination of the notches Blundell found that he was five inches shorter than Charles, which he was quick to emphasise was the result of an injury sustained in the King's service during the Civil War.[1] Blundell's notes from this period continue in euphoric form and suggest that he was overwhelmed not only by the return of monarchy but also by the anticipated removal of the penal laws in recognition of Catholic loyalty to the throne, which he believed was epitomised in the injury that he gladly bore for the King.[2] Yet within one year Blundell complained that due to the advice of 'Eevel Councellors about the King' the persecution of 'his Majesties most faithful subjects' continued, a grievance that stayed with him till his death in 1698.[3] Throughout his life Blundell projected the image of a staunch recusant who voluntarily drew an easy distinction between religion and politics, being at once both a loyal Englishman and a devoted Catholic. The few secondary works that consider his life have generally accepted these claims at face value, distinguishing him from his namesakes with the epithet 'the Cavalier'.[4]

This book considers the extent to which Blundell's reputation was justified by his actions. His surviving correspondence provides an overview of the activities that he was involved in, from which it is clear that he was neither the passive victim nor the entirely loyal subject that he and others have claimed. Blundell actively defended his family from the extremes of the penal laws, particularly through creating sprawling kin and social networks, which included both Catholics and Protestants. The relative freedom that this support offered Blundell allowed him to patronise other Catholics. In his locality he ensured that the township of Little Crosby was populated almost entirely by his co-religionists, on a national level he circulated arguments supporting the removal of the penal laws, and on an international level he worked as an agent for the Poor Clares of Rouen. This view of Blundell's life is further supported by the notes on his reading. Not only did Blundell rewrite the histories of recent civil conflicts to show that Protestants were prone to rebellion and Catholics to loyalty to monarchy, but we also find a different take on his religious beliefs. Though he was a committed Catholic, his commonplaces suggest an underlying tension with a number of central tenets of Catholicism, which do not accord with the image of an unquestioning believer. This tension was manifest throughout his notes on his practical engagement with the world, which reveal the nuances and anxieties in his thinking across a wide spectrum of social, political and personal issues. Blundell's papers offer a unique insight into the political culture of an early modern Catholic and a valuable contribution to our understanding of Catholic agency and gentry reading practices. An examination of his political and cultural worlds complicates generalisations about early modern religious identities and challenges a historical determinism which removes Catholics from the mainstream of early-modern society. Before we turn to consider these points in detail it is vital that this book is situated within its historiographical context.

I

Until the 1970s English Catholicism was generally excluded from mainstream historiography. Catholics were either ignored altogether or portrayed as effeminate, absolutist in inclination and subversive of all that it meant to be English.[5] Consequently, the writing of Catholic history has often been left to Catholic historians, which has led to another set of problems. In an effort to show how Catholics were marginalised and persecuted, emphasis was placed on the penal laws, without consideration of the extent to which they were applied. Contemporary Catholics were thus presented as a homogeneous group of victims.[6] This is not to say that this work can be dismissed lightly. J. C. H. Aveling, a one-time Benedictine monk, wrote a number of extensively researched studies of post-Reformation Catholicism in the north of England which, though inclined to highlight the victimhood of contemporary Catholics, successfully drew attention to previously ignored Catholic archives, as well as reinvigorating interest in this topic through an animated writing style.[7] However, while such work is often based on detailed engagement with particular archival material, the approach tends to be uninformed by broader work on the period, which has led Ethan Shagan to remark that Catholicism has become 'a historiographical sub-field or occasionally a ghetto' and Christopher Haigh to state that Catholic history remains 'an intellectual backwater, mainly worked at by Catholics who publish in house journals'.[8]

In the 1970s John Bossy completed his seminal study of English Catholicism, a work that radically challenged widely accepted axioms. Crucially he argued that, far from being a decreasing minority in its death throes, English Catholicism was a thriving nonconformist sect. Losing its state sponsorship gave Catholicism a vitality that it had hitherto not enjoyed, and through the efforts of entrepreneurial missionary clergy Catholicism developed a distinctive identity. However, though not for confessional reasons, Bossy's work agreed that by the seventeenth century English Catholics formed a homogeneous, politically inactive and hermetically sealed community, properly Catholic only when it was fully separated from Protestantism.[9] For Bossy, 1603 witnessed the Catholic 'retreat from the political engagements which had marked the Elizabethan period'.[10] Therefore, though Bossy's work highlighted the vigour of early modern English Catholicism, his conclusions still removed it from mainstream historiography, allowing Catholicism to retain its status as an interesting, but largely irrelevant, subfield of English history. This remained into the 1990s a staple of mainstream historiography, the focus of which was the language used to articulate anti-popery and the impact that these fears had on English politics, as opposed to the actual activities of Catholics.[11]

Over the last twenty years post-Reformation English Catholicism has received increasing attention. Historians such as Peter Lake, Michael Questier and Alexandra Walsham have paved the way for a new approach that views Catholics not as a homogeneous group but as individuals who played an active role within both their communities and the body politic.[12] Although the focus of these studies is English Catholicism in the late sixteenth and early seventeenth centuries, their arguments significantly revise our understanding of early modern English Catholicism in general.

Recent work on early modern England has challenged the view that religious belief necessarily marked distinct delineations within society. Instead, for many, religious belief was fluid and contemporaries gravitated between varieties of worldviews that defy precise categorisation.[13] Changing views on religious polarisation in this period have been, in part, a result of revisionist work on the English Reformation. It is now generally accepted that England's conversion to Protestantism was not an overnight phenomenon and that the pre-Reformation church was not crumbling with dissent. Instead many contemporaries slowly took on Protestant forms of worship, harbouring sympathies for the old religion.[14] This has a direct impact on how we view Catholicism in the early modern period.

The main focus of Catholic histories has been recusants, those Catholics who refused to attend Anglican Church service. Indeed, the foremost journal of English Catholic history is entitled *Recusant History*, while Walsham states that the history of post-Reformation English Catholicism has been 'traditionally and unashamedly "recusant history"'.[15] Recusants provided a perspective of post-Reformation English Catholicism that suited the needs of early modern Catholic clergy keen to emphasise the staunch commitment of lay Catholics, as well as according with more modern-day views that maintained that they were a homogeneous group of victims. Furthermore, recusants are relatively easy to identify as their failure to attend church often meant that they were proceeded against by the authorities and left a quantifiable paper trail behind.[16]

The main sources for the study of recusants are the recusant rolls that record the fines they paid for failure to attend church.[17] On the basis of these sources most estimates maintain that recusants accounted for around one per cent of the English population during the seventeenth century.[18] However, to end any study of English Catholics here would present a distorted picture, and it is vital that views of recusancy should be supplemented by two further categories of Catholic: the exile and the church papist.

Exiles were those who felt bound by their conscience, or were forced by government authorities, to flee the country and live abroad in parts of Catholic Europe, particularly France.[19] Many entered religious orders and kept in regular contact with family and friends in England, forming an important component of the networks that many English Catholics operated within. During the Interregnum exiled Royalists made vital use of these networks, sending messages through the complex mail service that had developed between nuns in the Low Countries and their family and financiers in England.[20] Many studies of English Catholicism fail to consider exiled English Catholics because of pragmatic factors: records pertaining to them are often held in foreign record offices and written in a foreign language. None the less, excluding exiles from a study of English Catholicism fails to highlight an important component of the English Catholic population.

The final group of English Catholics are the so-called 'church papists', individuals who attended Anglican Church service while secretly committed to the Catholic faith. Categories of church papist include heads of Catholic households who conformed to protect their property and those who attended Anglican services but refused to accept Holy Communion. As their identities resided in the mind, church papists 'defy statistical analysis'.[21] A central presupposition underlining Bossy's work is that the church papist had virtually disappeared by 1600.[22] Walsham has shown that this was far from being the case: fear of church papists continued throughout the seventeenth century, a number of previous conformists exposed their Catholic faith as the Stuart court became more sympathetic to Catholicism, and the small amount of Catholic correspondence that survives for this period regularly acknowledges the existence of church papists. Furthermore, the statistically high occurrence of law-abiding heads of household with recusant wives supports the view that occasional conformity was a widespread practice.[23] That church papists have often been ignored is partly a reflection of the difficulties in identifying them and also a product of the picture that Catholic contemporaries sought to project of a unified Catholic population staunch in their religious belief and unified in their suffering.[24] However, this was propaganda and should not be accepted at face value. Though it is impossible to measure numbers of church papists, to see Catholicism as a set of beliefs as opposed to an easily definable criterion (church attendance) is historically more accurate.[25] This recognition gives some credence to Protestant fears of a Catholic fifth-column demonstrates that English Catholics must be viewed as an ideologically heterogeneous group and 'may well subvert persisting notions of the "Catholic community" – if not the Protestant nation itself'.[26] This is not the only flaw in traditional conceptions of the English 'Catholic community'.

The notion that English Catholics formed an isolated enclave in the seventeenth century was perpetuated both by contemporary Catholics who portrayed themselves as removed from traditional spheres of influence and by Protestants seeking to fuel fears of popish conspiracies. This view still holds ground with many modern-day historians. The argument that there was a discernible Catholic community in early modern England was best articulated in the work of Bossy, most notably in his monograph *The English Catholic Community*.[27] Bossy's position was subsequently revisited by Caroline Hibbard, who maintained that Catholics were detached from parish communities and instead operated within a network of Catholic family alliances: the so-called 'Catholic connection'.[28] Certainly, there is significant evidence to support this view. Post-Reformation English Catholicism emerged as a predominantly seigneurial religion, surviving under the protection of households of Catholic Lords of Manors.[29] Catholics shared secret marriage ceremonies and a unique educational upbringing that usually entailed periods in seminaries on the continent.[30] Furthermore, in many cases Catholics congregated in areas with other co-religionists, particularly evident in Lancashire and Yorkshire.[31] However, there are important qualifications to this view concerning the nature of the confessional divide and the level of unity amongst contemporary English Catholics.

The blurred boundaries between Catholicism and Protestantism undermine attempts to identify any clearly defined Catholic community. The option of occasional or even outright conformity for church papists meant that Catholicism was not confined to seigneurial status. Church papistry was often undetectable to government authorities, meaning that the individual did not require the protection of a Catholic Lord of the Manor to avoid the penal laws.[32] Furthermore, recent work on the relationship between Catholics and Protestants has shown that recusants were regularly protected by Protestant friends and family and rarely persecuted to the full extent that the law allowed. Many Protestants continued to hold a deep fear of 'popery' as a malign political force, but went out of their way to protect their Catholic neighbours from the laws that had been put in place as a result of that fear.[33] Anthony Milton has argued that, though it may have been 'politically correct' for contemporaries to vehemently hate all things Catholic, early modern English society was littered with remnants of the old religion and many harboured sympathy for some aspects of Catholicism. For Milton, anti-Catholicism was not outright prejudice but a form of qualified intolerance that allowed its adherents to protect Catholic friends secretly, while at the same time calling for stricter enforcement of the penal laws.[34]

The traditional conception of an English Catholic community also fails to recognise the depth of intra-Catholic division, an embarrassment that both early modern and modern-day Catholics have tried to ignore.[35] Debate over occasional conformity caused internal fissures within English Catholicism, with a number of Catholic clergy critical of their colleagues who demanded staunch recusancy from an already heavily persecuted minority.[36] It also separated many lay Catholics from clergy, as a number of zealous Catholic clergy placed severe restrictions on already struggling lay Catholics.[37] Further divides were brought about by regular clergy obstructing efforts to appoint English bishops. A group of secular priests, known as Appellants for their regular appeals to Rome, supported Episcopal government, and between 1598 and 1602 conducted a propaganda campaign against Jesuits, branding them a political fifth-column. The debate over the leadership of the English Catholics continued throughout the century, with the full impact being evident in the late 1620s when Jesuits effectively procured the resignation of Bishop Richard Smith by reporting him to the regime.[38] These squabbles obstructed efforts to present English Catholicism as a unified community, and into the Restoration period anti-Jesuit literature written by Catholics was being released into the public forum which 'was as virulent as any Puritan publication'.[39]

A further central issue that separated English Catholics in the early seventeenth century surrounded loyalty to a temporal ruler. In 1606 English Catholics were divided over how to respond to an oath of allegiance, the main area of contention being whether the Oath concerned religious belief or merely civil order. Questier has argued that the Oath successfully provoked internal argument within the Catholic community as it raised the much-debated papal deposing power, while juxtaposing it with statements that covertly suggested Roman doctrine was heretical.[40] These internal controversies were made public in a tirade of pamphlets that seriously damaged the Catholic pretence of a unified community, and internal division was cited by contemporaries as being responsible for the apostasy of many Catholics throughout the period.[41] In light of these findings it is clear that early modern Catholics did not form a homogeneous and unified community, and neither were they fully excluded from mainstream Protestant society.

That early modern Catholics were distinguished solely by their victimhood has also been the subject of recent debate. This view does hold some ground. Throughout the majority of the seventeenth-century English Catholics were subject to a wide range of penal laws that imposed social and financial restrictions on them owing to their religious persuasions.[42] Despite promises and hopes to the contrary James I and Charles I brought little relief for Catholics, Charles II made sporadic attempts to introduce some form of limited toleration but was forced to abandon his efforts to get financial support from Parliament, James II's reign was despairingly brief and William never succeeded in introducing a toleration based on the model in the Netherlands.[43] However, to end on this note would give an unbalanced view of the place of Catholics in early modern English society.

The focus of many Catholic historians on the penal laws can be misleading. As Hibbard argues, 'the existence of harsh legislation was often mistaken for evidence that it was enforced'.[44] In light of arguments that Protestants and Catholics were not as opposed as once thought, it is hardly surprising to find reluctance on the part of many Protestants to bring about prosecutions for recusancy. In many cases openly recusant families escaped fines for years at a time, while some avoided being charged altogether. In a rare case in Sussex, a county with strong Catholic links, Henry Compton of Brambletye, the head of a staunchly recusant family, held office as a Justice of the Peace and Deputy Lieutenant from the early 1620s to 1642, when he was presented for failure to attend communion.[45] Elsewhere, in the early eighteenth century the recusant Nicholas Blundell was selected by his Protestant neighbours as the local church warden.[46] Even in cases where Catholics were legally attacked for their recusancy, Hibbard claims that while religion may have served as the pretext there were often ulterior financial or social motives.[47] Finally, a focus on the penal laws fails to consider Catholic responses to them. The thrust of recent work on English Catholicism emphasises Catholic agency in developing strategies to survive in a Protestant environment, which often involved hiding both the extent of their wealth and their Catholic practice from government commissioners.[48]

Catholic agency also included political machinations. In light of recent work on the early modern period, Bossy's claim that 1603 signalled the Catholic 'retreat from the political engagements which had marked the Elizabethan period' has become increasingly untenable.[49] Throughout the seventeenth century Catholicism held an influential position in the Stuart court, with the Stuart kings developing a penchant for Catholic wives, mistresses and courtiers.[50] The zenith of Catholic influence at court in this century was the deathbed conversion of Charles II to Catholicism and the accession of the openly Catholic James II to the throne in 1685.[51] However, Catholic involvement in politics was not limited to the court. Throughout the seventeenth century Catholic aristocratic and gentry families used the importance their wealth conferred to periodically influence politics on both a local and a national level. Arguments by Keith Lindley that Catholics were overwhelmingly neutral throughout the Civil War have been discredited on the grounds that the evidence he used excluded vital data about Catholic activity.[52] Other studies, most notably by Peter Newman, have shown that 'the Catholic commitment to armed support of the King was out of all proportion to the size of the community'.[53] During the Interregnum, Catholics played a vital role in the survival of the exiled Royalists, distributing money and messages between the exiles and England as well as offering lodgings.[54] Catholics were even responsible for ensuring the safety of Charles Stuart when he fled the Battle of Worcester in 1651.[55] Their involvement in James II's efforts to Catholicise public office have been well documented, and throughout his reign Catholics held the most senior governmental posts.[56] That this was the case goes some way to explaining contemporary anti-popery, a factor that becomes more apparent when their interactions with their co-religionists on the continent are considered.

The activities of English Catholics, and Protestant fears of these activities, can be understood only in relation to Catholicism within the British Isles and Europe as a whole. A. D. Wright has argued that the internal problems in English Catholicism, such as the division between secular and religious clergy, mirrored wider issues that were exported to the missions.[57] In a comparison of English Catholicism with early modern Catholicism in Sicily and Japan, Wright highlights the similarities between each, and asserts that 'the English Catholic community was part of the European Catholic world, not just an insular denomination'.[58] This position is given credence by the workings of the Catholic educational system, which relied on a ministry of priests trained abroad, making English Catholics unlike any other sectarian group.[59] Therefore, while the English recusant community may have been relatively small, to understand fears of Catholicism one must take a wider perspective. Daniel Szechi asserts that by c.1692 'if we take into account the religious demographies of the British Isles as a whole ... about 20 per cent of the population was Catholic'.[60] Furthermore, in Europe Protestantism was on the defensive and Jonathan Scott estimates that it had been reduced by armed force from fifty per cent of the land area of Europe to less than twenty per cent throughout the century.[61] Thus, essential to any understanding of English Catholics is a notion of how they related to their co-religionists abroad both in real terms and in the minds of their Protestant contemporaries.

These new approaches to Catholicism are often based on a disparate range of sources because of a paucity of surviving material. A significant amount of primary material, including much of the information in the State Papers, concerns Protestant fears of Catholicism, which were often exaggerated by contemporaries for political purposes. Recusant rolls give some idea of how many Catholics refused to conform, but little more, while records of Quarter Sessions and Episcopal Visitations often fail to distinguish between Protestant Dissenters and Catholics.[62] Surviving material allowing these issues to be explored in relation to individual Catholics is scanty. In many cases all that survives for this period, in otherwise rich family archives, are estate records and leases. Much can be gained from these sources concerning family connections and economic standing, however, much is left to speculation as there are often huge gaps in the family correspondence. The Aston (Staffordshire), Brudenell (Northamptonshire) and Giffard (Staffordshire) families, for example, all fall into this category. Despite their having an abundance of surviving correspondence for the sixteenth and eighteenth centuries, comparatively little or no correspondence or personal papers survive for the seventeenth century.[63]

In the last decade or so a number of groundbreaking studies have followed the fortunes of particular early modern Catholics, considering both their political activity and the extent to which their Catholicism had an impact on their lives. Most notable are Questier's study of the Viscounts Montague from the mid-sixteenth century to the outbreak of the Civil War, Sandeep Kaushik's work on Thomas Tresham (1543–1605), and Gabriel Glickman's study of Catholic Jacobites.[64] However, while Questier and Kaushik provide new interpretations of pre-Civil War Catholicism, and Glickman reassesses Catholicism after the Revolution of 1688, the late seventeenth century has received comparatively little attention. This is particularly perplexing given the central role that both Catholics and Protestant fears of popery played in English politics throughout this period. Through a study of William Blundell, this book contributes to redressing this imbalance.

II

William Blundell, who lived from 1620 to 1698, was the head of a staunchly recusant landowning family that had been based at Crosby Hall in Lancashire since the mid-fourteenth century.[65] He inherited the family estates in 1638 as a minor, following the death of his grandfather and namesake, as his father had died in 1631. In 1642 Blundell accepted a Captain's commission and fought for the King, receiving a serious wound in his first engagement that disabled him for life, earning him the nickname 'Halt-Will' due to the bizarre gait he developed as a result.[66] With his bald head, 'grosse full body' and cumbersome walk, Blundell felt it necessary to warn those who saw him for the first time since the outbreak of war to 'not you feare for ... the thing is no Goblin; but the very party we talk on'.[67] To avoid imprisonment he left his estate in the hands of his wife and sister and spent two periods of less than a year during 1646 and 1648 in exile on the Isle of Man and a brief, unspecified, period living a low-key existence in Wales, though concern for his estate at Crosby quickly drew him back home.[68] While he adopted the name Cicely Burton in two of his surviving letters to keep his identity secret, the fanciful claim of his biographer and kinswoman, Margaret Blundell, that he dressed as a woman and spent long periods sitting in the kitchen, unfortunately finds no corroboration in surviving evidence.[69] In 1646 an Ordinance was passed that held that no popish delinquent could compound for his estate; accordingly

Blundell's property was seized and held by commissioners for almost a decade. Throughout the Interregnum Blundell was imprisoned on a number of occasions, later noting that 'I was 4 tymes imprisoned and paid my ransom twice', and in 1660 on the eve of the restoration of monarchy he made his way to Breda and accompanied the future Charles II on his voyage to accept the throne.[70]

Despite Blundell's initial hopes, it rapidly became clear that the plight of English Catholics would not be relieved by Charles and in 1680 Blundell was driven into exile, recording in his application for a travel pass that 'The reason I would give for my travel is very true ... to avoyd the penal lawes which we hear have been lately ordered to be put in Execution'.[71] Having spent over a year abroad he returned to Crosby, where in 1685 his wife Ann died. Far from submitting to grief, Blundell soon made his way to London, taking full advantage of the lull in the penal laws brought by James II's accession. His letters show that he was in London for at least a year, during which he lodged in Vere Street.[72] While there he successfully brought a law suit at Chester Consistory Court against the Churchwardens of Sefton who had tried to force him and his tenants to pay for the creation of a road to Sefton Mill.[73] Blundell immersed himself in city life, his letters recording that he frequently drank wine or 'took a dish at the Coffee house' with friends, that he saw James II deliver an Address at Hampton Court, and that he went 'sometimes to the Court to gaze & look about as some others do; sometimes I go to pray & to hear the sermons'.[74] In May 1687 he spent seventeen days in Gravelines, after picking up 'an unexpected wind', where he left his granddaughter Margaret.[75] On his return he petitioned John Warner, who was shortly to become Royal Confessor, to recommend him 'for some small advantageous employment upon a civil account', though apparently without success and by September 1688 he had returned to Little Crosby.[76]

Following the Revolution of 1688 Blundell noted that he was imprisoned for eight months, and after his release claimed he wanted nothing more than to live a quiet life in the country.[77] His peace was shattered in 1694 when commissioners for the new regime brought a warrant for his arrest, which claimed that he and a number of other Lancashire Catholics had been involved in Jacobite conspiracy.[78] Finding him to be a sickly old man they fraudulently took his son and namesake instead. After a brief trial his son was released and Blundell lived the last four years of his life relatively unmolested until his death in 1698.[79] He was buried at his request in Sefton Church alongside his ancestors, an act which highlighted the complex relationship that many Catholics had with the Church of England.[80]

Throughout a marriage of nearly fifty years Blundell and his wife Ann, daughter of Sir Thomas Haggerston of Northumberland, had fourteen children. Three boys and seven girls survived into adulthood. Blundell's eldest son Nicholas chose to join the Jesuits rather than inherit the family estates, a vocation also followed by the youngest son Thomas. Blundell's heir was his second son and namesake who married Mary Eyre, daughter of Rowland Eyre, a prominent Derbyshire recusant.[81] Of his seven daughters, five joined the Poor Clares: Jane, Margaret, Alice, Mary and Clare Frances. His daughter Emilia married Richard Butler, the heir to the Mountgarret estates. After encouraging his youngest daughter, whom he affectionately referred to as 'the thing called Bridget', to take religious orders, Blundell eventually relented and in 1692, at the age of thirty-three, she married John Gerard 'Dr of Phisick', of whom Blundell was to comment in 1694 that 'They live in the City of Durham and have yet no issue'.[82]

The extent to which Blundell's position differed from other English Catholics is open to debate. Seventeenth-century Lancashire held the largest concentration of Catholics in England at the time.[83] Bossy maintained that this was a result of Lancashire's geographical isolation, the limited perspective of most gentry who focused all their attention on events in Lancashire, and the high number of missionary priests in the county.[84] While geographical isolation may be one factor in the survival of Catholicism in the rugged terrain of the north of Lancashire, in the easily accessible south-west this interpretation holds little value.[85] Conversely, Haigh has argued that Lancashire remained Catholic as Protestantism never took hold in the county, conservative ministers throughout Lancashire were protected by the gentry, while church discipline was always weak. Thus, missionary priests merely helped reinforce Lancashire's Catholic links, as opposed to building up from a grassroots level.[86] But as recent work on the divisions between Protestantism and Catholicism and the rediscovery of church papistry has shown, one need not have lived in an area dominated by recusants to find individuals sympathetic to Catholicism.[87] For this reason, it is increasingly accepted that the dichotomy between a backward and Catholic north of England and a progressive Protestant south is a false one.[88] As Questier argues, 'Put bluntly, what it means ... is that many English counties were more like Lancashire than everyone has thought'.[89]

Although Blundell was subject to the same laws and undertook the same common religious practices as other recusants, in many ways he was exceptional. He lived for seventy-eight years and, despite regularly claiming that he was 'old & crasy', his writings indicate that he was fully in control of his faculties at least until the year of his death, though it appears that the length of his life was a surprise to him as he had been saying his goodbyes to friends and family from his early fifties.[90] Unlike many contemporaries, and in spite of both his physical disability and the restrictions placed on him because of his recusancy, Blundell travelled widely within the British Isles and continental Europe.[91] The surviving records that he made on these trips vary greatly in detail. For his visit to Scotland in 1657 he kept a meticulous travel diary, though for other trips we are left with less descriptive material, sometimes as little as brief mentions in an account book explaining gaps in entries or references in his commonplace books to his having engaged with a particular culture during a visit. From these sources it is apparent that he lived in both Wales[92] and the Isle of Man[93] for a period during the Civil Wars, he visited London at least seven times, often for extended periods,[94] Scotland in 1657[95] and York in 1673,[96] Ireland at least four times,[97] and continental Europe at least three times, during which he visited Flanders, Holland and France.[98] Most important is the sheer volume of his surviving writings.

Responsibility for his estate from an early age meant that Blundell never received the education abroad that many of his co-religionists shared. Little is known of his education or any formative pedagogical influences, though it seems likely that he attended the Catholic school at Scarisbrick Hall.[99] If so, he would have been taught by a Jesuit tutor who had been educated at St Omer.[100] He persistently complained of a lack of grammar and Latin, though his letters specifically state, and his reading practices imply, that he could read and speak Latin far better than he could write it, no doubt a reflection of the way he had been taught.[101] However, the extent of Blundell's failings may have reflected false modesty, as in his commonplace books he kept lists in which he criticised others' use of Latin.[102] Despite his lack of formal education he developed a love of learning. It seems apparent that by his twenties Blundell had become a compulsive reader and writer. It may be that his experience of exile played an important part in this. The importance of writing as a means by which to stay in touch with those who remained in England was central to adjusting to life in exile. Geoffrey Smith argues that 'opportunities for communication with family and friends in England, for both personal and economic reasons, were a factor that determined both the choice of place of exile and the duration of the ordeal'.[103] In his study of the reading practices of William Drake, Kevin Sharpe discusses the urgency of Drake's reading during the Civil War and Interregnum periods, when Drake voluntarily withdrew from England on an intermittent seventeen-year period of exile. This prompted him to become a 'revolutionary reader': not only did he read at a revolutionary time, but he read old texts with new knowledge, which consequently saw him read in distinctively adversarial ways.[104] Blundell's surviving writings date from the Civil War period and took on new urgency in light of the political developments in post-Civil War England. As we will see, his commonplace books provided him a forum within which to engage with contemporary political issues, from which he was excluded as a result of his recusancy: thus, he engaged in a form of 'bookish exile'.[105] By the time he returned home, he had developed an 'itch after knowledge' that could be remedied only by reading, while he frequently apologised to recipients of his letters for writing 'a preface as long as a letter and a letter as long as a book', stating that the only thing that could stop him was his candle burning out.[106] He also sought to read other languages and by the end of his life he had taught himself Spanish, Italian and French by painstakingly translating and rereading books in each of the languages. His notebooks record a mass of information varying from notes on contemporary politics, summaries of books he read and drafts of letters, to observations of the weather, travel logs and the weights of family members.

During Blundell's life at least two of his writings were printed. In the Blue Book there is a work spanning fifty-two single sides of folio entitled 'A Short Discourse of the Paenall Lawes against the Roman Catholicks of England'.[107] Though a printed version of the text no longer survives, Blundell's marginal comments on the manuscript in the Blue Book state that it was printed in sections during 1661, while in 1880 Thomas Ellison Gibson recorded having discovered a small quarto manuscript of the work at Crosby Hall that can no longer be identified, in which Blundell stated that 'a few copies were printed in London'.[108] An entry in the Adversaria notes that Blundell was the author of a printed text entitled *Quid me Persequeris?*, while a transcription of a letter in the Great Hodge Podge entered under this title states that the 'Author of a book so called received a letter written unto him' that contained a series of positive comments about the text, a thinly veiled attempt at discretion in a notebook that circulated around the family and as such was not a secure forum in which to admit authorship.[109] From Blundell's comments it is probable that 'A Short Discourse' and *Quid me Persequeris?* were the same work. Both are noted as having been printed in 1661, entries detailing both refer to the same content, and the question 'Quid me Persequeris?', as heard by St Paul on the road to Damascus before his conversion to Christianity, is a far punchier title for the contents of the surviving draft, suggesting that *Quid me Persequeris?* was the title under which 'A Short Discourse' was printed.[110] Regarding the circulation of the book, Blundell recorded that 'In the yeare 1661 I printed a small book ... which I have shewed to few & I think it was never exposed to sale', suggesting that it was distributed selectively amongst the reading networks of which Blundell was part.[111] Searches in the *ESTC* under both titles indicate that no printed versions of 'A Short Discourse' survive, though Blundell's marginal comments suggest that the surviving version was close to, if not the final draft.[112] In addition, a single printed broadside documenting observations of a woman with a cutaneous horn growing from her head is extant. The broadside was printed in 1668 with the signature 'William Blundel, Cresby' and internal evidence suggests that the author was resident in the north-west of England.[113] As we will see, though Blundell's surviving papers include no mention of the work, his extensive interest in monster literature and the manner in which the account was documented leave little doubt that it was the product of this William Blundell.

Blundell also wrote a number of manuscripts that were circulated amongst friends and family. 'A History of the Isle of Man' was probably written by Blundell during his exile there, though not printed until the nineteenth century by the Manx Society.[114] Authorship of the document is, however, not as clear as has been suggested by previous secondary works. At no stage throughout the manuscript is the author named and the manuscript is not in Blundell's hand.[115] In a 1702 history of the Isle of Man, William Sacheverell stated that he used two sources, one of which his references suggests was the work that has been attributed to Blundell, which he referred to as the history written by 'the gentleman who has not been so kind as to transmit his name to posterity'.[116] The earliest mention of Blundell as author, upon which it appears that all other attributions rest, was made in 1736 in John Seacombe's history of the Stanley family. In a brief description of the Isle of Man, he noted that he used a history that was written by

> the Great and Learned Mr. *Blundell* of *Crosby*, who prudently retir'd thither during the time of the Usurpation, whereby he preserv'd his Person in peace and security, and his Estate from all manner of depredation: This Gentleman being a Person of Polite Learning, employ'd his leisure hours in collecting the History and Antiquities of the *Isle of Man*; and by his Manuscript, which I have seen, gave posterity the clearest and most correct Account thereof.[117]

Blundell's papers confirm that he spent at least one period in exile in the Isle of Man in 1646, while the history states that the author spent two periods there in 1646 and 1648.[118] The author also notes, like Blundell, that he spent a brief period of exile in Wales.[119] Finally, quotations from ancient history in the work suggest that the author was reading a number of the texts that Blundell's notes from this period refer to, while authorship of such a text was certainly consistent with Blundell's interests.[120] However, there is no reference in Blundell's surviving papers to a history of the Isle of Man, and there is no trace of such a manuscript in either the Lancashire County Record Office or Crosby Hall. Therefore, it is clearly possible that Blundell was the author of the history, but not certain. It is also likely that Blundell was the author of two brief works found in his papers that argue for the removal of the penal laws, which pick up on many of the same arguments he developed in 'A Short Discourse'.[121] Although these manuscripts were not printed, the central ideas were distributed widely by Blundell in his letters to friends and family.

The surviving manuscripts relating to Blundell include a huge range of material. There are the standard miscellaneous papers relating to the management of the Blundell estate, including copies of bonds and acquittances as well as a tenants' book that includes letters relating to the latter period of Blundell's life.[122] The most revealing sources are lodged in an addition to the Blundell collection, which was held at Crosby Hall and deposited at Lancashire County

Record Office in the late twentieth century.[123] The collection includes a small register for the Catholic burial ground established by Blundell's grandfather and updated by successive generations, which gives the names of 131 individuals buried between 1611 and 1753 along with the deceased's date of death, place of residence and any aliases by which they were known.[124] Three of Blundell's letter books survive. The Draft Letter Book consists of four volumes of letters that were bound together at some stage in the 1890s. Each volume was labelled separately: 'L:15', which includes drafts of letters from 1672 to 1673; 'Liber 16', which includes letters from 1673 to 1675; 'Letters L:18', which includes letters from 1677 to 1680, and an untitled volume of letters from 1686 to 1693. Many of the letters from these volumes were also transcribed into the other two surviving letter books.[125] The first of these was a book of 132 folios, into which Blundell transcribed more than 120 letters he deemed particularly important along with details of the recipient and in most cases the date sent.[126] Maintained in parallel with this was a 165-page book of letters that were written to Blundell, which were often transcribed along with additions detailing the author, the date received and small entries outlining the context of the letter.[127] In addition to these letter books, there survive three notebooks of which Blundell was the sole author. These volumes functioned in a similar manner to the waste books of contemporary merchants and the material included within each was inserted in an *ad hoc* pattern, with little consistency in the dates that material was entered or in the placing of material of different genres.[128] The Small Account Book is a small (7 by 5½ inches) notebook of ninety-three folios that contains a miscellany of information, including financial accounts, Blundell's diary of his trip to Scotland and drafts of letters.[129] The ninety-folio Blue Book and ninety-three-folio Hodge Podge the Third are large vellum-bound manuscripts. Amongst the contents are an array of financial accounts and rough letters, though both were mainly repositories for Blundell's literary jottings, including, amongst other items the draft of 'A Short Discourse'.[130]

The Blundell collection includes also two commonplace books and a selection of transcribed texts, which are discussed in detail in Chapter 3. The Historica is a single volume spanning 209 folios and the Adversaria 423 folios, which though continuously numbered is split into two separate volumes at folio 201.[131] As we will see, they were mainly used for Blundell to record his thoughts about books that he read. Despite initial attempts to organise the topics that each of these commonplace books contained, the distinction rapidly broke down and both include a crossover of topical material, though, as a general rule, the Historica is concerned with historical issues and the Adversaria with religious. The transcribed sources consist of a loose-leaf collection of excerpts from works on the Reformation made in 1647, extracts from religious works made in 1677, sixty-three pages of transcription of a translation of Joannus

Petrus Maffeus's *The Affairs of the Portuguese in India* made by Blundell in 1653, and a large transcription of the first part of Juan Eusebio Nieremberg's *A Treatise of the Difference Betwixt the Temporal and Eternal*, which Blundell referred to in his commonplaces as 'The Touchstone of Truth'.[132]

A family commonplace book, referred to by its authors as the 'Great Hodge Podge', also survives. As the title suggests it contains an apparently random collection of material, including poetry, brief histories of the Blundell family, accounts and occasional letters, spread over nearly three hundred folios. Unlike the sources discussed above, the authorship of the Great Hodge Podge did not reside solely with Blundell. The earliest entries were made intermittently, at various locations within the volume, by Blundell's grandfather and namesake (1560–1638). The Blundell with whom this study is concerned made entries covering more than 150 single sides of folio, with the rest of the volume being written by Blundell's son and namesake, and his grandson Nicholas Blundell.[133] As we will see, for Blundell the volume played a vital role as a site of family history, from which he established a sense of continuity and identity. Finally, two manuscripts appear in the Blundell collection that were exclusively written by other family members, but contain pertinent material. An account of the Jacobite trial of 1694 copied by Nicholas Blundell the diarist (1669–1737) survives, which appears to have been based on other contemporary accounts, and was transcribed and printed under the auspices of the Chetham Society in 1864.[134] A collection of letters spanning fifty-one-folios written by Blundell's son and namesake contributes the final major source relating to William Blundell in the Blundell collection.[135]

The extant Blundell papers formed part of a much larger corpus of material that can no longer be identified. In the surviving texts Blundell regularly cross-referenced to volumes such as the 'Little Hodge', 'the red book', 'the little whyte book' and 'Hodge IId', which do not appear in the Blundell papers, nor can be found at Crosby Hall.[136] A series of letter books has also disappeared. There is frequent reference to the seventh, eighth and ninth letter books, the existence of which is further suggested in that the letter books bound into the Draft Letter Book begin with one that Blundell numbered as 'L:15'.[137] Finally, Blundell regularly referred to letters in 'the crowd' or 'the throng', probably a large collection of loose-leaf letters which have not survived.[138] In light of these missing papers it seems evident that the surviving material provides only a small sample of the entire correspondence and writings of Blundell. Papers written before the Civil War and during the period surrounding the accession of James II are particularly scanty, though it is impossible to know if this was because they have disappeared by chance, Blundell did not have time to write during these periods or the content was deemed so sensitive that it was destroyed.[139]

Entries in Blundell's papers provide an insight into the way in which he categorised and stored his writings as physical objects. It would seem that all those topics that Blundell deemed important were accorded an individual titled box, such as 'Franks box', 'Malls box', and 'Rouen box', in which he placed relevant letters.[140] Miscellaneous letters were placed in 'the crowd' or 'the throng'.[141] A single entry in the Great Hodge Podge, which states that a newsbook 'lyeth upon shelf X', suggests that these boxes of correspondence and notes were accorded a place on a particular shelf, alongside other written material which was catalogued in a library system Blundell developed.[142]

Internal evidence in the surviving papers suggests that Blundell's motivation for keeping these records varied. Letter Book One and Letter Book Two were apparently constructed for posterity. There are few letters in these volumes that could implicate him in any activity that the government seriously frowned upon, and a number of names of individuals are given as 'A. B.' or 'N. N.' in an attempt to hide their identities.[143] That these letters were transcribed neatly and in full suggests that Blundell had specific reasons for maintaining them in such a condition. Two motives can be identified through a close reading of the volumes. Annotations and corrections in the margins suggest that Blundell read them on different occasions.[144] In one letter to an anonymous friend who had not written for some time, Blundell claimed that he often reread his correspondence to remind him of his friends and family, as he viewed letters as being 'lyke the lively picture of some deare deceased friend'.[145] However, another more subtle motivation behind these letter books may exist. Collectively they present a picture of Blundell as a loyal cavalier who voluntarily separated religion and politics, yet was punished excessively by brutal Protestant regimes. Blundell's rereading of his own correspondence would have helped him reinforce his sense of self-identity during difficult times, and presumably he also recognised that they would help his family remember him in the same way. Blundell's entries in the Great Hodge Podge, the family notebook that had been used by both his father and his grandfather, also support this view, recording Royalist songs and the trials recusants faced on the same folio.[146] The other surviving sources are of a very different nature. Much of the material contained within the Draft Letter Book, Hodge Podge the Third, the Blue Book and the Small Account Book appears to have been for Blundell's eyes only. Many of the letters that appear in the transcribed letter books with an anonymous author or recipient were drafted in these notebooks with their full name.[147] These volumes also contain sensitive material detailing Blundell's financial and familial links with religious houses abroad, the real value of his estates (which differed from that presented to the authorities) and notes on disputes amongst Blundell's family members.[148] In one case a large entry in Hodge Podge the Third concerning a family disagreement is subscribed by Blundell with the following note, 'If any body find these things concerning my Niece Selby when I am gone, they are desyred to deface them. I was forced to commit them to writing for the help of my memory: and I was greatly concerned to medle in those things by reason of the trust which I undertook at her marriage in sundry respects.'[149]

Not all of the material in Blundell's notebooks was written by him. Sometimes he allowed servants to write receipts and records of land measurements, presumably under his supervision.[150] A small number of letters written by his wife and sisters also appear in the manuscripts, some directly written in by them, others later transcribed by Blundell.[151] From the late 1660s with Blundell's increasing age also came a severe shake in his hand that meant that his writing was all but illegible. In a letter to his son, Thomas, Blundell outlined how this affected his writing, stating that the cold turned his hand into a 'perfect quaker' and that he could only 'write (with much paine I do assure you) about 10 or 12 lines an hour; and these very unstable characters'.[152] That Blundell developed this unfortunate problem is of great benefit to the historian: not only is his hand completely distinct from any other as a result but a comparison with his handwriting in papers where the date is known permits a general assessment of the date that entries were made. Blundell's 'wretched old limb' failed to slow his passion for writing. Initially he continued regardless, though as the pain got worse he employed one of his servants as a scribe.[153] From December 1675 most of his writings were produced by his trusted servant Walter Thelwall. A marginal note to one letter records that 'The letter above written the first letter that Walter Thellwal copied out for me; which he did on the 14 of Decem: 1675', after which many of Blundell's letters opened by informing the recipient that 'I must begg your leave to make use of another mans pen, for the ease of my shaking hand'.[154] The majority of letters and notes transcribed in Thelwall's distinctive hand were subscribed in Blundell's erratic hand with the abbreviation 'Exmd' alongside corrections written in the margin.[155] It is worth noting that Thelwall was not merely Blundell's scribe, but various footnotes to material indicate that he also became Blundell's reading partner. Material was often read aloud and then both men discussed the issues that appeared in the texts. For example, a footnote to a transcription of a parliamentary speech made in 1679 reads 'Examined 10th May 1679 by us Wm Blundell Walter Thelwall'.[156] As we shall see, throughout the later part of Blundell's life, Thelwall was the first contact in Blundell's reading networks.

The extent to which Blundell was writing freely is an area of debate. We have already seen that his letter books and notebooks were each written for different purposes, which meant that in some cases he disguised the names of contacts.[157] However, even when Blundell provided a full transcription of a letter he was not always completely open. His correspondence regularly voiced concerns of interception and as such he could not write as freely as he wished, often stating that he was unable to include important news in letters because the 'Country doth not afford it'.[158] Indeed, Blundell complained at least twice to the Comptroller of the Post Office about lost mail, once orally and once in writing, noting in one letter that 'I am the meanest of many thousands who injoy the convenience of the post; yet do I adventure to tell you that I think there is some defect in these parts by the want of due order there in ... Many years agoe I made my verball complaint of the very same miscarriage at your Office in London.'[159] This contributed to Blundell's concern to disguise the contents of his correspondence. Throughout his life he developed a number of different codes for correspondence to hide the names of recipients or individuals mentioned, whereby each was referred to by a letter of the alphabet, avoiding the risk of exposing the names of correspondents if mail was intercepted.[160] A need for discretion was a common theme in early modern writing. In recognition of this, Jonathan Barry has argued that historians 'cannot take expressions of conservative and consensual values at their face value, but have to look out ... for hidden meanings and subversive innuendos of every type'.[161]

Blundell's papers are unique in offering such an insight into the world of a seventeenth-century Catholic gentleman, though they have been virtually ignored by mainstream historians. In the late nineteenth century Gibson edited two collections of the Blundell papers, the first primarily concerned with Blundell and the second with his grandfather and namesake.[162] A further volume of primary sources with limited commentary was published by Margaret Blundell, kinswoman of William Blundell, in 1933.[163] Both Gibson and Margaret Blundell's collections were constructed in a haphazard manner, using selections of letters from a variety of Blundell's notebooks with no references and with no discussion of the source material. In 1955 a local historian, Frank Tyrer, produced an unpublished three-volume study of the Blundell papers, which gave a history of the family up to the period in which he was writing.[164] Although the text followed the same format as Margaret Blundell's, with large sections of transcribed source material and only limited commentary, the work is far more reliable. Tyrer detailed the primary sources he used, provided accurate transcriptions and used the occasional source outside the Blundell collection. However, all three of these early works showed little awareness of mainstream historiography and consciously portrayed Blundell as a victim, emphasising his staunch Catholicism and unwavering loyalty to the monarchy.

Since the 1970s Blundell has had a number of cameo appearances in historical works, though none specifically focuses on his activity. Michael Galgano's 1971 PhD thesis on north-west recusancy alludes to the Blundells throughout, but uses only a limited selection of the Blundell papers, relying on earlier published works.[165] In recent years historians have begun to pay increasing attention to the Blundell family. In particular Blundell's grandfather and namesake has received a significant degree of scholarly attention. Daniel Woolf has provided an overview of his reading practices based on entries in the family commonplace book, while Margaret Sena's article on his survival was the first to concentrate on his agency, as opposed to the more traditional narrative of victimhood.[166] However, while Blundell's grandfather has received increasing attention, Blundell himself has escaped any specific study. Aside from Andrew Gritt's excellent work on land management in Little Crosby, discussed in Chapter 2, since the 1970s there has been no sustained, scholarly work on Blundell and the few studies that briefly mention him have generally accepted the volume of correspondence recorded by Margaret Blundell as definitive. Therefore, historians have missed a mass of rich primary source material and the nature and extent of Blundell's activity has remained obscured.

III

This book provides a detailed examination of Blundell's political and cultural worlds. The first part considers the extent to which his public activities corroborate his claims of passive victimhood. Chapter 1 considers Blundell's activities in relation to his family and friends. Far from being the passive victim he claimed in his correspondence, it will be shown that Blundell created a series of defence mechanisms that protected him from the full force of the penal laws. Not only did he maintain kinship and social networks that provided him with both personal security and protection for his estate but he used the freedom that these strategies afforded him to protect other Catholics in his networks. Chapter 2 discusses Blundell's claims that he was a loyal subject in light of his activities outside these networks, and suggests that such claims represented loyalty to the monarchy not the regime, which Blundell undermined. He constructed a series of written defences of Catholicism, which sought the removal of the penal laws. Though surviving evidence indicates that only one of his works on this topic was printed, the arguments were disseminated amongst his contacts in manuscript and through close investigation it can be shown that their impact was widespread. Furthermore, Blundell patronised Catholics on his estate and developed close links with Catholics in Ireland, collecting money for their relief and keeping abreast of the latest news there, behaviour that many of his Protestant contemporaries would have viewed as directly contradicting his claims of loyalty. Blundell's links with Catholics outside England were most apparent in relation to religious orders. Not only did he encourage all of his children to take religious orders, but evidence from his notebooks suggests that he was one of the Poor Clares of Rouen's primary agents in England, holding significant sums of money on their behalf and lending it out at interest to ensure the continued prosperity of the order. In light of this it will be argued that Blundell's activities posed a direct threat to the Protestant state.

The second section of this book examines Blundell's reading practices as documented in his commonplace books: the Adversaria and the Historica. Written between 1658 and 1698, these sources allow a unique insight into the reading practices of a seventeenth-century Catholic gentleman, providing an outline of how he appropriated printed and manuscript texts, as well as outlining a worldview often contradictory to that found in his public claims. Chapter 3 considers the way in which Blundell constructed his commonplace books and the extent to which they support Ann Moss's argument that by the end of the seventeenth century commonplace authors abandoned the forms expounded in printed guides on structuring commonplace books and exerted autonomy over the style that they employed.[167] Far from sticking stringently to established methods of commonplacing, Blundell designed a method that suited his purposes and accorded with his reading practice. The agency evident through Blundell's public activities can be seen also in his reading. Blundell read for utility, often with a specific end in mind, and consequently mined books for material that supported his worldview. In cases when a text contradicted his beliefs he either ignored the sections he disagreed with or used his commonplace books as a forum within which to challenge them.

The ways in which Blundell appropriated and engaged with specific genres of material are considered in the final two chapters of this section. Chapter 4 analyses his entries on devotional writing and religious histories. Here we find further evidence that historians have been overly keen to accept his professions of loyalty and unquestioning Catholicism. Blundell's commonplaces suggest that certain aspects of Catholicism caused him problems. Amongst other issues, he did not accept many details of saints' lives, he thought that a number of miracles contradicted reason and had serious doubts about original sin. None the less, when engaging with work on Catholic history he rose to the defence of his co-religionists, including a passionate argument that maintained that the Irish Rebellions of the 1640s had little to do with Irish Catholics, but were instead the result of decades of brutal Protestant repression. The ways in which Blundell's anxieties about aspects of Catholic belief and practice affected his practical engagement with the world are discussed in Chapter 5. Through an analysis of his commonplaces on the social order and the place of women, his ethnographic entries and his notes on natural phenomena it is shown that Blundell was frequently torn between an approach to the world concomitant with his religious beliefs, and the approach advocated by Francis Bacon, of whom Blundell claimed to be a committed follower. The effect of this tension was that Blundell steered a distinctly idiosyncratic middle way through the two approaches.

The Conclusion holds that, in light of the findings of this book, early modern English Catholics cannot be seen as having been politically, intellectually or religiously inactive. Blundell's surviving papers clearly demonstrate that he actively ensured his own survival and played a prominent part in local and national politics. Blundell neither acceded thoughtlessly to the wishes of the Protestant regime or the Catholic Church. Furthermore, his political culture was not solely defined by his recusancy. Other issues such as his standing in the social order and his gender also had an impact on his worldview. A study of Blundell's political and intellectual worlds provides a unique window into early modern English Catholicism, as well as an insight into the way that one individual navigated the demands that were placed on him by different aspects of his belief system.

NOTES

1 Adversaria, fols 121–b; Historica, fol. 44b.

2 William Blundell to Charles Parker, 3 May 1660, in Letter Book One, fols 45–b.

3 Blue Book, fols 6, 7.

4 See, for instance: Blundell (ed.), *Cavalier: Letters*, passim.

5 T. B. Macaulay, *The History of England*, ed. H. Trevor-Roper (Harmondsworth: Penguin, 1986), pp. 70–86, 132–42; J. R. Western, *Monarchy and Revolution: The English State in the 1680s* (London: Macmillian, 1972), pp. 187–91. As discussed in: C. M. Hibbard, 'Early Stuart Catholicism: revisions and re-revisions', *Journal of Modern History*, 52 (1980), pp. 3–4; A. Shell, *Catholicism, Controversy and the English Literary Imagination, 1558–1660* (Cambridge: Cambridge University Press, 1999), p. 14.

6 As discussed in: M. C. Questier, 'Conformity, Catholicism and the law', in P. Lake and M. C. Questier (eds), *Conformity and Orthodoxy in the English Church, c.1560–1660* (Woodbridge: Boydell, 2000), pp. 238–9; Hibbard, 'Early Stuart Catholicism', pp. 3–4; Shell, *Catholicism, Controversy and the English Literary Imagination*, pp. 3–5.

7 H. Aveling, 'The Catholic recusants of the West Riding of Yorkshire 1558–1790', *Proceedings of the Leeds Philosophical and Literary Society*, 10 (1963), pp. 191–306; H. Aveling, *Northern Catholics: The Catholic Recusants of the North Riding of Yorkshire 1558–1790* (London: Geoffrey Chapman, 1966); J. C. H. Aveling, *Catholic Recusancy in the City of York 1558–1791*, Catholic Record Society Monograph Series, 2 (London: Catholic Record Society, 1970); J. C. H. Aveling, *The Handle and the Axe: The Catholic Recusants in England from Reformation to Emancipation* (London: Blond and Briggs, 1976).

8 E. H. Shagan, 'Introduction: English Catholic history in context', in E. H. Shagan (ed.), *Catholics and the 'Protestant Nation': Religious Politics and Identity in Early Modern England* (Manchester: Manchester University Press, 2005), p. 1; C. Haigh, 'Catholicism in early modern England: Bossy and beyond', *Historical Journal*, 45 (2002), p. 493.

9 J. Bossy, *The English Catholic Community, 1570–1850* (London: Darton, Longman and Todd, 1975).

10 J. Bossy, 'The English Catholic community 1603–1625', in A. G. R. Smith (ed.), *The Reign of James VI and I* (London: Macmillan, 1973), p. 92.

11 P. Lake, 'Anti-popery: the structure of a prejudice', in R. Cust and A. Hughes (eds), *Conflict in Early Stuart England: Studies in Religion and Politics 1603–1642* (Harlow: Longman, 1989), pp. 72–106; R. Clifton, 'Fear of popery', in C. Russell (ed.), *The Origins of the English Civil War* (Basingstoke: Macmillan, 1973), pp. 144–67.

12 Examples of their work include: P. Lake with M. C. Questier, *The Anti-Christ's Lewd Hat: Protestants, Papists and Players in Post-Reformation England* (London: Yale University Press, 2002); M. C. Questier, *Conversion, Politics and Religion in England, 1580–1625* (Cambridge: Cambridge University Press, 1996); M. C. Questier, *Catholicism and Community in Early Modern England: Politics, Aristocratic Patronage and Religion, c.1550–1640* (Cambridge: Cambridge University Press, 2006); A. Walsham, *Church Papists: Catholicism, Conformity and Confessional Polemic in Early Modern England* (Woodbridge: Boydell Press, 1999).

13 Questier, 'Conformity, Catholicism and the law', pp. 240–1, 248, 254–7, 260; M. C. Questier and S. Healy, '"What's in a name?": A papist's perception of Puritanism and conformity in the early seventeenth century', in A. F. Marotti (ed.), *Catholicism and Anti-Catholicism in Early Modern English Texts* (Basingstoke: Macmillan, 1999), pp. 140–3, 149.

14 See, for example: C. Haigh, *Reformation and Resistance in Tudor Lancashire* (Cambridge: Cambridge University Press, 1975); C. Haigh, *English Reformations: Religion, Politics, and Society Under the Stuarts* (Oxford: Clarendon Press, 1993); C. Haigh (ed.), *The English Reformation Revised* (Cambridge: Cambridge University Press, 1987) J. J. Scarisbrick, *The Reformation and the English People* (Oxford: Blackwell, 1984); E. Duffy, *The Stripping of the Altars: Traditional Religion in England 1400–1580* (London: Yale University Press, 1992).

15 Walsham, *Church Papists*, p. 5.

16 J. A. Williams, 'Sources for recusant history (1559–1791) in English official archives', *Recusant History*, 16 (1983), pp. 331–443.

17 Williams, 'Sources for recusant history', pp. 367–77.

18 J. Miller, *Popery and Politics in England, 1660–1688* (Cambridge: Cambridge University Press, 1973), pp. 9–12.

19 The major study of English Catholics on the continent remains P. Guilday, *The English Catholic Refugees on the Continent 1558–1795* (London: Longmans, Green and Co., 1914).

20 C. Walker, 'Prayer, patronage, and political conspiracy: English nuns and the Restoration', *Historical Journal*, 43 (2000), pp. 1–23; C. M. K. Bowden, 'The Abbess and Mrs. Brown: Lady Mary Knatchbull and Royalist politics in Flanders in the late 1650s', *Recusant History*, 24 (1998), pp. 288–308.

21 Walsham, *Church Papists*, p. 118.

22 Bossy, *English Catholic Community*, p. 193.

23 Walsham, *Church Papists*, p. 78.

24 Walsham, *Church Papists*, pp. 2, 22–49; M. C. Questier, 'Clerical recruitment, conversion and Rome c.1580–1625', in C. Cross (ed.), *Patronage and Recruitment in the Tudor and Early Stuart Church* (York: Borthwick Institute of Historical Research, 1996), p. 86.

25 C. Haigh, 'The fall of a church or the rise of a sect? Post-Reformation Catholicism in England', *Historical Journal*, 21 (1978), p. 185.

26 Walsham, *Church Papists*, p. 3.

27 Bossy, *English Catholic Community*, passim.

28 Hibbard, 'Early Stuart Catholicism', pp. 2–3.

29 Hibbard, 'Early Stuart Catholicism', p. 3. See also: M. B. Rowlands (ed.), *Catholics of Parish and Town 1558–1778*, Catholic Record Society Monograph Series, 6 (London: Catholic Record Society, 1999).

30 A. C. F. Beales, *Education Under Penalty: English Catholic Education from the Reformation to the Fall of James II* (London: Athlone Press, 1963); H. Aveling, 'The marriages of Catholic recusants, 1559–1642', *Journal of Ecclesiastical History*, 14 (1963), pp. 68–83.

31 Bossy, *English Catholic Community*, p. 79.

32 Walsham, *Church Papists*, passim; Questier and Healy, 'What's in a name?', pp. 137–53.

33 Miller, *Popery and Politics*, pp. 1, 58, 149; A. Hobson, '"The King's most loyal subjects": the relationship between Anglican loyalists and Roman Catholics in the reign of Charles II', *Royal Stuart Review* (1996), pp. 6–15; S. Pincus, *Protestantism and Patriotism: Ideologies and the Making of English Foreign Policy, 1650–1668* (Cambridge: Cambridge University Press, 1996), pp. 365–8.

34 A. Milton, 'A qualified intolerance: the limits and ambiguities of early Stuart anti-Catholicism', in Marotti (ed.), *Catholicism and Anti-Catholicism*, pp. 85–115; A. Milton, *Catholic and Reformed: The Roman and Protestant Churches in English Protestant Thought, 1600–1640* (Cambridge: Cambridge University Press, 1995).

35 A factor observed in T. H. Clancy, 'A content analysis of English Catholic books, 1615–1714', *Catholic Historical Review*, 86 (2000), p. 264.

36 M. C. Questier, 'What happened to English Catholicism after the English Reformation?', *History*, 85 (2000), p. 42; Walsham, *Church Papists*, p. 56.

37 Hibbard, 'Early Stuart Catholicism', p. 19; A. Walsham, '"Domme preachers?" Post-Reformation English Catholicism and the culture of print', *Past and Present*, 168 (2000), p. 102.

38 Questier, *Catholicism and Community*, p. 473.

39 Hibbard, 'Early Stuart Catholicism', p. 24; Bossy, 'English Catholic Community', pp. 94–7.

40 M. C. Questier, 'Loyalty, religion and state power in early modern England: English Romanism and the Jacobean Oath of Allegiance', *Historical Journal*, 40 (1997), pp. 311–29.

41 Walsham, 'Domme preachers?', p. 93; Questier, *Conversion, Politics and Religion*, pp. 40–75; M. C. Questier, 'Crypto-Catholicism, anti-Calvinism and conversion at the Jacobean court: the enigma of Benjamin Carier', *Journal of Ecclesiastical History*, 47 (1996), pp. 49–52, 64. Intramural bickering was also a motive for apostasy in Scotland: D. Szechi, 'Defending the true faith: Kirk, state, and Catholic missioners in Scotland, 1653–1755', *Catholic Historical Review*, 82 (1996), p. 407.

42 J. A. Williams, 'English Catholicism under Charles II: the legal position', *Recusant History*, 7 (1963), pp. 123–43.

43 K. Fincham and P. Lake, 'The ecclesiastical policy of King James I', *Journal of British Studies*, 24 (1985), pp. 169–207; K. J. Lindley, 'The lay Catholics of England in the reign of Charles I', *Journal of Ecclesiastical History*, 22 (1971), pp. 199–221; J. Spurr, 'Religion in Restoration England', in L. K. J. Glassey (ed.), *The Reigns of Charles II and James VII & II, 1660–1689* (Basingstoke: Macmillan, 1997), pp. 90–124; J. Israel, 'William III and toleration', in O. P. Grell, J. I. Israel and N. Tyacke (eds), *From Persecution to Toleration: The Glorious Revolution and Religion in England* (Oxford: Clarendon Press, 1991), pp. 129–70.

44 Hibbard, 'Early Stuart Catholicism', p. 3.

45 A. Fletcher, *A County Community in Peace and War: Sussex 1600–1660* (London: Longman, 1975), pp. 97–8.

46 J. Albers, 'Seeds of Contention: Society, Politics and the Church of England in Lancashire, 1689–1790' (DPhil thesis, Yale University, 1988), p. 496.

47 Hibbard, 'Early Stuart Catholicism', p. 4.

48 See, for example: J. Callow, 'The last of the Shireburnes: the art of death and life in recusant Lancashire, 1660–1754', *Recusant History*, 26 (2003), pp. 589–615; M. Mullett, '"A recepticle for papists and an assilum": Catholicism and disorder in late seventeenth-century Wigan', *Catholic Historical Review*, 73 (1987), pp. 391–407.

49 Bossy, 'English Catholic community', p. 92.

50 C. Hibbard, *Charles I and the Popish Plot* (Chapel Hill: University of North Carolina Press, 1983).

51 A relation of Charles's deathbed conversion was made by Catherine of Braganza and members of her entourage while staying with the Poor Clares of Rouen: 'many wou'd not believe that the King her husband dy'd a Catholick: which certainly he did ... he dy'd a true Catholick, & that no man cou'd dy with more repentance than he did': PCRA, Chronicles of the Poor Clares, Rouen I 1644–1701, p. 339.

52 K. J. Lindley, 'The part played by the Catholics', in B. Manning (ed.), *Politics, Religion and the English Civil War* (London: Arnold, 1973), pp. 126–76; Lindley, 'Lay Catholics of England', pp. 199–221.

53 P. R. Newman, 'Catholic Royalists of northern England 1642–1645', *Northern History*, 15 (1979), p. 88; P. R. Newman, 'Catholic Royalist activists in the north, 1642–46', *Recusant History*, 14 (1977), pp. 26–38; P. R. Newman, *Old Service: Royalist Regimental Colonels and the Civil War, 1642–1646* (Manchester: Manchester University Press, 1993); A. J. Hopper, '"The popish army of the north": anti-Catholicism and Parliamentarian allegiance in Civil War Yorkshire, 1642–46', *Recusant History*, 25 (2000), pp. 12–28; B. G. Blackwood, *The Lancashire Gentry and the Great Rebellion, 1640–60*, Chetham Society, 3rd Series, 25 (1978), p. 64; M. Bennett, 'Roman Catholic Royalist officers in the north midlands, 1642–1646', *Journal of Military and Strategic Studies*, 6 (2003), pp. 1–15; Questier, *Catholicism and Community*, pp. 499–507.

54 Walker, 'Prayer, patronage, and political conspiracy', passim.

55 B. Weiser, 'Owning the King's story: the escape from Worcester', *Seventeenth Century*, 14 (1999), pp. 43–62.

56 J. Miller, *James II: A Study in Kingship* (London: Methuen, 1989), pp. 167–87; A. Barclay, 'James II's "Catholic" Court', *1650–1850 Ideas, Aesthetics, and Inquiries in the Early Modern Period*, 8 (2003), pp. 161–71.

57 A. D. Wright, 'Catholic history, north and south', *Northern History*, 14 (1978), pp. 150–1.

58 Wright, 'Catholic history', p. 138.

59 Beales, *Education Under Penalty*, pp. 185–262; Hibbard, 'Early Stuart Catholicism', p. 31.

60 D. Szechi, 'A blueprint for tyranny? Sir Edward Hales and the Catholic Jacobite response to the Revolution of 1688', *English Historical Review*, 116 (2001), p. 365.

61 J. Scott, 'England's troubles: exhuming the Popish Plot', in T. Harris, P. Seaward and M. Goldie (eds), *The Politics of Religion in Restoration England* (Oxford: Basil Blackwell, 1990), p. 118; J. Scott, 'Radicalism and restoration: the shape of the Stuart experience', *Historical Journal*, 31 (1988), p. 460.

62 M. J. Galgano, 'Restoration Recusancy in the Northwest of England: A Social History, 1658–1673' (DPhil thesis, Vanderbilt University, 1971), pp. 80–3.

63 SRO, D590, Giffard Papers; SRO, D240, Aston Papers; NRO, FH3000–FH4653, Finch Hatton Papers.

64 Questier, *Catholicism and Community*, passim; S. Kaushik, 'Resistance, loyalty and recusant politics: Sir Thomas Tresham and the Elizabethan state', *Midland History*, 21 (1996), pp. 37–72; G. Glickman, 'John Caryll and the Context of English Catholic Jacobitism 1679–1712' (MPhil thesis, Cambridge University, 2002); G. Glickman, 'Politics, Culture and Ideology in the English Catholic Community 1688–1727' (DPhil thesis, Cambridge University, 2006).

65 D. R. Woolf, 'Little Crosby and the horizons of early modern historical culture', in D. R. Kelley and D. Harris Sacks (eds), *The Historical Imagination in Early Modern Britain: History, Rhetoric, and Fiction, 1500–1800* (Cambridge: Cambridge University Press, 1997), p. 98.

66 LCRO, DDBl 2/1, Sir Thomas Tyldesley to William Blundell, Captaincy of Dragoons, 22 December 1642; William Blundell to A. B., 9 July 1657; William Blundell to Unnamed Recipient, 29 December 1681, in Letter Book One, fols 29b–30, 122.

67 William Blundell to Margaret Haggerston, 27 February 1652, in Letter Book One, fols 55b–6.

68 See the discussion of Blundell's *History of the Isle of Man* later in this chapter. That he spent two periods in exile on the Isle of Man is based on the premise that he wrote the history. Blundell's letters specifically allude only to one period of exile there in 1646: William Blundell to Timothy Child, 17 October 1693, in Draft Letter Book, IV, fol. 70b.

69 William Blundell to Francis Parker, 6 June 1647, in Letter Book One, fols 62b–3; Cicely Burton [William Blundell] to Ananian Baker [Richard Masters], 1647, in Great Hodge Podge, fol. 89; Blundell (ed.), *Cavalier: Letters*, p. 17.

70 William Blundell to Constantia Masey, 26 November 1672, in Draft Letter Book, I, fol. 17b; Adversaria, fols 121–b; Historica, fol. 44b.

71 William Blundell to John Paget, 16 March 1680, in Draft Letter Book, III, fol. 60b.

72 The most detailed reference about his residence is a postscript to a letter which states 'From my lodging next door above the Crown in Veere-Street': William Blundell to Peter Shakerley, 2 November 1686; William Blundell to James Clifton, 17 October 1687, in Draft Letter Book, IV, fols 8b–9, 30. The earliest letters marked from London are from late September 1686 and the latest early October 1687. Further letters show that he was back in Crosby by September 1688, though the exact date on which he left London is not given: William Blundell to John Hulton, 4 September 1686; William Blundell to James Clifton, 17 October 1687; William Blundell to Thomas Cartwright Bishop of Chester, 5 September 1688, in Draft Letter Book, IV, fols 5b, 30, 36.

73 The case is documented in letters that Blundell sent to John Hulton, who acted as his Proctor: William Blundell to John Hulton, 4 September 1686; William Blundell to John Hulton, 25 September 1686; William Blundell to John Hulton, 16 November 1686, in Draft Letter Book, IV, fols 5b, 6, 9b. See also: CCA, EDC 5, Consistory Court Papers, 5, Sefton: William Blundell v. Churchwardens. In a letter to John Hulton Blundell claimed that issues relating to the road were 'my chief tho' not my only motive of coming to London'. What Blundell meant by this is unclear as the case was tried in Chester and it may have reflected an attempt to maximise the perceived distress it had caused him to elicit compensation: William Blundell to John Hulton, 8 January 1687, in Draft Letter Book, IV, fol. 15b.

74 William Blundell to William Gerard, 5 October 1686; William Blundell to John Gilli-

brand, 28 May 1687; William Blundell to John Entwistle, 22 March 1687, in Draft Letter Book, IV, fols 7, 22b, 24–b.

75 William Blundell to John Gillibrand, 28 May 1687; William Blundell to Margaret and Frances Blundell, 4 June 1687, in Draft Letter Book, IV, fols 24–b, 25b.

76 William Blundell to John Warner, 2 May 1687, in Draft Letter Book, IV, fol. 29.

77 William Blundell to Richard Bellings, no date, in Draft Letter Book, IV, fol. 42.

78 A copy of the warrant for Blundell Esq. can be found in: Great Hodge Podge, fol. 60b.

79 For an outline of Blundell's life see M. Gratton, 'Blundell, William (1620–1698)', in *ODNB*.

80 Hodge Podge the Third, fol. 3. That many Catholic landowners were buried in and offered financial support for the local parish church is also remarked on in Glickman, 'John Caryll and the Context of English Catholic Jacobitism', p. 12.

81 SA, Bagshaw Collection, C2705, Postnuptial Settlement between William Blundell the son and Mary Eyre now his wife, 12 April 1668.

82 William Blundell to Winifred Giffard, 14 October 1674, in Draft Letter Book, II, fol. 26b; William Blundell to Clare Frances Blundell, 2 January 1694, in Draft Letter Book, IV, fol. 75. Information for this paragraph was taken from the lists of members of his family who took religious orders and lists of his children with the dates of their births and deaths, initially made by Blundell and later updated by his son and grandson, in Great Hodge Podge, fols 89b–90, 184.

83 Bossy, *English Catholic Community*, p. 92.

84 Bossy, *English Catholic Community*, pp. 91–5.

85 Albers, 'Seeds of Contention', p. 485.

86 Haigh, *Reformation and Resistance*, pp. 247–94.

87 Milton, 'A qualified intolerance', passim; Walsham, *Church Papists*, passim.

88 See John Miller's claim that 'Catholicism was strongest in the more backward areas of the country': Miller, *Popery and Politics*, p. 13.

89 Questier, *Catholicism and Community*, p. 30.

90 William Blundell to Henry Stanley, 1677; William Blundell to Thomas Preston, 28 September 1678; William Blundell to Unnamed Recipient, 7 January 1682, in Letter Book One, fols 8b, 113b. 118b; Small Account Book, fol. 84.

91 Historians have emphasised the ubiquity of migration and mobility in early modern England. What is unusual about Blundell was the number of trips that he embarked on and, as we will see, the formative impact that they had on his worldview: I. D. Whyte, *Migration and Society in Britain 1550–1830* (Basingstoke: Macmillan, 2000), pp. 1–7; P. Clark, 'Migration in England during the late seventeenth and early eighteenth centuries', in P. Clark and D. Souden (eds), *Migration and Society in Early Modern England* (London: Hutchinson, 1987), pp. 213–52.

92 Only a brief reference to Blundell's time in Wales survives in a letter to an anonymous correspondent written after the Restoration, when he thanked 'my good friend who hath been so mindful of me in Wales' and held some books in trust during the unsettled times: William Blundell to Unnamed Recipient, 28 September 1665, in Letter Book One, fol. 85b.

93 Harrison (ed.), *Isle of Man*, I, pp. xiv, xxiii; William Blundell to Henry Stanley, 1677, in

Letter Book One, fol. 8b; William Blundell to Timothy Child, 17 October 1693, in Draft Letter Book, IV, fol. 70b.

94 William Blundell to Gilbert Crouch, 29 April 1653; William Blundell to Ann Blundell, 27 September 1658; William Blundell to Gilbert Ireland, August 1658; William Blundell to Charles Parker, 3 May 1660, in Letter Book One, fols 18b, 23, 36, 45–b; Hodge Podge the Third, fols 7, 19, 50b; Historica, fols 139b–40.

95 A journal for this trip survives, detailing distances travelled and a tour Blundell received around Edinburgh Castle: Small Account Book, fols 46–58b. The journal is transcribed and discussed in G. Baker, 'An unpublished account of an English Catholic's tour to Edinburgh in 1657', *Scottish Historical Review* (Forthcoming).

96 William Blundell to Richard Langhorne, 14 May 1673, in Letter Book One, fol. 102; William Blundell to Thomas Masey, 5 June 1673, in Draft Letter Book, I, fol. 38.

97 In 1639: William Blundell to A. B., 9 July 1657, Letter Book One, fols 29b–30. In 1662: Hodge Podge the Third, fols 46b–7. In 1666: William Blundell to Richard Bradshaigh, 14 November 1666; William Blundell to Francis Butler, 9 April 1667; William Blundell to Edmund Ballard, 30 June 1666, in Letter Book One, fols 88b–9, 94, 131; Small Account Book, fol. 83b; Hodge Podge the Third, fol. 57. In 1674: Small Account Book, fols 50, 51b; Hodge Podge the Third, fol. 26b.

98 In 1660: Small Account Book, fol. 78b; Blue Book, fol. 55b; William Blundell to Luisa Clare, 3 April 1660; William Blundell to Charles Parker, 3 May 1660; William Blundell to R. B., 12 June 1660, in Letter Book One, fols 45, 45b, 62. In 1680–81: William Blundell to Roger Midford, 9 April 1681; William Blundell to Unnamed Recipient, 7 January 1682; William Blundell to Thomas Blundell, November 1680, in Letter Book One, fols 118–22b; Hodge Podge the Third, fols 64b–5, 72b, 74, 90b. In 1687: William Blundell to John Gillibrand, 28 May 1687; William Blundell to Margaret and Clare Frances Blundell, 4 June 1687, in Draft Letter Book, IV, fols 24, 26.

99 This claim is based on the proximity of Little Crosby to Scarisbrick Hall (less than 15 miles) and that Blundell's papers relating to his kinsmen, the Scarisbrick family, suggest a close familiarity. See, for example: Blue Book, fol. 63b. In his study of the Jesuits, Henry Foley estimated the period that the school at Scarisbrick Hall was open. On the basis of dates of inscriptions in school textbooks he states that 'the school may have been in existence in 1618, probably from 1628 to 1639, certainly from 1648 to 1652, continuing probably in 1679'. Thus, it is likely to have been in existence before Blundell succeeded to the family estates, when he would have received his education. Further indications can be found in Foley's list of signatures extracted from the fly-leaves of textbooks from the school, in which the signature 'Blundell' appears, though no first name is given: H. Foley, *Records of the English Province of the Society of Jesus: Historic Facts Illustrative of the Labours and Sufferings of its Members in the Sixteenth and Seventeenth Centuries*, 7 vols (London: Burns and Oates, 1883), VII, pp. 1414–15. The archives from Scarisbrick Hall include further material suggesting close links between Blundell and the school during his adult life. These include two manuscript works of devotion authored by, and a series of printed books signed by, Thomas Blundell, William's son, from which it appears likely that he taught at the school in the 1680s: DAA, MS 54, Thomas Blundell, De Virtutibus Theologicus & Tractatus De Paenitentia, 1687; DAA, MS 38, Thomas Blundell, The Catholic Doctrine of Transubstantiation, 1687–1688. A signature on the fly-leaf to J. Childrey, *Britannia Baconica, or the Natural Varieties of England, Scotland and Wales* (1661) (DAA, B4) states that the book was given to John Grene, who had been at Scarisbrick Hall in the 1680s, by William Blundell. I am grateful to Maurice Whitehead and Geoffrey Scott for

discussions about Catholic education and for turning my attention to the archives at DAA.

100 On the basis of surviving records about the priests at Scarisbrick, this would probably have been Robert Grosvernor: Foley, *Records of the English Province*, VII, pp. 323–4. Foley argues that it was to Grosvernor (operating under the alias Henry Howard) that Blundell appealed for advice in 1654 on the management of the leases on his estate (discussed in detail in Chapter 2). This is certainly a possibility, though the constant changing of aliases means that we cannot be certain.

101 William Blundell to Christopher Bradshaigh, 14 February 1657, in Small Account Book, fol. 39b; William Blundell to William Selby, 13 May 1655; William Blundell to Charles Parker, 16 May 1659; William Blundell to J. Stevens, 3 September 1653; William Blundell to A. B., June 1654, in Letter Book One, fols 19, 20b, 42b, 54b, 57, 57b. Note Blundell's comment that between 1687 and 1688 he had many conversations 'in Latin with a natural Chinese whom I did sundry times meet with by reason that he went to the Latin school at the Savoy': Historica, fol. 139b.

102 Adversaria, fols 29, 94.

103 G. Smith, *The Cavaliers in Exile 1640–1660* (Basingstoke: Palgrave Macmillan, 2003), p. 91.

104 K. Sharpe, *Reading Revolutions: The Politics of Reading in Early Modern England* (London: Yale University Press, 2000), pp. 71, 170–1.

105 A phrase borrowed from A. Hughes, *Gangraena and the Struggle for the English Revolution* (Oxford: Oxford University Press, 2004), p. 15.

106 William Blundell to Roger L'Estrange, 31 May 1664; William Blundell to Thomas Blundell, November 1680, in Letter Book One, fols 65, 119b.

107 The draft of the work is spread (with signposting indicating where to finish and start again) throughout the volume: Blue Book, fols 2b–5b, 7–17, 19, 21–5, 32–41.

108 Gibson (ed.), *Cavalier's Note Book*, p. 78; Blue Book, fol. 39: '... thus far printed Decem: 5 1661'.

109 Adversaria, fol. 237b; Great Hodge Podge, fol. 199b.

110 'Saul, Saul, why persecutest me?': Acts 22:7.

111 Adversaria, fol. 237b.

112 Blue Book, fol. 39.

113 W. Blundell, *A Letter Writ to a Friend: Being a Description of a Horn, which Grows in the Back Part of the Head of an Ancient Woman ... Living at Saughal* (1668). (Owen H. Wangensteen Historical Library of Biology and Medicine at the University of Minnesota: TC Bio-Med Wangensteen Folio 617.3 B62). I am grateful to Elaine Challacombe and James Curley from the Wangensteen Historical Library for making this document available.

114 Harrison (ed.), *Isle of Man*; P. W. Caine, 'William Blundell and his Manx history', *Isle of Man Natural History and Antiquarian Society Proceedings*, New Series, 5 (1946–1950), pp. 128–35.

115 Only three manuscript copies of the document now survive, which are held at the Manx National Heritage Library. Of the three, only one contains the full text, a definite contemporary binding and is written in a seventeenth-century hand. The catalogue entry plausibly speculates that this manuscript was the original, and it was this that was the basis for William Harrison's transcription. MNHL, MS 741C: Manuscript history

of the Isle of Man, 1650. I am grateful to Roger Sims, Archivist at the MNHL, for assistance with analysing this manuscript.

116 W. Sacheverell, *An Account of the Isle of Man, its Inhabitants, Language, Soil, Remarkable Qualities* (1702).

117 J. Seacome, *Memoirs Concerning a Genealogical and Historical Account of the Ancient and Honourable House of Stanley, From the Conquest to the Death of Late Earl of Derby, In the Year James 1735; As also a full Description of the Isle of Man, &c* (Liverpool, 1741), II, pp. 1–2.

118 Harrison (ed.), *Isle of Man*, I, pp. xiv, xxiii; William Blundell to Timothy Child, 17 October 1693, in Draft Letter Book, IV, fol. 70b.

119 William Blundell to Unnamed Recipient, 28 September 1665, in Letter Book One, fol. 85b.

120 Adversaria, fol. 8b.

121 'Catholicks why they should not be persecuted' written in 1672, Blue Book, fols 55–7b; 'A discourse concerning the punishment of Roman Catholicks in England' written in 1666, Letter Book Two, pp. 145–62.

122 LCRO, DDBl 54/41 Tenants' Book, 1659–1728.

123 To avoid confusion, the titles are listed (see abbreviations section) as they are given in the hand-list for the collection. However, these are not accurate. For instance 'William Blundell the Cavalier's Letter Book 1681–90' includes significant material from the Civil War period onwards. See, for example: William Blundell to Unnamed Recipient, July 1650, in Letter Book One, fol. 53.

124 Harkirk Burial Register.

125 Draft Letter Book. As each of the four volumes bound into this document was numbered separately by Blundell, for the purposes of this study they are given as different volumes of the Draft Letter Book. I am grateful to Mark Walmsley, Conservator at the LCRO, for assistance in dating the binding.

126 Letter Book One.

127 Letter Book Two. The division of this source into pages as opposed to folios is in accordance with Blundell's own method of numbering the sheets. However, in most cases Blundell numbered his papers by folio.

128 P. Beal, 'Notions in garrison: the seventeenth-century commonplace book', in W. Speed Hill (ed.), *New Ways of Looking at Old Texts: Papers of the Renaissance English Text Society, 1985–1991* (New York: Renaissance English Text Society, 1993), pp. 131–47.

129 Small Account Book.

130 Hodge Podge the Third; Blue Book.

131 Historica; Adversaria. As the pages of the Adversaria are continuously numbered over the two volumes, for the purposes of this book the manuscript is referenced as a single entity.

132 LCRO, DDBl acc. 6147, Box 1, Loose Leaf Transcripts by William Blundell; LCRO, DDBl acc. 6121, Box 6, Extracts from religious books, 1677; LCRO, DDBl acc. 6121, Box 3, Transcription of *The Affairs of the Portuguese in India*; LCRO, DDBl acc. 6121, Box 3, Transcription of 'The Touchstone of Truth', transcribed from J. E. Nieremberg, *A Treatise of the Difference Betwixt the Temporal and Eternal* (1672).

133 Great Hodge Podge.

134 Account of Jacobite Trial; A. Goss (ed.), *II – The Trials at Manchester in 1694*, Chetham Society, 1st Series, 61 (1864). Because of the similarities between the two sources, Goss speculates that the text had a common origin in another account of the Jacobite trials copied by one John Jesse, which was transcribed in a volume of contemporary accounts of the Jacobite trial edited by William Beamont in the mid-nineteenth century. Beamont believed Jesse's work was copied from a manuscript written by Robert Wagstaffe, a nonjuring clergyman, who wrote the *Letter out of Lancashire* documenting the trials. This is largely speculation, but the similarities between the sources suggest that they were likely to have been based on the same original source(s): Goss (ed.), *The Trials at Manchester*, pp. xvi–xvii; W. Beamont (ed.), *The Jacobite Trials at Manchester in 1694*, Chetham Society, 1st Series, 28 (1853); R. Wagstaffe, *A Letter out of Lancashire to a Friend in London, Giving some Account of the late Tryals there* (1694).

135 Letters of Blundell Junior.

136 Blue Book, fols 55b, 80–b, 87; Small Account Book, fols 80, 85; Great Hodge Podge, fol. 192.

137 Hodge Podge the Third, fols 5b, 18b, 19, 37, 41, 67; Letter Book One, fol. 64b; Draft Letter Book, I.

138 For example: Hodge Podge the Third, fols 17, 40b, 64; William Blundell to Mrs Selby, 5 July 1672, in Draft Letter Book, I, fol. 5.

139 A lack of surviving papers from the pre-Civil War period may be explained in Blundell's comment to his son in 1686: 'A great number of ... coyness ... I had in my own keeping till the yeare 1642, when I sent them into Wales for better security with writeings and other goods which were finally lost'. This is the only comment that survives on this subject, and one is left to wonder exactly what was lost and to whom the goods were sent for safe keeping: William Blundell to Thomas Blundell, 29 December 1686, in Draft Letter Book, IV, fol. 13b. Elsewhere, in a note on a book he copied, Blundell recorded that 'the Copy (with many other bookes of myne) is allmost all perished, in the Late Warrs': Great Hodge Podge, fol. 83.

140 Hodge Podge the Third, fols 17b, 23b, 24b, 31b, 57b, 63b, 65b, 66b, 71b, 90.

141 Hodge Podge the Third, fols 17, 40b, 64.

142 Great Hodge Podge, fol. 88b.

143 See, for example: William Blundell to N. N., 23 April 1653, in Letter Book One, fol. 12b. On occasion Blundell also used the initials 'N. N.' to cover his own identity in his writings.

144 For examples of Blundell's marginalia see Letter Book Two, pp. 46, 57, 121, 127.

145 William Blundell to N. N., 19 April 1653, in Letter Book One, fol. 13.

146 See, for example: Great Hodge Podge, fols 258–b.

147 One example is the letter to Father Walton, the name of the recipient given in full in the Small Account Book, but as 'N. N.' in Blundell's Letter Book: William Blundell to N. N., 17 January 1657, in Letter Book One, fol. 33; William Blundell to Father Walton, 17 January 1657, in Small Account Book, fol. 33.

148 See, for instance: Hodge Podge the Third, fols 36, 53, 68b–77.

149 Hodge Podge the Third, fol. 36.

150 Blue Book, fol. 65; Hodge Podge the Third, fols 27b, 39.

151 For example: Ann Blundell to Nicholas Blundell, 20 November, in Small Account Book, fols 28b–9; Winifred Blundell to Unnamed Recipient, 26 September 1666; Frances Blundell to Lady Mountgarret, 3 June 1667, in Letter Book Two, pp. 39–41, 43–4.

152 William Blundell to Thomas Blundell, November 1680, in Letter Book One, fol. 119.

153 William Blundell to Thomas Blundell, November 1680, in Letter Book One, fol. 119.

154 William Blundell to Roger Bradshaigh, 14 December 1676; William Blundell to Unnamed Recipient, 14 July 1677; William Blundell to Unnamed Recipient, 23 January 1691, in Letter Book One, fols 104, 105, 129.

155 For example: Letter Book Two, pp. 41, 44, 49, 55, 58, 67.

156 Letter Book Two, p. 52.

157 See, for example: William Blundell to N. N., 23 April 1653, in Letter Book One, fol. 12b.

158 William Blundell to Gilbert Crouch, March 1657, in Small Account Book, fol. 41; William Blundell to Mrs Selby, 7 July 1672, in Letter Book One, fol. 6b.

159 William Blundell to the Comptroller of the Post Office, 17 December 1675, in Draft Letter Book, II, fols 53–b. In a letter to Thomas Masey he expanded on the problem, noting that 'In truth we have been often scurvily used by the Warrington post, & I do not doubt at all but the fault doth lye now at that dore. I have formerly complained of it at the letter office in London, & I do purpose againe to do so ... I shall therefore when the state of affaires will permit (espetially for larger packets) make use of some cheaper way then by the common post': William Blundell to Thomas Masey, 11 December 1674, in Draft Letter Book, II, fol. 33.

160 Two examples of different codes with keys survive: Great Hodge Podge, fol. 107b; Hodge Podge the Third, fol. 60.

161 J. Barry, 'Literacy and literature in popular culture: reading and writing in historical perspective', in T. Harris (ed.), *Popular Culture in England, c.1500–1800* (London: Macmillan, 1995), p. 87.

162 Gibson (ed.), *Cavalier's Note Book*; T. E. Gibson (ed.), *Crosby Records: A Chapter of Lancashire Recusancy*, Chetham Society, New Series, 12 (1887).

163 Blundell (ed.), *Cavalier: Letters*.

164 Tyrer, 'Recusancy'.

165 Galgano, 'Restoration Recusancy in the Northwest'.

166 M. Sena, 'William Blundell and the networks of Catholic dissent in Post-Reformation England', in A. Shepard and P. Withington (eds), *Communities in Early Modern England: Networks, Place, Rhetoric* (Manchester: Manchester University Press, 2000), pp. 54–75; Woolf, 'Little Crosby and the horizons of early modern historical culture', passim.

167 A. Moss, *Printed Commonplace Books and the Structuring of Renaissance Thought* (Oxford: Clarendon Press, 1996).

Part I

Family, friends and connections

Chapter 1

William Blundell's family and friends

With the exception of letters to close friends, the material that Blundell released into the public domain concentrated on his manifold sufferings under a Protestant state. However, these claims should not necessarily be taken at face value. Blundell developed defences that helped him to navigate the extremes of the penal laws, the most significant of which was the creation of Catholic and Protestant networks of friends and family who offered him protection. These networks had their limits, the most obvious example being during the Interregnum when his lands were confiscated by government agents and he was forced to repurchase them. Yet, even during the most trying times it can be shown that Blundell's initiative remained consistent and at least partially effective. This chapter focuses on Blundell's efforts to protect himself from the penal laws, and the ways in which he used the relative freedom this gave him to promote Catholicism amongst his family and friends. Far from supporting the view that Blundell was defined by his victimhood, the picture that will emerge is that of a wily, intelligent operator who actively ensured the survival of the Blundell dynasty.

I

Blundell's papers record both his victimisation and his expressed loyalty to the monarch. He felt a deep loyalty to monarchy, as he emphasised in his frequent statements that during the Civil War 'I lost for my duty to the king, to a pack of … Arch-villaines … My limbs, my Goods, my liberty'.[1] His letters regularly stated that during the late 1640s and 1650s 'My Estate was ten years sequestered, and afterwards bought off the Usurpers, with moneys which I borrow'd. I was 4 tymes imprisoned and paid my ransom twice'.[2] He was shocked to find that when Charles II ascended to the throne he did not protect his Catholic subjects from the penal laws in recognition of the support that they had given his father: a failure Blundell, like many of his contemporaries, attributed to 'Eevel Councellors about the King'.[3] With the exception of the years 1685 to 1688 when a Catholic monarch, James II, sat on the throne, from 1660 to the end of his life Blundell was subject to a series of penal laws. Applied sporadically, in line with the waves of anti-popery that panicked the country, these laws enforced social limitations and fines on the Catholic population for failure to attend Anglican services. Catholics were theoretically subject to a range of such penal laws, including financial penalties such as the 12*d* fine for each absence from the parish church on a Sunday and the £20 fine for failing to receive the sacrament, which increased by £20 for every year thereafter. Social penalties included being barred from holding public office and the inability to move more than five miles from the usual abode without special licence.[4] After James II fled the country Blundell was imprisoned again, and, despite claims to Protestant acquaintances that he was pleased with the way the country was run under William and Mary, in letters to close friends he stated that 'the world growes wors & wors dayly: and our everlasting & double taxes make us poorer and poorer'.[5] Blundell's papers demonstrate that he was embittered at this treatment. His frustration was evident in his statement that 'If Catholicks be disloyal, hang them: If loyal and serviceable to the king, why is the King deprived of their service? It would be thought a great hurt to the crown if Any one ... County of England were exempted from duty in civil and military affaires'.[6] He closed one letter to a friend by stating that 'I think that none but madmen can execute those cruel things that are threatened against his majestyes Catholic subjects'.[7] However, to end on such a superficial reading of his papers would be misleading.

That Blundell often referred to himself as a passive victim in his correspondence may reflect more his efforts to manipulate recipients of his letters than his real position. For instance, Blundell's relation of his sufferings during the Civil War and Interregnum in a letter to the Poor Clares of Rouen was designed to ensure that he negotiated the cheapest portion for his daughter's entry, which he secured at markedly below the average rate.[8] His claims that he was a 'wretched poore creature' bogged down by 'Age and infirmity, Debts and cares' were frequently used to excuse failure to respond to correspondence or late payment of dues.[9] Indeed, Blundell could play the part of the victim well when he knew that it would help provide security for his own position. Furthermore, the reiteration of his victimisation appears to have stemmed from Blundell's belief that his sufferings were actually a positive part of his identity and the historical legacy of his family. Throughout his papers, Blundell listed his sufferings next to those of his grandfather and father, boasting how his grandfather 'was 5 years imprisoned for his conscience ... yet prospered much in the world all though he payd much for his Conscience to his dying day'.[10] Therefore, Blundell's expressions of victimhood should not necessarily be accepted without question. For example, in letters to friends he frequently spoke of the 'mutilation of my best limbs' and how his disability had resulted in the near ruin of his life, requiring him to wear a 'long heeld shoe' and often resort to the use of crutches.[11] That Blundell had a pronounced limp received some external support, such as evidence presented at the 1677 Quarter Sessions that, following a dispute over some land between Hugh Reynolds and Blundell, Reynolds exclaimed, 'I will shoot him [Blundell] with a brace of bullets, calling him Halt Will & that he cared not a turd for him'.[12] However, it is unlikely that his disability proved as much of a barrier for Blundell as he claimed. He travelled extensively throughout the British Isles and continental Europe from the mid-1640s onwards, which required reasonable mobility. There is also a mention in a letter to Alice Haggerston, Blundell's mother-in-law, at his upset that an unnamed family member could stay no longer, as in regular games with them he had found 'a most excellent player at Shuttle-cock'.[13] A similar pattern can be seen in the incongruity between Blundell's claims about his financial situation in his correspondence, and the activities that his private papers show he was involved in.

Despite his claims, Blundell was never reduced to poverty and the Crosby estate was far from being reduced to rack and ruin during the seventeenth century. Though a number of annual accounting records were written in a volume that no longer survives, the Small Account Book contains nine years of detailed accounts and a summary of accounts for a further twelve years.[14] From these records it is evident that Blundell spent a great deal of time monitoring his finances and adjusting his lifestyle to suit his income. He was particularly successful in this endeavour and by 1658 his goods had exceeded the value of his debts by just over £208 despite the fact that he had been forced to repurchase the entirety of his estate only five years earlier.[15] By 1667 he was worth just over £891 and by 1674 just over £1250.[16] The Crosby estate was massively developed during Blundell's tenure as Lord of the Manor. In 1660 he spent an unspecified amount on 'the building of my Hall dyning room Starrcase &c', in 1663 ordered that a wainscot of the finest wood be constructed in his dining room, by 1667 had made 'a large Addition to my house in Building' and in 1672 he spent more than £100 on a new stable.[17] Blundell frequently complained of the cost of these buildings to his friends, noting in 1672 that 'I have spent too much this year in the making of some out buildings, which I trust will be the last that I or my Heires shall need to build for sondry ages to come'.[18] Blundell also improved his land by marling the soil, a process whereby lime and clay is added to the ground, reducing soil acidity and freeing up nutrients for future crops.[19] Having enquired into the effectiveness of this technique from neighbours and friends, he invested heavily in the process, which he continued to do even in the 1650s, when he spent £28 in 1652 and £40 in 1659 to marl specific plots of land on his estate.[20]

Blundell's financial interests were not restricted to his estate, and on various occasions he made investments that paid significant dividends for himself and his family. Though not a spectacular investment, in 1658 Blundell recorded how he bulk purchased oats, which kept the cost low while ensuring that he had a suitable supply of food in case of future civil disturbances.[21] The most rewarding speculative investment that he made was his 'venture at sea'.[22] Blundell's papers show that on at least two occasions he invested in shipping. Though only a brief mention is made of his 1664 investment, full accounts are provided for 1666 to 1667 which demonstrate a marked increase in his funds.[23] In September 1666 Blundell invested in 'an adventure to the Barbados in the good ship called the Antilope of Liverpoole' at a cost of £40, though his sister Winifred persuaded him to let her buy out £5 of his portion.[24] A full list of the goods that the Antelope transported survives in the Great Hodge Podge, which includes clothing, barrels of preserved food and building supplies, though the most significant of the goods on board the vessel was 3332 yards of linen cloth, at a value of £130 15*s* 9*d*.[25] So successful was this venture that on the vessel's return to Liverpool in August 1667 Blundell received a return of between £89 and £90, more than doubling his investment.[26]

Blundell's papers also show that he spent significant sums of money on expensive pastimes. Alongside building works, the lavish entertainment of friends at Crosby Hall provided a frequent obstruction to his financial targets for the year.[27] Furthermore, he was deeply involved in the horse racing scene in Lancashire. The Blue Book contains a mathematical formula that he developed to calculate how far horses could run, while in letters he enquired about the fortunes of particular horses, such as 'the late successe of the Gray mare in Cumberland'.[28] In response to a request from William Molyneux, five large single sides of folio in the Blue Book are taken up with a detailed list of articles concerning the rules and regulations for a racing cup in Lancashire. Not only did Blundell expend significant effort in constructing the document, but he was one of the subscribers who sponsored the event.[29] His extravagance can also be seen in the purchase of luxury goods. Correspondence with one David Cooke, a merchant in Liverpool, refers to a large consignment of dates that Blundell bought. While he did 'well approve of the Dates which you sold to my servant', Blundell refused to buy more unless Cooke could ensure that no extraordinary taxes were levied on the items.[30] Finally, despite comparing his likeness to that of a goblin, Blundell was something of a fashion connoisseur.[31] In a list of clothes purchased from his tailor, Richard Ayrey, among other costly items he recorded having paid £2 17*s* 'for a sky coloured silk hair coat' for his daughter Mary and £23 5*s* for 'my suit with the Gold buttons & for other things'.[32] As we will see, Blundell was deeply concerned with his wife's purchasing of clothing and complained how at one time clothes were passed between the generations for decades and women knew nothing more of London than its name, 'Now they know the streets as well as the Porters of the Town: & they pay not for their Gownes & silk stockings till there be half a dozen on the schore'.[33] Therefore, Blundell's emphasis on his sufferings may not provide an accurate account of his position, but an example of one way in which he facilitated his own survival. He no doubt hoped that through projecting the studied pose of a financially and physically weak individual the authorities would ignore him.

Before we look at the more subtle ways in which Blundell evaded the penal laws, it is worth noting that a concentration on his victimhood ignores many well known occasions when he proved an effective advocate of his needs and wishes. The most obvious example was his behaviour during the Civil War. Far from disappearing into obscurity Blundell took a Captain's commission, acquiring his disability during his first serious engagement.[34] In 1647 when he returned to his estate he rapidly found himself in further conflict with Parliamentarian troops when a number of Thomas Fairfax's soldiers refused to pay for quarters. In an anonymous draft letter, written to an unnamed representative of the regime in 1647, Blundell claimed that, when he refused to let the soldiers' horses out of the stables until they paid, the soldiers 'drew their swords so did I myne, my servants had sticks and stones but noe one blow was stricken on eyther side'. He was quick to assure the recipient that he appeared 'in right of my wife' and not as a landowner in his own right, as at the time Ann had leased the estate from sequestrators.[35] In 1673 Blundell refused to provide a horse and horseman for the county, a cost he believed unfair as it was originally divided between him and another individual. His persistent complaints resulted in the suspension of the charge until, it appears, 1680 when the other half of the cost was met by one Richard Hesketh.[36] As we have seen, Blundell's refusal to accept treatment that he deemed unfair extended to complaints over land disputes, one of which resulted in a threat against his life, and a warning to a local merchant that he would not pay arbitrary taxes on dates.[37]

During the reign of James II, Blundell went to London and petitioned for a civil position. The extent of Blundell's links at court is unclear and contradicted within his correspondence. Despite claiming to Peter Shakerley that 'I have not such access to his Majestie as you seem to think', elsewhere he boasted that 'I do not greatly doubt but that my Interest will be sufficient by the help of a second hand to present a paper even to the King himself'.[38] What is clear is that despite claiming in a letter to the Protestant Shakerley his 'passion ... against a most unseasonable Bigottry which I have observed in severall persons both of your Perswation and mine', Blundell watched with enthusiasm as Catholics were given senior civil and military positions and himself sought to grasp the opportunities for self-advancement that James II's reign brought.[39] However, Blundell not only challenged behaviour that he believed was demonstrably unlawful and exploited opportunities to increase his own fortunes when they were within the law, but he also negotiated routes around the penal laws.

II

Although an open recusant, Blundell kept the full extent of his Catholicism covert. We have already seen that he devised secret codes for letters that he sent to prominent co-religionists during unsettled times to carry on the correspondence safely.[40] Blundell often referred to letters to Rouen as being 'expressed by a dark Character, such as passeth between us in these bad tymes', and never gave full details of his dealings with the order in any of the family commonplace books, the security of which could not be guaranteed.[41] During the brief period that Blundell spent in hiding during the Civil War, he adopted a system of pseudonyms, referring to himself as 'Cicely Burton', and to the recipient of one letter, Richard Masters, as 'Ananian Baker'. Through this means he felt comfortable discussing news about the fate of the Royalists and hopes that new troops would be sent from Ireland.[42] Blundell's more blatant political and religious dealings with other Catholics or his own religious beliefs are conspicuously absent in any of his letters beyond the cryptic references discussed above. While his commonplace books and his personal notebooks contain politically sensitive material, Blundell had more control over their audience. Thus, unlike those contemporaries who have received historical attention, such as Edward Coleman and William Howard, Lord Stafford, Blundell was circumspect in his behaviour.[43]

Essential to Blundell's efforts to survive was a commitment to the gathering and interpretation of information. Blundell developed extensive networks of friends and family who sent him a wide range of material regarding local, national and international news. Local information that Blundell recorded mainly concerned how taxes would be distributed in Lancashire, as well as material specific to events in Little Crosby that was passed on to him by friends or officials in the township.[44] His national concerns were focused on the fortunes of recusants, though friends and family who were either visiting London or had heard news from the capital also kept him informed of developments such as the fate of parliaments during the Interregnum, military preparations during the Anglo-Dutch wars and efforts to grant William III aid.[45] In 1666 Richard Langhorne sent Blundell details of 'the late votes of Parliament, and his Majesties assent given for the putting of the Penall Lawes in speedie execution against all Catholick Priests & others of that profession', which concluded that all that Catholics could do under such circumstances was continue to confirm their loyalties to the King.[46] He was sent a handwritten copy made by John Gillibrand from the *Observator* of a list of recusants that Parliament intended to banish from Lancashire in 1680, which included Blundell's name.[47] Blundell also hired an attorney, Samuel Andrews, who kept him informed of developments about both his own conviction for recusancy in 1673 and laws against recusants in general.[48] This information was supplemented by Blundell's monitoring of published debates over the penal laws. For example, the pamphlet *The Case of Divers Roman Catholicks as it was Lately Stated* that proposed that Catholics 'not be excluded from the general Indulgement to tender consciences' was read by Blundell, examined and discussed with his friend Richard Haile and fully transcribed in Blundell's notebooks within a year of its publication.[49] His concerns abroad ranged widely from the success of the Catholic mission in China to the treatment of Huguenots under Louis XIV.[50] Blundell claimed that knowledge of affairs abroad was essential to his survival in England. As a landowner, information about foreign affairs, particularly the Anglo-Dutch war, helped him predict fluctuations in the cost of living and prepare accordingly; while events in Europe allowed him, as a recusant, to forecast future laws concerning Catholics as he believed that they offered 'an occasion here to justify the rigours used against the Catholicks of England who have few to favour or help them in these troublesome sad times'.[51] Therefore, Blundell made every effort to ensure that he was well informed about the position of Catholics in England, and his subsequent actions were often dictated by his understanding of how the changing fortunes of recusants would affect both himself and his family.

One of the crucial aspects of Blundell's survival was the continuation of the practice of strict settlement of the family estate.[52] Strict settlement of an estate meant that the heir to any lands became a life tenant as opposed to an outright owner, and the estate was most commonly entailed on his sons. Therefore, the heir was limited in what he could do to it, while the period for which a lease could be given was significantly reduced.[53] Strict settlement was employed during the seventeenth century as a method to help further dynastic ambition by ensuring that estates were not divided or treated in a destructive manner, but it played a particular role in securing the estates of recusant families.[54] Fines for recusancy and after the Civil War, delinquency, were charged on the basis of the legal interest that the individual had in their estate. As John Habakkuk has shown, fines for both were significantly lower if only a life interest was held as the full rate of any fine could be charged only on land held in fee-simple; only half was charged on those lands in which the individual held a reversionary or life interest.[55] Therefore, in sacrificing individual autonomy over the estate, landed recusant families could reduce the impact of fines for failure to attend church.

The practice of strict settlement was adopted in the Blundell family following the untimely death of Blundell's father. The marriage of Blundell at the age of fifteen to Ann provided the opportunity to draw up the settlement.[56] His charges for delinquency and the basis for repurchase were consequently charged at a lower level as he held only a reversionary interest. This was a practice that made survival for the recusant Blundell family easier and was continued into the following century with subsequent heirs revising wills during times of political upheaval. Nicholas Blundell, William's grandson, made six successive wills during the early eighteenth century in response to changes in his family situation, while he quickly reviewed and settled his estates after the outbreak of the 1715 Jacobite Rebellion, 'foreseeing difficult times for those of his religion'.[57]

III

The way in which Blundell drew on these survival mechanisms can be seen in his protection of his estates between 1643 and the Restoration. For all contemporaries the Civil War brought huge burdens, both financial and social.[58] The impact of war was felt most by Catholic Royalists, like Blundell, who qualified as 'delinquents' for both their stance during the conflict and their recusancy.[59] On 27 March 1643 Parliament passed an Ordinance of Sequestration, whereby the estates of Royalists were confiscated and the moneys accruing from them made available for the war effort.[60] Catholics were denied the opportunity to compound their fines in a single payment and regain their estates. However, the wives of Catholic landowners maintained a right to both the manor house and one-fifth of the estate in order to preserve the well-being of the family.[61] Between 1651 and 1652 three Acts of Sale were introduced which were directed at Catholic Royalists, those who refused to compound, and prominent Royalists who were not allowed to compound. Their estates were put on the open market, allowing those delinquents who could afford it to repurchase their lands, while others lost all rights to their estates.[62] A further Act in 1656 made blatant the government's efforts to deal forcefully with recusants, specifically penalising Protestants who held land in trust for Catholic friends to prevent it from falling into the hands of sequestrators.[63]

For Blundell the period 1643 to 1660 was one of hardship that he repeatedly recollected in correspondence and personal notes. In the mid-1640s Crosby was regularly looted by Parliamentarian troops and Blundell claimed that not only were the family valuables taken but he even had to bury bread to prevent soldiers from stealing it.[64] During this period Blundell was imprisoned four times and had his land confiscated by Parliament. In a letter written in 1654 he claimed that he had a 'sequestration sicknesse' and that his life had become 'a perpetuall clatter with Affidavits, Reprizalls, Conveyances, Fynes, Fees, Attournments, Recoveryes and Certificates'.[65] He was distraught that his only financial concern was 'more how to borrow more the next tyme, then to pay what I had borrowed the last'.[66] Although he devised ways of preserving his estate in Little Crosby, other land that he owned in Liverpool and a smaller estate in Ditton remained confiscated from 1643 to 1653.[67] Thus, in a discourse on the loyalty of Catholics written during the Restoration period, Blundell remarked that while more Protestants might have been killed in the King's service during the Civil War, it was Catholics who paid the most in terms of liberty and finance, stating that including fines for recusancy that Catholics paid 'at a 2fold charge higher rate ... then most of the Protestants had done'.[68] After the Restoration in 1660 Blundell was never recompensed for the massive outlay he made to preserve his estates. Yet survive these trying times he did.

Between 1643 and 1653 when Blundell's estate was sequestered and he spent intermittent periods in prison or hiding, it was his wife Ann who managed the estate. It was probably to this period that Blundell was referring when he stated that his wife was 'the Ark who hath saved our little cockboat at Crosby from sinking in many a storm'.[69] Ann had access to one-fifth of her husband's estate and the manor house at Little Crosby.[70] The 'fifth' was to be further broken into three parts, one of which was for her maintenance and the other two for the maintenance of her children. The condition of the allowance was that 'if any the said Children shall refuse to be Educated in the Protestant Religion, then such Child or Children for refuseing to losse their part allowed them'.[71] It is not recorded how Ann and the rest of the Blundell family responded to this condition, though the staunch Catholic beliefs of all the children would suggest that it was either ignored altogether or the young age of the children, who ranged from less than a year old to six years of age at the time, was used as an excuse to bypass the possible consequences.[72] Ann was no mere figurehead on the estate. In his brief and sullen account of the period, Blundell recorded that in 1645 Ann paid a fine to manage the remaining four-fifths of the estate in Little Crosby, which included a small mill.[73] Signatures on estate papers from this period suggest that all work was vetted by her and that she shrewdly sought to preserve the estate, purchasing a horse and two oxen to 'make up a teame' due to 'all her quick goods being lost' during the war.[74] Ann continued to maintain the estate throughout the decade. During Blundell's periods of exile she appears to have had sole charge, though surviving correspondence and his signatures on estate papers indicates that Blundell was again taking an active role in its management from the early 1650s onwards.[75] The family's fortunes began to change from 1652 as they prepared to repurchase the estate after the Act of Sale was introduced.

As a Catholic delinquent Blundell could not buy back his estates directly and was forced to seek the aid of two Protestant intermediaries, his cousin Roger Bradshaigh and the Protestant lawyer Gilbert Crouch, who purchased Blundell's estates in Little Crosby and Ditton and held them in trust until 1660.[76] None the less, Blundell retained charge over the estate in practice, and in a letter of attorney dated 1657, was appointed as their deputy.[77] The first issue that had to be resolved when Blundell repurchased his land from sequestrators in 1653 was for Blundell's heirs to prove their interest in the estate, as William held only a life interest.[78] The cost of the repurchase of the estate was £989 13*s* 5½*d*, plus a number of fines and legal fees that took the total cost to £1109 7*s*.[79] Blundell appears to have raised the money through three main sources, though his notes on this matter are vague. The first contributor was Blundell himself. Although unclear how much money he had available, his accounts for the previous year state that he was worth just under £150.[80] He also stated that he repurchased his estate with the help of an unspecified sum of money 'borrowed of my friends'.[81] However, the most significant contribution towards the repurchase came from Blundell's two sisters, Winifred and Frances, who both lived as spinsters at Crosby. Astonishingly, following the repurchase of his estate Blundell's accounts state that he was indebted at '£520 to my sisters: *and* £80 more to them upon certain conditions not like to be performed by them'.[82] Little is known of Blundell's two sisters beyond the occasional reference to them in his papers; however, one would presume that much of this money had been saved from their portions. After the repurchase of his estate, Blundell's sisters agreed that in lieu of an outright repayment they would be given £25 each, every year for the rest of their lives.[83] In providing this money and giving Blundell a way of spacing out payment, Frances and Winifred effectively saved the Blundell estate.

In the mid-1650s attempts were made by the Exchequer to charge Blundell an additional £1361 15*s* 6*d* for ancient rents owed to the Crown for the recusancy of his forefathers, which dated back as far as 1594.[84] However, there is no evidence that he actually paid this as a lump sum as Margaret Blundell and Frank Tyrer have both implied.[85] Neither the entries concerning Blundell in the Committee for Compounding papers nor Blundell's own accounts mention this money.[86] Attempts in 1656 by government officials to get Blundell to pay £60 for what he describes as 'dead mens faults' possibly refer to one instalment of this money. Discussion about this payment continued until the Restoration, suggesting that the money was in dispute and Blundell either failed to pay anything or paid only a very small proportion of the total amount due.[87] Indeed, the final entry in the document listing the ancient rents owed suggests that the debt may have reverted to the new owners of the estate, Bradshaigh and Crouch, and following negotiation they were eventually acquitted of the charge.[88]

As was the case with much of his life, Blundell's representations of himself as being a broken cripple who lost everything in the King's service are misleading.[89] While the period brought social and financial costs for him and his family, his condition was not as fraught as he suggested. Even during the late 1640s Blundell found time to read and write for leisure, a factor epitomised in a prologue to a stage play that Blundell wrote in 1647. In the heading of the small surviving extract, in which the end to conflict is heralded, Blundell noted that it was written 'at the intreaty of some Country Neighbour who were to Act the play about the yeare 1647'.[90] As we have seen, between 1643 and 1660 Blundell travelled widely, initially for necessity's sake to avoid apprehension by the regime, later for pleasure. It was during the late 1650s that he spent a week in Scotland, for which a diary of his travels survives. His notes do not elaborate on how he navigated around the five-mile limit placed on him, but as we will see he was quite prepared to be economical with the truth to acquire travel permits.[91] Furthermore, while the periods that Blundell spent in prison were difficult, Lake and Questier have shown that the experience could offer unprecedented opportunities for Catholic expression. Imprisoned Catholics were able to discuss their political and religious beliefs in a manner often too dangerous to do in public.[92] Blundell was no exception to this, his 'chamber-fellow and companion in restraint' was his uncle, Christopher Bradshaigh, while he remarked that the knowledge that other recusants were in a similar situation gave him 'a sad kynd of Comphort'.[93] Indeed, Blundell met his future son-in-law Richard Butler, heir to the Mountgarret estates, while in prison, a connection with a suitable Catholic that he might otherwise have been unable to make. As we have seen, financially Blundell was not in as dire a position as a superficial reading of his correspondence would have us believe. During this period he made a number of minor developments to his land and by 1658 his goods exceeded the value of his debts by just over £208.[94] However, the most striking aspect of Blundell's survival concerns the extent to which he was able to pursue his religious beliefs.

Although the Interregnum brought severe penalties for harbouring priests, Blundell was particularly active on this account. During this period a number of itinerant Catholic priests, such as Father John Smith, stopped at Crosby while travelling to other destinations. In a letter dated 1648 addressed to Mr Manley, the pseudonym of the Catholic Priest Robert Charnock, Blundell referred to having provided him with lodging and regretted that 'You have been too often my Intelligencer' although he had received only meagre board in exchange.[95] Furthermore, though Blundell's papers only occasionally alluded to the ways in which he gained access to priests, we are given a brief insight for the Interregnum period. In the surviving papers there is a farewell to Father John Walton written in 1657, who had been chaplain at Crosby Hall for an unspecified period and whose poor health necessitated that he move on.[96] Both Tyrer and Margaret Blundell state that he began at Crosby in 1652, suggesting that they had access to another source that has since disappeared.[97] It appears that, after Walton's departure from Little Crosby, Father Francis Waldegrave took over as chaplain, a position he apparently held until the early 1670s, when Little Crosby is referred to as his home.[98] That Crosby Hall had a chaplain throughout this period indicates how effective Blundell and his family were at evading the penal laws. However, as we have seen, Blundell did not achieve this alone, and it is to his networks of family and friends that we now turn.

IV

Both Blundell's first line of defence against the penal laws and his patronage of Catholicism began at home. We have already seen that his wife and sisters played a vital role in maintaining the estate. He also turned to them for support with personal matters. For example, following the marriage of his daughter Emilia to Richard Butler and the subsequent breakdown in communication between the two families, it was to his sister Frances that Blundell entrusted the job of rebuilding the relationship. When Emilia and Richard were effectively evicted from Crosby, Blundell sent Frances with the couple to Ireland in the hopes of eliciting suitable support from the Butler family estates, and after Emilia's death at the age of thirty-eight Frances stayed with Richard and helped raise his young children until they were sent to Crosby to be looked after by Blundell himself.[99] Blundell's reliance on immediate family members also extended to his second son, heir and namesake. After his return from St Omer in the early 1660s, William Blundell junior was given increasing responsibility for managing the estate. In the early 1670s it appears that the estate was divided in some manner between father and son, as Blundell stated in a letter to a family member 'My son (who is happily marryd) shares almost the one half of my real Estate'.[100] From 1673 Blundell referred to his son as his 'chief secretary' and 'houskeeper' of the estate and by the late 1680s and early 1690s, as he reached his eighth decade of age, Blundell became a figurehead at Crosby, his son either managing the estate, or 'alwayes abroad to provide for the family'.[101]

Blundell's commitment to his family was a driving force in his life. He prayed daily for their well-being, and absence from them left him distraught.[102] In 1657 Blundell's wife wintered with her parents, leaving him to remark that he wanted nothing more than to 'see my little round wife, come tumbling home to her Bratts, with a Bratt in her Belly'.[103] Writing in 1693, Blundell reflected that the death of his wife and sisters in addition to his children leaving home had left him 'the most forlorne & disconsolate Wight ... that he went mewing up and down like a kisling that had lost her Dam'.[104] Indeed, Blundell was the epitome of the caring family man, a factor that was most evident in his diligence as a father. He kept a strict watch on how his children were brought up, frequently enquiring into their progress in the various seminaries that they were enrolled in.[105] His priorities were to ensure a strongly Catholic and financially secure family, as seen in his approach to his children's marriages and their education.

Only three of Blundell's ten children who survived into adulthood were married. In 1668, before Blundell's heir and namesake had found a suitable partner, Blundell had begun drawing up 'heads for a Treaty of mariage with a person inferiour', and in a separate document for a marriage 'with a person above our degree'.[106] These two entries detailed methods to protect the estate from the charges that the future wife of the heir might incur, while ensuring her income in the event of her husband's death. Blundell offered a jointure of a tenth of her portion in the event of her husband's death if she be 'inferiour' and a third if she be 'above our degree'.[107] Later in the same year his son married Mary Eyre, a daughter of Rowland Eyre, a prominent Derbyshire recusant.[108] As she brought only £600 to the marriage she fell into Blundell's 'inferiour' bracket and her jointure was drawn up accordingly.[109] Interestingly, one of Blundell's letter books contains a letter written from Blundell junior to Mary before the two were married, in which he pleaded with her that 'This paper shall take the boldness to kiss your fair hand, from whence I am incouraged to hope for such a favorable return as may keep my hopes alive'.[110] That such a personal document should remain extant in Blundell's papers suggests that the father was more involved in the arrangement of his son's marriage than a cursory glance would suggest. Whilst we are left to speculate about his involvement in his son's marriage, Blundell was forced to defend himself on a number of occasions against allegations that he had manipulated a situation whereby his daughter Emilia married Richard Butler.

During his imprisonment in Liverpool in 1658 Blundell befriended Richard Butler, heir to the 'much impayred Fortunes' of the House of Mountgarret.[111] Despite being first in line to the estate, Butler had no income and on his release from prison allegedly had only 20*s* to his name.[112] Blundell invited the young man to recover at his home, where he fell in love with Blundell's daughter, Emilia. Correspondence from Butler's father in the same year stated that he did 'detest and abhorre' the thought of him marrying Emilia, as it would 'dash all my desygnes which concerne my self & house' and threatened to disinherit him if he did.[113] None the less, although Butler was evicted by Blundell from his estate after his family's failure to provide any financial support for their son, by 1661 he had returned to Crosby and renewed his suit to Emilia.[114] Blundell recorded how he 'purposly removed my Daughter, before he came, some half a score of myles from my house'; however, by the end of the year the couple were married.[115] From here on Butler's father effectively ignored his son for five years.[116] During this time Blundell recorded that he 'went twice to London & twice into Ireland to sollicit their grand concerns at my own charge, with a great expence of money & tyme; for I spent no lesse than 15 or 16 months in those four journeyes; how much money God-allmighty knows; but the sums were very great'.[117] By the early 1670s Richard had been reconciled with his family and the couple had moved to Ireland with Blundell's sister Frances to offer support, leaving one of their sons in Blundell's care.[118]

However, Emilia died at the age of thirty-eight in 1681, leaving her widowed husband and their numerous children distraught and Frances to manage the family, until Blundell eventually stepped in and took over the upbringing of the children.[119] Though he continued a close relationship with his grandchildren, Blundell himself by the early 1680s had fallen out with Richard Butler, with whom he claimed 'I have lost my interest', and noted that he 'expresses an unkindness' to his eldest son Edmund.[120]

The Butler family alleged that Blundell had arranged the marriage against the best interests of Richard Butler, whose poverty at the time of meeting Emilia had driven him to desperation.[121] Letters that Blundell wrote to anonymous friends in 1658 and 1659 show that he too was worried about Butler's motivation for the marriage, cautioning 'the danger of an indiscret marryage sollicited perhaps by the Good Gentleman, (in so great distresse and neglect of all his friends) no lesse to get him Bread than a Wife'.[122] None the less, the marriage was a move into more prosperous Catholic circles for the Blundell family and from 1658 Blundell had begun investigating the value of the Mountgarret estates, estimating that while they were poorly managed and not bringing in their full due they consisted of between seven and eight thousand acres of land.[123] Furthermore, whilst he supported Richard when the Butlers ignored him, he did not do so without hope of recompense. Blundell regularly reminded his son-in-law of the support that he had given him, no doubt expecting reward when Butler inherited his estates, while in 1667 Emilia entered into an agreement with her father that if Richard died before her she would cover the cost of his debts to her father, an agreement that she claimed was 'free without compulsion, my husband (as far as I know) not knowing of it'.[124] Thus, despite his protestations that he lost a fortune battling for the rights of his son-in-law, Blundell did all in his power to ensure that he would not be out of pocket when the negotiations concluded.

Blundell's involvement in the education of his children and grandchildren was as intimate as his concerns with their marriages. As we have seen, despite his brief formal education he developed a passion for learning, a passion that he tried to pass on to his children. It seems likely, as Tyrer has suggested, that during both Father John Walton's and Father Francis Waldegrave's residencies at Crosby Hall they had some involvement in teaching the Blundell children, while there is a strong possibility that they also attended the Catholic school at Scarisbrick Hall.[125] However, Blundell also held a pivotal position in their education.

In an entry in the Blue Book entitled 'An exercise for the children to Embolden them in speaking', written by Blundell in 1663, we find an insight into his efforts to facilitate his children's learning.[126] The entry is a play that details an imaginary incident in which Blundell's daughter, Mary, was chastised for behaving in a manner unacceptable for a good Catholic. Mary retorts by asking her father if he had ever committed a sin, and, being left to reflect, Blundell decided not to whip her on the promise that she would henceforth behave in an appropriate manner.[127] However, bolstering his role as the patriarch, Blundell reminded his daughter that 'you must know that the Rod in your fathers hand is the same to a chyld offending, that purgatory & other temporal paines are in Gods, when he pleaseth to inflict them on sinners'.[128] On Blundell's exit from the scene, Mary is faced with a new challenge as her two sisters Clare Frances and Bridget enter, the latter being driven before Clare Frances 'tyed (lyke a horse) with a string in her mouth'.[129] After chastising her sisters for such behaviour, Mary tells them how her new found maturity 'came from Heaven in a clap of thunder. And my father was the Thunderer by Gods command.'[130] The play ends with Mary's rapid downfall to her old ways after being taunted by her younger sisters. Having dressed up a bass viol as their father the three girls dance around it, remarking that not only did it look like an ass but it would play like one too. Eventually after threatening to destroy the instrument it responded by playing in great haste 'the olde wives didle' and the play closes with the children dancing around in circles.[131] Commenting on a version of this play in Margaret Blundell's edited collection of papers, Alison Shell has argued that this attempt to acculturate the girls into appropriate adult spirituality shows 'how little girls could be seen as possessing moral authority within the home, up-ending conventional familial hierarchies and re-channelling the directions of instruction'.[132] The play was presumably written for each of the named characters to act their role, thereby encouraging both reading and oratorical development. Blundell's use of drama as an educational tool is consistent with broader Catholic trends across Europe. This was particularly the case in Jesuit approaches to education and may go some way to explaining references to Blundell having written his own plays and the occasional citations of works by Ben Jonson and John Dryden in his commonplace books.[133] The play that Blundell wrote for his daughters demonstrates the significant role that he held in the intellectual upbringing of his children, both daughters and sons, and the Catholic prism through which their worldview was developed.

Blundell encouraged his children to attend Catholic seminaries on the continent, and seven of his ten surviving children took religious orders. However, his commitment to his family's learning did not end when they attended Catholic seminaries, as he kept in regular contact with them and their tutors. When his eldest son Nicholas went to St Omer, Blundell wrote to his tutor, Charles Parker, checking on his son's progress and blamed any faults in his learning on himself as he had 'never had the lucke or capacity to know the meaning of a Gramer'.[134] Elsewhere, in response to a brief note from his grandson Nicholas, Blundell bemoaned his writing style, stating that while the letter may 'be humble & loveing ... I am very sorry to perceive that the character of your letters do still grow wors & wors. I may say the same of your spelling & of your leaveing out of words. Your Sister Mary is 4 years younger then you yet she writes a very laudable hand ... Now as for your small progress in the schoole ...'[135] He closed his letter offering advice on how to avoid these mistakes in future. Religion was central to Blundell's view of education, which he believed should result in 'a competent good schollar, and a grounded Catholick'.[136] Although Blundell did not elaborate on what he meant by a 'grounded Catholick', in his other writings he noted that being educated in the Christian faith was a central aspect of being a good Catholic.[137]

For the late Stuart period Blundell's correspondence shows how he believed a child should be brought up, as his grandson, Edmund Butler, had been left in his care because of the financial difficulties of his parents.[138] Blundell conscientiously supervised Edmund, and his papers reveal the boy's syllabus. The tone of his lessons was set by a prayer said before study, which begged that God would allow him to use knowledge for his honour '& to my soules eternal welfare'.[139] As we have already seen, Blundell viewed himself as a loyal Englishman and a devotee of the monarchy, a factor that is clearly evident in one essay title from this period, which required that a short treatise be written on how 'Roman Church and English Monarchy and Civil State have great resemblance'.[140] By the age of thirteen Edmund's programme not only included history, literature and Catholic theology in both Latin and English but he was also made familiar with a number of texts critical of Catholicism.[141] Thus, Blundell informed one correspondent, 'Of late I have read unto him some of the harmless Colloquies of the roguish Erasmus; but he hath not tasted the egg which Luther hatched'.[142] Initial hiccups in his education were caused, Blundell speculated, by the fact 'that his brain is no little oppressed with flegme or moysture. He spits exceeding much & I think when he spits the most his memory is the most defective.'[143] Elsewhere, Blundell blamed deficits in Butler's behaviour on 'playing with the rude Boyes of our Neighbourhood'.[144] By the late 1670s, as Edmund overcame his difficulties and advanced in his studies, so Blundell pressed the boy's mother and father to allow him to attend a Catholic college on the continent, including in one letter a detailed list with notes on the strengths and weaknesses of each of the major Catholic colleges.[145] As soon as he had his son-in-law's permission, Blundell used his Catholic connections to ensure Edmund a place at Flamsteed, the college of St Omer. This was achieved through correspondence with a distant relative, Father Edward Scarisbrick (of the family based at Scarisbrick Hall), the Prefect of St Omer, in which he reported on Butler's progress to date and requested him to remember their ties of religion and kinship.[146] Although Butler was admitted into the college his parents had trouble paying the fees of £25 per annum, and on a number of occasions Blundell stepped in to ensure that his grandson's education was adequately provided for.[147]

In 1689, having returned to Ireland, Edmund rebelled against the government by raising a troop of horse and storming Londonderry, during which he was quickly outnumbered and imprisoned. In a letter to his grandfather about the incident, Edmund implied that his behaviour was a direct product of his upbringing, following in the footsteps of the staunch Catholic loyalism that had been embedded in his identity while at Crosby Hall. He claimed he could bear the confinement as 'imprisonment may in a manner be termed my inheritance, my Father, Grandfathers, and almost all my Ancestors haveing undergone it for their Masters sake'.[148] Although Blundell noted that 'I am mightily glad' that Edmund had been commissioned as a soldier in James II's army, his response to his grandson's actions in 1689 is not recorded. It seems likely that the education which he provided Edmund informed his subsequent behaviour.[149] However, on his release from prison over a year later, Blundell assured Edmund that he was 'far from blaming you for not risqueing your All in France', a sentiment no doubt informed by the increasing strength of William and Mary.[150] While Blundell's immediate family provided both an opportunity to promote Catholicism as well as crucial support and protection for the Crosby estate, they were only the first line of defence that he developed.

V

Essential to Blundell's negotiating around the penal laws were networks of friends and family who helped to protect him. Hibbard has argued that early modern Catholics were often detached from county and parish communities, operating instead within a network of Catholic family alliances; the so-called 'Catholic connection'.[151] Blundell's papers demonstrate that he had links with almost every significant Catholic in Lancashire, whether through friendship or through marriage connections. A list of the friends that Blundell sent gifts to in 1664 mentions members of the Scarisbrick (Scarisbrick), Gerard (Bryn) and Bradshaigh (Haigh) families, while in a list entitled 'the day of the death of some of my Friends', Blundell recorded the names of almost all the prominent Lancashire Catholics, including members of the Clifton (Lytham), Gillibrand (Chorley), Tyldesley (Leigh) and Molyneux (Croxteth) dynasties (see Appendix for a map of Little Crosby and surrounding area).[152] While we know little about the access that Blundell had to priests in Lancashire, in one letter he mentioned the death of 'two of my dearest friends in Lancashyre' who were 'religious men & Priests', and he corresponded with Mr Ballard, the priest of the Butler family in Ireland, whom he described in a marginal note as 'a very antient prudent and vertuous priest belonging to that family'.[153] Blundell's Catholic connections spanned much further than Lancashire, a reflection of the manner in which the Catholic educational system operated.[154] He had close family members throughout continental Europe in Catholic seminaries and religious houses, many of whom held senior positions. For example, his sister Ann was Mother Abbess of the Poor Clares at Dunkirk and his uncle Richard Bradshaigh was Rector at St Omer.[155]

Blundell used his Catholic networks to help him evade the penal laws. Although he generally avoided blatant disregard for the penal laws, many of his Catholic contacts were prepared to risk the consequences of such violation. In particular, they helped him evade the law that forbad recusants to travel more than five miles from their estates, which he referred to as the 'chaine'.[156] Blundell used Catholic agents, mainly itinerant Catholic priests, to purchase items, distribute money and exchange private letters with individuals throughout the British Isles and continental Europe. For example, one of Blundell's correspondents, Mr Ever, volunteered to transport 'Roman Treacle' from Paris for Blundell at a time of ill health.[157] In a letter written in 1678, Blundell asked Waldegrave, chaplain at Little Crosby, to purchase from London four French books and 'to buy me a peruke or to suffer me to expose this old bald pate of mine to cold and scorn'.[158] His cousin Cuthbert Clifton regularly transported money from England to religious houses on the continent, which enabled Blundell to provide financial support for those family members who had taken religious orders or were undergoing a period of education in a seminary.[159] Blundell frequently drew on his Catholic connections to ensure that his children were given an adequate Catholic education. For example, in 1657 when he was focused on ensuring the survival of his estate, Blundell's Catholic connections intervened to ensure that one of his daughters, most probably Jane, could join the Poor Clares. In a letter to his uncle Richard Bradshaigh, Blundell explained that he had 'lately receyved the promises [of] so great a charity from some noble frends that I shall be able to give her £15 per annum during lyf or one hundred and fifty to her portion'.[160] Furthermore, Blundell's contacts helped to extend his networks by speaking of him in person or correspondence. In a letter to 'Mr RB his intyre worthy friend', Blundell provided details of his 1660 trip to Paris alongside his thanks to the recipient for 'the great effect of your Letters to Mr Campian on my behalf', whose 'good company' delayed him by a full day.[161]

Blundell extended the support of his protective networks to other Catholics. In one letter to an unnamed friend he recorded that he was given the job of 'the keeping of your curious and costly Juel', which was held in trust during the Civil War period.[162] Presumably the owner was either in a more precarious position than Blundell, hence it was safer at Little Crosby, or one of Blundell's Protestant friends was holding it in trust on his behalf. He also held money for religious purposes on behalf of local Catholics. Thus, he was given £210 from Margaret Molyneux to be released when one of Luisa Grey's daughters took religious orders.[163] Blundell's efforts to preserve his estate meant that many of his Catholic correspondents viewed him as a legal expert and frequently consulted him for advice. For example, Blundell advised on a jointure for his nephew's wife if she failed to conceive a child, and acted as a mediator when the two met at Little Crosby to sign the final forms.[164] Furthermore, Blundell was frequently entrusted as executor of the wills of local Catholics. His surviving notes contain drafts of four wills for local Catholics and indicate that he had been executor to many more.[165] In one entry in the Great Hodge Podge there is a series of observations on how to be an effective executor, suggesting that it was a role that he took seriously.[166] Some of the wills contained clauses such as that found in Elizabeth Lithgoe's will that left Blundell £25 for unspecified uses, which a secret note in the Blue Book stated was for Blundell to 'give out of that for her soul to the priests, according to my discretion £15. £5 to one of my own children who is to be religious, or for want of such, then to one of myne that is religious. And lastly £5 I must give to some maid next of kin to the Testator which intends to be Religious.'[167] Thus, Blundell extended his own support networks and knowledge acquired from experience to help his Catholic friends.

Blundell also passed on information he received to other Catholics throughout the country. For example, in 1659 he wrote to an unnamed Catholic correspondent with news of how 'the Godly ministry of these parts, are afraid of loosing theire Tythes', and in 1660 he wrote to Charles Parker at Flamsteed informing him how Charles II's Restoration 'hath allmost set London on fyre'.[168] This exchange of news with other Catholics was particularly evident with the crucial information that Blundell received from his Protestant friends, which he disseminated, for example, with the same unnamed Catholic neighbour with whom he placed a joint subscription to the *Publick Intelligence*.[169] Like many of his contemporaries, Blundell's correspondence suggests that he viewed news as a currency, and he tried to offer an adequate 'exchange' for information that he received.[170] On the rare occasions that Blundell found that news in Lancashire was unreliable or out of date, he was overly apologetic. In a letter to an unnamed Catholic correspondent, Blundell was so mortified that his intelligence networks 'will not afford me newes to maintaine the Trade with you, by an equal exchange' that he instead sent him four ounces of expensive 'Quarto' tobacco, which had recently been shipped to Chester. His reasoning for the gift was that 'words are nothing but wind, wind is lesse then smoke, & an Emblem of Smoke is Tobacco'.[171]

The most striking example of the extent of Blundell's intellectual networks concerns his involvement in Catholic book sharing. Blundell's letters regularly thanked recipients for the loan of texts.[172] Much of the material circulated concerned the position of Catholics in England, the penal laws and relations of miracles that had occurred through the means of Catholic priests.[173] From his surviving correspondence it is clear that this book-lending community encompassed the majority of his Catholic correspondents, including his cousin Laurence Ireland and his nephew Thomas Selby.[174] It was kept up to date with material sent by family members attending Catholic seminaries on the continent. For example, while at St Omer Blundell's grandson Edmund Butler successfully defended a series of printed theses, the notes of which were sent to Blundell to keep him abreast with the latest theological developments.[175] This was a two-way process, and between the years 1666 to 1676 Blundell listed a range of books and pamphlets that he lent out, including the text he referred to as 'The Touchstone of Truth', as well as 'the Liturgie of the mass' and '8 other several pamphlets most of them concerning Ireland'.[176] The exchange of Catholic texts in this way not only allowed a large number of individuals access to often-expensive works but also created an underground community of information and ideas that helped its adherents maintain a stalwart Catholic identity in the face of religious persecution. Furthermore, those involved in these unofficial networks not only exchanged printed and manuscript texts but also commented on the contents, thereby forming a network of Catholic readers.[177] The importance of these networks was most apparent with regard to the exchange of stories relating to conversions to Catholicism.

As Questier has shown, conversion stories played an important role in strengthening the beliefs of Catholics during the seventeenth century. Such stories were 'discussed almost exclusively in doctrinal and, indeed, polemical terms' and highlighted the success of the faith in the battle for believers, suggesting that God was working in their favour.[178] This genre of news and reactions to it was a staple for the networks of which Blundell was part. Thus, he received a six-page letter written in 1669 from Laurence Ireland detailing the conversion of John Warner after his wife converted and joined the Poor Clares.[179] This focus on conversions also included material about conversion from the secular to religious life. The longest surviving letter that Blundell received was a thirty-six-page report on the conversion of his brother, Richard, to the religious life while studying at St Omer. Richard was motivated by some form of religious revelation and took Jesuit orders on his deathbed. The letter was written after his death by Father Gray, the Provincial of the Jesuits in England, and sent to Father Richard Bradshaigh, only to be copied by Blundell's sister Ann and sent to Blundell. The circulation of the letter was increased as Blundell recorded that he and others read the letter twice and it seems most likely that Blundell, who was so proud of his family's achievements in religious orders, would have circulated the account widely among his friends and family.[180] Blundell's preoccupation with conversions to Catholicism was not limited by national boundaries. In a transcription of a letter from one Henry Bryth, an account of Catholic conversions in China is provided. The letter claimed that almost all of the conversions in the country had been made by Jesuits, and estimated that 'The number of

Christians is about 100000 or more. In great Towns at a Mass or Sermon 5 or 6000 came together.'[181] It is not clear who the recipient of the letter was, the only indication being a footnote stating that 'the Copy or extract of a letter from Rome which extract was left amongst us at Crosby by Mr Tarsborough. April the 16th 1685'. It appears that Blundell junior copied the letter under his father's instruction, demonstrating the enlarged readership of such correspondence.[182] These conversion stories helped instil in English Catholics a sense that their religion was blossoming in parts of the world, and that they were not alone in supporting the cause.

The extent of these networks was far wider than may initially appear. References in letters sent to Blundell suggest that his correspondence was not only read by the person to whom it was addressed. The most striking example of this is from his cousin Laurence Ireland, who told Blundell that his letters 'are very welcome not only to me but to many more with whome I comunicate them, not withstanding your commands to the contrary'. Ireland went on to ask Blundell to 'Pardon my cryme, and here after if you please: put your casuall deaths and other accidents in the end of your letters: for I cannot deny a sight of them to severall who importune me without a note of disrespect'.[183] Blundell in turn frequently recorded having allowed others to read letters sent to him. He confessed to Thomas Masey that at a funeral that he had recently attended, as soon as was polite he circulated the letters that Masey had written, proclaiming them to be 'the freshest newes'.[184] This Catholic network was further extended as Blundell frequently read aloud with his friends and his servant Walter Thelwall, often recording their comments in his commonplace books for reflection.[185] Furthermore, when he had finished them, Blundell gave a number of books to Catholic neighbours and tenants who could not afford them. Given that Blundell regularly referred to marginal notes he made in the books that he read, it is likely that some form of intellectual exchange occurred for those who accepted this charity and subsequently engaged with both the content of the book and Blundell's marginal additions.[186]

Blundell's concern for providing a suitable Catholic education extended to those Catholics who were part of his network. For instance, in a visit to Ireland in 1674 Blundell found an individual whom he believed to be a suitable tutor for Scarisbrick Hall. The tutor was the son of one Thomas Grene, to whom Blundell explained that he would have had him for the tutor of his own children, but that he had no employment for a man of his quality. Instead he believed that Grene's expertise in Latin would make him valuable in the Scarisbrick household and wrote to them giving a detailed appraisal of Grene's worth.[187] Following the birth of the first child of his sister-in-law, Margaret Haggerston, Blundell sent a letter of congratulations, noting that his main wish for his nephews was that their parents leave them 'aboundantly ritch in all spiritual and temporal Blessings', while in another letter to her he hoped that all of his 'pretty sweet Nephews ... may largely correspond to that liberall and free Education which I know you will afford them'.[188] As with his immediate family, Blundell encouraged all around him to take religious orders, inviting his nephew Thomas Selby at St Omer to think of a time 'when you shall sit lyke an Oracle in the Highlands of Northumberland giving Councel and assistance, to all your friends & Neighbours', a barely veiled reference to his entry into the priesthood and eventual return to England.[189] This interest in providing a suitable Catholic education for the children of family and friends was also shared by Blundell's wife: a letter from her cousin Laurence Ireland, who had recently enrolled his daughters in the Poor Clares at Dunkirk, thanked Ann 'for your care and labours in their education: what they have I ascribe to you, and if they have any thing more then you gave them, tis but a smalle structure upon your foundations'.[190]

Not only was Blundell an adept networker on his own behalf, but he frequently made connections between Catholics. For example, in a letter to 'James C: in Dublin', Blundell informed him that he would be visited by an unnamed individual and as he was Blundell's friend 'Ergo he must be yours'.[191] Blundell's patronage of Catholic networks is most evident in his involvement in Catholic marriages throughout the country. He believed himself an expert in finding the best companion 'of the same religion and rank' for any individual looking for marriage.[192] In a letter written to one Mrs Talbot of Dinkley he advised her that a suitable Catholic would appear before her daughter 'encouraged by relations from my self' to court her for marriage. Blundell noted that he had fully investigated the young man, having 'chanced to learn from credible hands' that both his religious persuasions and monetary backing were suitable for the union.[193] In another letter he named the man as William Talbot, son of Robert Talbot, and though he noted that 'he have a body a little to gross for so young a man', he asserted that his mother was 'the Lord Baltomores Daughter', giving a full valuation of his estate and his hopes for inheritance.[194] As with his marriage negotiations for his immediate family, Blundell quickly found himself in trouble, and in 1678 was forced to write to the mother of his cousin Gerard to explain that he had nothing to do with a match between Gerard and a local widow, Madam Poole. Although he admitted having discussed it with his cousin, Blundell excused himself by explaining that he 'had a private wish of my own, that Cozen Gerrard might rather fix upon a person to whom my obligations are greater then to madam Poole'.[195] Thus, Blundell held a significant role in preserving the Catholic networks of which he was part by ensuring that Catholics were both educated by appropriate tutors and married to appropriate partners.

VI

Although the religious beliefs of some in Blundell's networks may be open for debate, he was certainly in contact with a number of church papists. Unfortunately for the historian Blundell was especially discreet when alluding to them and the presence of so many anonymous letters in the collection may have been an attempt to disguise their identities. A footnote to one letter stated that the recipient was 'Colonel R L a late acquaintance of his & privately a Catholick'.[196] The most striking example of Blundell's connections with a church papist was his relationship with Richard Langhorne. Langhorne was an exemplar of a church papist, he ran a legal practice in London and the Whig Bishop Gilbert Burnet claimed that he 'passed as a Protestant'.[197] However, of his four children, two became priests, two Catholic non-jurors, and three attended St Omer, he gave legal and financial advice to the Jesuits and he was executed for alleged involvement in the Popish Plot after his son used Titus Oates as a carrier for an incriminating letter to him.[198] In Blundell's copy of Langhorne's speech at the gallows he recorded that one of Langhorne's last statements was 'I die a Member (though an unworthy one) of that Holy Catholick and Apostolick Church of Christ'.[199] Blundell and Langhorne were in frequent communication from the mid-seventeenth century till his death, a relationship that according to Langhorne became much closer after Blundell had performed an unspecified act of 'Charity to my deare deceased Brother-in-law'.[200] Langhorne helped Blundell obtain the latest news and predict the impact it would have on English Catholics, as seen in the closing lines of one of Blundell's letters:

> The noyse which was made at London hath been heard a great waie off, and it makes us very sollicitous concerning the war with Holland concerning the kings Majesty & concerning ourselves. What do your wise men think in relation to these matters? Will money be got for the war? Shal we preserve our repute at home and abroad whether money be raised or no? Shal the Catholicks be all destroyed & they alone?[201]

Langhorne also gave Blundell legal advice on matters regarding recusancy and land issues and he was entrusted with raising money for Emilia and Richard Butler. So close was the relationship that Blundell paid nothing for the privilege, as Langhorne expounded in one letter, begging Blundell 'that from this day forward you will give me leave on all occasions of your owne to be of Councell for you, upon the score of true & noble friendship, and without not only offering but without making mention of any other fee then that of your love & affection'.[202] However, as important as Blundell's Catholic connections were, to understand fully how he avoided the extremes of the penal laws we must also look elsewhere.

VII

Although anti-Catholicism seemingly permeated almost every aspect of contemporary English life, Blundell's most important protection came from Protestants. In his commonplace entries, he reflected that while rigid penal laws were on the statute books, ultimately 'the magistrate must punish or release Offenders according to his own pleasure'.[203] However, he did not rely on the charity of benevolent Protestants unknown to him. A network of Protestant agents in his locality provided Blundell with news and ensured the survival of his fortunes by holding money, and on a number of occasions the Crosby estate itself, in trust during periods of political instability. Glickman has discussed this process used by recusants into the mid-eighteenth century, in which Catholic landlords effectively became 'tenants for life', while Anglican friends nominally held the estates, 'with the intention, as the Lancashire Tory Sir John Statham assured Maria Shireburne [in 1742], "to returne 'em if the times mend"'.[204]

Blundell benefited from links with a number of well placed Protestants in his locality. Although John Chorley, Mayor of Liverpool from 1678 to 1679, had links with prominent Whigs and entertained the Duke of Monmouth on his quasi-royal progress through Liverpool in 1682, he was vital to Blundell's survival.[205] Throughout the late seventeenth century, particularly during the Popish Plot, Chorley held money in trust for Blundell to prevent it from falling into the hands of government agents and even invested money on Blundell's behalf, holding the interest for him until it was safe to return.[206] In October 1678 Blundell leased the entire Crosby estate in trust to Chorley, renting it back for a token £50. An endorsement on the lease document, which appears to be in the hand of Nicholas Blundell his grandson, states that 'I take this to have been a Lease in Trust made in times of Oats his Plot'.[207] Furthermore, in January 1680 Blundell sent a messenger to Chorley with the note that 'I do send you by this Bearer a considerable sum of money which I desyre you to put out in your own name & that when the same is so affected you will please to assyne the bonds to me. yet nevertheless that you make that assignment with such caution as that you may thereby be secured from all manner of hazard which may happen by the kindness which you lately shewed here.'[208] Others amongst Blundell's Protestant friends helped him by providing intelligence material. For instance, in a letter written in 1680 Blundell thanked John Entwistle, a Protestant magistrate, for advance warning of a house search.[209] Thus, at a time of widespread anti-Catholic hysteria, Blundell's Protestant friends not only maintained contact with him but also stepped up their activities on his behalf helping to ensure his survival.

A vital element of Blundell's support came from his Protestant cousin Roger Bradshaigh. Bradshaigh was the son of zealous Catholic parents and had uncles, aunts and brothers who had taken religious orders. His uncle

Richard, for example, held the posts of Provincial and Rector of the College of St Omer from 1656 till his death in 1666.[210] However, though born into Catholicism, following the death of his father when he was thirteen, Bradshaigh's education was entrusted to Protestants, and in 1641 he became a Protestant. From the Restoration onwards he played a significant part in local affairs, serving as MP for Lancashire from 1660 to 1678 and Mayor of Wigan in 1661 and 1681, in recognition of which he was given a baronetcy.[211] Throughout his life Bradshaigh expended considerable effort on Blundell's behalf. He monitored closely Blundell's affairs and his surviving letter book contains a number of entries relating to 'My Cosen Blundell', including copies of a petition to the Deputy Lieutenants and personal letters from Blundell requesting that Bradshaigh resolve particular issues for him.[212] As we have seen, he played a vital role in Blundell's repurchase of his estate during the Interregnum. Blundell also appealed to Bradshaigh for help in acquiring a travel pass in 1673 to visit Richard Langhorne who was 'sorely tormented ... with a villainous Rheamatisme' and again in 1679 when he sought to flee the country in anticipation of stringent application of the penal laws in light of the Popish Plot allegations.[213]

While all would agree that Bradshaigh 'made little secret of his desire to protect his Catholic relatives and friends from the full force of the militant Anglican reaction of the 1660s', his most recent biographer accepts at face value Blundell's claim of Bradshaigh that 'His own religion is such as that he is no friend at all to ours. Yet to me and all mine he hath allwise been incomparably faithfull and loving', implying that Bradshaigh's activities on behalf of Catholics stemmed merely from familial duty.[214] While there is no evidence to suggest that Bradshaigh was anything other than a committed Anglican, his activities on behalf of Blundell did not end with ensuring his financial survival. Although he may not have known the purpose of the transactions, Bradshaigh was deeply involved in Blundell's efforts to loan out at interest moneys belonging to the Poor Clares of Rouen.[215] However, Bradshaigh was fully aware of other aspects of Blundell's more blatant Catholic dealings as indicated in the postscript to a letter from Blundell instructing his Jesuit son, Nicholas, how to behave on meeting him: 'If Sir Roger do inquire concerning his Nephewes at Flamsteed, I think you ought to answer him plainly without shewing of any distrust'.[216] Thus, Bradshaigh proved a vital element in Blundell's networks, and both his apparently strong Anglicanism and his quiet support for Blundell's blatant Catholic dealings support Milton's argument that the line between Protestant and Catholic was neither as clear nor as aggressively divided as historians and contemporaries have suggested.[217]

The nature and effect of the Protestant support that Blundell and his family received was also seen during the Manchester Jacobite trials. In 1694 John Taaffe and John Lunt, two professional informers, claimed that there was a Catholic Jacobite Plot in Lancashire to raise troops on behalf of the exiled

James II and to assassinate King William.[218] One of the accused was William Blundell, now seventy-four years old. Throughout July eight Lancashire Catholics were arrested: Lord Molyneux, William Gerard, Rowland Stanley, Thomas Clifton, William Dicconson, Philip Langton, Bartholomew Walmesley and William Blundell junior.[219] Government agents illegally arrested Blundell's son on finding that Blundell was too sick to travel and his son conveniently had the same name.[220] The trial began on 17 October 1694 and following a farcical case by the prosecution the defendants were found not guilty within one week.[221] The prisoners led a successful character assassination of Lunt, whereby he was exposed as a one-time thief and a bigamist who was married to two women and had promised marriage to three further women as a means to engage in sexual relations.[222] The witnesses for the government were given a final blow when Taaffe defected to the side of the defendants and brought disguised friends of the prisoners to Lunt, who asked them to become perjured witnesses with him.[223]

Although the eight defendants at the Manchester Jacobite trial were Catholic they received significant support from Protestant contemporaries both locally and nationally. The prisoners were met with supportive crowds in Manchester and the witnesses for the prosecution were chased out of the town at the end of the trial, following which there were celebrations throughout the county.[224] Printed and manuscript pamphlets, newsletters and poems were circulated before and after the trial that condemned Lunt and extolled the virtues of the defendants.[225] A number of surviving contemporary letters written by both Protestants and Catholics also voiced concerns about the motives of the witnesses for the prosecution, with one letter claiming that the trial was 'a refined piece of villany to destroy several wealthy men to enrich others that want money'.[226] Even Bishop Gilbert Burnet was prepared to concede that the motivation for the trial was financial, that there were flaws in Lunt's testimony and that another supporting witness was 'so prolifigate a man that great and just objections lay against giving him any credit'.[227] That the trial went in favour of the defendants was largely due to the support they received from Protestants.

Shortly after the trial Blundell's sister claimed that the accused were preserved thanks to God's will, 'who by his mercy and singular providence has preserved our friends when on the very brink of utter ruin and destruction'.[228] Most subsequent narratives have accorded the victory for the defendants as being the responsibility of the changing sides of John Taaffe. Certainly, Taaffe's revelations aided the defendants, demonstrating that Lunt had tried to suborn perjured witnesses to aid his case. However, another individual was active in protecting the interests of the defendants: Roger Kenyon, Clerk of the Peace for Lancashire. Kenyon held a prominent position in Lancashire politics for much of his life. During the Tory Reaction he excelled as a collector of recusancy fines and his obstruction of efforts to repeal the penal laws resulted in his removal as Clerk of the Peace in December 1687. After the Revolution, Kenyon remained a Tory and was returned for the first time to the Commons in 1690.[229] His attitude to his Catholic neighbours is open to some debate. Paul Hopkins refers to him as 'the anti-Catholic'.[230] However, this fails to recognise the complexities in the way anti-Catholicism functioned and ignores Kenyon's pivotal role in supporting the accused at the Manchester trials.

The defendants were already known to Kenyon before the trial: their religion and his legal responsibilities meant that their paths had often crossed. Blundell felt comfortable enough with Kenyon that his letters record him asking for a 'favour' concerning an update on the penal laws.[231] As soon as the trials began, Kenyon collected a mass of information against Lunt, which forms the most complete biography of the informer that survives. His writings focus on Lunt's dubious character while minimising his connections with genuine Jacobite conspiracy in the early 1690s.[232] During and after the trials well-wishers of the defendants directed their expressions of sympathy and later congratulations to the defendants via Kenyon, leading Lady Molyneux to remark that 'she never expected him to be a friend to the Roman Catholics'.[233] In fact, Kenyon was directly involved in the defence that the leading spokesman of the accused, William Dicconson, built up, using his detailed legal knowledge to provide instructions on how Lunt and the other witnesses should be examined.[234] Finally, Kenyon's involvement did not end when the defendants were found not guilty at Manchester, as his comments in the House of Commons helped bring about an enquiry into the handling of the case, in which he hoped 'you will ... pass your sensure on the wrong-dooers', meaning Lunt and the other witnesses for the prosecution.[235]

Kenyon was not the only Protestant who supported the defendants. Other prominent Protestants testified on behalf of the witnesses during the trial, including the MP for Preston.[236] The factors that motivated Protestants such as the usually anti-Catholic Kenyon to help the Catholic defendants may have been resentment at the use of perjured witnesses. Contemporaries were ambivalent towards the use of informers, and, while some may have viewed them as a necessary evil, it was also recognised that they were 'corrupt, unreliable and liable to commit perjury'.[237] Support for the defendants may also have been brought about by the perception that the case was a Whig tool to gain more power, or simply that they wanted to help protect neighbours in need. Whatever the cause of their sympathies, the support that Blundell and the other defendants received indicates that Catholics were not completely marginalised. It seems evident that most Protestants were happy to live peaceably with their Catholic neighbours, supporting Bossy's argument that after the Revolution the term 'persecution' is not appropriate to describe the predicament that English Catholics found themselves in.[238] These Protestant connections also kept Blundell informed about the latest news pertaining to English Catholics.

That Blundell did not exist in an isolated Catholic community is also evident from the news networks of which he was part. Blundell's attorney, Gilbert Crouch, sent him news throughout the Interregnum and Restoration periods, including 'the Abstract of the Declaration of the 5th monarchy men that rose in London the 7th of Jan: 1660', extracts of which were copied into the Blue Book.[239] Blundell also kept in regular contact with John Greenhalgh, the staunchly Royalist Governor of the Isle of Man, until his death in 1651.[240] The pair exchanged contemporary news and discussed their shared experiences of sequestration.[241] Finally, Blundell was in frequent correspondence with Edmund Borlase, a doctor of medicine whose practice was based in Cheshire from 1660 onwards.[242] In response to a letter in which Blundell enclosed 'an Epitaph on the D of Albermarle', Borlase sent Blundell a copy of his latest work on Latham Spa in Lancashire.[243] Borlase was also the author of a history of the Irish Rebellion, which as we will see was the centrepiece of a debate between the two.[244] Blundell's relationship with these individuals supports Geoffrey Scott's argument that during the reigns of the first three Stuart monarchs there was a 'remarkable degree of convergence and literary "commerce" between Anglican and English Catholic circles'.[245] Indeed, Blundell's most useful source of information came from a surprising contact.

Throughout the Restoration period Blundell developed a close friendship with the loyalist journalist and press censor, Roger L'Estrange. From 1662 L'Estrange, a future Tory activist, established a reputation as a 'scourge of dissent and bloodhound scenting republican intrigue'.[246] Despite his claims that cheap print fuelled sedition, he used the same popular medium to humiliate his adversaries. In a multitude of letters between Blundell and L'Estrange, which began in the early 1660s and continued to at least 1681, when Blundell mentioned that they had met in London, the pair exchanged information, varying from local and national news to discussions about the penal laws.[247] Four transcriptions of letters from L'Estrange to Blundell and nine copies of letters from Blundell to L'Estrange survive, although references to other letters in the correspondence and Blundell's claim that 'I converse with you constantly twice a week' indicate that this represents a small proportion of their actual correspondence.[248] L'Estrange was so eager to hear of affairs in Lancashire that he asked Blundell that 'if you love me, if you have but a chickin com into the world whole footed let me hear on't'.[249] Blundell was only too happy to oblige, and his letters to L'Estrange are among some of the longest that survive. In one letter he informed L'Estrange that he would illegally 'break [his] chaine and take an other frisk in the world' specifically to collect news for him, for 'if this club foote of my owne could do you any service, you may use it, with the rest of the silly Animall, according to your pleasure'.[250] In exchange L'Estrange sent Blundell packets of weekly news books and personally wrote with the latest news.[251] Furthermore, following Blundell's offer to L'Estrange that 'if you have any other thing, which is fit ... to be made lesse publick I should be ... somtymes a suitor for it', the two began to discuss more sensitive issues.[252]

Although only a proportion of the correspondence survives, it seems evident that L'Estrange used the 'plain and naked friendship' with Blundell to discuss his ideas on religion.[253] Blundell frequently gave his opinion of anti-Catholic works, criticising William Prynne in particular, while in one letter Blundell offered L'Estrange 'a charge or two for your gun' if he decided to continue 'destroying the kings Enemyes with your paper bullets'.[254] Much of Blundell's own writing in defence of removing the penal laws was similar to the arguments developed by L'Estrange, such as his contention that nonconformists and regicides were indistinguishable, and his argument that Catholics had shown themselves more loyal than Puritans; a factor that will be discussed further in future chapters.[255] Although L'Estrange built up strategic relations with individuals who had access to vital information or country-wide news networks, such as that with Samuel Pepys, his relationship with Blundell apparently stemmed from genuine friendship.[256] It is also apparent that L'Estrange was sympathetic to his religious beliefs. Despite the claims of Whig propaganda during the Exclusion Crisis, most modern-day accounts maintain that L'Estrange was a staunch Anglican. As Harold Love states, 'a man who was so definite in all his opinions should be allowed to be so about his religion, which he always insisted was that of the Church of England'.[257] However, his correspondence with Blundell indicates some respect for Catholicism. In response to Blundell's notice that his wife would 'not fail to use her beades for your best advantage', L'Estrange replied 'that I have a greater reverence for her Beades then eyther her self or you perhaps are aware of'.[258] L'Estrange's sympathy for Catholicism was also evident in his work as a censor of the press and throughout his career he was far harsher on Protestant nonconformist works than on Catholic.[259] Though as official censor of the press he should have been excluding Catholic influence on printed works, L'Estrange was both receiving and disseminating information from Blundell throughout the Restoration period. He was the most significant and well connected individual in Blundell's news network, access to which was clearly not dictated by religious belief.

VIII

Despite both the image of himself that Blundell projected and the arguments of later historians, it is clear that he was not a passive victim. Like other contemporary Catholics, Blundell constructed survival mechanisms that ranged from more obvious strategies such as writing sensitive letters in code to the creation of reciprocally supportive networks of Protestants and Catholics that extended throughout the country and into continental Europe. These networks can be usefully considered in three groups. His familial network centred on familial obligations, ties and mutual economic advantage. These interlaced with his broader Catholic networks where he secured social capital by facilitating important social contacts through marriage, education and promoting communal discussions on Catholic doctrine. Finally, he made use of both geographical and social proximity to obtain support from key Protestants, whom he took care to repay with both affection and the exchange of valuable information. The extent of Blundell's Protestant connections shows that a failure to integrate Catholics into mainstream narratives of the period has not only obscured Catholic history but has also provided an overly simplified interpretation of Protestant histories and identities. However, the scope of Blundell's activity extended far beyond these networks.

NOTES

1 William Blundell to Richard Langhorne, 14 May 1673, in Draft Letter Book, I, fol. 36, transcribed in Letter Book One, fol. 101b.

2 See, for example: William Blundell to Constantia Masey, 26 November 1672, in Draft Letter Book, I, fol. 17b.

3 Blue Book, fol. 6. It is generally accepted that while there was an initial feeling of relief amongst English Catholics at the Restoration, discontent at Charles II for failing to recognise the support Catholics gave him and his father rapidly spread amongst the Catholic population: A. J. Loomie, 'Oliver Cromwell's policy toward the English Catholics: the appraisal by diplomats, 1654–1658', *Catholic Historical Review*, 90 (2004), pp. 29–44; N. H. Keeble, *The Restoration: England in the 1660s* (Oxford: Blackwell, 2002), pp. 10, 29, 123; J. Spurr, *The Restoration Church of England, 1646–1689* (London: Yale University Press, 1991), p. 66.

4 Williams, 'English Catholicism under Charles II', pp. 123–44.

5 William Blundell to William Atwood, 23 January 1691, in Draft Letter Book, IV, fol. 51, transcribed in Letter Book One, fols 129–b; William Blundell to Mrs Gerard, 22 November 1693, in Letter Book Two, p. 78; William Blundell to Bridget Blundell, 22 December 1693; William Blundell to Edmund Butler, 20 June 1690, in Draft Letter Book, IV, fols 47b, 71b.

6 Blue Book, fol. 55.

7 William Blundell to Richard Langhorne, 14 May 1673, in Draft Letter Book, I, fol. 35b, transcribed in Letter Book One, fol. 101.

8 William Blundell to Elizabeth Bradshaigh, 5 February 1657, in Small Account Book, fols 59b-63.

9 William Blundell to Margaret Haggerston, 23 October 1665, in Letter Book One, fol. 73.

10 Blue Book, fol. 58.

11 William Blundell to A. B., 9 July 1657; William Blundell to Richard Bradshaigh, 1666; William Blundell to Unnamed Recipient, 29 December 1681, in Letter Book One, fols 30, 89, 122.

12 Blue Book, fol. 67; LCRO, QSP/468/4, Quarter Sessions Papers, 1677.

13 William Blundell to Alice Haggerston, 22 October 1654, in Letter Book One, fol. 59.

14 Small Account Book, fols 42b–52, 69b–85b.

15 Small Account Book, fols 63, 84b. These figures also provide the most reliable gauge of Blundell's worth at a given time. As we will see, the system of tenure that Blundell operated on his estate works against an estimation of his wealth based on rental income. His tenants paid low ancient rents, which in 1668 Blundell estimated to total £58 yearly, but paid variable, individually negotiated fines to renew leases, which brought Blundell the bulk of his income from his tenants. This is evident in the estimation of the value of Little Crosby made during negotiations for Blundell junior's marriage to Mary Eyre, where Blundell stated that 'The yearly fines from the Tenants upon the making or renueing of Leases depend so much on the contingence of life & death, that they cannot be valued at any certain revenue': SA, Bagshaw Collection, C365, William Blundell to Rowland Eyre.

16 Small Account Book, fols 44b, 51.

17 Small Account Book, fols 49b, 85, 87; Hodge Podge the Third, fol. 28; Great Hodge Podge, fols 206b–7.

18 William Blundell to Thomas Haggerston, 16 September 1672, in Draft Letter Book, I, fol. 11.

19 W. M. Mathew, 'Marling in British agriculture: a case of partial identity', *Agricultural History Review*, 41 (1993), pp. 97–110.

20 Small Account Book, fols 84b-5.

21 Great Hodge Podge, fol. 199b.

22 Small Account Book, fol. 44b.

23 The entry for 1664 is very brief and alludes only to the cost and repairs of a ship. It does not provide information about the amount Blundell invested or how much he made: Hodge Podge the Third, fol. 19b.

24 Hodge Podge the Third, fol. 59.

25 Great Hodge Podge, fol. 194.

26 Hodge Podge the Third, fol. 59.

27 Hodge Podge the Third, fol. 42.

28 Small Account Book, fol. 92b; William Blundell to Thomas Haggerston, 25 May 1657, in Letter Book One, fols 29–b.

29 Blue Book, fols 66b–8b.

30 William Blundell to David Cooke, 10 September 1675, in Draft Letter Book, II, fols 47–b, transcribed in Letter Book One, fol. 102b.

31 William Blundell to Margaret Haggerston, 27 February 1651, in Letter Book One, fols 55b–6.

32 Hodge Podge the Third, fol. 28b.

33 Adversaria, fol. 204.

34 LCRO, DDBl 2/1, Sir Thomas Tyldesley to William Blundell, Captaincy of Dragoons, 22 December 1642.

35 LCRO, DDBl 24/16, Draft letter from William Blundell complaining of soldiers of Thomas Fairfax, 1647.

36 LCRO, DDBl 24/37, Order of Deputy Lieutenants suspending charge on William Blundell, 12 November 1673; William Blundell to Henry Houghton, 7 June 1675, in Draft Letter Book, II, fol. 40; William Blundell to Roger Hesketh, 13 April 1680, in Draft Letter Book, III, fol. 25.

37 Blue Book, fol. 66; William Blundell to David Cooke, 10 September 1675, in Draft Letter Book, II, fols 47–b, transcribed in Letter Book One, fol. 102b.

38 William Blundell to Peter Shakerley, 15 December 1686; William Blundell to John Entwistle, 22 March 1687, in Draft Letter Book, IV, fols 11, 22b.

39 William Blundell to Peter Shakerley, 15 December 1686; William Blundell to John Gillibrand, 9 June 1687, in Draft Letter Book, IV, fols 11b, 26.

40 Hodge Podge the Third, fols 55b, 64b, 68b, 69b; Great Hodge Podge, fol. 108.

41 Hodge Podge the Third, fol. 68b.

42 Cicely Burton [William Blundell] to Ananian Baker [Richard Masters], 1647, in Great Hodge Podge, fol. 89.

43 See: A. Barclay, 'The rise of Edward Colman', *Historical Journal*, 42 (1999), pp. 109–31; J. Miller, 'The correspondence of Edward Coleman, 1674–78', *Recusant History*, 14 (1977), pp. 261–75; S. A. H. Burne, *The Trial of William Howard Viscount Stafford* (1964).

44 Blue Book, fols 31b, 58b, 62–3.

45 William Blundell to Gilbert Crouch, 29 April 1653; William Blundell to Thomas Masey, 25 May 1672, in Letter Book One, fols 18, 79b; Hodge Podge the Third, fol. 79b.

46 Richard Langhorne to William Blundell, 3 November 1666, in Letter Book Two, p. 42.

47 Letter Book Two, pp. 67–9.

48 Great Hodge Podge, fol. 107b.

49 Great Hodge Podge, fols 113b–14; Anon., *The Case of Divers Roman Catholics as it was Lately Stated to a Person Eminent in the Law and Thought not Unfit to be made Publicke* (1662), p. 1.

50 William Blundell to Unnamed Recipient, 29 December 1681, in Letter Book One, fols 122–b; Edmund Butler to William Blundell, 4 July 1689, in Letter Book Two, pp. 73–4.

51 Small Account Book, fol. 83b; William Blundell to Unnamed Recipient, 29 December 1681, in Letter Book One, fol. 122b.

52 That Blundell held a life interest in his estate is shown in the proceedings of the Committee for Compounding, where Ann Blundell begs that her children are able to prove their title for the estate: TNA, SP23/69, Proceedings of the Committee for Compounding, p. 510; M. A. Everett Green (ed.), *Calendar of the Proceedings of the Committee for Compounding, &c., 1643–1660*, 5 vols (London: HMSO, 1892), V, p. 2692.

53 B. English and J. Saville, *Strict Settlement: A Guide for Historians*, Occasional Papers in Economic and Social History, 10 (Hull: University of Hull Press, 1983), pp. 27–8.

54 J. Habakkuk, *Marriage, Debt, and the Estates System: English Landownership 1650–1950* (Oxford: Clarendon Press, 1994), pp. 5, 12; English and Saville, *Strict Settlement*, p. 11.

55 H. J. Habakkuk, 'Landowners and the Civil War', *Economic History Review*, 18 (1965), p. 133.

56 Gibson (ed.), *Cavalier's Note Book*, p. 21.

57 English and Saville, *Strict Settlement*, pp. 38, 40.

58 A. Hughes, *Politics, Society and Civil War in Warwickshire, 1620–1660* (Cambridge: Cambridge University Press, 1987), pp. 255–90; C. Carlton, *Going to the Wars: The Experience of the British Civil Wars, 1638–1651* (London: Routledge, 1995), pp. 342–50.

59 J. Thirsk, 'The Restoration land settlement', *Journal of Modern History*, 26 (1954), pp. 315–28.

60 C. H. Firth and R. S. Rait (eds), *Acts and Ordinances of the Interregnum 1642–1660*, 3 vols (London: HMC, 1911), I, pp. 106–17.

61 TNA, SP23/69, Proceedings of the Committee for Compounding, p. 512.

62 Firth and Rait, *Acts and Ordinances*, II, pp. 520–45, 591–8, 623–52.

63 Firth and Rait, *Acts and Ordinances*, II, p. 1178.

64 William Blundell to Constantia Masey, 26 November 1672, in Draft Letter Book, I, fol. 17b.

65 William Blundell to Unnamed Recipient, 1654, in Letter Book One, fols 57–b.

66 William Blundell to Thomas Selby, 16 May 1650, in Great Hodge Podge, fol. 87.

67 Small Account Book, fol. 85; LCRO, DDBl 30/15, Note relating to holding of demesne of Ditton during sequestration, 1643–1660.

68 Blue Book, fol. 7b.

69 This appears as a single quotation in Margaret Blundell's work, with no suggestion of the context in which the quotation was found, nor the date. However, she believes that the phrase is 'alluding, no doubt, to the years of their youth when he roamed a fugitive and she ... gallantly held the remnants of their possessions together and waited for better times': Blundell (ed.), *Cavalier: Letters*, p. 54.

70 TNA, SP23/69, Proceedings of the Committee for Compounding, p. 512.

71 LCRO, DDBl 30/16, Order for the allowance of fifth of profits of estate to Ann wife of William Blundell and five children, 19 August 1646.

72 Tyrer, 'Recusancy', I, p. 179.

73 Ann could not compound in the usual sense, but was allowed to become the tenant of the estate on payment of a fine, in effect leasing the estate from government commissioners. That Blundell's notes mention 'composition fees' paid by Ann no doubt reflects his shorthand understanding of the payments: LCRO, DDBl 30/18, Agreement: William Blundell to the Commissioners of Sequestration, 19 April 1651.

74 Small Account Book, fol. 84; LCRO, DDBl 30/14, Certificate of Peter Ambrose that composition has been made in respect of the demesne of William Blundell, 12 March 1646.

75 See, for instance, signatures on acquittances for fines allowing the Blundells to farm the remaining four-fifths of their estate: LCRO, DDBl 30/3, Acquittances for composition money, 1627–1658.

76 William Blundell to Gilbert Crouch, 29 April 1653, in Letter Book One, fols 18–b; TNA, SP23/69, Proceedings of the Committee for Compounding, p. 508; TNA, SP23/77, Proceedings of the Committee for Compounding, p. 492.

77 Copy of a Letter of Attorney, 24 October 1657, in Small Account Book, fol. 42; LCRO, DDBl 30/25, Account of repurchase of estate from government.

78 TNA, SP23/69, Proceedings of the Committee for Compounding, p. 510; Everett Green (ed.), *Calendar of the Proceedings of the Committee for Compounding*, IV, p. 2692.

79 Small Account Book, fol. 84b.

80 Small Account Book, fol. 84.

81 A receipt from Crouch made in 1660 acquits Blundell of all money owed, though it is not clear if this was for legal services, or, as Tyrer speculates, the final payment of a loan: Tyrer, 'Recusancy', I, pp. 215–16; LCRO, DDBl 30/26, Final receipt by Gilbert Crouch from William Blundell, 28 November 1660.

82 Small Account Book, fol. 84b.

83 Small Account Book, fol. 85.

84 LCRO, DDBl 30/4, Enrolment of recusancy fines in Little Crosby, 1595–1656.

85 Blundell (ed.), *Cavalier: Letters*, p. 41; Tyrer, 'Recusancy', I, p. 225

86 Though there is a gap in Blundell's accounts from 1654 to 1658, as he 'was so far over charged with care debts business & imprisonments that I think tooke no exact account of the value of my goods till the year 1658', it is highly unlikely that such a large sum would have gone unmentioned. Certainly a full outline of the cost of the repurchase of his estate survives: Small Account Book, fol. 84b.

87 William Blundell to Gilbert Crouch, 7 November 1656, in Small Account Book, fol. 18b.

88 'it is Considered and adjudged by the said Barons that they, the said Roger Bradshawe and Gilbert Crouch, of and from the payments of all and euye Sume and Sumes of money and other penaltyes and forfeitures happeninge in respect or by reason of the said Composicion or Lease against his highnesse the Lord Protector and his Successors shalbee Acquitted and Dischardged': LCRO, DDBl 30/4, Enrolment of recusancy fines.

89 For examples of Blundell's contemporary and retrospective claims of this nature see: William Blundell to A. B., 9 July 1657; William Blundell to Unnamed Recipient, 29 December 1681, in Letter Book One, fols 30, 122.

90 Great Hodge Podge, fol. 48b.

91 Small Account Book, fols 52b–8b.

92 P. Lake and M. Questier, 'Prisons, priests and people', in N. Tyacke (ed.), *England's Long Reformation 1500–1800* (London: UCL Press, 2000), pp. 195–233; Questier, *Catholicism and Community*, p. 518; Lake with Questier, *The Anti-Christ's Lewd Hat*, pp. 199–207.

93 William Blundell to Elizabeth Bradshaigh, 5 February 1657, in Small Account Book, fols 62–3.

94 Small Account Book, fols 63, 84b.

95 William Blundell to R. Manley [Robert Charnock], 1648, in Blundell (ed.), *Cavalier: Letters*, pp. 30–1. I have been unable to locate this letter.

96 William Blundell to John Walton, 17 January 1657, in Small Account Book, fols 32–b.

97 Blundell (ed.), *Cavalier: Letters*, p. 40; Tyrer, 'Recusancy', I, pp. 195–201.

98 William Blundell to Thomas Haggerston, 16 September 1672; William Blundell to Henry Heton, 23 October 1672, in Draft Letter Book, I, fols 11, 15.

99 Frances Blundell to William Blundell, 22 March 1682; Frances Blundell to William Blundell, 3 April 1682; Frances Blundell to Lady Mountgarret, 6 November 1694, in Letter Book Two, pp. 53–5, 57–8, 122–4; William Blundell to Thomas Blundell, November 1680, in Letter Book One, fol. 120.

100 William Blundell to Constantia Masey, 26 November 1672, in Draft Letter Book, I, fol. 17b. Elsewhere Blundell noted that 'I purpose the next spring eyther to contract my family in a little corner of this little house, or else to table with my Son': William Blundell to John Walton, 20 May 1673, in Draft Letter Book, I, fol. 37.

101 William Blundell to Mrs Gerard, 22 November 1693, in Letter Book Two, pp. 77–8; William Blundell to Thomas Blundell, November 1680, in Letter Book One, fol. 120; William Blundell to Madam Selby, 13 July 1673, in Draft Letter Book, I, fol. 43b.

102 William Blundell to Mrs Gerard, 22 November 1693, in Letter Book Two, p. 79.

103 William Blundell to Alice Haggerston, 20 July 1657, in Letter Book One, fol. 50b.

104 William Blundell to Mrs Gerard, 22 November 1693, in Letter Book Two, p. 78.

105 See his enquiries, relayed by his wife Ann, as to the intellectual well-being of his eldest son, Nicholas: Ann Blundell to Nicholas Blundell, 20 November, in Small Account Book, fols 28b–9.

106 Blue Book, fols 53b, 57.

107 Blue Book, fols 53b, 57. The use of a jointure in a marriage settlement was common practice: A. L. Erikson, 'Common law versus common practice: the use of marriage settlements in early modern England', *Economic History Review*, 43 (1990), pp. 24–5.

108 The activities of this staunchly Catholic family are discussed in M. Rosamond, 'A Derbyshire family in the seventeenth century: the Eyres of Hassop and their forfeited estates', *Recusant History*, 8 (1965), pp. 12–77.

109 LCRO, DDBl 55/91, Settlement pursuant to marriage of William Blundell junior and Mary, 12 April 1668; SA, Bagshaw Collection, C2705, Postnuptial Settlement between William Blundell the son and Mary Eyre now his wife, 12 April 1668.

110 William Blundell junior to Mary Eyre, no date, in Letter Book Two, p. 17.

111 William Blundell to Pears Butler, 16 July 1677, in Letter Book One, fol. 107b.

112 William Blundell to Unnamed Recipient, 26 December 1658, in Letter Book One, fol. 40b.

113 Lord Mountgarret to Richard Butler, 3 November 1658, in Great Hodge Podge, fol. 74b.

114 William Blundell to Unnamed Recipient, 26 December 1658; William Blundell to Unnamed Recipient, 14 June 1659; William Blundell to Mervin Touchet, 2 May 1661, in Letter Book One, fols 39–40b, 49, 93–5. Note that this is Mervin Touchet, fourth Earl of Castlehaven, son and namesake of the notorious second Earl. Blundell was in correspondence with him because Edmund Butler was his nephew.

115 William Blundell to Mervin Touchet, 2 May 1661, in Letter Book One, fol. 93; Great Hodge Podge, fol. 74b.

116 The correspondence between the families was temporarily maintained by the senior females: Lady Mountgarret to Ann Blundell, 4 June, in Letter Book Two, p. 46.

117 Small Account Book, fol. 87.

118 William Blundell to Lady Willoughby, 28 July 1667; William Blundell to Thomas Blundell, November 1680, in Letter Book One, fols 95b–6b, 120b.

119 Frances Blundell to William Blundell, 22 March 1682; Frances Blundell to William Blundell, 3 April 1682, in Letter Book Two, pp. 53–5, 57–8.

120 William Blundell to Thomas Blundell, 29 December 1686, in Draft Letter Book, IV, fols 11b–13b.

121 Blundell was so worried by these accusations that he had a solicitor help him draw up a written copy of his version of events: Hodge Podge the Third, fols 43b–6.

122 William Blundell to T. B., 26 December 1658, in Letter Book One, fol. 39.

123 Great Hodge Podge, fol. 104b; William Blundell to Thomas Blundell, November 1680, in Letter Book One, fol. 120b.

124 Blue Book, fol. 50; William Blundell to Unnamed Recipient, 12 September 1681, in Letter Book One, fols 125b–6.

125 Tyrer, 'Recusancy', I, pp. 199–201.

126 Blue Book, fols 26b–8b. A second, less dramatic exercise follows in which Clare Frances tries to teach her young sisters how to behave as ladies, but to little avail as all the girls will do is rhyme or talk about 'Fryd pudding': Blue Book, fols 29b–30b.

127 Blue Book, fol. 26b.

128 Blue Book, fol. 27.

129 Blue Book, fol. 27.

130 Blue Book, fol. 27b.

131 Blue Book, fol. 28b.

132 A. Shell, '"Furor juvenilis": Post-Reformation English Catholicism and exemplary youthful behaviour', in Shagan (ed.), *Catholics and the 'Protestant Nation'*, p. 198.

133 Shell, 'Furor juvenilis', pp. 192–3.

134 William Blundell to Charles Parker, 16 May 1659, in Letter Book One, fol. 42b.

135 William Blundell to Nicholas Blundell, 7 July 1686, in Draft Letter Book, IV, fol. 3b.

136 William Blundell to Henry Blundell, 1650, in Letter Book One, fol. 53b.

137 William Blundell to Edmund Butler, 2 October 1693, in Draft Letter Book, IV, fol. 68.

138 Blundell (ed.), *Cavalier: Letters*, p. 89; Great Hodge Podge, fol. 185b.

139 Blue Book, fol. 41b.

140 Blue Book, fol. 54.

141 William Blundell to Richard Butler, 19 January 1677; William Blundell to Edward Scarisbrick, 14 July 1677, in Letter Book One, fols 7b–8, 104b–7.

142 William Blundell to Edward Scarisbrick, 14 July 1677, in Letter Book One, fols 105b–6.

143 William Blundell to Edmund Ballard, 9 April 1673, in Draft Letter Book, I, fol. 31.

144 William Blundell to Emilia Butler, 11 May 1674, in Draft Letter Book, II, fol. 21.

145 William Blundell to Emilia Butler, 21 August 1678, in Draft Letter Book, III, fols 18b–9.

146 William Blundell to Edward Scarisbrick, 14 July 1677, in Letter Book One, fols 105b–6.

147 William Blundell to Frances Blundell, 9 October 1681, in Letter Book One, fol. 123b; William Blundell to Emilia Butler, 21 August 1678, in Draft Letter Book, III, fol. 18.

148 Edmund Butler to William Blundell, 4 July 1689, in Letter Book Two, p. 74.

149 William Blundell to Edmund Butler, 8 March 1687, in Draft Letter Book, IV, fol. 21.

150 William Blundell to Edmund Butler, 15 February 1692, in Draft Letter Book, IV, fol. 54.

151 Hibbard, 'Early Stuart Catholicism', pp. 2–3.

152 Great Hodge Podge, fols 184b–5; Hodge Podge the Third, fol. 16b.

153 William Blundell to Richard Langhorne, 14 May 1673, in Letter Book One, fol. 102; Frances Blundell to William Blundell, 3 April 1682, in Letter Book Two, p. 57.

154 See Beales, *Education Under Penalty*, passim.

155 William Blundell to Richard Bradshaigh, 14 November 1666, in Letter Book One, fol. 88b; Great Hodge Podge, fol. 185.

156 William Blundell to Roger L'Estrange, 9 December 1665, in Letter Book One, fol. 76.

157 William Blundell to Ralph Ever, 28 June 1681, in Letter Book One, fol. 5b.

158 William Blundell to Francis Waldegrave, 18 April 1678, in Draft Letter Book, III, fol. 12.

159 Ann Blundell to Nicholas Blundell, 20 November, in Small Account Book, fol. 28b.

160 William Blundell to Richard Bradshaigh, 7 February 1657, in Small Account Book, fol. 64b.

161 William Blundell to R. B., 12 June 1660, in Letter Book One, fol. 62.

162 William Blundell to Unnamed Recipient, 9 November 1653, in Letter Book One, fol. 13b.

163 Blue Book, fol. 29.

164 Hodge Podge the Third, fols 25b, 35b–7, 41.

165 Small Account Book, fol. 17; Blue Book, fols 44–7b, 51b, 59–b, 60b.

166 Great Hodge Podge, fols 102–3.

167 Blue Book, fol. 47.

168 William Blundell to Charles Parker, 3 May 1660; William Blundell to Unnamed Recipient, 14 June 1659, in Letter Book One, fols 45b, 48b–9.

169 William Blundell to Roger L'Estrange, 31 May 1664, in Letter Book One, fols 64b–5.

170 William Blundell to Unnamed Recipient, 14 June 1659, in Letter Book One, fol. 48b. For the transmission of news in early modern England see: R. Cust, 'News and politics in early seventeenth-century England', *Past and Present*, 112 (1986), pp. 60–90; I. Atherton, 'The itch grown a disease: manuscript transmission of news in the seventeenth century', in J. Raymond (ed.), *News, Newspapers and Society in Early Modern Britain* (London: Frank Cass, 1999), pp. 39–65.

171 William Blundell to Unnamed Recipient, 4 October 1654, in Letter Book One, fols 58b–9.

172 See, for example, the postscript to a letter to Christopher Bradshaigh which states 'I do purpose to send with this the booke which I borrowed of you ... Lassels Voyage to Italy': William Blundell to Christopher Bradshaigh, 15 October 1673, in Draft Letter Book, II, fol. 3b.

173 See, for example: William Blundell to Robert Manley, 11 July 1663, in Great Hodge Podge, fol. 194b. Manley was a Jesuit priest who used the alias Robert Charnock.

174 William Blundell to Unnamed Recipient, no date; William Blundell to Edmund Borlase, 17 July 1672; William Blundell to A. B., 19 January 1659; William Blundell to Thomas Blundell, November 1680, in Letter Book One, fols 9b, 11, 41b, 120b; William Blundell to Laurence Ireland, 28 December 1669, in Letter Book Two, pp. 31–6.

175 Edmund Butler to William Blundell, 14 December 1680, in Letter Book Two, p. 59.

176 Hodge Podge the Third, fol. 42b.

177 For example: William Blundell to Unnamed Recipient, September 1650, in Letter Book One, fols 50b–1b.

178 Questier, *Conversion, Politics and Religion*, p. 12.

179 Laurence Ireland to William Blundell, 28 December 1669, in Letter Book Two, pp. 31–6. The Warner discussed in Ireland's letter may have been the same John Warner who published controversial Catholic works and became an ardent Jacobite after the Revolution of 1688: J. M. Rigg, 'Warner, John (1628–1692)', in *ODNB*.

180 George Gray to Richard Barton, 21 December 1649 (copied by Ann Blundell, 23 June 1664), in Letter Book Two, pp. 85–121.

181 Henry Bryth to Unnamed Recipient, 6 January 1686, in Letter Book Two, p. 71.

182 Henry Bryth to Unnamed Recipient, 6 January 1686, in Letter Book Two, p. 73.

183 Laurence Ireland to William Blundell, 28 December 1669, Letter Book Two, p. 36.

184 William Blundell to Thomas Masey, 25 May 1672, in Letter Book One fol. 80.

185 For example, see the footnote to 'The Lord Chancellors Speech', in Letter Book Two, p. 52. 'Examined 10th May 1679 by us Wm Blundell Walter Thelwall'.

186 Hodge Podge the Third, fol. 19.

187 Blue Book, fol. 63b; William Blundell to Alexander Causey, 25 February 1672, in Draft Letter Book, I, fol. 25.

188 William Blundell to Margaret Haggerston, 1651; William Blundell to Margaret Haggerston, 23 October 1665, in Letter Book One, fols 55, 74b.

189 William Blundell to Thomas Selby, 16 May 1650, in Great Hodge Podge, fol. 87b.

190 Laurence Ireland to Ann Blundell, 30 September 1670, in Letter Book Two, p. 83.

191 William Blundell to James C., no date, in Letter Book Two, p. 37.

192 William Blundell to Mrs Talbot, 6 November 1677, in Letter Book One, fol. 112.

193 William Blundell to Mrs Talbot, 5 November 1677, in Letter Book One, fol. 110.

194 William Blundell to Mrs Talbot, 6 November 1677, in Letter Book One, fol. 111–b.

195 William Blundell to Mrs Gerard, 12 October 1678, in Letter Book One, fol. 115.

196 William Blundell to Colonel R. L., 1656, in Letter Book One, fols 26–b.

197 Cited in: T. M. McCoog, 'Langhorne, Richard (c. 1624–1679)', in *ODNB*.

198 T. M. McCoog, 'Richard Langhorne and the Popish Plot', *Recusant History*, 19 (1988), pp. 499–508; J. Kenyon, *The Popish Plot* (London: Phoenix Press, 2000), pp. 185–8.

199 Langhorne's speech was recorded in Letter Book Two, pp. 133–43, quotation at p. 140.

200 Richard Langhorne to William Blundell, 18 September 1666, in Letter Book Two, p. 16; William Blundell to Richard Langhorne, 14 February, in Letter Book One, fol. 79.

201 William Blundell to Richard Langhorne, 21 March 1672, in Draft Letter Book, I, fol. 27.

202 Richard Langhorne to William Blundell, 13 July 1665, in Letter Book Two, p. 9.

203 Adversaria, fol. 172b.

204 Glickman, 'Politics, Culture and Ideology', p. 90.

205 For Chorley's entertainment of Monmouth, see: D. E. Ascott, F. Lewis and M. Power, *Liverpool 1660–1750: People, Prosperity and Power* (Liverpool: Liverpool University Press, 2006), p. 168; M. Mullett, 'The politics of Liverpool, 1660–88', *Transactions of the Historic Society of Lancashire and Cheshire*, 124 (1972), p. 50.

206 Records of Blundell's acquittances to John Chorley dating from 1672 can be found in Blue Book, fol. 50b; Draft Letter Book, I, fol. 15.

207 LCRO, DDBl 50/72, Lease for 5 years 11 months and 2 weeks at £50 rent: John Chorley, Mayor of Liverpool, to William Blundell of Little Crosby, 28 October 1678. A copy of this lease can be found in Draft Letter Book, III, fols 33–6b.

208 William Blundell to John Chorley, 9 January 1680, in Draft Letter Book, III, fol. 37.

209 William Blundell to John Entwistle, 23 January 1680, in Draft Letter Book, III, fol. 37b. This was not forgotten. In a letter dated March 1687 Blundell offered to appeal to James II on Entwistle's behalf: William Blundell to John Entwistle, 22 March 1687, in Draft Letter Book, IV, fol. 22b.

210 A. J. Hawkes, *Sir Roger Bradshaigh of Haigh, Knight and Baronet 1628–1684 With Notes of his Immediate Forbears*, Supplement to the *Transactions of the Lancashire and Cheshire Antiquarian Society* (Manchester: Lancashire and Cheshire Antiquarian Society, 1945), pp. 4–6; B. Coward, *The Stanleys: Lords Stanley and Earl of Derby 1385–1672*, Chetham Society, 3rd Series, 30 (1983), p. 186.

211 Hawkes, *Sir Roger Bradshaigh*, pp. 8–9; J. Langton, 'Bradshaigh, Sir Roger, First Baronet (1628–1684)', in *ODNB*.

212 MCL, L1/48/6/1, Letter book of Roger Bradshaigh of Haigh, pp. 168–9, 353.

213 William Blundell to Roger Bradshaigh, 24 April 1673, in Draft Letter Book, I, fols 34–b; William Blundell to Roger Bradshaigh, 28 July 1679; William Blundell to Roger Bradshaigh, 4 August 1679; William Blundell to Roger Bradshaigh, 4 September 1679, in Draft Letter Book, III, fols 46, 47b, 50.

214 John Langton attributes this quotation to Nicholas Blundell. It was, in fact, made by William in a letter to his son Nicholas: Langton, 'Bradshaigh, Sir Roger', *ODNB*; Coward, *The Stanleys*, p. 181; Hawkes, *Sir Roger Bradshaigh*, p. 39; William Blundell to Nicholas Blundell, 18 February 1677, in Draft Letter Book, III, fol. 8.

215 Hodge Podge the Third, fols 50b, 68b, 87. When Bradshaigh first handled money belonging to the Poor Clares, Blundell noted that 'Sir R knows not so much', though we do not know if Bradshaigh remained ignorant as to the purpose of his work: William Blundell to John Rigmaiden, 28 May 1675, in Draft Letter Book, II, fol. 39.

216 William Blundell to Nicholas Blundell, 18 February 1677, in Draft Letter Book, III, fol. 8b.

217 Milton, 'A qualified intolerance', pp. 85–115; Milton, *Catholic and Reformed*, passim.

218 P. A. Hopkins, 'The commission for superstitious lands of the 1690s', *Recusant History*,

15 (1980), pp. 265–82; P. A. Hopkins, 'Aspects of Jacobite Conspiracy in England in the Reign of William III' (PhD thesis, Cambridge University, 1981), pp. 449–50; Beamont (ed.), *The Jacobite Trials at Manchester*, pp. xxvii–xxxiv, 1–3, 13–40; J. Addy, J. Harrop and P. McNiven (eds), *The Diary of Henry Prescott, LL.B., Deputy Registrar of Chester Diocese*, 3 vols, Record Society of Lancashire and Cheshire, 127, 132, 133 (1987, 1994, 1997), III, pp. 897–8; R. Kingston, *A True History of the Several Designs and Conspiracies Against his Majesties Sacred Person and Government; as they were Continually Carry'd on from 1688 till 1697* (1698), pp. 100–30, 231–6, 249–58, 287–302; E. L. Lonsdale, 'John Lunt and the Lancashire Plot, 1694', *Transactions of the Historic Society of Lancashire and Cheshire*, 115 (1964), pp. 94–6; HMC, *The Manuscripts of Lord Kenyon*, HMC 14th Report, Appendix Part IV, (London: HMC, 1894), pp. 292–304; Account of Jacobite Trial, pp. 2, 5, 8–9.

219 Beamont (ed.), *Jacobite Trials*, p. xxxiv. An important exception was William Standish, for whom a warrant had been issued, but he eluded officials by going into hiding.

220 Blundell (ed.), *Cavalier: Letters*, p. 279; HMC, *Manuscripts of Lord Kenyon*, p. 362; Beamont (ed.), *Jacobite Trials*, p. 47; Account of Jacobite Trial, pp. 49–51.

221 P. K. Monod, *Jacobitism and the English People, 1688–1788* (Cambridge: Cambridge University Press, 1993), p. 311; HMC, *Manuscripts of Lord Kenyon*, pp. 309, 348; Kingston, *True History*, p. 132; LCRO, Kenyon Papers, DDKe/8/3, Accounts of the joint trials of the Lancashire plotters, 14–20 October 1694, fol. 2.

222 Beaumont (ed.), *Jacobite Trials*, pp. 81–100; Lonsdale, 'John Lunt', pp. 96–104; Account of Jacobite Trial, pp. 17–63.

223 Frances Blundell to Lady Mountgarret, no date, in Blundell (ed.), *Cavalier: Letters*, p. 278; Beamont (ed.), *Jacobite Trials*, pp. 92–5. Although further evidence was later discovered during the renovation of Standish Hall in 1757 that indicated that William Standish may have been involved in some form of intrigue, it is unlikely that this ever developed into the level of plotting alleged by Lunt. Blundell's name appears neither in these papers nor on a list of Jacobite commissions for this period that survives in the papers of David Nairne, the undersecretary of John Caryll at St German, and it is unlikely that he was ever involved in preparations for a Jacobite rebellion: T. C. Porteus, *A History of the Parish of Standish, Lancashire* (Wigan: J. Starr & Sons, 1927); T. C. Porteus, 'New light on the Lancashire Jacobite Plot, 1692–4', *Transactions of the Lancashire and Cheshire Antiquarian Society*, 50 (1934–35), pp. 1–64; WRO, D/DSt. M1/1–20, M2/1–25, M3/1–34, Standish Hall plot papers; WRO, D/DAn9/7, Anderton Papers, Jacobite cipher; Bodl., Carte MSS. 181, Nairne Papers, List of commissions required by and sent to Colonel Parker by Standish, fols 558–62.

224 Addy, Harrop and McNiven (ed.), *Diary of Henry Prescott*, pp. 898–9; Blundell (ed.), *Cavalier: Letters*, p. 281.

225 For example: R. Ferguson, *A Letter to Mr. Secretary Trenchard* (1694); Wagstaffe, *A Letter out of Lancashire*; NUL, Portland Papers, PwA2460, Verse entitled 'A letter to Dyer ... upon the Lancashire Plot'.

226 HMC, *Manuscripts of Lord Kenyon*, pp. 305, 307, 375; NUL, Portland Papers, PwA2706, Victual Office to Godart van Ginkel, first Earl of Athlone, 11 February 1695, fol. 1.

227 G. Burnet, *Bishop Burnet's History of his own Time* (London: Henry G. Bohn, 1850), pp. 608–10, at p. 609.

228 Frances Blundell to Lady Mountgarret, no date, in Blundell (ed.), *Cavalier: Letters*, p. 282. I have been unable to locate this letter and Margaret Blundell's transcription offers no indication as to its provenance.

229 Kenyon has received little scholarly attention, the only narrative of his life being in the *History of Parliament* series: E. Cruickshanks, 'Roger Kenyon', in E. Cruickshanks, S. Handley and D. Hayton (eds), *History of Parliament: The House of Commons 1690–1715*, 5 vols (Cambridge: Cambridge University Press, 2002), IV, pp. 545–8.

230 Hopkins, 'Aspects of Jacobite Conspiracy', p. 399.

231 HMC, *Manuscripts of Lord Kenyon*, p. 375, see also pp. 356, 379–81; William Blundell to Roger Kenyon, 18 January 1689, in Blundell (ed.), *Cavalier: Letters*, p. 255.

232 Lonsdale, 'John Lunt', p. 94; HMC, *Manuscripts of Lord Kenyon*, pp. 292–394; Hopkins, 'Aspects of Jacobite Conspiracy', p. 411; P. Hopkins, 'Sham plots and real plots in the 1690s', in E. Cruickshanks (ed.), *Ideology and Conspiracy: Aspects of Jacobitism, 1689–1759* (Edinburgh: Donald, 1982), p. 106.

233 HMC, *Manuscripts of Lord Kenyon*, p. 310, see also pp. 307, 371–2, 378–9.

234 HMC, *Manuscripts of Lord Kenyon*, pp. 292, 305, 320, 357, 375; Porteus, 'New light on the Lancashire Jacobite Plot', p. 24.

235 HMC, *Manuscripts of Lord Kenyon*, pp. 370–2.

236 Beamont (ed.), *Jacobite Trials*, pp. 98–9; Porteus, 'New light on the Lancashire Jacobite Plot', pp. 38–9; Account of Jacobite Trial, pp. 57–60.

237 M. Gaskill, *Crime and Mentalities in Early Modern England* (Cambridge: Cambridge University Press, 2000), pp. 165–6, 170.

238 J. Bossy, 'English Catholics after 1688', in O. P. Grell, J. I. Israel and N. Tyacke (eds), *From Persecution to Toleration: The Glorious Revolution and Religion in England* (Oxford: Clarendon, 1991), pp. 369–87. This does not mean that Catholics were not subject to adverse discrimination or that the population did not support discrimination in general, whatever exceptions they made in individual circumstances.

239 Blue Book, fol. 87b.

240 J. R. Dickinson, *The Lordship of Man Under the Stanleys*, Chetham Society, 3rd Series, 41 (1996), p. 355; J. R. Dickinson, 'Greenhalgh, John (1588/9–1651)', in *ODNB*.

241 William Blundell to John Greenhalgh, 1647, in Letter Book One, fols 51b–2b.

242 A. Clarke, 'Borlase, Edmund (1620–82)', in *ODNB*. Receipts copied into Hodge Podge the Third show that Blundell was Borlase's patient throughout the 1670s at least. Hodge Podge the Third, fol. 6b.

243 The brief title in the correspondence, *A Further Account of Latham Spaw*, suggests that Blundell received either the second half or the entire manuscript of E. Borlase, *Latham Spaw in Lancashire with some Remarkable Cases and Cures Effected by it; Together with a Further Account of it* (1672). Edmund Borlase to William Blundell, May 1670, in Letter Book Two, p. 47; William Blundell to Edmund Borlase, 17 July 1672, in Draft Letter Book, I, fol. 8b, transcribed in Letter Book One, fol. 11.

244 E. Borlase, *The History of the Execrable Irish Rebellion Trac'd from many Preceding Acts, to the Grand Eruption, the 23 of October, 1641, and then Pursued to the Act of Settlement, 1662* (1680); Clarke, 'Borlase, Edmund', *ODNB*.

245 G. Scott, 'A Benedictine conspirator: Henry Joseph Johnston (c.1656–1723)', *Recusant History*, 20 (1994), p. 58.

246 J. Raymond, *Pamphlets and Pamphleteering in Early Modern Britain* (Cambridge: Cambridge University Press, 2003), p. 324.

247 William Blundell to Roger L'Estrange, 19 November 1681, in Letter Book One, fol. 117.

248 Roger L'Estrange to William Blundell, 26 September 1665; Roger L'Estrange to William Blundell, 7 October 1665; Roger L'Estrange to William Blundell, 2 December 1665; Roger L'Estrange to William Blundell, 16 December 1665, in Letter Book Two, pp. 21–7; William Blundell to Roger L'Estrange, 11 May 1664; William Blundell to Roger L'Estrange, 1 June 1664; William Blundell to Roger L'Estrange, 23 June 1664; William Blundell to Roger L'Estrange, July 1664; William Blundell to Roger L'Estrange, 27 December 1664; William Blundell to Roger L'Estrange, 18 September 1665; William Blundell to Roger L'Estrange, 9 December 1665; William Blundell to Roger L'Estrange, 2 October 1665; William Blundell to Roger L'Estrange, 19 November 1681, in Letter Book One, fols 63–9b, 72–b, 75b–6b, 86b-7, 117–b.

249 Roger L'Estrange to William Blundell, 2 December 1665, in Letter Book Two, p. 26.

250 William Blundell to Roger L'Estrange, 9 December 1665, in Letter Book One, fol. 76.

251 William Blundell to Roger L'Estrange, 31 May 1664, in Letter Book One, fol. 64b.

252 William Blundell to Roger L'Estrange, 31 May 1664, in Letter Book One, fol. 65.

253 William Blundell to Roger L'Estrange, 7 October 1665, in Letter Book Two, p. 23.

254 William Blundell to Roger L'Estrange, 31 May 1664; William Blundell to Roger L'Estrange, 23 June 1664; William Blundell to Roger L'Estrange, 9 December 1665, in Letter Book One, fols 65, 68, 76b.

255 N. H. Keeble, *The Literary Culture of Nonconformity in Later Seventeenth-Century England* (Athens: University of Georgia Press, 1987), pp. 102–10; H. Love, 'L'Estrange, Sir Roger (1616–1704)', in *ODNB*. The most complete articulation of L'Estrange's views on the subject can be found in R. L'Estrange, *Toleration Discuss'd* (1663).

256 Love, 'L'Estrange', *ODNB*; R. Latham and W. Matthews (eds), *The Diary of Samuel Pepys 1664*, 11 vols (London: Harper Collins Publishers, 2000), V, p. 348.

257 Love, 'L'Estrange', *ODNB*. However, Love notes that his attempts 'to free himself from this accusation [of popery] were strangely muted and did little to convince either his opponents or many on his own side'. The most complete articulation is in R. L'Estrange, *L'Estrange No Papist* (1681).

258 William Blundell to Roger L'Estrange, 2 October 1665, in Letter Book One, fol. 87; Roger L'Estrange to William Blundell, 7 October 1665, in Letter Book Two, p. 23.

259 Love, 'L'Estrange', *ODNB*.

Chapter 2

William Blundell and the wider world

Blundell's patronage of Catholicism extended beyond the networks of friends and family that aided his survival. His support for his co-religionists emanated from the Little Crosby estate to include Catholics throughout the British Isles and those exiled on the continent.[1] He used his estate as a refuge for Catholicism, making every effort to protect his Catholic tenants. This protection was not selfless and through the employment of a leasing system he ensured that his leaseholders stayed Catholic. Not only did he seek to alleviate the sufferings of English Catholics by offering both religious and practical support, but at risk to himself and his family he also provided charity for Irish Catholics. Furthermore, Blundell was a zealous supporter of English religious houses on the continent and by 1660 he was entrusted with vast sums of money to farm out on behalf of the Poor Clares of Rouen and became one of their foremost financial agents in England. Finally, in his writings he provided arguments for the removal of the penal laws and the admission of Catholics into every area of English social life. This chapter examines these activities and shows that Blundell made a significant contribution to safe-guarding the prospects of English Catholicism.

I

Blundell owned almost the entirety of the manor and township of Little Crosby. This was a balance that he deliberately maintained, claiming that 'tis not proper to have more freeholders in town if it can be avoided', and the leases that he gave out were non-freehold, ensuring that they would revert to the Lord of the Manor at the end of a fixed period and he would retain his local hegemony.[2] This provided him with a power over his estate that he used to support Catholics. Since the Reformation Little Crosby had been established as a Catholic refuge, as successive Lords of the Manor invited their co-religionists to become tenants and employees. Blundell strictly adhered to this tradition and in Little Crosby he surrounded himself with Catholics. A return of papists in the township made in 1678 listed over a hundred Catholics, and Blundell was later to claim that it was often remarked of Little Crosby that there was 'No Rebell in the town, no Alehous, no beggar, no Protestant'.[3] Elsewhere he boasted how 'There are not (thro' the Grace of God) any other but Catholicks in it [Little Crosby], except, peradventure, one or 2 dayly labourers'.[4] An incident from the 1690s may suggest how keen Blundell and his tenants were to keep Little Crosby Catholic.[5] In 1692 Martha Tomson, one of a few Protestants, or even the only Protestant, in the township, petitioned for relief at the Quarter Sessions. In the petition she claimed that her husband had been beaten to death by a neighbour, and unable to provide for herself after the loss of income she had been thrown out of her home. The Justices ordered the Overseers of the poor of Little Crosby to pay her an annual sum of 40s.[6] However, in 1697 she petitioned the Quarter Sessions again when this payment stopped, arguing that she had been forced to go out of the town for work, not finding any available to her in Little Crosby, and that 'the rest or most of the Said Township beinge Roman Catholicks and shee not of the same perswasion was very cruell and severe with her'.[7] Given Blundell's close involvement with his tenants it is unlikely that he would have been unaware of this case, and, if the story was true, one can only speculate as to his reaction to it.

Although Blundell managed his estates diligently, he was prepared to forgo the loss of money to maintain his Catholic tenants. He was an exemplary paternalist landowner, his actions being driven by a desire to protect his co-religionist tenants' interests as well as his own. He gave a number of 'lease gratis' to individuals whom he believed had shown their worth and loyalty to either himself or the monarchy. Thus, Robert Tomson, a seaman, was given 'a lease gratis, for the great service he had done to his late Majesty in time of the war, which was truly great & remarkable in many respects', while in 1690 Blundell gave Walter Thelwall his servant a lease for one lifetime, which was later extended to his son and namesake by Blundell's grandson.[8] Even when Blundell was apparently stretched to the limit ensuring the survival of his estate, he found resources to help his tenants, a factor most evident during the Interregnum. Given that Blundell bragged at one stage that all of his tenants were Catholics, it should come as no surprise that a number had their land sequestered at the same time as Blundell. Although the repurchase of Blundell's estate went relatively smoothly, seven of his tenants spent a further five years negotiating the repurchase of sequestered lands.[9] Blundell went out of his way to help, offering to pay his lawyer, Gilbert Crouch, with his own money if Crouch could ensure the rapid repurchase of the estates.[10] In 1657 Crouch joined the cases of all the tenants in one plea to the Exchequer. Blundell agreed that if successful Crouch could keep an unspecified debt he owed Blundell, in addition to which Blundell stated that 'in case the sayde tenants can be cleared either in this or the next terme I will add to the consideration afforesaid some such remembrance as shall not (I hope) be thought much unsuitable to your merit'.[11] However, the best example of how Blundell's land management strategies helped protect Catholic tenants was the system of lease holding employed on the Crosby estate.

Throughout the seventeenth century the three-life leasehold was commonplace in Lancashire. The system of tenure functioned so that a high entry fine was taken up to begin the tenancy, usually paid within a few months, followed by a low annual rent based on ancient fixed rents. The tenancy was invested in the lives of three individuals: the tenant, typically followed by the heir and a third person connected by family links or an investor; the lease usually being given for a period of ninety-nine years.[12] There is some debate as to the extent to which the operation of the three-life leasehold aided economic development; however, at the time it was seen as vital to maintaining the established social hierarchy because of the power it enabled the landowner to exert over tenants.[13] Entry fines were usually calculated on a set amount of the annual value of the tenancy. By the mid-eighteenth century entry fines were as much as twelve to fourteen times the annual value of the estate.[14] Gritt argues that the success of a three-life leasehold could vary dramatically. In some cases a tenant could pay a massive entry fine and then all three lives could expire in rapid succession, in other instances favourable terms could be given and the tenant and heir could benefit from low annual rents and security of tenure for many years. Immediate payment of entry fines meant that tenants often went into debt and were unable to invest in the tenancy. Consequently, on many estates in Lancashire merchants were called on for loans and increasingly they appeared as the third name on three-life leases to ensure that they made a profit in the event of the tenant's death.[15] The manipulation of the system of leasehold by recusant landowners has been identified by Bossy as 'strong-arm action', and nowhere is this more evident than Blundell's management of his estate.[16]

Blundell used the operation of the three-life leasehold to control his tenants, both ensuring their obedience to him as landlord and facilitating his role as a protector of Catholicism. During his tenure as Lord of the Manor entry fines were usually calculated on a basis of five, seven or ten times the annual value of the estate for a ninety-nine-year lease.[17] However, Blundell differed from most landowners through the use of an additional tenant-right on the standard three-life leasehold system. In his case study of leasehold systems on the Blundell estate, Gritt views this as a deliberate attempt to manipulate tenants.[18] Tenant-right was a system whereby the family of deceased tenants were offered reduced entry fines and first refusal when a lease expired on lands historically farmed by the family. Though attempts were made by some tenants to sell tenant-right, generally the use of this system ensured that Catholic heirs of Catholic tenants inherited tenements.[19] Thus, Blundell commonly demanded seven years' value from an old tenant for a three-life leasehold for ninety-nine years and ten years' from a stranger for the same.[20] Although practised by the Blundell family for a number of generations before Blundell inherited the estate, tenant-right was not legally enforceable. Having enquired into the issue as 'a matter of conscience' in 1654, Blundell was advised that 'there is no tenement at all remaininge when their leases are fully expired' and that the use of such a system was at the discretion of a generous landlord.[21] None the less, although tenants had no legal right to tenant-right, it was common practice for the Blundells to buy back tenant-right from the heir if they did not take up the estate following the death of the tenant.[22] For instance, in 1674 when the lease of Elizabeth Bolton was not extended following the death of her grandfather, out of goodwill Blundell offered her a pension of £3 a year.[23]

The use of tenant-right had a number of positive aspects for Blundell. Most obviously he ensured the continued strength of Catholicism in Little Crosby, protecting himself and other Catholic tenants from possible Protestant infiltration. Furthermore, given that tenements passed through generations of the same family there was more likelihood that they would be well maintained.[24] While no evidence can be found to support his argument, Bossy plausibly suggests that tenant-right may have been used to ensure that no individuals holding tenements from Blundell could marry outside Catholicism: 'If, after all, the families of landlord and tenant were to live as neighbours for the decades, indeed centuries, which tenurial arrangements like the Blundells' imply, a landlord was entitled to be interested in whom the tenants married', especially when given the preferential deals the Blundells were offering.[25] Although Blundell clearly had trouble with some tenants, he had the ultimate decision over whether to suspend, reduce or altogether remove tenant-right from a troublesome individual.[26] Despite his recognition in 1663 that the preferential rates offered to Catholic heirs of Catholic tenants had a negative impact on the financial success of the family estate, Blundell continued the practice, retaining his control over his tenants and ensuring the sustained vitality of Catholicism in his locality.

Blundell's protection of Catholic tenants included the provision of charity for those in need. As we will see, this accorded with the active life that Blundell believed was the aspiration of gentlemen.[27] He frequently wrote testimonials for those he deemed as worthy poor, though from the information that survives it appears that they were all either Catholics or Royalists such as Edward Conyers of Northumberland, who 'served very long in the cause of our Late King & was an officer of good rank in the first and second war'.[28] Blundell also provided social support for his neighbours, such as the four visits he paid to Madam Moore of Bank Hall following the death of three of her sons.[29] His support for his Catholic neighbours is most evident in the donations that he provided. Although accounts of Blundell's charity only exist for short periods, it is clear that he was generous in his support for the poor. In 1661 alone, in addition to his contributions to the poor tax, he gave out £7 14*s* 2*d* in money to the poor, a range of clothes, food surplus to his family's requirements and a weekly 'Noggin full of oat meale' to any who turned up at his home, which as he noted was very expensive, 'wheat being sold for 8*s* the bushell, & other graine accordingly'. Additionally, in the same year he estimated that he gave approximately £3 9*s* 10*d* as small gifts, much of which was given to tenants 'after they had payd fines or other dutyes by giving them back 5 or 10*s*'.[30] It should also be noted that almost all of this money was given to individuals whose names he knew. He very rarely gave money to strangers and recorded that he gave 'but little or nothing to wandering beggars'.[31] Blundell's failure to provide charity for strangers may have been motivated by contemporary perceptions of the poor, who were increasingly viewed as a nuisance, but it also resulted in almost all of his charity going to Catholics.[32] Thus, as with other aspects of Blundell's protection of those in his locality, it was both generous and religiously exclusive.

Although few records survive about the priests that Blundell supported, it is clear that he contributed to the maintenance of a well provided priesthood in the area. We have already seen that two of Blundell's sons became Jesuits, while he encouraged other local Catholics to become priests and return to serve in their native Lancashire.[33] The cost of training his son at St Omer was one that Blundell was prepared to bear, for if Nicholas returned 'home with the Grounds of Religion & vertu the Commoditie will be very usefull'.[34] Though Blundell rarely named them, he was well connected to the priests in Lancashire, speaking of his upset in one letter that two local priests had died and offering his home as a refuge for the Jesuit Father Walton.[35] Furthermore, we have already seen that he was frequently the executor of wills leaving money for the support of priests.[36] We also know that Blundell had a resident priest, Father Walton from 1652 to 1656 and then Father Francis Waldegrave probably from the late 1650s to the late 1670s. It seems likely that they provided religious and educational support for those on the Crosby estate.[37]

Blundell's role as a protector of Catholics in his locality is well illustrated by the burial ground on his property maintained by his family since the early seventeenth century for poor Catholics and priests. The burial ground was constructed in 1611 on part of the Little Crosby estate known as the 'Harkirk', after 'a bitter storm of Persecution extended its fury in these parts to the bodyes of deceased Catholicks' as parish churches refused them burial.[38] Having heard about a woman's corpse that had been interred in Common Lane, only to be unearthed and eaten by hogs, Blundell's grandfather and namesake began its construction. While building the enclosure his grandfather 'found in the Grownd dyvers hundereds of old Saxon Coyne each about 3*d* or a groat in weight all of them silver and coyned by Christian Princes', remarkably, Blundell claimed that their value was exactly the cost of building the enclosure.[39] The discovery of these coins became family legend and was highlighted as an example of providential intervention in support of Catholicism. In times of particular persecution Blundell found solace from the tale, relaying it to family members who were also experiencing hardship.[40] This practice of providing a Catholic burial ground for priests and the poor was continued by William, and a burial register amongst his papers records the burial during his tenure as Lord of the Manor of six priests, not all of whom were from Crosby, indicating that the site was used beyond the immediate locality.[41]

The limited surviving correspondence from the late 1680s suggests that during the reign of James II Blundell's support for Catholicism in his locality took a different turn. He wrote to the Lancashire Catholic John Gillibrand in May 1687 advising him to make haste to London, where he should apply for employment from the King, who was 'in truth ... very graciously disposed especially towards his Catholick subjects and it is my opinion ... you may find a great capacity to improve yourself & your fortunes'.[42] While in London Blundell kept in touch with developments in Lancashire, writing to John Chorley of his delight in finding in a letter sent by an unnamed Deputy Lieutenant that Chorley had supported the removal of the penal laws and encouraged him to continue his work on behalf of Catholics in the area.[43] As late as 5 September 1688, having returned to Crosby, Blundell wrote a letter to the Anglican Lord Bishop of Chester recommending the curate at Sefton, James Jackson, as curate for Liverpool. Blundell's sole basis for the recommendation was that Jackson 'is one of the few that did most cheerfully discharge the duty of reading the kings declaration for Liberty of Conscience'.[44] As significant as Blundell's support for Catholicism in his locality was, his practical support for the survival of Catholicism was not limited to England.

II

Throughout his life Blundell maintained close links with Ireland. He was in regular contact with many individuals there, including 'Mr A. B.' with whom he still corresponded after the 'very great respects you shewed me, so long a tyme agoone, that this month & weeke make it 18 years', reminiscing about his first visit to Ireland when 'the glory of Straford your Great Lord Deputy was mounted to its meridian'.[45] Following the marriage of his daughter Emilia, Blundell frequently visited the country trying to arrange adequate financial support for his son-in-law.[46] Individuals in Blundell's information network regularly sent him news of Ireland.[47] Blundell also kept notes on the King's declaration concerning the Irish land settlement following the Restoration in 1660, while a brief poem in the Great Hodge Podge entitled 'The Irish Question' asked that 'Most gratious Soverayne graunt that we may have, our auntient faith and laws thats all we crave' and went on to explain that all that Irish Catholics wanted was to remove the King from the bad council of 'sum English and the Schotts' after which they would obey his every command.[48] As we will see, in his commonplace books Blundell made extensive notes on the activities of Catholics in Ireland, engaging adversarially with works that blamed them for the 1641 Rebellion. His justification of the behaviour of Irish Catholics was circulated in letters to his various correspondents.[49]

Blundell frequently made connections between English and Irish Catholics, such as in the letter to 'Rob R:', in which Blundell explained that the unnamed bearer was a great friend and introduced the individual as someone with whom the recipient would have much in common.[50] Furthermore, Blundell's charitable accounts show that he gave to the Irish. In 1663 he gave money to three Irish men, and 'Sent unto the poore in Ireland by a priest 5*s*'.[51] Again, in 1665 he recorded giving 1*s* 4*d* to two Irish women and an Irish man.[52] In a letter written to Lady Mountgarret discussing ways of transferring money to cover Butler's stay at Crosby, Frances Blundell alluded to an established method of transferring money across to Ireland, previously for charitable uses. Mountgarret was instructed to send money 'by meanes of such in Dublin as trade to Leverpoole', where the money would be safe and the transport rapid.[53] However, Blundell's strongest links with Catholics outside England arose from his relationships with religious houses in continental Europe.

III

Blundell was highly supportive of the religious life. While he made sure that of his ten children who survived into adulthood that there were enough lay members to manage the estate and secure a couple of strategic marriages, seven of his children joined religious houses. Two of his sons became Jesuits, while five of his daughters joined the Poor Clares.[54] Blundell's papers demonstrate that he viewed having his children in religious houses as both a source of prestige and a spiritual necessity. He told his daughter Jane, who had recently joined the Poor Clares, that he did 'much rejoyce for your great content & chearfullnesse, whilst you labour amongst Strangers, in the service of Religion'.[55] He eagerly collected details of religious houses for men and women, alongside records of 'Religious persons of Both sexes & priests of my kindred' that detailed more than 120 of his relatives, from both immediate and distant family.[56] His attitude was encapsulated in his comment following the death of his Jesuit son, Nicholas, when he told one correspondent that 'If my own observations faile not and the judgement of sondry others also who knew him much better than I, he was truly a Religious man: and this was all

I could wish or hope for after he had left the world'.[57] When his cousin James Scarisbrick took orders at St Omer, Blundell sent him a letter stating that 'you are now setting a coppy, for the youth of our whole Country to imitate'.[58] Blundell was hopeful that more of his kin would join religious houses, and was already predicting whether his children and grandchildren would enter before they had reached their seventh birthdays.[59] So keen was he, that despite that 'shee saith [that she] hath no vocation to Religion' his daughter Mary was pressurised into joining the Poor Clares. Even while Mary was refusing to take religious orders Blundell was negotiating her portion with the Abbess, taking great delight in her eventual conversion to the religious life after years spent as a scholar.[60] In the same vein Blundell tried to persuade Emilia to join the Poor Clares as late as 1660, the year before she was married, though this urge apparently faded when Blundell realised how beneficial a Butler marriage could be.[61] Even during the most difficult times Blundell ensured that his children were able to join their respective religious houses. In 1658 he arranged for his daughter Jane to take orders at Rouen. Not satisfied with sending her across alone, he set about making preparations to escort her. After a number of attempts, Blundell secured a pass to travel to London.[62] Once there he secretly crossed over to France where he bade farewell to his daughter and went on to tour continental Europe.[63]

While supportive of religious orders in general, Blundell and his family had particular links with the Poor Clares and St Omer. The Poor Clares, a female order at Gravelines, Dunkirk and Rouen, and St Omer, a male Jesuit house, were both connected to Lancashire. Blundell could demonstrate strong familial links to both, which no doubt contributed to his decision to send his children to these particular orders.[64] In the list of 'Religious persons of both sexes & priests of my kindred' covering individuals kin to Blundell 'eather in the forth degree or nearer', all took religious orders with the Poor Clares or the Jesuits.[65] In keeping with Blundell's view of himself as a staunch Englishman, it is not surprising that the character of these orders was also strongly English. After some debate, the Poor Clares of Rouen said holy communion daily for the Conversion of England, the Mother Abbess noting that the 'practise being observ'd by divers reform'd Orders, she thought none had more right to that priveledg, then the Children of Saint Clare'.[66] Furthermore, after having trouble with both an Irish Priest who assisted the order and an Irish Sister who 'gave publick scandal in the Community & perpetually disquieted their repose', the decision was made to limit members of the community solely to the English.[67] In its concluding remarks about the unspecified indiscretions of the Irish Sister, the Poor Clares' Chronicle concluded that the order 'must also be very careful not to turn the house into any other nation than English since it was founded for them it is just that preferably to, any others, they should find a shelter here from the dangers of their heretical country'.[68]

Blundell's efforts to support the faith in this manner did not come cheap. In 1674 his daughter Clare Frances entered the Poor Clares of Rouen. In his accounts for that year, he estimated that her endowment to establish her in the house totalled 'upon all accounts about £140', the largest of his extraordinary expenses for the year, though still relatively cheap when compared to the dowries demanded by other cloisters.[69] The significance of this figure can be seen in his account books where Blundell claimed that the total of his money and goods in that year amounted to just over £1250.[70] However, the various negotiations that he conducted to ensure his children a place show that he was not prepared to bear unnecessary costs for his faith. Negotiations for the portions for his daughters began many years before they were ready to join, ensuring that the financial aspects of their religious life could be smoothed out well in advance.[71] Immediately after ensuring a place for his eldest daughter Jane, Blundell wrote to his aunt, Elizabeth Bradshaigh, a Poor Clare, acknowledging that he had persuaded 'some frends of myne to represent me lately to your house', and after having listed his financial hardships he requested that he might 'make more reasonable propositions to your house for some other of my Daughters'.[72] Payment for his daughters could be made in the form of either a one-off lump sum or an annuity for the rest of their lives. The portions for Blundell's daughters varied greatly and were subject to the success of his bartering skills. Thus, in 1657 he proposed admitting his daughter Jane for £100, but was refused. Later an annuity of £12 10*s* was agreed for Jane and the same for his second daughter Margaret, though the costs of Margaret's annuity were picked up in full by unnamed friends.[73] The cost of these two daughters going to Rouen was further increased by their travel expenses, which totalled £60 for both their travel and Blundell's journey to see them off.[74] His intense negotiations to keep his daughters' portions as low as possible could cause problems for them when they arrived at the chosen religious house. When Mary joined the Poor Clares at Ghent Blundell negotiated for an annuity of the meagre sum of £5.[75] However, she eventually moved to the Poor Clares at Gravelines, giving as her reason that her fellow sisters 'were allwaies telling me that I might not expect soe to have what the rest of the scholers had being I did not pay so much & such kynd of words which I had not vertu enough to beare'.[76] For the privilege of moving Mary to the Poor Clares at Gravelines, Blundell paid the more reasonable portion of £120.[77]

Blundell's negotiations with religious orders were so calculated that he effectively insured against his daughters' deaths. Where he paid for an annuity for his daughters he also arranged that on their deaths it would be transferred to another daughter, which surprisingly the Poor Clares agreed to, as usually on the death of one of their number they benefited financially as they no longer had to cover their living costs.[78] The success of Blundell's negotiations over his children's portions can be seen when compared to the massive sums that were demanded by most religious houses. For example, in the Poor Clares' Chronicles we find references to Henry Howard, the Earl of Arundel, having given £1000 for his daughter's portion, while £300 to £500 was not an uncommon amount to pay.[79] Blundell was not as successful in negotiating bargain annuities for his sons, for whom he paid the standard rate of £20 per year for their education and lodgings at St Omer, besides supplying a range of goods such as clothes and books to support their studies.[80] None the less, while Blundell was not prepared to pay unreasonable costs for his children to join religious houses, he was extremely supportive of religious orders in general, offering his children both moral and financial support to attend.

Blundell also offered support for other families hoping to send their daughters to join religious orders. In 1665 he held £210 in 'trust and confidence' for Margaret Molyneux until her daughters were old enough to take orders.[81] Again, in 1672 Blundell held £100 for the mother of John Houghton, to fund his daughter 'D' to take religious orders.[82] In both cases, Molyneux and Houghton did not specify which religious house the individual should be enrolled in, only that they should 'have made their profession of a religious life' before the money was released.[83] While Blundell offered support for his own children and the children of others in his locality to take up religious orders, he developed a much stronger role working as an agent for the Poor Clares of Rouen.

The links that English religious orders on the continent maintained with their homeland are shrouded in mystery. The risks run by those in England meant that many records were written in code or destroyed during times of particular anti-Catholicism. As Ann Forster writes, little has been uncovered about 'the shadowy system of local alms-collection in England for the Poor Clares of Rouen during penal times'.[84] While the records of the Poor Clares show that they often relied on patrons local to the houses who made specific gifts as well as paying fees for funeral services and annual masses, much of their regular income was sent by individuals in England, as gifts or as portions of novices, while the order used contacts there to lend out surplus funds at interest.[85] Blundell's notes show that the religious orders that he was involved with each had a system of agents across the country. Thus, John Banks appears as 'the Agent for the Fathers' at St Omer in 1670, Robert Hill agent for Flamsteed, John Rigmaiden the agent for the Poor Clares of Rouen and William Gowin the 'procurature' for the Poor Clares of Gravelines.[86] It is also evident that the agents frequently changed, possibly as a result of increased government pressure making their position more dangerous. In most cases those charged with the most dangerous parts of the operation, such as the physical transfer of funds from London to the religious houses, were obscure individuals. However, in his notes on Mr Mawson, agent for the Poor Clares of Rouen from 1675 onwards, Blundell mentioned that he was 'a Goldsmith who is back in Fleetstreet in London'.[87] Such a position would have given Mawson easy access to merchants who could transport moneys to continental Europe, while he would have been adept at managing large sums of money. The 'Receyvers in England', as Blundell called them, were only the first stage in this underground network.[88] From here money was farmed out to a nexus of friends of the orders, who in turn lent it out at interest to suitable candidates and collected further voluntary donations, which were returned to the order when requested. Thus, in 1669 when the Poor Clares of Rouen extended their convent to include a new wall and an infirmary, the 'Rd Mother Abbess writt to our friends in England, who had had money of ours, in their hands, to make it over'.[89] Blundell was one of the agents acting for the Poor Clares, and his incessant note taking provides an insight into the functions of such an agent.

Blundell's role as an agent for the Poor Clares involved a variety of tasks. He disseminated letters on their behalf. His transcriptions of correspondence from the order often mentioned that 'Within this letter were some Letters inclosed', which he delivered to various local Catholics including Margaret Molyneux and Cuthbert Clifton.[90] He also collected gifts for the order, including the small tokens of commitment to the Poor Clares from Blundell's tenants and friends, such as the 3*s*–4*d* that Blundell received from James Smith.[91] Blundell acted as a broker on behalf of the Poor Clares, ensuring a suitable deal for the portions of Molyneux's daughters, and arranging for agents to collect the portion and transfer it to Rouen.[92] However, as with agents working for other orders, Blundell's most important job was the loaning out of money, in trust, and the collection of interest on behalf of the order. In a letter from the Poor Clares in 1666 he was instructed to loan their money out at a rate of '£6 in the hundered', a rate of six per cent which apparently remained stable throughout the period that Blundell held the position.[93] From Blundell's notes it appears that he worked in this capacity from 1660, when he was entrusted with the significant sum of £300, until 1685 when his last surviving accounts for the order were settled.[94] As with other religious orders, Blundell was one in a chain of agents and when called on he returned the money to Rouen through brokers in London.[95] Although the Poor Clares' records never explicitly named the agents they used, references in their own papers about the amounts of money that they had invested in brokers throughout England indicate that Blundell was one of the primary agents that the order used.[96]

Blundell's papers show that his work for the Poor Clares was supported by his family. Entries in his accounts show that his wife, his heir and his sisters collected interest on money loaned out on behalf of the Poor Clares while he was in exile, though he was later to complain of his wife's handling of the affair that 'Her accounts seeme to me to be confused'.[97] That the Blundell womenfolk were involved in this blatantly illegal activity should come as no surprise. In her work on English nuns Claire Walker has argued that women were able to participate easily in such activities precisely because authorities did not view them capable of such intrigues.[98] This was a cause of frustration for some males. For instance, the failure of his contemporaries to recognise the power that women could exert was commented on by the MP George Hungerford during the second 'Exclusion Parliament' of 1680. Hungerford argued that a Bill for banishing Catholics from England was necessary for Protestant security, but exclaimed, 'I hope, sir, that if you banish the men, you will banish some women too; for I do believe, that some of that sex have been great instruments in bringing about our ruin'.[99]

All those to whom Blundell lent Poor Clares' money can be identified as either kin or regular correspondents. Thus, in his list of Poor Clares' money lent out, Thomas Selby his nephew, Christopher Bradshaigh his uncle and Thomas Masey his cousin appear frequently as having borrowed sums ranging from £50 to £100.[100] A number of prominent Protestants also benefited from these loans, including John Chorley the Mayor of Liverpool and Roger Bradshaigh, who was also used to collect money on more than one occasion.[101] On closing his accounts Blundell boasted 'what profit I have made of their money', despite the fact that when the penal laws were strictly enforced or when trade was bad he noted that the money was left 'lying dead'.[102] He carefully laid out money belonging to the Poor Clares of Rouen on the basis of his interpretation of the political climate. As he noted in a letter to Elin Bradshaigh after being given £50 for the order, 'It now lyeth saf without profit and in regard that the penal laws do now look upon us with a more rigid & threatening face I think shall not venture it out again nor any other of your money that shall chance to com to my hands hereafter unless I have new instructions to do so'.[103] Blundell's accounts show that from the original £300 that he was given in 1660, in over twenty-five years of service he more than doubled their money.[104] Blundell frequently claimed that his work as an agent for the Poor Clares cost him a small fortune. Not only did he spend hours managing the accounts, but the correspondence he kept with them also cost a significant amount, which he did not reclaim until the end of his service.[105] When he finally tallied up the expenses that he had accrued in 1685 he estimated that he had spent a total of £10 which he had not reclaimed, and took only £2 to cover these costs.[106]

There were a number of advantages to Blundell's position that he exploited as an agent for the Poor Clares. Blundell was head of a patronage network and had the final say as to whether a potential recipient could receive significant loans at a preferential rate. Both Blundell and his son borrowed extensively from the fund in times of need. Records in the accounts record that Blundell himself repaid interest on loans of £50 and £100, while his son and namesake appeared as having borrowed £50.[107] When it came to negotiating his daughter's annuities for the order, Blundell used his work as an agent as leverage, oscillating in the same paragraph between requests to reduce the annuity and a conspicuously unrelated discussion of the amount he was loaning out.[108] Finally, the presence of John Chorley and Roger Bradshaigh in the lists suggests that he used the money to reward Protestant friends. Thus, while Blundell risked apprehension from the authorities and took on considerable responsibility to help support the Poor Clares of Rouen, his relationship with them brings into doubt many of the protestations made in his correspondence. He derived a number of fringe benefits from completing the work, which facilitated his own survival during times of financial trouble by allowing him easy access to large sums of money at preferential interest rates. Furthermore, despite his professions of loyalty to the regime, his aiding and abetting of religious orders overseas, who in turn sent agents to England with the aim to convert new Catholics, or said daily mass for the conversion of England, posed a direct threat to the Protestant regime.

IV

Blundell was also the author of a series of works that sought to alleviate the position of English Catholics. While a variety of drafts and collections of ideas for future publications were circulated, only one work was published in printed form, 'A Short Discourse of the Paenall Lawes against the Roman Catholicks of England'. As we have seen, it is probable that this was printed in 1661 under the title *Quid me Persequeris?*[109] The main aim of these works was to show that Catholics should be able to 'Exercise and professe their owne Religion, without forfeiting all that is Deare', a move that Blundell claimed was consistent with protecting the safety of the Kingdom.[110] Blundell hoped his writing would 'contribute something of myne to the taking away of the *Prejudice* under which we have all beene sufferen'.[111] The date of publication of 'A Short Discourse' suggests that its overall purpose may have been to lobby the Restoration regime for toleration when it was becoming increasingly clear that little protection would be given to Catholics, despite their support for the King during the Civil War.

The way in which Blundell wrote followed a common pattern throughout both his notes on the position of Catholics and in 'A Short Discourse'. He appealed to what he saw as the logic of removing the penal laws, supporting his argument with historical and religious citations from works regarded as authorities. For example, when discussing Charles II's apparent favour for Protestants who had fought against his father, and the lack of reward that he had given Catholics, Blundell found a comparison from the Bible. He quoted Judges 11:7 when the elders of Gilead went to fetch Jephthah the son of a prostitute, who had been driven from his country, 'And they sayd unto Jephthah come and be our Captain that we may fight with the children of Ammon. And

Jephthat sayd unto the Elders of Gilead, are not ye they that hated me & cast me out of my Fathers house? why are ye comme unto me now, when yee are in distresse?'[112] At the same time, Blundell often directed his arguments against those he blamed for hostility towards Catholics, most notably Marchamont Nedham and William Prynne. Thus, writing about Nedham's claims that Catholics had fought against the King, Blundell returned a classical comparison: 'When Nero had burned Rome he layd the blame and the punishment on the innocent Christians'.[113] The text to which Blundell referred most regularly was James I's *Basilicon Doron*, particularly as an authority on rebellion, arguing that he did so because 'We do not alledge K James as a favourer of Popery ... but only as an able judge (by a sad experience of his owne) betwixt Rebellion and Loyalty'.[114] That he chose this text as his main authority no doubt reflected an attempt to emphasise the loyalty of Catholics to the monarchy. Having used historical and religious texts to support his argument and add authority to his position, Blundell developed a distinctive case for the removal of the penal laws.

It is hardly surprising that the basis of Blundell's argument for the removal of the penal laws was that Catholics were passive victims. Referring to the English Catholic as 'a distressed Creature', and comparing the English Catholic population to the children of Israel, Blundell's 'A Short Discourse' began by listing all of the penal laws to which Catholics were subject from the reign of Elizabeth I onwards.[115] As in his correspondence, he maintained that Catholics suffered far more than Protestants during the Civil Wars, claiming at one stage that Catholic Royalists paid double what Anglican Royalists were forced to pay owing to the extra fines for recusancy levied on them.[116] Blundell maintained that this strengthened the case for the removal of the penal laws: 'it is evident I hope by our sufferings, that we have reason to lay hold upon his majestyes most gracious Indulgence in the favour of tender consciences'.[117] In his concluding remarks about the victimisation of English Catholics, Blundell claimed that he did not want revenge on those that had dealt him a blow, merely the ability to 'cure the wound that the blow hath given me'.[118] Having argued that Catholics were passive victims, with the use of vague evidence, Blundell went on to offer specifics, based on their loyalty to the monarchy, their distance from a small radical element of Catholics in England, and a discussion of the behaviour of their co-religionists on the continent.

Blundell maintained that English Catholics had always been loyal to the monarchy, referring to them as 'His Majesties most faithful subjects'.[119] His efforts were far from unique and from the Restoration onwards English Catholics 'were determined to prove how far they had risked all for the Royalist cause'.[120] Blundell not only argued that the representation of Catholics in the Royalist forces was out of all proportion to their actual numbers but, in an exceptional entry, he gave a precise estimation of the number of Catholic gentry involved in the war.[121] He claimed that the Catholic gentry formed one-fifteenth of the entire gentry on the eve of Civil War 'And it hath beene lykewaies supposed that a third or 4th part of the English Gentlemen that fought for their Majestyes here consisted of their Catholic Subjects. If these Conjectures be anything nere the mark it may then appear that the fidelity and affection of the Catholicks in this particular, was 4 or 5 fold more then that of other Religions being taken ... all in grosse.'[122] In addition to their manifold sufferings on behalf of the King, Blundell stated categorically that no Catholic had ever fought against the King.[123] However, he complained that the tide had instantly turned on Catholic fortunes at the Restoration. Far from popery being synonymous with Royalism as it had been during the Civil Wars and Interregnum, it had become linked to Parliamentarianism, a link that Blundell claimed was self-evidently nonsense.[124] In fact, he juxtaposed the plight of Catholics with the monarchy, maintaining that those who hoped to bring down popery were the same who hoped to bring down monarchy.[125] Blundell reminded readers of the risks Catholics took ensuring the survival of Charles II after the Battle of Worcester, and the use that he had made of Catholic priest holes, into which he was again forcing the English Catholic population.[126] However, Blundell was prepared to concede that a small group of Catholics had been disloyal to the monarchy, and for these instances he offered a clear solution.

Blundell felt it necessary to give specific mention to the Gunpowder Plot, where he tried to exonerate Catholics. He remarked that for fifty-six years since the 'accursed and damnable plot' English Catholics had 'continuewed in a singular obedience to their Kings acting and suffering allwayes according to their Majesties pleasure'.[127] Essential to Blundell's position on the Gunpowder Plot was the separation of mainstream law-abiding Catholics, who Blundell claimed were the vast majority, and small radical groups who had no connection to other Catholics and were acting against the teachings of Catholicism.[128] This view has received some support from modern-day historians, such as Jenny Wormald, who argue that the plotters were a group of disparate poor gentry who had been plotting before James came to the throne, and it was almost incidental that they were Catholic. They were, according to Wormald, motivated equally by xenophobia as by religious partisanship.[129] Blundell held that the broadsheets that equated Catholics with those involved in the Gunpowder Plot were cast from 'a blacker dye then the powder itself'.[130] He argued that by isolating a tiny minority of radical Catholics the government would ensure the continued loyalty of the vast majority and expose any surviving radical elements, about the punishment for whom Blundell was quite clear: 'If Catholicks be disloyal, hang them'.[131]

Another element of Blundell's work was the reconceptualisation of the Catholic movement outside England. We have already seen how important

Blundell believed this was, as the activities of Catholics on the continent often justified the treatment of Catholics in England. In 'A Short Discourse' Blundell disputed Prynne's view that all Catholics were involved in the 1641 Irish Rebellion, asking 'What were all of them privy to the Irish Plot? Did all intend a Massacre? Indeed it is hardly credible'.[132] Blundell did not shy away from the military successes of continental Catholicism, but suggested that this was a further reason why Catholics should be viewed favourably, arguing that 'Their victoryes and conquests abroad have beene as large and wonderful: Hospitalls & other monuments of Piety have not beene at all inferiour, to any of thos that the Puritan or Independants have since erected'.[133] Attempting to highlight the virtues of Catholicism by alluding to Catholic victories over Protestants was a dangerous strategy when trying to get support to remove the penal laws. Blundell's motives for this reflect the precise group that he wanted to win over.

'A Short Discourse' was aimed at a group that Blundell called 'the honest Episcopal party', by which he meant Royalist Anglicans, whom he claimed to 'have beene the truest partakers in all their Kings Concernements since the beginning of the War that any story hath recorded'.[134] In an effort to gain the support of this group, 'A Short Discourse' included a vehement attack on Puritans and sectarian groups alongside a fundamental criticism of the iniquity of the penal laws. According to Blundell, Catholics had shown themselves no more disloyal than Protestant sectarians and yet the laws affecting the two groups were massively different.[135] Blundell blamed the Civil War on the freedom that was given to Puritans, arguing that had a distinction been made between 'the honest Episcopal Protestant, and those of other persuasions, it had questionlesse prevented the greatest part of the Troubles which the nation hath felt'.[136] He landed the blame for this squarely on Charles I, stating that 'the bountyes of a meeke and indulgent King, by a generation of ungrateful persons, were turned against him self', a stark warning to Charles II and his advisers about giving leeway to any other Protestant group than Royalist Anglicans.[137] Blundell concluded his position on this issue as being that 'Catholicks no lesse then the Puritans who have merited no more than we and deserved as ill, do stand in a fair capacity at the present, of the Royall indulgence'.[138]

Looking at laws against Catholics in England, Blundell first tackled the Oaths of Allegiance and Supremacy. His papers demonstrate a preoccupation with the Oaths, which he saw as the major barrier to Catholic integration into mainstream society.[139] As late as 1673 Blundell remarked that he was praying that 'God grant us a better test of Allegiance a more lucky othe'.[140] The essence of his argument was that the elements of the Oaths that related to the spiritual power of the Pope (and Blundell was keen to highlight that he was referring *only* to the spiritual) meant that they could not be taken by Catholics.[141] Blundell argued that the Oaths were themselves no guarantee of loyalty as the same hands that signed them, and the orders against Catholics for their failure to do so, had also signed Charles I's death warrant.[142] Indeed, he claimed there was 'not a great Traytor in the first wars which had not taken the Oath of Allegiance' and tartly suggested that the only thing that could be added to the Oaths to ensure the protection of the monarchy was a clause that Parliament stealing power was treason.[143] Blundell's argument in 'A Short Discourse' concerning the Oaths was based on those of the Catholic George Digby, Earl of Bristol, who had campaigned earlier in the year that the pamphlet was published for the removal of the penal laws.[144] A full transcription of two of Digby's speeches is extant in the Blue Book, which pleaded, like Blundell, for 'ease of Conscience from certaine Oathes' for Catholics, arguing that they could not take the purely spiritual Oath of Supremacy because they held the Pope to have supreme authority 'in things mearley spiritual', neither could they take the Oath of Allegiance because, whilst they were completely loyal to the King, the wording of the Oath made Catholicism heresy.[145] The conclusion of Blundell's work on Catholics and the Oaths was that semantics had obscured the fact that 'whilest the Catholicks always denyed the words, have duly performed the sense'.[146]

Echoing classic non-resistance arguments, Blundell's position on the future of the penal laws was clear: if they continued Catholics would remain passive victims loyal to the monarchy and true to their religion; 'If it shal chance to be made felony for any of our profession to eat or sleep, we must eyther perish starve or hang'.[147] Blundell argued that, if the aims of Puritans and others who wished to see the removal of Catholicism were realised, those Catholics who converted would be hypocrites, not better subjects.[148] He maintained that Catholics deserved the same treatment as all other groups who deviated from the line advocated by the Church of England: thus the penal laws should be removed and the Oaths of Allegiance and Supremacy no longer required, as Catholics had repeatedly proved that they were the most loyal of all subjects. Blundell concluded by challenging parliamentary legislation that forbade Catholics from holding weapons other than those deemed sufficient to defend the household: a series of laws put in place, as Brian Quintrell noted, 'in the interests of national security' to prevent Catholics from rising against the Protestant regime.[149] In a stark inversion of this, Blundell argued that for the safety of the kingdom Catholics should all be armed, allowed to 'trayle their old pykes, in The Militia of the Kingdom', for it was they alone who had shown themselves capable of defending the monarchy's interests against dangerous sectarians.[150]

Blundell's patronage of Catholicism involved the development of a forceful argument for the repeal of the penal laws and a level of toleration for Catholics in England, but it is unclear how much impact his work had. It would be erroneous to presume that because 'A Short Discourse' only had a small print run its impact was also limited. Blundell disseminated the arguments he developed in his letters which were in turn shared by the recipients with their friends and family.[151] Recent work on the history of the circulation of ideas has stressed the importance of scribal or manuscript publication and argued that its content was often given more credence as a result of the selective nature of the medium.[152] Blundell himself referred to various texts which demanded an equal amount of his time, but were 'never printed'.[153] The historian is not always left to speculate on such things. As we have seen, many of L'Estrange's views on the work of Prynne, the penal laws and the position of Protestant nonconformists were developed through discussion with Blundell.[154] Furthermore, in a letter of 1666, Roger Bradshaigh complained to the Earl of Derby that he could not enlist Catholics in the militia. This was an issue about which Blundell spoke frequently with Bradshaigh, and correspondence between the two from 1678 suggests that this continued to be discussed until Bradshaigh's death.[155] Bradshaigh's letter to Derby repeated almost point by point the same argument put forward by Blundell in 'A Short Discourse' and asked Derby not to judge all Catholics 'like Phanaticks; they weare otherways esteemed in the late Warr and accrewd a good opinion by theire faythfull servise ... I have heard it frequently from them, with many serious conversations, that though the Pope himselfe should endeavour to invade, they would be as ready to sheath a sword in his gutts as any enemy whatsoever.'[156] Therefore, while Blundell's printed works may have had only a minor impact, through his Protestant and Catholic networks he ensured that his arguments were widely disseminated.

V

Blundell's activities show that he was no passive victim and he avoided the extremes of the penal laws while carving himself out a role as a protector of English Catholics, locally, nationally and internationally, in defiance of Protestant authorities. Blundell's estate was a fully Catholicised space, where both he and his tenants did all in their power to keep Little Crosby Catholic. Beyond Lancashire Blundell sent charity to Ireland and provided significant assistance to religious orders on the continent, working for more than twenty years as one of the primary agents for the Poor Clares of Rouen. While time-consuming, Blundell's work on behalf of this order allowed him to head a patronage network, which could loan out significant amounts of money at preferential rates. Finally, Blundell worked as a Catholic apologist, arguing for the removal of the penal laws in manuscript and printed works, the circulation of which was demonstrably aided by members of both his Catholic and Protestant networks. Clearly then, Blundell's correspondence with close friends and entries in his notebooks show that his protestations of passivity formed one aspect of a misleading pose that he presented to his contemporaries. It is in his notes on his reading, discussed in the second part of this book, that the stark divergence between Blundell's public demeanour and his more private beliefs and behaviour can be seen most clearly.

NOTES

1 In her work on Blundell's grandfather and namesake, Sena has shown that this tradition began two generations before: Sena, 'William Blundell and the networks of Catholic dissent', pp. 54–75.

2 LCRO, DDBl 54/41, Tenants' Book, fol. 1b; A. J. Gritt, 'Aspects of Agrarian Change in South-west Lancashire, c.1650–1850' (DPhil thesis, University of Central Lancashire, 2000), p. 109. I am grateful to Andrew Gritt for discussion about the issues presented here.

3 Great Hodge Podge, fols 207b–8b; Blue Book, fol. 58; Draft Letter Book, IV, fol. 34.

4 Draft Letter Book, IV, fol. 33.

5 I owe the discovery of this case to Frank Tyrer. Tyrer, 'Recusancy', II, pp. 363–5.

6 LCRO, QSP/718/10, Quarter Sessions Papers, 1692.

7 LCRO, QSP/811/1, Quarter Sessions Papers, 1697.

8 Hodge Podge the Third, fol. 69; LCRO, DDBl 54/41, Tenants' Book.

9 LCRO, DDBl 30/15, Note relating to holding of demesne of Ditton during sequestration, 1643–1660; LCRO, DDBl 30/23, Acquittances of sequestered properties in Little Crosby and Ditton of Thomas Rice, Thomas Marrow, Francis Rowson, Richard Bryanson, William Johnson, Ellin Worrall and Richard Marrow, 1658–1659.

10 Small Account Book, fols 11–b, 25b–8.

11 William Blundell to Gilbert Crouch, 21 January 1657, in Small Account Book, fols 33b–4.

12 Gritt, 'Aspects of Agrarian Change', p. 83; A. J. Gritt, 'The operation of lifeleasehold in south-west Lancashire, 1649–97', *Agricultural History Review*, 53 (2005), p. 6; B. G. Blackwood, 'The Lancashire cavaliers and their tenants', *Transactions of the Historic Society of Lancashire and Cheshire*, 117 (1965), pp. 17–32; C. Clay, 'Lifeleasehold in the western counties of England 1650–1750', *Agricultural History Review*, 29 (1981), p. 83.

13 Gritt, 'Aspects of Agrarian Change', p. 83; Gritt, 'Operation of lifeleasehold', pp. 1–2; Clay, 'Lifeleasehold in the western counties', pp. 94–6.

14 Gritt, 'Aspects of Agrarian Change', p. 86; Clay, 'Lifeleasehold in the western counties', p. 89.

15 Gritt, 'Aspects of Agrarian Change', pp. 86, 99, 101.

16 Bossy, *English Catholic Community*, p. 177.

17 Gritt, 'Aspects of Agrarian Change', p. 88; Gritt, 'Operation of lifeleasehold', p. 9.

18 Gritt, 'Aspects of Agrarian Change', p. 106; Gritt, 'Operation of lifeleasehold', p. 10.

19 Gritt, 'Aspects of Agrarian Change', pp. 106–7; Gritt, 'Operation of lifeleasehold', pp. 10–11.

20 LCRO, DDBl acc. 54/41, Tenants' Book, fol. 1b.

21 Hen: Ho: to William Blundell, 11 October 1654, in Great Hodge Podge, fols 115b–7. It is possible that the author of the document was the Jesuit priest Robert Grosvernor, operating under the alias Henry Howard: Foley, *Records of the English Province of the Society of Jesus*, VII, pp. 323–4.

22 Gritt, 'Aspects of Agrarian Change', p. 110; Gritt, 'Operation of lifeleasehold', p. 10. See Blundell's offer of a 'free gieft' to Richard Roson if he chose not to extend a lease: William Blundell to Richard Roson, 19 November 1673, in Draft Letter Book, II, fol. 9b.

23 Blue Book, fols 64–5.

24 Gritt, 'Aspects of Agrarian Change', pp. 109, 112.

25 Bossy, *English Catholic Community*, p. 181.

26 Gritt, 'Aspects of Agrarian Change', pp. 112–13.

27 As discussed in Chapter 5.

28 Blue Book, fol. 52.

29 William Blundell to Mrs Selby, 7 July 1672, in Letter Book One, fol. 6b.

30 Hodge Podge the Third, fols 7–8.

31 Hodge Podge the Third, fol. 7.

32 P. Slack, *Poverty and Policy in Tudor and Stuart England* (London: Longman, 1988), p. 22; A. L. Beier, *Masterless Men: The Vagrancy Problem in England 1560–1640* (London: Meuthuen, 1985), p. 7.

33 William Blundell to Thomas Selby, 16 May 1650, in Great Hodge Podge, fol. 87b.

34 William Blundell to William [probably Selby], 12 November, in Small Account Book, fol. 22b.

35 William Blundell to N. N. [Father Walton], 17 January 1657; William Blundell to Richard Langhorne, 14 May 1673, in Letter Book One, fols 33, 102; William Blundell to Father Walton, 17 January 1657, in Small Account Book, fol. 32.

36 Blue Book, fol. 47.

37 Frank Tyrer seemed certain that Walton was 'engaged in teaching Mr Blundell's children, and perhaps also the children of neighbouring Catholics', suggesting that he may have had access to information concerning Walton's ministry from a source that no longer survives: Tyrer, 'Recusancy', I, p. 200. For Waldegrave's period as Chaplain see William Blundell to Thomas Haggerston, 16 September 1672; William Blundell to Henry Heton, 23 October 1672, in Draft Letter Book, I, fols 11, 15.

38 William Blundell to Mr [probably James] Scarisbrick, 29 April 1655, in Great Hodge Podge, fol. 85b.

39 William Blundell to Mr [probably James] Scarisbrick, 29 April 1655, in Great Hodge Podge, fol. 86.

40 William Blundell to Mr [probably James] Scarisbrick, 29 April 1655, in Great Hodge Podge, fols 85–6b. See also D. Woolf, *The Social Circulation of the Past: English Historical Culture 1500–1730* (Oxford: Oxford University Press, 2003), pp. 246–55.

41 Harkirk Burial Register, pp. 1, 23–5, 33.

42 William Blundell to John Gillibrand, 28 May 1687, in Draft Letter Book, IV, fol. 24.

43 William Blundell to John Chorley, 12 January 1687, in Draft Letter Book, IV, fol. 32b.

44 William Blundell to Lord Bishop of Chester, 5 September 1688, in Draft Letter Book, IV, fol. 36.

45 William Blundell to A. B., 9 July 1657, in Letter Book One, fols 29b–30.

46 Accounts for these trips can be found at Small Account Book, fol. 87.

47 William Blundell to J. Stevens, 1653; William Blundell to J. Stevens, 3 September 1653; William Blundell to Lady Fitz Morris, 18 January 1663, in Letter Book One, fols 49b, 53b–5, 83–b.

48 Great Hodge Podge, fols 105b–6, 165b.

49 In a list of books that Blundell lent out, he recorded having lent '8 other several pamphlets most of them concerning Ireland': Hodge Podge the Third, fol. 42b.

50 William Blundell to Rob. R., no date; William Blundell to James C., no date, in Letter Book Two, pp. 28–9, 37–8.

51 Hodge Podge the Third, fols 7b, 18b–9.

52 Hodge Podge the Third, fol. 19.

53 Frances Blundell to Lady Mountgarret, 6 November 1694, in Letter Book Two, p. 124.

54 PCRA, Miscellaneous Rouen manuscripts: notebook describing foundation, fol. 1b; PCRA, Miscellaneous Rouen manuscripts: extracts of death notices, pp. 1–4; D. A. Bellenger, *English and Welsh Priests 1558–1800* (Bath: Downside Abbey Press, 1984), p. 40.

55 William Blundell to Jane Blundell, 1658, in Letter Book One, fol. 81b.

56 Great Hodge Podge, fols 70b–1, 75, 89b–90b, 112.

57 William Blundell to Unnamed Recipient, 7 January 1682, in Letter Book One, fol. 118b.

58 William Blundell to Mr [probably James] Scarisbrick, 29 April 1655, in Great Hodge Podge, fol. 85.

59 William Blundell to Luisa Clare, 3 April 1660; William Blundell to Thomas Blundell, November 1680, in Letter Book One, fols 44b–5b, 120.

60 Hodge Podge the Third, fols 24–b, 66b.

61 As he noted in a letter to Luisa Clare, Abbess of the Poor Clares at Gravelines: William Blundell to Luisa Clare, 3 April 1660, in Letter Book One, fol. 44b.

62 William Blundell to Gilbert Ireland, 16 August 1658, in Tyrer, 'Recusancy', I, pp. 238–9. Tyrer's reference for this letter states that it was from 'Cavalier's Small Letter Book', no record of which survives in either LCRO or Crosby Hall.

63 William Blundell to Charles Parker, 3 May 1660; William Blundell to R. B., 12 June 1660, in Letter Book One, fols 45–b, 62.

64 William Blundell to Ann Blundell, 27 September 1658, in Letter Book One, fol. 23b.

65 Great Hodge Podge, fols 89b–91, 112.

66 PCRA, Chronicles of the Poor Clares, Rouen I, pp. 149–50.

67 PCRA, Chronicles of the Poor Clares, Rouen I, pp. 177–8, 304.

68 PCRA, Chronicles of the Poor Clares, Rouen I, pp. 317–18.

69 Small Account Book, fols 51–b; Hodge Podge the Third, fol. 87; C. Walker, *Gender and*

Politics in Early Modern Europe: English Convents in France and the Low Countries (Basingstoke: Palgrave Macmillan, 2003), p. 32.

70 Small Account Book, fol. 51.

71 As documented in regard to his daughter Mary: Hodge Podge the Third, fols 24–b.

72 William Blundell to Elizabeth Bradshaigh, 5 February 1658, in Small Account Book, fols 62b–3.

73 Small Account Book, fols 59b–60, 64–b; Hodge Podge the Third, fols 23b, 68b.

74 Small Account Book, fol. 85.

75 Hodge Podge the Third, fol. 24.

76 Hodge Podge the Third, fol. 66b.

77 Hodge Podge the Third, fol. 66b.

78 Hodge Podge the Third, fol. 90b. There is not, however, any evidence that this actually occurred.

79 PCRA, Chronicles of the Poor Clares, Rouen I, pp. 157, 276.

80 Hodge Podge the Third, fol. 21b.

81 Blue Book, fol. 29.

82 Blue Book, fol. 60b.

83 Blue Book, fol. 29.

84 A. M. Forster, 'The Chronicles of the Poor Clares of Rouen – II', *Recusant History*, 18 (1986–87), p. 191.

85 PCRA, Chronicles of the Poor Clares, Rouen I, pp. 100, 102, 125, 157, 158, 159, 162, 165, 168, 327, 364–5, 368–9, 375–7.

86 Hodge Podge the Third, fols 21b, 40b, 42, 66b.

87 Hodge Podge the Third, fol. 64.

88 Hodge Podge the Third, fol. 52.

89 PCRA, Chronicles of the Poor Clares, Rouen I, p. 238.

90 Hodge Podge the Third, fols 25, 27b.

91 Hodge Podge the Third, fol. 63b.

92 Hodge Podge the Third, fols 23, 25.

93 Hodge Podge the Third, fol. 27.

94 Hodge Podge the Third, fols 27, 77, 90b; William Blundell to Winifred Giffard, 10 July 1673, in Draft Letter Book, I, fol. 42b; William Blundell to Thomas Masey, 14 October 1673, in Draft Letter Book, II, fol. 3.

95 Hodge Podge the Third, fols 65–7. When money was recalled it was usually for building works: William Blundell to Winifred Giffard, 22 July 1675, in Draft Letter Book, II, fol. 43b.

96 PCRA, Chronicles of the Poor Clares, Rouen I, pp. 101, 125, 158, 159, 165, 376, 377.

97 Hodge Podge the Third, fols 23b, 51b, 58, 72b, 77.

98 Walker, 'Prayer, patronage, and political conspiracy', p. 21.

99 W. Cobbett (ed.), *Parliamentary History of England from the Norman Conquest in 1066 to the Year 1803*, 36 vols (London: R. Bagshaw, 1806–20), IV, p. 1238.

100 Hodge Podge the Third, fols 16b, 62b, 63.

101 Hodge Podge the Third, fols 50b–2, 58, 62b, 65, 72b.

102 William Blundell to Winifred Giffard, 3 April 1673, in Draft Letter Book, I, fol. 29b.

103 William Blundell to Elin Bradshaigh, 27 August 1673, in Draft Letter Book, I, fol. 50.

104 Hodge Podge the Third, fols 27, 64, 90–b; William Blundell to Winifred Giffard, 8 July 1678, in Draft Letter Book, III, fols 15b–16.

105 Hodge Podge the Third, fol. 25.

106 Hodge Podge the Third, fol. 77.

107 Hodge Podge the Third, fols 63b, 65, 72–b, 73b.

108 William Blundell to Winifred Giffard, 14 January 1674, in Draft Letter Book, II, fols 13b–14.

109 Gibson (ed.), *Cavalier's Note Book*, p. 78; Adversaria, fol. 237b; Great Hodge Podge, fol. 199b; Blue Book, fol. 39.

110 Blue Book, fol. 6.

111 Blue Book, fol. 25b.

112 Blue Book, fol. 36b–7.

113 Blue Book, fol. 8.

114 Blue Book, fol. 37b; James I, *Basilikon Doron. Or His Majesties Instructions to his Dearest Sonne, Henrie the Prince* (1603).

115 Blue Book, fols 4, 5–b, 6b.

116 Blue Book, fol. 7b.

117 Blue Book, fol. 22.

118 Blue Book, fol. 15.

119 Blue Book, fol. 7.

120 Questier, *Catholicism and Community*, p. 501.

121 Blue Book, fols 4, 5, 23, 55–b, 80.

122 Blue Book, fol. 7.

123 Blue Book, fol. 7b.

124 Blue Book, fols 6, 8, 9, 55b.

125 See the essay title that he presumably set his grandson Edmund Butler, which required him to write a short treatise on 'Roman Church and English Monarchy and Civil State have great resemblance': Blue Book, fols 5b–6, 54.

126 Blue Book, fol. 10.

127 Blue Book, fol. 13b.

128 Blue Book, fols 13b–14b.

129 J. Wormald, 'Gunpowder, treason and Scots', *Journal of British Studies*, 24 (1985), pp. 141–68.

130 Blue Book, fols 14b, 19.

131 Blue Book, fol. 55.

132 Blue Book, fol. 34.

133 Blue Book, fol. 6.

134 Blue Book, fol. 23.

135 Blue Book, fols 5b–6, 8, 9, 12.

136 Blue Book, fol. 22b.

137 Blue Book, fol. 22b.

138 Blue Book, fol. 37b.

139 See his seven-page transcription of reasons why Catholics could not take the Oaths in his notes for/on (authorship of the document is not clear) 'A discourse concerning the punishment of Roman Catholicks in England, in the yeare 1666', in Letter Book Two, pp. 154–62.

140 William Blundell to Richard Langhorne, 14 May 1673, in Draft Letter Book, I, fol. 35b, transcribed in Letter Book One, fol. 101b.

141 Blue Book, fols 23–b.

142 Blue Book, fol. 23b.

143 Blue Book, fols 24b, 55b.

144 Digby 'committed political suicide' in January 1659 when he converted to Catholicism, from which point he sought to protect his co-religionists through his arguments in the House of Lords: R. Hutton, 'Digby, George, Second Earl of Bristol (1612–1677)', in *ODNB*.

145 Blue Book, fols 81b–6b.

146 Blue Book, fol. 23b.

147 Blue Book, fol. 12.

148 Blue Book, fol. 22.

149 B. W. Quintrell, 'The practice and problems of recusant disarming, 1585–1641', *Recusant History*, 17 (1985), pp. 208–22, at p. 208.

150 Blue Book, fol. 24b.

151 See, for instance, his letter to Richard Langhorne written in 1673 that briefly alluded to all the central arguments from 'A Short Discourse': William Blundell to Richard Langhorne, 14 May 1673, in Letter Book One, fols 101–2.

152 Atherton, 'The itch grown a disease', pp. 39–65; H. Love, *Scribal Publication in Seventeenth-Century England* (Oxford: Clarendon Press, 1993), passim; H. Love, *English Clandestine Satire 1660–1702* (Oxford: Oxford University Press, 2004) pp. 248–302.

153 Blue Book, fol. 55.

154 Blue Book, fols 8b, 16, 32–5, 36–b, 80–b, 87–8.

155 Blundell encouraged Bradshaigh to 'Deale as severely as you will (I mean as severely as you can) against the Leviathan of Parrise but be not too angree against the poor subjects at home'. Elsewhere, he told Bradshaigh that 'When France or Rome it self (upon any civil account or national quarrel) shall chance to be Enimies to England

I shal hold myself obleeged and all other English subjects, according to our several capacityes to pay, to pray, or to fight most heartily against them'. William Blundell to Roger Bradshaigh, 18 February 1678; William Blundell to Roger Bradshaigh, 7 March 1678, in Draft Letter Book, III, fols 9, 11.

156 NLS, Acc. 9769, Crawford Muniments, Personal Papers 42/2/5, Draft reply of Sir Roger Bradshaigh, first Bart, to Charles Stanley, eighth Earl of Derby, 1666. I am grateful to Robert Alexander Lindsay, Earl of Crawford and Balcarres, for permission to cite this letter and to Kenneth Dunn, curator in the Department of Manuscripts, for assisting my research in this collection.

Part II

Reading and reflections

Chapter 3

Reading and the construction of commonplaces

Of all of Blundell's surviving papers, his commonplace books have been paid the least attention, receiving only a single mention in the secondary work on his life, where they are listed as a source without discussion in his brief entry in the *ODNB*.[1] This reflects a general pattern, and until recently commonplace books were generally 'ignored' and their full potential as historical and literary sources rarely recognised.[2] Over the last two decades, work in the fields of English literature and history has sought to redress this, emphasising the significance of the commonplace book as a source for documenting reading practices and for understanding the political and cultural worlds of contemporaries.[3] Indeed, Peter Beal has argued that the commonplace book is 'a unique document, a unique witness to the tastes, values, and thinking of a specific person or group', while Kenneth Lockridge claims they are 'the ultimate source for the study of reading, the book, and identity'.[4] This is certainly the case with Blundell's commonplace books, where we find a very different perspective on his religious and political beliefs from that offered in his correspondence.

I

The term 'commonplace book' has often been confused by historians and literary scholars alike, being applied to a range of manuscripts including letter books, account books, and miscellaneous volumes of personal papers compiled in a haphazard manner that contemporaries often referred to as 'wastebooks', under which category Blundell's Hodge Podge volumes fall.[5] In fact, the 'commonplace book' is a specific genre of text, containing information, usually but not exclusively quotations and sententious sayings from textual material compiled under headings so that the author could easily access specific information.[6] Commonplace books were not always in manuscript format and throughout the early modern period there was a penchant for those who did not have the time to compile them to purchase printed commonplace books that brought together a selection of notable quotations.[7] The format reached the apex of its popularity during the early modern period. By the early sixteenth century they were used with increasing regularity throughout northern Europe, as the development and maintenance of a commonplace book became a central part of a humanist education.[8] Students were generally taught variations of the method whereby information was grouped under specific, often Latin, titles. The practice was further encouraged by printed guides to commonplacing, the most influential of which was Jeremias Drexel's *Aurifodina Artium et Scientiarum Omnium*, which had run to fourteen editions by 1695.[9] The use of commonplace books began to wane in popularity from the beginning of the eighteenth century, though their place in educational manuals remained into the nineteenth century.[10]

Despite the definition of the term 'commonplace book' being specific, the texts that fall under this heading still vary significantly. Throughout the early modern period contemporaries adopted different means to arrange information, and surviving texts demonstrate the idiosyncratic recording methods of their authors. For instance, the commonplace book of John Evans, compiled from 1655 to 1659, contains a collection of quotations from contemporary authors arranged alphabetically by subject, with a list at the end of the volume of both the authors and the works from which the quotations were taken. The most striking aspect of Evans's commonplace book is the meticulously accurate quotations and neatly written entries, which cover nine hundred pages, although they were entered in only four years.[11] The twenty-nine-folio commonplace book of Elizabeth Countess of Huntingdon has references carefully written in the margin next to which quotations are noted, with English titles separating topical groups of notes.[12] On the other hand the miscellaneous commonplace book Folger V.a.439 has entries spanning approximately seventy years, contains huge gaps and has different hands interspersed throughout.[13]

Not only did the format differ between individual commonplace books, but so too did the content. John Evans, for instance, recorded only quotations from texts. However, other contemporary commonplace books such as Theophilus Ayle's volume, constructed 1679 to 1716, and the anonymous early modern commonplace books Folger V.a.260 and Folger V.a.399 contain the standard quotations alongside the compiler's views of a text, recipes, poems, epitaphs, sketches and financial accounts.[14] Furthermore, many authors had different commonplace books for different topics. For example, the sixteenth-century French philosopher Jean Bodin mooted a three-volume system, where human themes, natural events and divine matters were each given a separate volume.[15] Thus, as Ann Blair argues, 'commonplace note taking does not imply a commonplace product'.[16]

The motives for using commonplace books were more complex than at first appear. Contemporaries viewed them as tools to manage large amounts of material, playing an important role in dealing with the 'multitude of books' that became a source of anxiety throughout this period.[17] Their role in facilitating memorisation meant that they developed as 'a pedagogical tool' in humanist approaches to education, part of 'a pedagogic tradition related to rhetoric and the art of memory that dated back to the classical period'.[18] Furthermore, the act of compiling material in a logical manner became synonymous with combating idleness and developing an ordered mind, so 'while collecting and ordering notes and thoughts, compilers also worked on their own intellectual, moral, and social edification'.[19] In this sense commonplace books performed a public service. However, the commonplace book was 'sidelined' by the end of the seventeenth century as intellectuals criticised the emphasis on memory, claming that it enabled the compiler to feign knowledge, without judgement or understanding.[20] There was also a concern over the blank spaces left in many commonplace books, something that John Locke sought to solve with his system of indexing that became popular from the early eighteenth century onwards.[21] Beal argues that the eventual decline of the commonplace book from the eighteenth century onwards may have been prompted by its commercialisation, 'when a uniform method becomes freely available to all and sundry and commonplace books are compiled not simply by gentleman scholars ... their sense of specialness is somehow felt to be dispersed'.[22] For Blundell they were an important part of his life and offer an insight both into the way he read and his worldview.

II

Two of Blundell's commonplace books survive: the Historica and the Adversaria. The Historica is a one-volume document that covers 223 folios or double pages. The Adversaria is bound in two volumes, the first containing folios 1 to 200 and the second 201 to 435. Each volume measures 8 by 6 inches and consists of small gatherings of paper bound in a full calf vellum cover. The binding dates from the mid- to late seventeenth century, and the presence of sewn on cords and the fact that the paper does not appear to have been clipped subsequent to having been written on, while the page numbering is sequential throughout, suggests that the volumes were bought readymade.[23] Both commonplace books were kept throughout the same period, possibly in response to an early modern 'midlife crisis'. As Blundell noted in his discussion of the provenance of both texts, 'I did not begin to take these notes until July the 15 1659 (being that day 39 yeares old)'.[24] He continued to make entries in the commonplace books at least until 1697, during the seventy-seventh year of his life, with the help of Walter Thelwall his scribe.[25]

Blundell had a clear view on the role and value of the commonplace book. Over four folios of notes in the opening pages of the Adversaria, entitled 'Electio Scribendorum', Blundell justified his practice and the way that he arrived at that particular compiling method. He read widely on the arguments for and against using a commonplace book before beginning his entries, making a series of commonplaces on commonplacing. Blundell briefly summarised John Sergeant's negative position stating that 'Mr Sarjaunt in his letter to Dr Casaubon ... seemes much to undervalue these kynd of Notebookes. And speaking of those who rely wholly on them, he repeateth the words of a Poet – Lord how they'd looke, if they should chance to loose their paper book.'[26] He counterbalanced this by noting the position of two authors he frequently used, Michel de Montaigne, who 'doth much approve the use of another mans words in our Writings', and Francis Bacon, who 'doth much value the use of particular Topiques (or common places) and he sheweth great reason for it: much contrary to a malevolunt opinion of some modern Wits, who are great enimyes to such kyund of collections as these'.[27] The physical position of this justification at the start of the Adversaria suggests that Blundell was sensitive to contemporary attacks on the practice of commonplacing. However, his own method addressed some common criticisms. Although he noted Bacon's generally positive view of commonplace books, he also recorded that 'he saith he hath not seen any good method of common place but such as rather carry the face of a schoole than of a word'.[28] With this in mind Blundell drew up general rules for the construction of his commonplace books that defined his compiling practice.

Blundell's commonplacing practice was informed by Bacon's criticism of standard methods. He adopted a fluid approach to his note-taking, stating that, while the use of topics is generally a good idea, sticking rigidly to such titles may obstruct the advancement of both the compiler and the collection, an approach outlined in his reflection 'Do not forbeare to note because you know not unto what letter or classe to reduce the things most properly. Besure to note it.' While the author must never fail to include a desired entry, Blundell added a further caveat, 'Collect only the best things, even a few of the very best, to avoyd contempt of your owne Collections, no lesse then Confusion'.[29] Finally, he was keen from the offset that his notes would remain of use, or 'serviceable', throughout his life: 'young men do collect such things, as to their ryper years do appeare, but toyes; therfore be sure to make your notes, a little more weighty ... than your present genius and inclination can yet fully relish'.[30] His views on commonplace books provide a counter-argument to those historians who have neglected them, believing them to be 'childish things'.[31] Instead, Blundell viewed them as an important tool for a rational, mature man, which he used and referred to throughout his life.

The motives for the construction of the Adversaria and Historica were mixed. Like his contemporaries, Blundell used his commonplace books to make sense of an array of information. Numerous marginal notes and additions to entries suggest that he regularly read and reread his comments. For instance, in the margin of a 1659 note about lending money for interest, Blundell stated that the same practice was evident in 1683.[32] It also appears that Blundell used the commonplace books to structure arguments for oral and written transmission, a common practice throughout the early modern period, with many contemporaries recycling fragments recorded in commonplace books in letters or speeches.[33] Thus, much of the material used in Blundell's 'A Short Discourse' was informed by and in turn informed records in his commonplace books.[34] Furthermore, in a remarkable entry concerning the Pope as Anti-Christ, Blundell noted that the material had been compiled for the use of Samuel Aspinwall, 'a zealous Puritan ... [who] ... professed that if he did not think that the Pope were Antichrist he would turn Papist ... whereupon I shall here note down for his use &c some thing which shall relating to that matter'.[35] That Blundell used information recorded in his commonplace books in everyday situations reflected his view that reading had practical application, seen in his advice to Edmund Butler on how to make the best of his imprisonment in 1693: 'you have now a fayr opportunity to improve your self by the reading of choice books for the service of your Prince & Country in future times and perhaps for the greater advancement of your Honorable but much declined house'.[36] This reminds us that reading was not always a private event – Blundell's commonplace books provided him with a forum in which he could rehearse for public action.

Turns of phrase and occasional brief entries suggest that the texts were not only for Blundell's reference, complicating notions that commonplace books were completely 'private'. While detailing an account of a duel in the Historica he concluded 'This let the following story teach you', and notes on two other books end 'They are truly worth your Reading' and 'his 3d volumne is worth the reading'.[37] Blundell's motive for including these signposts may be that he intended to pass the commonplace books on to his family after he died, a legacy befitting an individual who so prized education. Whether he planned this from the start, or whether it was a response to his ageing condition, in one of the final entries in the Adversaria written, as Blundell noted, when he was seventy-six years old, he recorded that his commonplaces were written 'for the use of those who survive me'.[38] His commonplace books may also have served further purposes. Lockridge argues that commonplace books provided a forum in which 'the public self is rehearsed in this intensely private arena', as they offered contemporaries an opportunity to test arguments that would later be discussed in public.[39] A study of Blundell's commonplace books suggests that, for individuals excluded from open activity in the public domain, the commonplace book offered a surrogate. The inclusion of material on the future of politics in England, the position of religion in society and comments on England's foreign policy meant that Blundell was able to use his commonplace books to engage in the political public life from which he had been excluded because of his recusancy: in this sense they facilitated a proxy public life. On the other hand, as we will see, Blundell's seemingly guilty noting of inconsistencies and contradictions within the Bible, his refusal to believe a number of miracles and his critical comments about members of the Catholic clergy, followed by apologies that he was not a better Christian and he could not state such things amongst his Catholic friends and family, suggest his commonplace books may also have offered a form of confessional.[40]

As with Blundell's letter books, all of the early entries were written by himself, though as the shake in his hand became more erratic Walter Thelwall took over. Though Thelwall wrote the later entries in both of Blundell's commonplace books, Blundell's direction is clearly stamped on them. Not only are many of Thelwall's entries checked over and annotated by Blundell but his control over what was written can be found in the entries themselves.[41] For example, in a note on the clipping of silver coin, the entry begins 'I received from my Servant Walter Thelwall (who writes this after my dictate and know the same to be true)', or the note on extreme weather that includes the comment 'Since the last word here was written I sent my Man, who takes these lines from me according as I dictate'.[42] The use of a scribe had an impact on the type of notes that were taken. Early entries in the commonplace books vary greatly in length and Blundell often entered notes as he came across them, regardless of their length. Thelwall's entries were less frequent, but much longer, tending to be ten- to twenty-page summaries of books, with headers indicating the topic of the volume summarised as opposed to a general header for a collection of thematic notes, such as the summary of the life of the Jesuit Father Rapin, which appears under the title 'Rapin Criticus'.[43] This presumably reflects the fact that, during the period Thelwall was scribe, Blundell was reliant on scheduling times when he and Thelwall could meet for this purpose. That Blundell and Thelwall read together also meant that Blundell was not appropriating texts in isolation. Although there is no indication of how significant Thelwall's role was, beyond simply writing what he was told, the relationship meant that the pair formed a micro-reading community where some form of negotiation may have taken place.[44] With the exception of Blundell and Thelwall, there are only three hands that appear in the commonplace books: a small verse written by Thomas Tyldesley, an epitaph copied by Richard Butler and an anonymous hand which detailed a method of killing birds.[45]

While the hand may have changed in the commonplace books, the format of entries remained roughly the same. Following common practice in Renaissance commonplace books, the overwhelming majority of entries have a header, mostly in Latin, written in the margin.[46] In some cases the header is the only overt reference to the subject being discussed, such as the entry 'Phoenix' under which we find the brief comment 'see much of it in the 205 French Conferrence, where the verrity of the story is strongly denyed & yet in some sort defended'.[47] Following common contemporary practice, a number of pages were left blank after particular headings, presumably so Blundell could further add to notes at a later date.[48] Evidence of this can be seen in those entries begun in an early hand, with much later additions that follow beneath.[49] Although this is less evident in the Historica, the single volume of which is almost full, the second volume of the Adversaria contains more than twenty-five blank pages interspersed throughout, which Blundell presumably hoped to fill before he died.[50]

Blundell initially outlined a precise format for commonplacing. In an early entry in the Adversaria, he devised a system of symbols and underling that would denote when he was detailing 'the sense, but not the words of the Author' marked by a dash in the main text, or a line in the margin, where he noted 'where you find a little marke lyke thes at the end of the lynes you may be sure those are the very words of the place ceited'.[51] However, though there are a small number of entries that follow this method, or a slight alteration whereby direct quotations were underlined, his good intentions soon eroded and direct quotations and summaries of an argument are often indistinguishable.[52] Failure to distinguish between direct quotations and the commonplace author's own words was not unique to Blundell. Jeremias Drexel's influential notes on commonplace methods did 'not call for a distinction to be made between an exact quotation and a summary or paraphrase'.[53] In the same manner, while Blundell had good intentions about keeping the content of his commonplace books distinct, as time progressed the topical division between them blurred.

There is significant overlap in material entered in both the Historica and the Adversaria. Both discuss natural wonders, contain ethnographic notes, and provide Blundell's take on important events in Protestant and Catholic history. However, there are also fundamental differences. Though never explicitly stated, it is clear that Blundell viewed each commonplace book as having its own select content. He frequently noted that material had been 'misplaced' in the wrong volume and cross-referenced to the section in which it should have been written.[54] For example, while documenting the sufferings of those who had opposed Catholicism in a section entitled 'Judicia in Catholicotum hostes' in the Historica, Blundell noted that the reader can 'See much of this in Adversaris wher I have misplaced it', while a note in the Adversaria under the same heading directs the reader back to the Historica 'for those relations are misplaced'.[55]

As a general rule, the Historica is concerned with historical issues and the Adversaria with religious. Each text contains material that is unique to that particular commonplace book. The Historica includes a series of short biographies from both Roman history and more recent history, which are not found in the Adversaria.[56] Furthermore, while the Bible appears as a source in both, the way in which it is used differs significantly. In the Adversaria it is referred to in religious terms, considering the impact its teachings should have on the lives of contemporaries, while in the Historica it is often used as a source of factual historical material. For example, in a discussion of weather in Palestine Blundell used Maccabees 13:22, which he quoted as 'Typhon prepared all the Horse men to come that night but ther was an exceeding great Snow and he came not into the Country of Galaad' as an example of how countries 'nerer the Sunne' at one time suffered from severe snow.[57] The sections specific to the Adversaria are detailed comments on religious matters, such as discussions of factual irregularities within the Bible and notes on his readings of religious literature.[58]

In some cases Blundell was unsure of exactly which volume to place material in, as in his discussion of the life of Descartes. While he noted that in error Adrien Baillet's life of Descartes had been summarised in both commonplace books, discussion of the text continued in each, apparently over the same period.[59] Furthermore, Blundell was conscious that he mistakenly entered the same information more than once. In a discussion of the burning of heretics, under the title 'Heretici Combrandi' Blundell speculated 'I suspect I have, by mistake, somtymes inserted the same things twice or thrise under this tytle'.[60] That each commonplace book had a different focus is further emphasised in the source material used. The overwhelming majority of texts cited in the Historica are concerned with history or antiquarianism, whereas religious or philosophical works make up the majority of texts cited in the Adversaria.[61] This is also reflected in Blundell's use of the Bible in both commonplace books. In the Historica the Bible is referenced on a total of thirty-three single sides of folio, in many cases being used as a historical source. In the Adversaria four different versions of the Bible are referenced on 296 single sides of folio, thirty-five per cent of the total volume.[62]

The two-text format of Blundell's commonplace books was seemingly adapted from the method outlined by Drexel, a Catholic intellectual writing in the mid-seventeenth century. In his notes on commonplacing Blundell recorded that in *Aurifodina Artium et Scientiarum Omnium* Drexel spoke of having '6 severall bookes (besydes the Indexes to each booke) that conteyned his notes of this kynd. 3 Bookes were for Sacred things, and 3 for profane'.[63] Drexel also outlined three types of notes suitable for commonplacing. The first consisted of bibliographical information only; the second, which he referred to as 'adversaria', involved direct transcriptions from a source with bibliographical material; and the third, 'historica', which 'comprises anecdotes of human behaviour taken from human history of all places and periods'.[64] It is probable that Blundell based the titles of his commonplace books on Drexel's and the initial inclusion of material on lives of notable individuals from Roman history in the Historica suggest that it may have been his intention to stick closely to the format, though this was unrealised. As we have seen, Blundell was deliberately flexible in his approach to his commonplace books and both contain a crossover of material, suggesting that he used Drexel's method as a rough guide adapted to suit his own purposes. Drexel also advocated the use of an index and there is little indication that Blundell ever intended to index his commonplace books.[65]

A close reading of the commonplace books shows that Blundell developed a common practice for the way in which he read and made notes. Throughout most of his life he made notes directly into the commonplace books either as he read, or shortly after reading a section of a source. This is evident in the exact and numerous page numbers in many of his citations, and the way his summaries appear to unfold, apparently not knowing what an author will conclude until the end of the summary. Indications that many entries were completed after reading a section of a source can be found in the examples where exact page references are given, but smaller points from the same source are given a non-specific reference. For instance, in the life of Bede taken from William Camden, which included regular page-numbered quotations, Blundell noted that Camden referred to Bede with different titles, and that 'he calleth him in some place (as I remember) Amator Veritatis'.[66] Blundell often read more than one text and made notes simultaneously. For example, he read Plutarch and Livy at the same time. Throughout the relevant sections he alternated between the two authors, noting on one occasion that 'These things above related, are taken cheefly out of Plutarche, and partly out of Livi'.[67] The practice of reading more than one text at a time was common in the early modern period. Anthony Grafton and Lisa Jardine have shown that the scholar Gabriel Harvey read a range of texts, which were probably spread out before him during a reading session, and he alternated between them at will.[68]

At times necessity forced Blundell to alter his commonplacing practice. During the early 1640s he first began making rough notes, which were later entered into his commonplace books. These notes, which no longer survive, were copied into the Historica during the early 1660s, as indicated by a number of footnotes to entries, such as 'All this above is out of Plutarch: and I have writ allmost verbatim out of notes which I extracted thence. AD1644', or the statement 'All above is drawne out of Curtis, according as I find it in my loose papers'.[69] A further reference is made in the Adversaria, in a discussion about the inception of the commonplace books, where Blundell mentioned that he started writing these notes in 1659, 'yet some few, espetially (or only) in the Historica were notes which I first tooke in loose papers about the years 1644 & 45. These were chiefly out of Plutarche's Lives.'[70] Blundell was again forced to make rough notes on to loose leaf paper in 1689 and 1690 when he was temporarily imprisoned in Manchester, and the header to a small section on a devotional treatise states that 'These two leaves next above were translated by me W: B: when I was Prisoner at Manchester in 1689: And now againe in 1696 I do make some farther reflections out of the same book'.[71]

By the early 1690s, at over seventy years old, Blundell was not only still reading but developing his note-taking practice to accommodate new books. During the last eight years of his life Blundell began to read entire tomes in different languages, telling one correspondent that 'I have no excuse that I spend some time now in the reading of foreign language but that Cato the learned Roman at 80 years of age betook himself to the Greek with good success'.[72] To help in this, he constructed a practice whereby he read a text, made brief notes on it, then returned to it in six to nine months and made full notes. This practice is outlined in his entry on Pietro Sforza Pallavicino's history of the Council of Trent, where he stated that

> I had twice read over the first Tome before the end of May 1693 and being unwilling to forget all that I read therin, I make these few memorandums out of so great a work ... After I had read it as above, I laid it aside, applying my self for 7 or 8 monthes at the least, to quite different studyes. The Abstract & memorialls which I had taken out of that tome are contained in less then in the 4th part of a sheet. With the help of these and with my labor (this present Easter week 1694) in turning over the book, to renew my notions, I make these farther observations as well as I can.[73]

The final entries in the commonplace books demonstrate another shift in the way Blundell read and made his notes, as a number suggest that he was noting from memory. Thus, on the life of Descartes, Blundell stated that 'The same Descartes in severall parts of his works which I do very well remember tho' I have not noted the places', and in a description of a battle in Ireland, Blundell guessed the number of dead, with the caveat 'if I mistake not, for I have not noted the number'.[74] This no doubt reflected that Blundell was not able to jot down small points as he came across them, as a scribe was writing for him.

III

The sources that Blundell used in his commonplace books were mainly textual. In addition to the Bible, 148 books, pamphlets, broadsheets, newspapers and distinct manuscript works were used in the Historica, and 393 books, pamphlets, broadsheets and newspapers as well as eight poems were used in the Adversaria.[75] The material defies simple classification. Many of the works overlap in topic, such as his histories of the Jesuits which contained both religious and historical information, and it is difficult to distinguish between 'Catholic' and 'Protestant' texts. Blundell's reading was broad and the texts that he chose were increasingly ambitious. The majority of the works that he used were central to the education and learning of individuals on both sides of the confessional divide, many overlapping with, for instance, the book lists of the Calvinist John Newdigate II.[76] Thus, Livy and Plutarch were used throughout the volumes, as were more recent chronicles, such as Baker's 1674 *Chronicle of the Kings of England.* Newsbooks and broadsheets, such as *The General Bill of Mortality*, works on science and education, particularly those by Francis Bacon, and a variety of books about travel can also be found. Blundell also read political works, one of the most frequently used authors being his friend, Roger L'Estrange. Like many of his contemporaries Blundell read texts that argued against his viewpoint.[77] In particular, he regularly used works that were identified by contemporaries as Protestant, if not Puritan, the most obvious examples being the works of William Prynne. There was also a 'Catholic' dimension to Blundell's reading list, including Nicolaus Orlandinus's history of the Jesuits and Pedro de Ribadeneyra's life of Ignatius Loyola, and the large body of Catholic devotional literature, including Daniel Brevint's *Missale Romanum* and Alfonso Rodriguez's *Treatise of Humility.* The other major difference between Blundell's reading list and the lists of his contemporaries can be found in the absence of a significant body of poetry. The few poems that he did record were mostly relegated to the family notebook, the Great Hodge Podge.

Blundell's meticulous records enable us to estimate how many of the books he read, he owned. Only two books from Blundell's original collection can be identified with certainty.[78] A two-volume Douai Bible has been passed through the Blundell family as an heirloom. Through both volumes Blundell has underlined text and made brief marginal notes.[79] A further printed text that Blundell used has been located. *An Epitome of Ortelius* was acquired as a single volume by a modern-day bookseller, with no indication of its provenance. The book was never cited in Blundell's commonplace books, but includes his underlining and marginalia throughout, as well as the signatures of three William Blundells (senior, the 'Cavalier' and junior) alongside those of Blundell's wife and one of his daughters, demonstrating how the text was passed around the family as a physical object.[80] In his study of book ownership in early modern Kent, Peter Clark states that 'by 1640 our evidence would suggest that almost every county landowner of note had several shelves of books at home'.[81] Blundell was no exception to this rule. Between 1668 and 1672 his inventories note that he owned £25 10s worth of books.[82] A comparison of this figure with the average cost of books for the late seventeenth century suggests that Blundell owned between fifty-one and seventy-three folios or 128 to 510 octavos, or a mixture thereof.[83] In his inventory for 1675 a symbol by the entry for books notes 'a more particular & exact valuation of the good next unto it, then had been formerly made'.[84] Here the value of Blundell's books is given at

£42 1s and the number of books that he owned as 447 (though the numbers he gives add up to 494). A caveat in the notes indicates that these figures are 'not valuing or numbering many scores of stiched Bookes', the small ephemeral pamphlets that were distributed in large numbers throughout this period.[85] These figures are expanded on further in Hodge Podge the Third under the title 'Bookes valued. In August I valued my bookes as I think they might then be sold in case I were dead. viz', where Blundell gives the following data:[86]

		£	s
47	in Folio worth	14	–
63	Quartos & Octavos, on oneshelf	6	–
32	Quartos on one shelf	1	10
48	Quartos, 8os & less on one shelf	2	–
33	4o & 8os	3	–
37	Octavos & Less	1	15
31	Octavos & Less	2	10
42	Controvercyes on the little shelf	2	2
40	Controversyes on the Great Shelf besydes the stiched bookes	2	10
62	(on 4 short shelves) in 4o 8o & less	3	15
59	Spiritual bookes & poets on the two high shelfs	2	19

Totall 447 / Value £42–1s.

A number of points can be ascertained from this information. Firstly, Blundell read texts in a range of formats, eagerly acquiring cheap pamphlets and more expensive quarto volumes. Secondly, the inventory provides an insight into the place of books in Blundell's home. Unfortunately, there are no notes recording the room in which he kept his books. However, it is clear that most had a specific place on certain shelves. 'Spiritual bookes & poets' were kept together, presumably in an accessible location so they could be enjoyed by the family, whom Blundell encouraged to partake in devotional literature. Perhaps the most interesting aspect is the fact that Blundell clumped 'Controvercyes' together on 'the little shelf' and 'the Great Shelf'. While this may have simply been a method for Blundell to categorise his own books, from other notes one might infer that they were kept so for pedagogical reasons. Blundell's home was alive with a community of young and enthusiastic readers: his children and grandchildren. Blundell's notes, such as his claim to one correspondent regarding his grandson Edmund, that 'Of late I have read unto him some of the harmless Colloquies of the roguish Erasmus; but he hath not tasted the egg which Luther hatched', suggest that Blundell viewed some of the polemical work that he read as being too sensitive for the younger readers in his household.[87] In this sense, his shelves of 'Controversyes' may have served a similar function to that of the modern-day Board of Film Classification, ensuring that texts were divided between those appropriate and those inappropriate for certain readers in his household. Finally, though Blundell may have borrowed books, given that he had 494 different volumes in his collection by 1674, not including 'stiched Bookes', it is likely that he owned the majority of books that he referenced.

A number of commonplace entries provide an insight into the methods that Blundell used to get physical access to the texts that he read. Some, such as his editions of Livy and Plutarch, may well have been part of his inheritance, though the majority he acquired himself. As we have already seen, Blundell was at the centre of a network of readers with whom he exchanged material, and from whom he gained access to manuscripts, such as Richard Bellings's *History of the Irish Wars.*[88] When Blundell found that a friend was visiting London, they were invariably sent with a list of books to purchase on his behalf, often including details of the best shops to try.[89] For instance, having asked Robert Scarisbrick to purchase an Italian history of the Jesuits, Blundell suggested that 'I know no place more likely to informe you then at the Feathers (or Princes Armes) in Little Brittain'.[90] He accessed texts 'in the Library at Manchester' on more than one occasion, presumably Chetham's Library, established at the bequest of Humphrey Chetham after his death in 1653.[91] During the last five years of his life, having developed a friendship with the bookseller Abel Swall, Blundell used a mail order system to get books. Swall sent books requested from a catalogue to Blundell, who on inspection either kept them and paid for both the book and postage or returned them and paid only for postage.[92]

Many of the texts Blundell used were recommended, as was the case with the *Collection of some of the Murthers and Massacres Committed on the Irish in Ireland*, which was recommended by Richard Bellings.[93] He also located books through advertisements in newspapers or other books, though he complained that 'We are ever at a loss when we find in the Advertisments no more expressed then the volume or price. The foreign Advises do usually ad folio 40, and sometimes they do give us the precise number of pages.'[94] When Blundell began to read in more than one language, his method of selecting texts took on a new dimension, as he read both the foreign edition and the English translation.[95] However, perhaps the most intriguing example can be seen in relation to polemical religious and political texts. Eager to engage with both sides of an argument, Blundell regularly read both the original and a refutation of texts, seen in his reading of Théophile Brachet La Milletière's *The Victory of Truth* alongside John Bramhall's *Answer*.[96]

Of equal interest to the way Blundell chose the printed books he used was the idiosyncratic way he referred to them. Blundell's references to the sources that he used in his commonplace books are as varied as the sources themselves. There is currently no major study of the significance of the way in which contemporaries referred to books, though historians and literary scholars have occasionally alluded to this. In response to a debate over the authorship of an early modern poem, Beal notes that the formulation of any reference is indicative of some aspect that drew the reader's attention, 'A man's name might become linked with a poem in the course of a manuscript transmission because he was the copyist, or because it was written by someone in his circle; or because he added his own stanzas to it ... and so on. There is usually a reason for the association – scribes were not wont to pluck names out of the air at random.'[97] A logical extension of this argument is that each reference that a contemporary compiler chose demonstrates the aspect of each text that was of particular importance to them. Paul Seaver briefly alludes to this in his study of the intellectual world of Nehemiah Wallington, a London Puritan reading in the mid-seventeenth century, recording that Wallington's references to the books that he used variously cited the title or the author's name or both, though he notes there was little pattern to such references.[98] Vivienne Larminie also states that in John Newdigate II's commonplace book the form of references varies greatly, describing the process of identifying the texts as an 'intricate matter'.[99] Although a complete analysis of the significance of attribution in early modern commonplace books is beyond the scope of this book, some observations can be made in relation to Blundell's commonplace books.

The majority of Blundell's references provide a brief title and the author's name, thus Francis Bacon's *The Historie of the Raigne of King Henry the Seventh* appears in Blundell's notes as 'Bacons Hen 7'.[100] Blundell also frequently referred to texts that he used regularly by just their author or title, at times adjusting the title slightly, or in some cases omitting it altogether. For example, he refers to the text *A General Collection of Discourses of the Virtuosi of France, upon Questions of all sorts of Philosophy, and other Natural Knowledge Made in the Assembly of the Beaux Esprits at Paris*, simply as 'French Conference', following the division of the book into 'Conferences' in its contents page.[101] Even more striking are those examples in which Blundell constructed a completely new title, most notably Nieremberg's *A Treatise of the Difference Betwixt the Temporal and Eternal*, which Blundell not only used throughout his commonplace books but also transcribed and referred to as 'The Touchstone of Truth' in both his transcription and his notes, offering no explanation for his actions.[102] Blundell often noted the name of the publisher also, though place of publication was usually only mentioned when outside England. For example, Jean Mabillon's *Traité des Études Monastiques* is noted as 'Jean Mabillion or Mabillon Benedictin in his treatise Des Etudes Monastiques printed at Paris in 1691'.[103] As a general rule Blundell rarely mentioned the translator of a work, tending to leave authorship with the individual who wrote the original text.[104] However, where Blundell's references are most revealing is when they concern the cost and physical appearance of a text.

The form of a number of entries in both the Historica and the Adversaria suggests that Blundell's interest in books bordered on bibliomania. First identified by contemporaries in France during the late seventeenth century, bibliomania as a phenomenon 'constructed books as material objects existing in particular spaces, as surfaces: it valued certain kinds of typography, binding, paper, illustrations, format, and even accidental contingencies, such as printing errors distinguishing one copy or edition from another. It also ascribed to books extrinsic value that was market-driven.'[105] Blundell included a number of references that mentioned the cost of a text, such as the regular entries: 'it cost me 11 shillings', 'price 30*s*', 'price 16*s*', or the entry for Hamon L'Estrange's *Alliance*, 'Ther is a booke of 7*s* price set out by Le'Strange which is a collection of all the Lyturgies or Common prayers which have been commanded in England since the Reformation'.[106] That the cost of texts was so prominent in Blundell's commonplaces suggests that he viewed the financial cost as being inextricably linked to its value as a literary source. He also meticulously recorded printing errors, most notably that in Luke Wadding's life of St Clare, in which Blundell noted 'Ther are 3 leaves in this booke p15.15.15 printed each of them, in a maner, with the same letters and word, but through what designe or error (the booke being dedicated to a Queene) I cannot sufficiently wonder'.[107]

The most frequently commented on aspect of a text was the physical form it took. Blundell's references were regularly followed by notes on the binding and format of a text, including 'a pamphlet', 'a pamphlet of 6 sheetes', 'printed in quarto', 'printed in 8o', 'printed in twelves', 'printed in folio', 'two large Tomes in folio', 'printed in octavo' and 'a notable small book printed in ocatavo'.[108] In one instance Blundell noted having read both the quarto and octavo editions of Edwin Sandys's *Europae Speculum*.[109] So important was the physical format of a text, that when they were bound together, either by the publisher or Blundell himself, they lost their individual identities. References such as 'See many notable things in Evangelium Armatum which I have bound up with other pamphlets in a red cover' are frequent in both of the commonplace books.[110] The most striking example of this is the writings of Joseph Scaliger, whose work Blundell referred to under the title 'Scaligeriana'.[111] A reference in the Adversaria reveals that the volume he was referring to was a collection of Scaliger's works that Blundell bound together himself, 'in the book I have intituled Scaligeriana'.[112] He was not unique in noting the physical formats of books. Christine Cerdeira has identified a number of wills in which books were referred to by their physical format, including medical works 'which are bounde in three books or volumes', or the statement 'I give to Robert Crudd my servant tenne of my bookes in 8o'.[113] As revealing as these references are, they also posed a significant obstacle in locating the texts referred to in the commonplace books.

Through a series of author, title, keyword, date of publication and topic searches on *EEBO* the *ESTC*, and holdings of various libraries, the majority of sources that Blundell quoted have been located.[114] In many cases this required entering a variety of spellings for each entry, as Blundell's spelling of a name or, as we have seen, his interpretation of a title, often differed from the published version. Once the text was located, through meticulous cross-referencing with either Blundell's page references or publication details, in many cases we can be certain that not only has the correct text been identified but also the correct edition. Aside from Bible references, of the 146 books, pamphlets, broadsheets and newspapers used in the Historica, 7 (5 per cent) cannot be traced because of the limited information provided in the reference, 10 (7 per cent) are non-specific references such as 'the Chronicles of those tymes',[115] 8 (5 per cent) references suggest probable sources, though there is not enough information to be certain, 46 (32 per cent) references can be matched up with the work quoted, though not the edition, and 75 (51 per cent) references can be matched up with the exact text and edition.[116] Of the 393 books, pamphlets, broadsheets and newspapers used in the Adversaria, 30 (8 per cent) cannot be traced, 20 (5 per cent) are non-specific references, 20 (5 per cent) references suggest probable sources, 161 (41 per cent) sources can be matched up with the work quoted, though not the edition, and 162 (41 per cent) references can be matched up with the exact text and edition.[117] There are two further genres of information that Blundell drew on: his experience and information derived from others.

A striking feature of Blundell's commonplace books is the interplay between oral and literate sources of information recorded. Both commonplace books contain information that had been passed on to Blundell by friends and family.[118] He developed a standardised method of recording such information, whereby the individual was named, followed by the date that she or he told him, such as 'Mr Frances Anderton told me thus Dec:30 1663'.[119] The majority of entries of this kind are from individuals with whom Blundell had regular correspondence, or whom he considered an authority on a subject, an issue that was expanded on in the reference. For example, following a relation of a wild buck being killed, Blundell noted 'This was tolld me by a Gentleman that was present when the Buck was killed, and the thing is very true'.[120] Having noted that one Edward Lloyd told Blundell his parents had an abnormally large tree growing in their garden, he included the note, 'But when I seemed not to credit this, he did seriously affirm that he had been assured that it was eyther 5 or 7 fathem in compas, but that indeed he had never measured it'.[121] The veracity of Blundell's oral sources was an issue of concern, and when a source was of a dubious nature, his suspicions were noted. When comparing the Bible's claim that Abraham was one hundred years old when he fathered Isaac, and the claim of a friend that Thomas Parr of Shropshire 'being aged 152 had ... a Bastard chyld', Blundell noted that 'we have not so good Authority for the tru fathering of the one chyld, as we have for the other'.[122] More striking is how Blundell often turned to literary sources to support oral.[123] Thus, having been told a story 'by a Gentleman that travailed long in Spain' about a beggar who was condemned to death for selling a slipper given to him by a lady, but was saved after praying to an image of Mary, which 'threw unto him the other slipper', Blundell found corroboration for this kind of event in classical sources, noting that 'Ther was an excellent discourse, concerning these accidents and signes in Images in Plutarch'.[124]

Blundell also included information drawn from his own experience.[125] These notes include small anecdotes, such as the fact that he saw the portrait of Thomas Parr while in Cardinal Mazarin's Palace in 1660, or that he saw the Bishop of Angers while travelling, and he was 'extreamly old & thin'.[126] He also made specific, detailed notes on his observations, including the claim whilst discussing the dimensions of the ship the *Royal Sovereign* that 'This I can ad: that her firme flat side in the port holes was 17 inches thick as nere as may be'.[127] When entering information gained from personal experience, Blundell regularly closed the point with his initials, as though his signature added veracity to its content. For example, 'I saw the Tomb of this Prince at Delph, which is a stately piece. WB'.[128] Indeed, he was prepared to counter the information found in textual sources with speculation based on his experience. Thus, in his notes on John Ray's *Observations*, Blundell disputed Ray's claim that there were twenty thousand Jews in Amsterdam, stating that 'I saw them in their Sinagogue AD 1660 but I do not think they are so many. WB'.[129]

That Blundell's commonplace books combine literary and oral sources with such ease reflects broader contemporary practice. As Adam Fox has argued, 'England in the sixteenth and seventeenth centuries was far from being an oral society; and yet it was not a completely literate one either'.[130] That contemporaries did not divorce oral and literate cultures has already been seen in Blundell's commonplace books. Having read John Sergeant's *Sure-Footing* he engaged directly with this debate, noting that Sergeant 'acknowledges *Oral* tradition to be the greatest (or chief) and he seemeth to mean by this, that tradition which is now oral & passing so from father to Son'.[131] Blundell was not alone in this practice: Jean Bodin, for instance, incorporated into his commonplace books a range of entries that he observed himself or gathered from acquaintances.[132] The practice of incorporating material gathered from different media was also promoted by Drexel, who recommended including notable items that are 'heard and seen'.[133] Thus, while the commonplace book in its original form was designed to hold material accumulated from textual sources, it could accommodate a range of material, handling 'each entry independently of its source, as potentially useful knowledge equivalent to every other entry'.[134]

Not only did the type of source that Blundell used vary but so too did the information that he extrapolated from it. The policy of taking different information from different sources is outlined in his commonplaces on commonplacing, where he included a near-exact quotation from James Howell: 'some books are to be tasted only, some chewed & some swallowed. Some to be dissected and anatomized into Epitomes & notes'.[135] Thus, for those books that Blundell deemed important, he included page by page summaries of the whole book.[136] In other instances he adopted a different approach, such as in his summary of Adrien Baillet's life of Descartes, for which Blundell stated that 'There are so many things handled in the 5th book that it would be too long here to give a particular account of all. I shall therfore first take the titles of the severall chapters in brief: and then perhaps I shall mention certain particular things to give farther light therin.'[137] A number of entries contain direct quotations with the source listed at the end. As we have seen, despite initial good intentions many of these quotations are indistinguishable from Blundell's summary, and are entered with no markings to indicate that they are direct quotations, such as the note that 'A woman lived, dyed and is buryed at Dunstable (where is her Epitaph) who had 19 children at 5 births', which is a direct, though unacknowledged, quotation from *Anglorum Speculum*.[138] Furthermore, at times Blundell recorded information from one source, which he had cited in another, such as his summary of Seneca's *De Ira*, which he noted as being 'Ceited by Ho: Court'.[139] Finally, some of the most interesting notes within Blundell's commonplace books are those in which he provides an evaluation of a work, such as his notes on Arrigo Caterino Davila's history of the French Civil Wars, in which he gave both a summary and a section entitled 'Some observations of my own concerning this History of France'.[140] It is to an analysis of this material and its indications about the way in which Blundell appropriated what he read that we now turn.

IV

Recent work on the history of reading has challenged the view that readers passively accepted the arguments of the material they read. Challenges against this 'receptive fallacy' have come from all periods of historical study. For instance, in his work on British working-class readers from the late eighteenth to mid-twentieth centuries, Jonathan Rose has shown that 'Even when literature was deliberately written as propaganda, it often had no appreciable impact on the politics of the reader – or an impact entirely different from what the author or publisher intended'.[141] Certainly, this was the case in the early modern period. Seventeenth-century readers actively interpreted the texts they read, projecting on to them their own opinions and viewpoints, reinventing them to suit their needs. As Stephen Zwicker has argued, 'just as books shaped readers, so we must also acknowledge that early modern readers shaped the books they read'.[142]

Readers approached their texts with a specific purpose or purposes in mind, which had an impact on the way in which they appropriated the material they read. Thus, in the early seventeenth century the scholar Gabriel Harvey read with a view to ensuring the continued patronage of his employers, extracting from books material that would be of benefit to the position that they found themselves in at a given time, reading Roman history 'in a way directly applicable to contemporary affairs of state'.[143] In his analysis of the commonplace books and notebooks of William Drake, a landowner based in Buckinghamshire who lived from 1606 to 1669, Sharpe has shown that Drake read for efficacy, mining texts for information that could offer personal instruction for the particular moment in which he found himself.[144] Drake often rejected the preferred reading of a text, twisting the meaning of literature to suit his own purpose, even building ideas that 'we or other contemporaries would consider against the grain of the text, let alone the authorial intention'.[145] This approach was not exclusive to scholars or gentlemen who had the time for such engagements. Seaver has shown that the Puritan turner Nehemiah Wallington read and recorded information from a range of sources throughout the mid-seventeenth century. His interpretation of texts was incorporated into a large corpus of material in which Wallington meticulously examined his life, providing him with an insight on living well and methods to glorify God.[146] Work on female reading practices in the early modern period has shown how women negotiated traditional power structures in their appropriation of texts, 'finding meaning and inspiration for themselves even in apparently conventional "patriarchal" writings'.[147] In her study of Ann Bowyer's early seventeenth-century commonplace book, Victoria Burke argues that reading and the compilation of private commonplaces 'could be the means for creative expression in a society which in general did not value women's writing'.[148] This approach has been identified also outside England, most notably in Carlo Ginzburg's seminal study of the reading practices of Menocchio, an Italian miller accused of heresy in the late sixteenth century. Inquisition records provide an insight into his reading practices and show that Menocchio's 'manner of reading was obviously one-sided and arbitrary – almost as if he was searching for confirmation of ideas and convictions that were already firmly entrenched'.[149] Blundell's commonplace books detail an approach to contemporary texts that supports the view that early modern readers were not passive receptors of information, while reminding us that 'there is no such thing as *a* typical reader'.[150]

Blundell's reading techniques were marked by a deep level of engagement with a given text and the manipulation and reconstruction of an author's position. Throughout his commonplace books he stamped his authority on the texts that he used, referring to authors as 'my' or 'our' author.[151] Whether this was a deliberate or a subconscious act Blundell clearly viewed himself as a consumer of the text, who could do with it what he would. This notion is borne out in his comments on the works he used. Far from appearing as a passive receptacle of information Blundell's notes suggest that his approach to texts was similar to that of an unfavourable reviewer, an approach that defined his reading of both Protestant *and* Catholic works. That Blundell approached the texts he used in this manner was facilitated by the commonplace method. Although commonplace books initially appear to promote a formulaic approach, in which the author copied extracts from 'a storehouse of wisdom' under agreed headings, the very act of choosing which section to extract, and under which title to place it, put the compiler in an elevated position.[152] This is particularly evident in Blundell's use of the Roman historians.

Blundell engaged with Roman histories in different ways during the course of his life. As we have seen, the short lives at the start of the Historica are the earliest entries in the commonplace books, being made on loose-leaf papers while he was exiled in the mid-1640s and copied into the Historica during the early 1660s.[153] While Blundell used the Roman historians Suetonius and Quintus Curtius, the focus of his reading of Roman history was undoubtedly Plutarch and Livy, central texts in the education of all early modern gentlemen, which appear in the book lists and commonplace books of such Protestant readers as William Drake, John Newdigate and Gabriel Harvey.[154] Initially, Blundell's engagement with these works follows a common practice amongst contemporaries, whereby the lives of individuals in the Roman histories are summarised and their virtues expounded; an 'archaic form' of commonplacing as conceived by Erasmus and the early humanists.[155] Thus, having commended his 'goodly personage' and his modesty towards women, Blundell concluded his notes on the life of the Roman statesman Publius Cornelius Scipio with the comment 'I do not find a more worthy Romain soldier then Publius Scipio, mentioned in any history'.[156] However, this relatively brief section at the start of the Historica, totalling no more than ten folios, is the only dedicated discussion of Roman history in Blundell's commonplace books.[157] None the less, Blundell continued to draw on both Plutarch and Livy as authorities on all manner of issues, apparently believing that incidents of dubious plausibility were given credibility if similar events had been recounted in their works.[158] The relatively scant attention Blundell paid to Roman history may reflect that engagement with these works was deemed essential to excel in public office, an arena from which he was excluded because of his recusancy.[159] This may also explain the absence of Machiavelli from the list of works to which Blundell referred. While Blundell continued to rely on the authority of the Roman historians, the focus of his commonplace entries increasingly turned to those issues of immediate relevance to his position at a given time. As he built up his confidence as a scholar and his control over his commonplace books became marked, this autonomy over the works he used became more pronounced. Indeed, a survey of Blundell's commonplace books shows that his reading practice was active, critical and at times adversarial.

Blundell read actively, making connections between the different sources he read and information he came across. Having noted that Nicolas Caussin's *The Holy Court* sums up 'ingeniously and eloquently the common trivial occations of the anger of great persons', Blundell concluded that he could well have demonstrated his point by relaying the story of when Philip III of Spain was stabbed in the foot by a spur that his page had negligently left in his shoe.[160] He also developed arguments in instances where he felt the author had failed to do justice to the material presented. Thus, when reading René Rapin's *Oeuvres Diverses*, a text that Blundell praised highly, he noted of his comments on Pythagoras that 'He can give no very clear account of Pythagoras: yet it seems to me by what we have in Rapin, that he was the greatest man that ever had been in the world for naturall knowledg, acquired by natural means'.[161] The most striking example, considering it was written by a Catholic, is Blundell's notes on the life of Descartes. Blundell was clear that 'Descartes was an excellent man' and in his notes on Adrien Baillet's life of Descartes, upon which Blundell lauded significant praise, he expressed dismay that no attempt was made to explain why Descartes lived so long in Holland and visited England, yet failed to promote his work in his native, Catholic France.[162] Blundell noted that he had found 'some hints in this book'.[163] After meticulous study of Baillet's work, Blundell speculated that Descartes was 'much alarm'd with the late proceeding in Italy against Galileo' who was being investigated by the Inquisition 'for his Doctrine about the motion of the earth (an opinion which seemed probable to Mr Descartes)'.[164] Blundell highlighted further overlap in the beliefs of Galileo and Descartes, noting that 'I have found in some part of this little history, that some of his own opinions were condemned at Rome'.[165] While Blundell read actively, he was also not averse to reading critically, identifying areas of failure in the texts that he read.

Whatever his position on the views of an author, Blundell regularly noted concerns over how their arguments were constructed. At its most superficial level this included comments on the use of language. Although Blundell claimed to have poor Latin skills, he regularly identified 'pityfull latin' in the works he read, and noted that in a blank sheet at the end of Thomas May's *Breviary* he had listed 'sondry faults in that author', going on to comment 'It is very remarkable that the English in this age have no great tallent in writing latin prose'.[166] Sections of his commonplace books are devoted to listing examples of poor Latin in his reading, though these caused him less concern than poor English.[167] A particular grievance of Blundell's surrounded the use of colloquial phrases that he believed were subverting the English language. Writing on the topic of Robert Loveday's *Letters*, 'esteemed by many to be most quaint and ingenious', Blundell claimed that they were 'a begging to be understood: The expressions indeed are nothing vulgar, but the sense is as plain as may be. For an example of which, I do propose, that one of the choyse Epistles be translated out of that new fashioned English phraze into plain honest English, and I think it will then looke lik a pluck't peacock.'[168] Blundell's concern that authors were shrouding their work in pretentiousness is also evident in his notes on Philippe Avril's *Travels into Divers Parts of Europe and Asia, Undertaken by the French King's Order to Discover a New Way by Land into China.*[169] Although he found the content otherwise satisfactory, he criticised 'the pompous style of the book' and noted that its author had 'never approached nearer to China then unto the Dominions of the Persian Empire'.[170]

Blundell was also mindful of the relevance and importance of what he read, and criticised a news book of 1665 for running a large section on a gift from the London citizenry of £61 to the poor, stating 'This I note as a ridiculous charity to be so published'.[171] He criticised Abraham van Wicquefort's concentration on ceremonies and formalities, stating that it is 'somwhat ridiculous in my opinion ... amongst all thos weighty affaires which our Author recounts', criticising both the author's choice of material and the pageantry of early modern diplomacy.[172] While inappropriate content was a particular bugbear for Blundell, lack of material was also equally obstructive to his enjoyment of a book, and in his notes on Sforza Pallavicino's work on the history of the Council of Trent he claimed that his observations of the fifteenth session ended too abruptly.[173] Indeed, though written by a Jesuit from the Catholic perspective, Blundell was heavily critical of Pallavicino because of omissions in the work. While he accepted Pallavicino's overall argument, he remarked that 'Our Author seems to be defective in sondry places, by neglecting to name the day & year of the most principall events in his history'.[174] Blundell also noted inaccuracies in texts, including Robert Stapylton's translation of Famiano Strada's *De Bello Belgico*, claiming 'in sondry places he mistakes the sense of the author'.[175] In 1693, having discovered that Camden's *Britannia* was to be republished, Blundell found an outlet for such comments, sending to the publisher a list of corrections covering more than six single sides of folio.[176] At times Blundell suspected that these errors may have been a result of the author's bias or faulty source material, and he routinely questioned the provenance of an author's information.

Whenever he approached a text, one of Blundell's primary concerns was how the author came upon the information discussed. He regularly praised individuals for 'citeing his Authors', noting of Abraham van Wicquefort that 'he takes an occasion to shew his great reading & to give his opinion concerning the best Historians of ancient & latter times'.[177] For information about contemporary events, Blundell was keen to use authors who had actually been present. Thus, when discussing Richard Bellings's unprinted manuscript on the history of the Irish wars, he stated that 'I do give the greater credit to it, by reason that the said R B was a witness of very many things which he writes there'.[178] Elsewhere he pointed out that Davila was 'present & heard every word' at the speeches he recorded, and was 'a souldier for the K and was wounded at the siege of Amiens' which was detailed in his work on the Low Country wars.[179] In instances where Blundell could not attest to the reliability of a text he noted so, as in a summary of an article on coins minted in 1696 from the newspaper *The Post Boy*, where he stated 'the Authority of which as to this particular I can neither greatly distrust nor comend'.[180] When he believed that an author had insufficient evidence to make an argument he noted his challenge. In some cases this might be nuanced, such as Blundell's disputation of the claim in *Fides Regia Britannica sive Annales Ecclesiae Britannicae* that a woman walked over coals: 'the truth may be doubted because the Author Alford knows no antient writer who hath recorded it'.[181] He also doubted some of the conclusions of Avril's comments on China as 'he had got his knowledg more by his ears then his eyes'.[182] The most blatant assault on an author's source material was reserved for Edwin Sandys's *Europae Speculum*, Blundell claiming 'that what he hath writ dependeth much upon conjectures & reports'. He added frequent scurrilous comments after small notes on Sandys' work, such as 'saith the Lyer'.[183]

Blundell was also wary of the impact that authors' bias might have, and when approaching any source he was keen to understand an author's perspective. Many of his notes on books include asides about the author, such as 'I take him most certainly to be a German Protestant', 'he is a bitter enemy to the Papists' or, in the case of a life of Descartes, 'that our Author is a great friend & admirer of this new philosopher; and I think we may lawfully suspect he favours him a little to much'.[184] Blundell held that any form of bias could obstruct accurate coverage of a topic, even if the argument added weight to his own beliefs. For instance, Blundell noted that in *Oeuvres Diverses* the Jesuit Father Rapin 'seems to me to be over-nice in the point somtimes; and not alwayes exactly just'.[185] On Sforza Pallavicino's work on the Council of Trent, Blundell claimed that Pallavicino had become so obsessed with disputing the work of one of the detractors of the Catholic Church that 'I conceive it has made our Author solicitous & perhaps a little too prolix, in returning a full answer'.[186] Elsewhere Blundell claimed that Ralph Winterton's translation of Drexel's *Considerations ... upon Eternity* was flawed because of the translator's bias, noting that 'his different opinions in religion hath made him often to mince and conceil the Authors sense'.[187] So concerned was Blundell about the impact that an author's motivation might have on what was written that he cross-checked accounts of the same event. This was the case with Abraham van Wicquefort's notes on the Council of Trent, of which Blundell recorded that 'My Author may be suspected as a Protestant writer; but I give the more credit to this, in regard it is suitable enough to Palavicin's history of the Council of Trent'.[188] Blundell's suspicions about Wicquefort's bias continued and later in his notes he compared his stance with that of Joseph Scaliger, again recording that the accounts corroborated each other.[189]

At times Blundell's readings can clearly be identified as adversarial. The comments that fall into this category will be discussed in more detail in following chapters, though an outline is offered here of how he handled these texts. Blundell's adversarial readings can be seen in a range of vicious comments that he made about the texts that he took issue with, including the claim that a polemical religious book was 'a most horrid one', that another was 'a notable knavish bitter discourse against the old Protestants of England', that an author's view of Jesuits was 'impertinent & malitious', or that to claim King James's performance at the Hampton Court Conference was equal to the greatest of divines was simply 'ridiculous'.[190] Blundell often developed counter-arguments against texts that he disagreed with. These were developed in two different ways. On the one hand he simply cross referenced texts that stated the opposite. For example, in an entry on tall men, he noted Bacon's claim that 'tall men are lyke high houses of 4 or 5 storyes wherin commonly the uppermost roome is worst furnished', which he juxtaposed with the view that 'the most eminently wise of this nation, of later years have beene tall men'.[191] For more contentious issues Blundell directly engaged with arguments that he disagreed with. The most striking example of this is in his refutation of Richard Cox's *Hibernia Anglicana*.[192] As before he drew on other secondary sources, noting that, despite Cox's claim that all the Catholics of Ireland were engaged in a conspiracy against the King, the Earl of Ormond had stated of Irish Catholics '*that the Nobility & greater part of the Gentry continued faithfull to his Majesty, obedient to his Authority & worthy of his favour*'.[193] Furthermore, he went on to compare the actions of the Irish with those of the Scottish, which he deemed far worse, and questioned why Cox had failed to discuss the actions of the English who Blundell thought had behaved more despicably than the Irish Catholics.[194]

That Blundell took issue with many of the texts he read did not mean that he rejected all of their content and recorded them in his commonplace books only to challenge them. Blundell regularly manipulated the words of his authors, twisting disagreeable material to support his own position. For example, though he noted that an article in *The Monthly Mercury* was 'unspeakably bitter against the French King', he overlooked its central thrust in favour of focusing on a small section from which he concluded that 'we do not read of any Prince better serv'd, either in the field, or at the Councell-table, or that lives more free from the attempts of conspiracy and infidelity'.[195] Blundell selectively read many of the texts that he used, taking factual information and some arguments from texts with an overall perspective that he found morally repugnant. Thus, he built up a large section on the history of Parliament taken from the work of William Prynne, including sections on the power of Parliament. However, he categorically stated that Parliament 'cannot (what ever Prin saith) take the life of the meanest subject, without the Kings consent'.[196] Furthermore, despite the fact that Blundell claimed Daniel Brevint's *Missale Romanum* was a 'blastphemus book', which was critical of Catholicism throughout, he plundered it for information about miracles.[197] Blundell regularly read against the grain of a text with an idiosyncratic reading practice that he developed over decades of reading and note-taking. As we have seen, he was not alone in this approach, and his commonplace books provide a further case study supporting the view that contemporaries did not unquestioningly accept everything that they read in print.

V

The following two chapters engage with specific aspects of Blundell's reading and commonplacing practice. Chapter 4 considers how Blundell used his reading to bolster his own religious beliefs. This includes a discussion of Blundell's religious beliefs based on his engagement with the Bible and other devotional works, and an analysis of how he read and rewrote Catholic and Protestant history to add credibility to the former. Chapter 5 shows how Blundell used reading to explore the world, analysing his comments on different nations and peoples, different beliefs (as distinct from different denominations of Christianity), the treatment of women and his observations on social hierarchy. Consideration of Blundell's work on natural wonders and how they influenced his worldview will also feature here. These divisions have been artificially imposed on to the commonplace books for the purposes of this book, as a means to manage the wealth of material found there, though, as will be shown, the material discussed in each chapter was usually clumped together by Blundell under a small selection of titles.

NOTES

1 M. Gratton, 'Blundell, William (1620–1698)', in *ODNB*.

2 K. Lockridge, 'Individual literacy in commonplace books', *Interchange*, 34 (2003), p. 337; V. E. Burke, 'Ann Bowyer's commonplace book (Bodleian Library Ashmole MS 51): reading and writing among the "middling sort"', *Early Modern Literary Studies*, 6.3 (2001), 1.4.

3 See, for example: Beal, 'Notions in garrison', pp. 133–47; Moss, *Printed Commonplace-Books*; Lockridge, 'Individual literacy'; A. Blair, 'Note taking as an art of transmission', *Critical Inquiry*, 31 (2004), pp. 85–107; Burke, 'Ann Bowyer's commonplace book'.

4 Beal, 'Notions in garrison', p. 133; Lockridge, 'Individual literacy', p. 337.

5 Blair, 'Note taking', p. 91; Beal, 'Notions in garrison', pp. 132–3.

6 K. Berland, J. K. Gilliam and K. A. Lockridge (eds), *The Commonplace Book of William Byrd II of Westover* (London: University of North Carolina Press, 2001), p. 4; Moss, *Printed Commonplace-Books*, pp. 1–2; L. Dacome, 'Noting the mind: commonplace books and the pursuit of the self in eighteenth-century Britain', *Journal of the History of Ideas*, 65 (2004), pp. 603–4; Burke, 'Ann Bowyer's commonplace book', 1.6. Peter Mack adheres to a strict definition of a commonplace book, maintaining that it can include *only* sententious material. The inclusion of other miscellaneous content such as occasional transcriptions of letters or transcripts from literature that cannot be classed as sententious makes the manuscript a notebook. While this sharp division may be sustainable for the Elizabethan period on which Mack is writing, during the seventeenth century attitudes to commonplacing were more fluid and Blundell, for example, regularly transcribed material that was not sententious in nature, but continued to view his manuscript as a commonplace book: P. Mack, *Elizabethan Rhetoric: Theory and Practice* (Cambridge: Cambridge University Press, 2002), pp. 44, 108.

7 Moss, *Printed Commonplace-Books*, p. 242, passim.

8 Moss, *Printed Commonplace-Books*, pp. 1, 133; A. Blair, 'Humanist methods in natural philosophy: the commonplace book', *Journal of the History of Ideas*, 53 (1992), p. 541; Lockbridge, 'Individual literacy', p. 337; Mack, *Elizabethan Rhetoric*, pp. 31–2, 103; A. Moss, 'The *Politica* of Justus Lipsius and the commonplace-book', *Journal of the History of Ideas*, 59 (1998), pp. 421–2.

9 Blair, 'Note taking', pp. 96–7; J. Drexel, *Aurifodina Artium et Scientiarum Omnium* (Antwerp, 1638).

10 Dacome, 'Noting the mind', p. 604.

11 FSL, V.b.93, Commonplace book of John Evans.

12 HL, mssHM 15369, Certain collections of the right Hon. Elizabeth late Countess of Huntingdon.

13 FSL, V.a.439, Miscellaneous commonplace book.

14 FSL, V.b.93, Commonplace book of John Evans; FSL, V.a.260, Miscellaneous commonplace book; FSL, V.a.399, Miscellaneous commonplace book.

15 Blair, 'Humanist methods', p. 543.

16 Blair, 'Note taking', p. 101.

17 R. Yeo, 'Managing knowledge in early modern Europe: essay review of Peter Burke, *A Social History of Knowledge: Gutenberg to Diderot*', *Minerva*, 40 (2002), pp. 301–14, at p. 308; R. Yeo, 'A solution to the multitude of books: Ephraim Chambers's *Cyclopedia* (1728) as "the best book in the universe"', *Journal of the History of Ideas*, 64 (2003), pp. 61–72; A. Blair, 'Reading strategies for coping with information overload ca.1550–1700', *Journal of the History of Ideas*, 64 (2003), pp. 11–28.

18 A. Blair and A. Grafton, 'Reassessing humanism and science', *Journal of the History of Ideas*, 53 (1992), p. 539; Dacome, 'Noting the mind', pp. 603, 610 at p. 603.

19 Dacome, 'Noting the mind', p. 615; Blair, 'Note taking', p. 98.

20 Moss, 'The *Politica* of Justus Lipsius', pp. 421, 435; Dacome, 'Noting the mind', p. 612; Blair, 'Note taking', p. 98; Lockridge, 'Individual literacy', p. 338.

21 R. Yeo, 'John Locke's "new method" of commonplacing: managing memory and information', *Eighteenth-Century Thought*, 2 (2004), pp. 1–38; Dacome, 'Noting the mind', p. 608.

22 Beal, 'Notions in garrison', p. 142.

23 I am grateful to Mark Walmsley for assistance in dating the bindings of these volumes.

24 Adversaria, fol. 8b.

25 Adversaria, fol. 356.

26 Adversaria, fol. 6b; J. Sergeant, *Sure-footing in Christianity, or Rational Discourses on the Rule of Faith* (1665), p. 336.

27 Adversaria, fols 6–b; M. de Montaigne, *The Essayes or Morall, Politike and Millitarie Discourses of Lo: Michaell de Montaigne* (1603), pp. 67–87; F. Bacon, *Of the Advancement and Proficience of Learning or the Partitions of Sciences* (1640), pp. 253–5.

28 Adversaria, fol. 6b; Bacon, *Of the Advancement and Proficience of Learning*, pp. 253–5. For Bacon's verdict on commonplace books see: Beal, 'Notions in garrison', p. 138; Blair, 'Note taking', p. 103; Blair, 'Humanist methods', p. 550;

29 Adversaria, fol. 1.

30 Adversaria, fol. 1.

31 As discussed in Moss, 'The *Politica* of Justus Lipsius', p. 423.

32 Adversaria, fol. 18.

33 Mack, *Elizabethan Rhetoric*, pp. 26, 44, 103, 105, 300. For example, William Drake's notes 'show him constructing a speech around a set of adages and observations from history': Sharpe, *Reading Revolutions*, p. 154.

34 See, for example, Blundell's notes on Prynne and the history of Parliament, which categorically state that Parliament 'cannot (what ever Prin saith) take the life of the meanest subject, without the Ks consent', a claim reiterated in Blundell's 'A Short Discourse': Adversaria, fol. 73; Blue Book, fols 24b, 55b.

35 Adversaria, fol. 142b.

36 William Blundell to Edmund Butler, 2 October 1693, in Draft Letter Book, IV, fol. 68b.

37 Historica, fols 26b, 30; Adversaria, fol. 58b.

38 Adversaria, fol. 368.

39 Lockridge, 'Individual literacy', p. 338.

40 I am grateful to Kevin Sharpe for discussion about the different functions of Blundell's commonplace books.

41 For examples of Blundell's corrections to Thelwall's entries see Adversaria, fols 333b, 341b.

42 Adversaria, fols 347, 356b.

43 Adversaria, fol. 329.

44 For a discussion of this phenomena see R. Chartier, 'Leisure and sociability: reading aloud in early modern Europe', in S. Zimmerman and R. Weissman (eds), *Urban Life in the Renaissance* (London: Associated University Presses, 1989), pp. 103–20.

45 Adversaria, fols 259b, 261b–2, 305.

46 Sharpe, *Reading Revolutions*, p. 181.

47 Adversaria, fol. 305.

48 Dacome, 'Noting the mind', p. 608.

49 For example: Adversaria, fols 163, 278.

50 Adversaria, fols 285b, 315, 315b, 338b, 343b, 344b, 346, 346b, 349b, 352b, 354, 354b, 355b, 358, 359, 364b, 367b, 380, 380b, 382, 396b, 398b, 400, 400b, 402b, 405, 412, 419.

51 Adversaria, fol. 8b.

52 For an example of this method in use see Adversaria, fol. 87. 'Camden speaking of the cutting of a part of a word, saith *Our delight is to speak short*'. This is a direct quotation from W. Camden, *Britain, or A Chorographicall Description of the most Flourishing Kingdomes, England, Scotland, and Ireland, and the Ilands Adjoyning* (1610), p. 171.

53 Blair, 'Note taking', p. 100.

54 See, for example: Adversaria, fols 36, 37, 51b, 61b.

55 Historica, fol. 31b; Adversaria, fol. 56.

56 See the examples of Blundell's short lives of St Francis and Julius Caesar: Historica, fols 9b, 15.

57 Historica, fol. 43b.

58 Adversaria, fols 75, 77b.

59 Adversaria, fol. 395; Historica, fol. 179; A. Baillet, *The Life of Monsieur Des Cartes Containing the History of his Philosophy and Works* (1693).

60 Adversaria, fol. 276.

61 This is a rough estimate based on the subject matter of the 330 printed books, pamphlets and broadsheets cited in the Adversaria and the 124 printed books, pamphlets and broadsheets cited in the Historica, identified for this book. Approximately half of the 330 texts cited in the Adversaria were religious and/or philosophical, 20 per cent were concerned with history and antiquarianism (from ancient to 1620), 10 per cent with science, medicine and geography, 10 per cent with politics, current affairs and law, while 10 per cent of sources were either literary or miscellaneous. On the other hand approximately half of the 124 texts cited by Blundell in the Historica were historical or antiquarian (from ancient to 1620), 25 per cent were religious or philosophical, 10 per cent were concerned with science, medicine and geography, 10 per cent with politics, current affairs and law, while 5 per cent were either literary or miscellaneous. In creating these figures individual titles have been counted only once, based on the main topic of the work. By nature these figures do not offer a fully accurate view of the subject matters of all works – for instance, the histories of religious groups or lives of religious figures have been listed as works of history, though they also offer political and religious material. (Note that the subject categories presented here are based on a slightly modified version of the five categories Daniel Woolf used to estimate the subject content of the books read by Henry Prescott, Deputy Registrar of Chester Diocese, in the early eighteenth century: D. R. Woolf, *Reading History in Early Modern England* (Cambridge: Cambridge University Press, 2000), p. 120). A full list and discussion of the sources that Blundell used can be found at G. Baker, 'The Political and Cultural Worlds of William Blundell (1620–1698), A Seventeenth-Century English Catholic Gentleman' (PhD Thesis, Keele University, 2007), pp. 298–392.

62 Baker, 'Political and Cultural Worlds of William Blundell', pp. 298–392.

63 Adversaria, fol. 1; Drexel, *Aurifodina Artium et Scientiarum Omnium*, p. 183.

64 Blair, 'Note taking', pp. 98–100, quotation at p. 100.

65 Blair, 'Note taking', p. 101. A single mention to an index survives, when Blundell stated that more information about a topic could be found by looking up the title 'in the Index of these Adversaria's'. However, subsequent comments as well as the fact that this is the sole reference to an index, suggest Blundell is referring to headers in the margin as opposed to a separate volume indexing the commonplace books: Adversaria, fol. 389.

66 Historica, fol. 46b.

67 Historica, fol. 14b.

68 L. Jardine and A. Grafton, '"Studied for action": how Gabriel Harvey read his Livy', *Past and Present*, 129 (1990), pp. 45–6. This was also the case with William Drake: Sharpe, *Reading Revolutions*, p. 184.

69 Historica, fols 16, 17b.

70 Adversaria, fol. 8b.

71 Adversaria, fol. 363.

72 William Blundell to Robert Scarisbrick, 10 March 1692, in Draft Letter Book, IV, fol. 55b.

73 Historica, fol. 145; S. Pallavicino, *Istoria del Concilio di Trento* (Rome, 1657).

74 Adversaria, fol. 388b; Historica, fol. 141b.

75 A full list of the works referred to can be found in Baker, 'Political and Cultural Worlds of William Blundell', pp. 298–392.

76 V. Larminie, *Wealth, Kinship and Culture: The Seventeenth Century Newdigates of Arbury and their World*, Royal Historical Society Studies in History, 72 (Woodbridge: Boydell, 1995), pp. 146–50.

77 See the example of the Godly Minister Ralph Josselin who 'acquired Catholic theology, even praising a work by Bellarmine on raising the spirit closer to God as a "pretty discourse"': Sharpe, *Reading Revolutions*, pp. 283–4.

78 I am grateful to Brian Whitlock-Blundell for discussion about the books extant at Crosby Hall.

79 English College of Doway, *The Holie Bible Faithfully Translated into English out of the Authentical Latin*, 2 vols (1609). The volumes referred to here are held in Crosby Hall.

80 I am grateful to Philip Burton for supplying me with photographs of this text. The volume referred to is part of his personal collection: A. Ortelius, *An Epitome of Ortelius his Theater of the World* (1601).

81 P. Clark, 'The ownership of books in England, 1560–1640: the example of some Kentish townsfolk', in L. Stone (ed.), *Schooling and Society: Studies in the History of Education* (London: Johns Hopkins University Press, 1976), p. 97.

82 Small Account Book, fols 43, 46, 49.

83 Based on the average cost of a folio being 7–10*s* and an octavo 1–4*s* unbound: D. Finkelstein and A. McCleery, *An Introduction to Book History* (London: Routledge, 2005), p. 111.

84 Small Account Book, fol. 51b.

85 Small Account Book, fol. 50b. For early modern pamphlets see Raymond, *Pamphlets and Pamphleteering*.

86 Hodge Podge the Third, fol. 10b.

87 William Blundell to Edward Scarisbrick, 14 July 1677, in Letter Book One, fols 105b–6.

88 Historica, fol. 63b, 95b.

89 William Blundell to Francis Waldegrave, 18 April 1678; William Blundell to Francis Waldegrave, 25 April 1678; William Blundell to Roger Bradshaigh, 19 May 1679, in Draft Letter Book, III, fols 11b, 13, 42; William Blundell to Bridget Blundell, 22 December 1693, in Draft Letter Book, IV, fol. 72b. Blundell's notes indicate significant knowledge of London booksellers. See his comment that one book he used 'was 'a notable small book printed in ocatavo at London in 1691 for Tymothy Child at the white hart in St Paul's Church yard (I think he is since remov'd to the Unicorn there) . Historica, fols 197–8b.

90 William Blundell to Robert Scarisbrick, 10 March 1692, in Draft Letter Book, IV, fols 55b–6.

91 Adversaria, fols 240, 313b; S. J. Guscott, *Humphrey Chetham 1580–1653: Fortune, Politics and Mercantile Culture in Seventeenth Century England*, Chetham Society, 3rd Series, 45 (2003).

92 William Blundell to Abel Swall, 6 July 1693; William Blundell to Abel Swall, 17 August 1693; William Blundell to Abel Swall, 9 March 1694, in Draft Letter Book, IV, fols 65–b, 66b, 77b.

93 Historica, fol. 96; R. S., *A Collection of some of the Murthers and Massacres Committed on the Irish in Ireland since the 23d of October 1641* (1662).

94 William Blundell to Abel Swall, 6 July 1693, in Draft Letter Book, IV, fols 65–b.

95 Historica, fol. 113b.

96 Adversaria, fol. 128b. In this case it is likely that he bought the two texts bound together in the edition: J. Bramhall, *The Victory of Truth for the Peace of the Church to the King of Great Britain to Invite him to Embrace the Roman-Catholick Faith* (1653).

97 P. Beal, 'Shall I die?', *Times Literary Supplement* (3 January 1986), p. 13. I owe the discovery of this reference to M. W. Thomas, 'Reading and writing the renaissance commonplace book: a question of authorship', *Cardozo Arts and Entertainment Journal*, 10 (1992), p. 665.

98 P. S. Seaver, *Wallington's World: A Puritan Artisan in Seventeenth-Century London* (Stanford: Stanford University Press, 1985), p. 5.

99 Larminie, *Wealth, Kinship and Culture*, pp. 146–7.

100 Historica, fol. 28; F. Bacon, *The Historie of the Raigne of King Henry the Seventh* (1622).

101 For example: Historica, fols 68b, 125b, 134, 135; Bureau d'adresse et de Rencontre, *A General Collection of Discourses of the Virtuosi of France* (1664), p. 1.

102 For example: Historica, fols 53b, 61b, 65, 68; LCRO, DDBl acc. 6121, Box 3, 'The Touchstone of Truth'; Nieremberg, *Treatise of the Difference.*

103 Adversaria, fol. 358b; J. Mabillon, *Traité des Études Monastiques, Divisé en Trois Parties* (Paris, 1691).

104 One exception to this is Blundell's reference of Cicero's *Principa Latine Loquendi*, which he notes as 'Cicero Epis: translated by Dr Web'. This was probably an attempt to distinguish the volume he used from other versions of Cicero, as opposed to any stance on the issue of ownership of a text: Adversaria, fols 94, 139, 183, 210, 261; M. T. Cicero, *A Very Necessary and Profitable Entraunce to the Speakyng and Writyng of the Latin Tongue*

(1575). For the relationship between author and translator and the ownership of a text, see H. E. Wicker, 'Negotiating the reader: narrative strategies in the preface to *The Breviary of Britayne*', in G. Baker and A. McGruer (eds), *Readers, Audiences and Coteries in Early Modern England* (Newcastle: Cambridge Scholars Press, 2006), p. 86.

105 N. Kenny, 'Books in space and time: bibliomania and early modern histories of learning and "literature" in France', *MLQ: Modern Language Quarterly*, 61 (2000), p. 256.

106 Adversaria, fols 92, 234, 285b, 301; H. L'Estrange, *The Alliance of Divine Offices, Exhibiting all the Liturgies of the Church of England Since the Reformation as also the late Scotch Service-Book, with all their Respective Variations* (1659).

107 Historica, fol. 9b; L. Wadding, *The History of the Angelicall Virgin Glorious S. Clare* (1635).

108 Historica, fols 94, 145, 197; Adversaria, fols 52, 145, 287, 303, 329, 359b, 386b.

109 Historica, fol. 23b.

110 See, for example: Adversaria, fols 130, 145b, 162, 218b, 247b, 266b, 298, quotation at fol. 266b.

111 See, for example: Historica, fols 95, 126; Adversaria, fols 58, 101, 119, 161b, 189, 211, 238b, 239, 253b, 261.

112 Adversaria, fol. 373.

113 C. Cerdeira, 'Early modern English medical wills, book ownership, and book culture', *Canadian Bulletin of Medical History*, 12 (1995), pp. 429, 431.

114 Details of individual texts can be found in Baker, 'Political and Cultural Worlds of William Blundell', pp. 298–392.

115 Historica, fol. 59b.

116 In the Historica Blundell also quoted two distinct manuscript sources: Richard Bellings's *The History of the Irish Wars*, and an account of Prince Rupert's time as Commander of the Royalist fleet from an unnamed friend: Historica, fols 63b, 95b.

117 In the Adversaria Blundell quoted or fully transcribed eight poems. Unfortunately, he does not attribute a source, meaning they may have been copied from books, sent to him in manuscript or been recited to him.

118 See, for example: Historica, fols 12, 83b, 137; Adversaria, fols 13, 62b, 116b, 162b, 180, 227, 259b, 308b.

119 Historica, fol. 12.

120 Historica, fol. 73.

121 Adversaria, fol. 182.

122 Adversaria, fol. 196.

123 The high estimation with which Blundell accorded oral testimony reflected the contemporary perception that truth-telling was a central component of gentlemanly behaviour: S. Shapin, *A Social History of Truth: Civility and Science in Seventeenth-Century England* (London: University of Chicago Press, 1994), pp. 65–125.

124 Historica, fols 22–b; Plutarch, *The Lives of the Noble Grecians and Romains* (1631), pp. 220–41.

125 See, for example: Historica, fols 25b, 41b, 87, 134b; Adversaria, fols 3, 45, 103, 198b, 203, 241, 320b, 347.

126 Historica, fols 41b, 134b.

127 Historica, fol. 39b.

128 Historica, fol. 34b.

129 Historica, fol. 25b; J. Ray, *Observations Topographical, Moral, & Physiological made in a Journey Through Part of the Low-Countries, Germany, Italy, and France* (1673), p. 41.

130 A. Fox, 'Remembering the past in early modern England: oral and written tradition', *Transactions of the Royal Historical Society*, 6th Series, 9 (1999), p. 233; Cust, 'News and politics', p. 65; A. Fox and D. Woolf, 'Introduction', in A. Fox and D. Woolf (eds), *The Spoken Word: Oral Culture in Britain 1500–1850* (Manchester: Manchester University Press, 2002), pp. 4–8; A. Shell, *Oral Culture and Catholicism in Early Modern England* (Cambridge: Cambridge University Press, 2008), p. 13.

131 Adversaria, fol. 125b; Sergeant, *Sure-Footing*, p. 333.

132 Blair, 'Humanist methods', p. 545.

133 Blair, 'Note taking', p. 97.

134 Blair, 'Humanist methods', p. 547.

135 Adversaria, fol. 1. Both William Drake and Ben Jonson used similar metaphors to describe the way they engaged with texts, the former stating that particular texts he would 'chew and digest' and the latter pleading that the poet be 'not as a creature that swallows what it takes in crude raw or undigested; but that feeds with an appetite and hath a stomach to concoct, divide and turn all into nourishment'. Quotations cited and discussed in Sharpe, *Reading Revolutions*, p. 182.

136 See, for example, the summary of Philippe Avril's *Travels* that covers thirty-six single sides of folio: Historica, fols 161–78b; P. Avril, *Travels into Divers Parts of Europe and Asia, Undertaken by the French King's Order to Discover a New Way by Land into China* (1693).

137 Historica, fol. 183b.

138 Historica, fol. 139; G. S., *Anglorum Speculum, or The worthies of England, in Church and State* (1684), p. 65.

139 Historica, fol. 27b; N. Caussin, *The Holy Court in Three Tomes* (1634), I, p. 177.

140 Historica, fol. 111; A. C. Davila, *The Historie of the Civill Warres of France* (1647).

141 J. Rose, 'Rereading the English common reader: a preface to a history of audiences', *Journal of the History of Ideas*, 53 (1992), pp. 48–9.

142 S. Zwicker, 'The reader revealed', in S. Baron (ed.), *The Reader Revealed* (London: University of Washington Press, 2001), p. 15. See also H. Brayman Hackel, *Reading Material in Early Modern England: Print, Gender, and Literacy* (Cambridge: Cambridge University Press, 2005), p. 17.

143 Jardine and Grafton, 'Studied for action', pp. 30–78, quotation at p. 56.

144 Sharpe, *Reading Revolutions*, pp. 96, 101, 115–16, 120, 121–2, 126, 160, 170, 189, 217, 235, 239, 262–3, 306.

145 Sharpe, *Reading Revolutions*, p. 269, see also pp. 95, 105–6, 268, 276. This is evident in Drake's reading of Francis Bacon: 'Drake picks up Bacon the Machiavel and silences the Bacon who has a more conventional and optimistic perception of human nature and state'. Sharpe, *Reading Revolutions*, pp. 188, 267.

146 Seaver, *Wallington's World*, passim.

147 Barry, 'Literacy and literature', p. 86.

148 Burke, 'Ann Bowyer's commonplace book', 1.28.

149 C. Ginzburg, *The Cheese and the Worms: The Cosmos of a Sixteenth-Century Miller*, trans. J. Tedeschi and A. Tedeschi (London: Penguin, 1992), p. 36.

150 Sharpe, *Reading Revolutions*, p. 270.

151 See, for example: Historica, fols 14, 37b, 109b, 155, 184, 190b, 201b; Adversaria, fols 332b, 334, 336, 372b.

152 Sharpe, *Reading Revolutions*, p. 278, see also pp. 41, 181, 279, 283.

153 Historica, fols 16, 17b.

154 Sharpe, *Reading Revolutions*, p. 101; Larminie, *Wealth, Kinship and Culture*, pp. 146–50; Jardine and Grafton, 'Studied for Action', passim.

155 Lockridge, 'Individual literacy', p. 337.

156 Historica, fols 14–b.

157 Historica, fols 12b–22b.

158 See, for example: Historica, fols 22–b; Plutarch, *The Lives of the Noble Grecians and Romains*, pp. 220–41.

159 See Malcolm Smuts's discussion of Roman histories and their role in interpreting court-centred politics in early modern England: M. Smuts, 'Court-centred politics and the uses of Roman historians, c.1590–1630', in K. Sharpe and P. Lake (eds), *Culture and Politics in Early Stuart England* (Basingstoke: Macmillan, 1994), pp. 21–44.

160 Adversaria, fol. 50; Caussin, *The Holy Court*, I, p. 185.

161 Adversaria, fol. 333b; R. Rapin, *Oeuvres Diverses* (Amsterdam, 1686).

162 Historica, fol. 191.

163 Historica, fol. 184b.

164 Historica, fol. 185.

165 Historica, fol. 185.

166 Adversaria, fols 29, 94; T. May, *A Breviary of the History of the Parliament of England* (1680).

167 See, for example: Adversaria, fols 94–b, 148b–9.

168 Adversaria, fol. 183; R. Loveday, *Loveday's Letters, Domestick and Forreign* (1662).

169 Avril, *Travels into Divers Parts of Europe and Asia.*

170 Historica, fol. 161.

171 Adversaria, fol. 185.

172 Adversaria, fol. 373b; A. van Wicquefort, *L'Ambassadeur et ses Fonctions* (The Hague, 1681).

173 Historica, fol. 156b.

174 Historica, fol. 147.

175 Adversaria, fol. 55b; F. Strada, *De Bello Belgico The History of the Low-Countrey Warres* (1650).

176 William Blundell to Abel Swall, 6 July 1693; William Blundell to Abel Swall, 17 August 1693; William Blundell to Timothy Child, 17 October 1693; William Blundell to Abel Swall, 9 March 1694, in Draft Letter Book, IV, fols 65–b, 66b–7b, 69–70b, 78. It is likely that Blundell first heard about Abel Swall's reprinting of the work, which was apparently the first time the two had corresponded, through one of two printed advertisements: A. Swall, *Proposals for Printing by Subscription, Cambdens Britannia* (1693); A. Swall, *New Proposals for Printing by Subscription, Cambdens Britannia* (1693).

177 Adversaria, fols 292b, 374.

178 Historica, fol. 95b.

179 Historica, fols 103b, 110b, 113b.

180 Adversaria, fol. 387; *The Post Boy*, 349, 31 July 1697.

181 Adversaria, fol. 214.

182 Historica, fol. 177.

183 Historica, fols 23b, 24, 25b.

184 Historica, fols 141, 191; Adversaria, fol. 368.

185 Adversaria, fol. 333b; Rapin, *Oeuvres Diverses.*

186 Historica, fol. 145b.

187 Adversaria, fol. 55b; J. Drexel, *The Considerations of Drexelius Upon Eternity* (1663).

188 Adversaria, fol. 370.

189 Adversaria, fol. 373.

190 Adversaria, fols 77b, 147, 212b; Historica, fol. 54.

191 Historica, fol. 36; J. Howell, *Epistolae Ho-elianae Familiar Letters Domestic and Forren* (1650), II, pp. 1–2.

192 R. Cox, *Hibernia Anglicana, or, The History of Ireland from the Conquest Thereof by the English to this Present Time* (1692).

193 Historica, fol. 142; Cox, *Hibernia Anglicana*, III, p. 34.

194 Historica, fols 142–3.

195 Adversaria, fol. 343; *The Present State of Europe: or, the Historical and Political Monthly Mercury*, October 1695.

196 Adversaria, fol. 73; W. Prynne, *A Seasonable, Legal, and Historical Vindication of the Good Old Fundamental Liberties, Franchises, Rights, Properties, Laws, Government of all English Freemen* (1657).

197 Adversaria, fol. 216; D. Brevint, *Missale Romanum, or, The Depth and Mystery of the Roman Mass* (1684).

Chapter 4

Reading the confessional divide

Blundell's commonplace books demonstrate an overriding concern with exploring Catholicism, in both religious and historical terms. A number of entries suggest his religious beliefs, which included a commitment to many aspects of Catholic practice and his views on what constituted a life of virtue. However, while he was a committed believer, his religious identity was more complex than he presented in his correspondence, and his commonplace books show that he struggled with particular aspects of Catholicism. None the less, he regularly read and, on occasion, rewrote history to argue that Catholics were passive victims, overwhelmingly loyal to the monarchy. These entries were juxtaposed with adversarial readings of Protestant histories, in which he maintained that Protestants represented a subversive element within society. This was supported through the meticulous documentation of what Blundell perceived as providential events in which Protestants had been punished while Catholics flourished. Reading and note-taking provided Blundell with a forum in which to develop and maintain his religious beliefs, and it is through a study of his commonplace books that we are offered the most revealing insight into this aspect of his life.

I

Blundell was an enthusiastic supporter of many areas of Catholic belief and practice, seen in the accumulation of commonplace entries that supported a commitment to mass, praised the leadership of the Catholic Church provided by the Pope and demonstrated an attachment to the Rosary as a tool for effective prayer.[1] One of Blundell's most obvious concerns was the Virgin Mary. He meticulously detailed comments on her life, noting at one stage that 'This present Octobr 1683 I have begun to read the New Testement & I propos to note the places where mention is made of our Bd Lady', which is followed by a list of references.[2] Blundell also constructed a defence for transubstantiation, listing instances in the Bible where Jesus had performed similar miracles, and providing a detailed summary of the 1666 French text *La Perpetuite de la Foy de L'Eglise Catholique Touchant L'Eucharistie*, which sought to undermine Protestant attacks on transubstantiation.[3]

Like most Catholics Blundell praised what he considered the virtues of virginity and marriage: his commonplaces regularly included authors who noted the same, such as Jeremy Taylor's *Great Exemplar*, from which he quoted the passage '*Ther is a Good & a Better in Virginity & Marriage*', though Blundell did not remark on which he viewed as the greater.[4] He was particularly averse to blasphemy, noting that 'He that blasphemes the name of the Lord dying let him dy', a view that facilitated his barely concealed joy when noting from Ephraim Pagitt's *Heresiography* that William Hacket, 'that blasphemous monster ... the first that brought into the world the execrations God Dame me: God confound me body & soul', was executed during the reign of Elizabeth.[5] His commonplace books also include musings on purgatory, such as the list of 'the best and the briefest arguments for Purgatory taken out of scripture', which he compiled himself, and a note on the *Question of Questions* where he claimed 'the doctrine of purgatory ... is most clearly proved'.[6] Part of Blundell's motivation for recording this material on purgatory and the nature of sinning appears to have been a fear of the Devil as much as a love of God. The Devil was a very real presence for Blundell; it appeared regularly in the stories of sin discussed above and his record of a Latin verse read backwards by a woman exorcised of the Devil through baptism.[7] This concern with the Devil was shared by many of Blundell's contemporaries on either side of the confessional divide: both Protestants and Catholics partook in anti-diabolic prayers. The major difference between the two was that Catholics emphasised 'temptation as an event rather than a condition of life' and anti-diabolic prayers therefore aimed at 'the removal of diabolic affliction rather than at its management'.[8] Thus, Blundell's concern with the Devil and belief that sin could be eradicated reflected broader contemporary Catholic practice.

Blundell highlighted the virtues of an unworldly religious life, saving particular praise for hermits. In his frequent recording of these accounts one may suspect that he was disappointed that he could not live in a more unworldly manner, giving up not only material possessions, but also his insatiable quest for knowledge. He recorded favourably that St Benedict spent his younger years as a hermit, so far removed from both people and books that he did not know when it was Easter.[9] Merely seeing a hermit could bring an individual closer to God, as Blundell noted in his account of how a man was converted to Christianity 'by seeing a monk eat wild Rootes' and two courtiers took religious orders having viewed a group of hermits reading.[10] He also regularly alluded to the moral lives of many religious, drawing selectively on praise for religious communities from historians and divines, including William Camden and Peter Heylyn.[11] This focus on religious life was reflected in his own concerns with avoiding sin, seen in a series of entries entitled 'Sententiae morales' and 'Sententiae Piae' where he recorded the thoughts of divine thinkers on morality, how to avoid sin and how to live a pious life.[12] However, Blundell's commonplace notes also identify areas of tension in his beliefs.

II

Blundell was wary of practical failings that prevented him from being a good Catholic, fearing that he was not intellectually capable of theological debate. For instance, writing on Pallavicino's history of the Council of Trent, he recorded that 'I question my own ability, whether I do rightly understand these matters, as well as some other higher points which are handled in our Authors work'.[13] He noted that he was not alone and that the Apostles could not understand aspects of scripture until Jesus explained them, while Augustine admitted that large sections of scripture were beyond his comprehension.[14] Blundell took steps to resolve this, regularly rereading the Bible and recording a method to remember the Apostles' writings, whereby a verb stood for the content of the events contained in each chapter.[15] Though Blundell left few clues as to his religious practices, he spent significant time praying throughout his life. In a brief note in the Adversaria on adverse weather conditions in 1697, written when Blundell was seventy-seven, he recorded that 'I was sitting in my chamber, over the hall at Crosby, with my face directly to the southwest casement there and being then at my prayer I did not make such observations as I might otherwise have done'.[16] None the less, his notes also include comprehensive instructions for what 'those persons ought to do in the time of prayer who by reason of their wandring fancyes cannot fix their minds long upon good thoughts', though we are not told whether these excerpts were for his own use.[17] This was not the only area in which Blundell fell short of the religious persona that he sought to present to the world.

The most striking revelation in Blundell's commonplace books is his scepticism about particular aspects of Catholicism. In a discussion of Nieremberg's work on miracles of the Passion of Christ, Blundell recorded that 'I do observe that bad Christians disbelieve and scorn such storyes, that cold Christians (such as I am) do doubt of the truth of them & that the devinest & best men do seem to believe them'.[18] Unfortunately Blundell does not elaborate on what it meant to be a 'cold Christian', though it is perhaps worth noting that, despite assiduously recommending religious orders for his children, he never seems to have countenanced them for himself. None the less, it is clear that Blundell was often frustrated that his approach to the world obstructed unquestioning belief and that he struggled to believe all that was in the Bible as the 'devinest & best men do', a struggle that can be identified throughout his notes.

Although Blundell held that the religious life was an ideal that all should aspire to, he frequently noted the failings of individual clergy. He recorded, without further comment, how one 'Jesuit stark mad, killd with a knif 3 of the Chief Fathers' in 1574 and how again in 1577 another member of the order killed a Jesuit 'with a penknif'.[19] Blundell also noted his own observations of lapses in clerical behaviour. In an account of family celebrations for the conception of the Virgin Mary in 1664, he stated that he spoke to his 'spiritual director' about the possibility of saying the Rosary together, but the priest (most probably Francis Waldegrave) refused, stating that he had 'weak health and finding that such excercises did spend him'. On returning later in the day he discovered that the priest had 'spent the most part of the afternoone of that holy day in playing tables and shovell board in the Dyning roome and in the hall'.[20]

Blundell's commonplace entries demonstrate a marked sympathy for the arguments of Jean Mabillon (1632–1707), the Benedictine scholar whose works caused controversy throughout the Catholic world. Mabillon developed an enquiry-based approach to historical religious events whereby every aspect of a story was questioned, most notably its evidentiary basis.[21] The most controversial aspect of his work was his challenge of the veneration of the lives of certain saints. He was frequently called to defend himself and was widely condemned by elements of the Catholic Church.[22] Blundell was keen to note of Mabillon's 1691 work, *Traité des Études Monastiques*, that 'I have read the whole consisting of 478 pages'.[23] Mabillon's work appears to have accorded with Blundell's approach to religious history, and he noted that in the text there were 'good things concerning the usefullness of history even for Religious persons and especially for Divines, which ought not indeed to be so called if they be not conversant in history'.[24] He was particularly sympathetic to Mabillon's criticisms of the way Catholic divines had approached history, and in a brief entry spoke favourably of his arguments on the saints' lives, noting that his work 'has some things worth reading ... especially & more particularly against some legends of Saints printed in these later times where we should not much regard an infinite number of storyes'.[25] Indeed, Mabillon's approach to religious history was one that Blundell had developed long before reading his work, seen most clearly in his reading of miracle stories.

Throughout the Adversaria there are large sections entitled 'Miracula', which include discussions on all aspects of miracles.[26] Interestingly these are all in Blundell's hand, perhaps suggesting that he did not want anyone, even his trusted servant Thelwall, to see his controversial musings on this topic. Blundell's definition of what constituted a miracle was based on a direct quotation from the *General Collection of Discourses of the Virtuosi of France*, where he stated that 'A *miracle* is defined (as I understand it) to be an Effect, wherof no naturall caus is seen'.[27] Blundell accepted the occurrence of many miracles. He credited all miracles found in scripture as truth, recording that Hugo Grotius's *Of God* 'proveth the truth of the mirackles mentioned in Scripture'.[28] His notes also positively relayed the story that on the same day that the English received Christianity, so the country received the first rain in three years, ending a famine.[29] Blundell held that miracles could still happen, alluding to a recent 'wonderfull authentick story of one returned from death' and emphasising the importance of making pilgrimages to shrines to seek healing.[30] Though not every one would return from such a pilgrimage in a fit state, he noted that this was also the case in John 5 where 'one only was cured although many waited for cure'.[31]

Though he accepted that miracles could still happen, Blundell's commonplaces indicate a marked scepticism about many modern-day accounts. He noted that he was not alone in this belief, alluding to incidents where worthy individuals had disputed the legitimacy of certain miracle stories. For instance, he recorded Gideon's restraint, in Judges 6, noting 'what great caution Gedeon used to find out the truth of such signes & mirackles as God had wrought before he would wholy rely on them'.[32] In part, this was motivated by Blundell's quest to add credibility to his own questioning of miracles, which on his account caused offence to many of his co-religionists. Following a relation of how the Jesuit Louis Maimbourg disputed a list of contemporary miracles as 'fables', Blundell recorded that 'I beleeve in case I had rejected the same but in table talk and on no better grounds then Maimburg gives, I should have given great offence to pious & learned Catholicks, as I have to often don upon much less ocation of the very same nature'.[33] Blundell had a proclivity for causing his co-religionists such upset during 'table talk', the most striking example being his questioning of the story of Ursula and her eleven thousand virgins: 'I think I gave great offence to a learned Priest Mr ____ A by saying that I doubted whether every one of the reputed 11000 virgins & martyres were virgins or no. He seem'd to beleeve most certainly & to think that I ought to beleeve that they were all virgins, becaus the church calls them so.'[34] While the examples of Mabillon and Maimburg show that Blundell was not alone in questioning certain miracle stories, particularly that of St Ursula which was questioned by Catholic intellectuals from the medieval period onwards, it is striking with what contempt he dismissed them as 'silly fables'.[35]

Though Blundell was to note that 'Hereticks have often wrought miracles in proufe of Christianity', his main target was the work of St Augustine.[36] As modern-day scholars have noted, Augustine included any form of miracle story that supported his point, a matter frequently observed in the Adversaria.[37] Blundell began a scathing attack on Augustine's work with a quotation from the chronicler Richard Baker, in which he recorded simply that 'Baker saith St Augustine gave credit to many Lying Mirackles'.[38] He continued with his own notes on Augustine's *Of the Citie of God* where he stated, 'see there ... very many stupendious miracles with the reising of 4 dead persons chiefly by the Reliques of or devotion to St Steven'.[39] Blundell's concern over the false recounting of miracle stories was motivated by his understanding of their importance. He noted that they 'are in some sort said to be of greater credit than the verbal testimony of the Apostles or even of Christ himself', later concluding that the high regard they were held in was due to them being 'the Extra ordinary effect of the hand of God'.[40] As such Blundell's adversarial readings of many latter-day miracles was motivated by his overriding belief that 'I think it is less damage to Christianity if we conceil 100 tru mirackles than if we publish one fals one'.[41]

Protestant propaganda frequently criticised Catholic use of miracles, claiming that miracles had ceased since Biblical times, and later accounts were 'paradigms of popish deceit'.[42] In response there was some initial effort by Counter Reformation forces to stem the hunger for miracles, but in England, where geographical isolation from continental Europe meant their arguments could be ignored, many remained attached to such accounts of supernatural intervention.[43] Indeed, recent research has challenged the notion that Tridentine Catholicism distanced itself from miracles, instead arguing that in post-Reformation England both Jesuits and secular priests 'harnessed supernatural power in their attempts to combat heresy, reinforce contested tenets, reclaim backsliders, and win converts to their cause', using miracles as 'proselytizing tools'.[44] They frequently appeared in accounts of martyrs' deaths, thaumaturgic wonders linked to material objects and exorcisms. Tridentine Catholicism did not deny the occurrence of contemporary miracles, it wanted to bring them under control.[45] At first glance Blundell's approach to miracles may appear to accord more comfortably with the Protestant perspective, which sought 'to align itself with the forces of enlightenment and knowledge'.[46] However, as with other areas of his life, Blundell's approach was idiosyncratic and cannot be pigeonholed as belonging to any one category of thought. Certainly he was sceptical about the occurrence of modern miracles, and as we will see he did not ascribe natural wonders to the supernatural. However, his belief that God regularly punished Protestants suggests that his approach to the supernatural was informed by a range of factors.

In a detailed investigation of providential belief in early modern England from the mid-sixteenth to the mid-seventeenth century, Walsham has shown that the belief that God regularly intervened in the world was not the preserve of zealous Protestants. Instead it was found amongst different groups of Protestants and on either side of the confessional divide: 'Providentialism was not a marginal feature of the religious culture of early modern England, but part of the mainstream, a cluster of presuppositions which enjoyed near universal acceptance'.[47] However, as Warren Johnston has argued, while it is held that 'questions of prophecy, providence and scriptural sanction carried enormous intellectual import in the 1640s and 1650s, it is often supposed that these factors disappeared as issues of consequence later in the century'.[48] Indeed, Walsham's work finishes in the 1640s, emphasising the increasingly divisive impact that belief in providential intervention had on English Protestants. Johnston has shown, however, that apocalyptic interpretations of events remained in vogue amongst Protestants after 1660, forming a central aspect of how contemporaries understood and justified the Revolution of 1688.[49] For Catholics, belief in providential intervention played a particular role, helping to shore up the beliefs of those who were victims of temporal punishment, relations of such divine intervention being 'designed to dint Protestant pride and inflame Catholic zeal'.[50] It was for this reason that Blundell collected such accounts of divine intervention, which he scrupulously detailed in his commonplace books.

Blundell's notes on history regularly implied providential intervention. For example, in notes on William Rufus, which were recorded in three separate entries based on his reading of Francis Godwin's *Catalogue of the Bishops of England* and Michael Alford's *Fides Regia Britannica*, Blundell wrote that 'King William Rufus was slayne by the glade of an arrow in the forrest for the making of which he had thrown down 30 churches. He was otherwaies very sacralegious.'[51] His commonplaces also include a folio-long list of providential events taken from Nicolas Caussin's *The Holy Court*, and his record of 'A whole Town, with men, Beasts, trees and all things turned into ston ... which is said to be the judgment of God for the unnatural & horrid sins of the people'.[52] This was a theme that Blundell returned to, and amongst his notes from *The Adventures of Mr T. S.* he recorded the author's account of finding in Africa a man turned to stone whilst in the unfortunate act of 'Buggering his Ass, which were by the Inhabitants ... affirmed to have been transmuted in the beastly act'.[53] Blundell's notes show that he believed such events continued to the present day. While his Protestant contemporaries were ascribing responsibility for the 1666 Fire of London to Jesuit conspirators, in a brief entry on the fire of Troy Blundell compared the two, noting that 'Troy had never offended the King nor the Gods. London had greevously offended both & therfore it was punished first by a warr at sea then by a rageing plague & the next year after by a fire which consum'd it from one side to the other.'[54] Blundell was no doubt motivated to make this claim to contest allegations that Catholics were responsible for the fire.[55] These notes on providence were not random entries illustrating God's power, but in most cases were organised in a specific manner with a specific aim.

In a series of entries entitled 'Judicia in Catholicotum hostes' ('Justice for the Enemyes of Catholicism'), Blundell detailed worldly events in which he believed God had deliberately intervened to punish those who obstructed Catholicism. The sources for the majority of these accounts were records of conversations that Blundell had with his friends, or transcriptions of correspondence. Many of these ideas never appeared in print, suggesting their sensitive nature. They included notes on incidents concerning individuals who had benefited from, or in some way aided, the dissolution of the monasteries or destruction of church property. Examples include, 'the tragicall and untymely death of the Duke of Somerset ... after he had built Somerset house upon many most Sacrilegious ruines' or the account of the Puritan minister who pulled down a cross and used the stone to make a well, only to find that 'his wife and sondry of his children became blynd & he drowned himself in the same well'.[56] In the Historica Blundell cross-referenced to an entry he mistakenly wrote in the Great Hodge Podge, in which he recorded that the First Viscount Scudamore had removed a marble altar from Abbey Dore to his home to press cheeses on. Unfortunately the cheese pressed there ran with blood and a continual banging sound was heard from the altar at night until Scudamore returned it to the Abbey.[57] Blundell also recorded incidents concerning individuals who had an impact on his own life, noting, for instance, how a local man named Edward Moore 'fell dead upon the road. He was a great persecutor & notorious.'[58] Such providential judgements extended to sequestrators, and Blundell recorded that 'The horrid Judgements upon sequestrators, commity men and farmours of Cathlicks Estates hath been remarkable'.[59] To support this he juxtaposed these stories with Biblical accounts in which similar apocalyptic acts had occurred. For example, he noted that, in Daniel 5, King Belshazzar was 'drinking with his Concubins &c in the sacred vessels which had beene taken from the Temple, was warned at the same tyme of his destruction, by a hand from heaven. And the same night he was slayn.'[60] However, while Blundell retold such stories to exemplify the righteousness of the Catholic religion and the errors of Protestantism, these beliefs also posed a problem.

Despite Blundell's belief that he was a follower of the true church who had been loyal to the monarchy, at various times he had been imprisoned, fined and had his estates confiscated; he was also left partially disabled during a battle, while many of his enemies prospered. This problem was dispatched in a single entry in his commonplace books. Though he noted that 'Those Judgments which God doth send dayly upon his Enemyes, espetially upon the Persecutors of the Catholick church, are most evident and numberable', he remarked that 'some strange disposalls of the Divine providence have hapened which carry the appearance of a quite contrary nature'. For this reason he saw fit to note down a list 'espetially of the Antient tymes, which may shew us if the like should happen now, that God hath sent us the same visitations which he sent to his Antient friends and faithfull servants'.[61] Thus,

Blundell sought to show that God had treated worthy individuals throughout time in the same way Blundell and his Catholic contemporaries were being treated in the seventeenth century. The main focus of these entries was Bede's *History of the Church of England*, from which Blundell noted the story of Edwin the first Christian King of Northumberland who was killed in battle while a young man, losing not only his life but also his two sons and his whole army. Within a year the Christian King Oswald took the throne, after which he was 'killed in Battle in the prime of his age against Infidells and his Armes cut from his body'.[62] Therefore, while the belief that God intervened in worldly affaires on behalf of Catholicism may have been a necessary component in maintaining Blundell's religious strength, his entries show that he was also capable of adversarial interpretations of such accounts. This approach to aspects of Catholic belief was taken not only to miracles outside scripture but also to the text of the Bible itself.

Reminding us that the Bible, like other texts, was subject to the interpretations of the reader, the Adversaria houses a number of sections entitled 'Scriptura Difficultis', the primary focus of which is the 'many appearing incongruityes' in the Bible.[63] Under this heading Blundell recorded a range of contradictions. This included 'that grand difficulty not to be cleared' in Genesis 11:12 where it is claimed that Arphaxad begot Sale, 'yet St Luke &c: placeth Cainan betwixt them, as the father of Sale and the Son of Arphaxad'.[64] Or the example in Matthew 23:9 where the reader is told 'Call no man father upon the earth', yet in Matthew 19:5 it is recorded that 'Man *shall* leave father & mother & cleave to his wife'.[65] Examples of contradictions in the sense of an argument are frequent, including the note that in 'John 3:2 it said plainly that Jesus baptized: yet chp: 4:2 it is sayd *Jesus did not baptize but his disciples*'.[66] However, of most concern to Blundell were examples from scripture where worthy individuals blatantly defied Biblical teachings, including the statement in Matthew 5 'Not to resist evil, to turne the other cheeke, to give to him that asketh', which he juxtaposed to Matthew 10:34, 'I came not to send peace, but the sword'.[67] The note that Galatians 5 recorded that 'If you be circumcised Christ will profit you nothing', though Acts 16:3 stated that Paul took Timothy to be circumcised, is repeated on two separate occasions.[68] Furthermore, Blundell gave examples of instances when individuals in the Bible claimed to have seen God's face, noting that 'Altho' it is els where sayd that one canot see God and live, yet it seems by sondry texts that he hath been seen by mortall eyes'.[69] Blundell also regularly drew attention to occasions when prophecies were not foretold, such as the claim in Exodus 9:6 that 'All the beasts of the Ægiptians dyed', which was juxtaposed with 'v10 there were made Boyles in men & *beasts*. And ch 14 v23 Pharao's horse were drowned. So that it seemes that some beasts were left alive.'[70] Blundell also turned to history to expose the failure of prophecy, seen in his notes on Ezekiel 26:7 which state that

Nebuchadnezzar would destroy Tyre so that it could never be rebuilt, 'Then how come it to be besieged long after by Alexander the Great?'[71] Furthermore, he found that the Bible regularly contradicted reason, most notably in the claim in Genesis 1 that God created light before he created the sun.[72] Finally, he questioned the morality of certain entries in the Bible, asking how God could have permitted the Jews, his chosen people, to fall, and the revealing personal reflection at the end of a section on sin, 'How coms an Infants *Soul* to be infected with original sin?'[73]

Blundell's notes on the Bible are most commonly juxtapositions of conflicting accounts, with little or no discussion. The nearest he came to directly criticising it was in his statement in a discussion of the New Testament that 'Ther seems to be much differrence in the 4 Gospells, concerning Christs bearing of his Cross, concerning the tyme and other circumstances of his Resurrection, & the like concerning St Peters deniall of Christ before the Cock crow once, twice &c'.[74] On only one occasion did Blundell speculate on the reasons for this, in a half-hearted allusion to the possibility that the errors that he listed were a result of problems in translation.[75] On the whole he steered clear of any speculation as to the reason for errors in the Bible, apparently believing it was his failure for even noticing such contradictions, holding that only 'the devinest & best men' would unquestioningly accept all that is contained within the text.[76] These 'Scriptura Difficultis' sections also highlight a further use of the commonplace books. His critical views of the world, seen in the way he approached his reading, were incompatible with the unquestioning approach to the Bible that was required of him by his faith. However, as outlined in modern-day works on dissonance theory, any outlet of such feeling can work to smooth over these beliefs.[77] In Blundell's case, it is as though writing down the contradictions that he noted with little or no further discussion, helped address his doubts, aiding him to expel feelings of religious inferiority. In this sense, as we have seen, the commonplaces may have offered a form of confessional.

III

The commonplace books may also have played a further role, helping Blundell deal with his feelings on controversial issues that were splitting contemporary Catholicism. There are some parallels here with Puritan works. Nehemiah Wallington's writings were 'given to endless and searching introspection' and he regularly considered the specific beliefs and areas of contention between different Protestant groups, reassuring himself that his was the correct interpretation of Christianity.[78] Throughout Blundell's surviving correspondence there is little engagement with any of the issues that were dividing English Catholics. However, his commonplace books provide some important, if brief, insights into his position on central divisive issues, most notably his attitude towards church papistry, his position on the divide between secular and regular clergy and his interpretation of the controversial work of Thomas White.

Although Blundell was an open recusant, we have already seen that he corresponded with church papists.[79] However, as was the case with his relations with Protestants, Blundell could befriend individuals while disapproving of their religious and political beliefs. Throughout the late sixteenth and early seventeenth centuries, the English Catholic population was divided over church papistry. Many clergy took a hard line against what they perceived as a desertion of the true religion.[80] On the other hand, as casuistry gathered strength, there was an increasing fear that condemnation of occasional conformity might push church papists into fully embracing Protestantism, and through the seventeenth century the hard stance against church papists eased. An examination of Blundell's commonplaces suggests that while in public he may have appeared sympathetic, in private he held that occasional conformity was a betrayal of Catholicism. Only two entries consider church papistry, both of which are overwhelmingly negative. The first is a generic note on conformity under which Blundell recorded 'See the notable observation out of St Agust: &c which shews the unlawfulnesse of Goeing to the Heretical Service'.[81] That the sentiments expressed in this passage reflected Blundell's own opinion is evident in a brief note in the Historica, where he recorded that 'My Ld Stourton a Church Papist, kept two priests in his house, that one might be sure to be ready in case he were sick'. Unfortunately for Stourton he died before receiving the attention of either priest. In light of this they agreed to pray for his soul, during which 'the person defunct appeared begging in his prayers & shewing his syde burnt with the fyre of Purgatory'.[82] That Blundell recorded this account under the heading 'Serious Repentance' suggests that he viewed the event as indicative of Stourton's sin and an indictment of church papistry.[83]

Notes in Blundell's commonplace books also reveal his views on the division between regular and secular clergy. Blundell was clearly not averse to regular clergy: two of his sons became Jesuits, as were many of his friends and family. His commonplace books contain numerous entries praising the Jesuits, epitomised in his quotation from Peter Heylyn's *Cosmographie* that 'they are now the greatest Politicians soundest scholers & chiefest upholders of the Romish see; so that the only way to reestablish the Romish Religion in any land is to plant a Colledge of Jesuits in it'.[84] Blundell also recorded, contrary to the arguments of their detractors, that 'The Jesuites are forbid ... to meddle with affayres of state'.[85] None the less, though a supporter of the Jesuits he never became intellectually embroiled in the issues arising from the Archpriest Controversy.[86] The absence of such material from his letters seemingly reflected his view that this was not an issue that should concern

Catholics. Instead, he believed that any division between secular and regular clergy was a result of Protestant machinations, as suggested in his notes on the reign of Elizabeth, where he claimed that 'shee had choyce intelligence, the incomparable arts of ... Bancroft, a jovial cunning Bishop of Canterbury, who divided the Catholick clergie and the Regulars'.[87] According to Blundell, enquiry into Jesuit activities in England revealed that, far from obstructing the secular cause, the Jesuits had aided it. This was supported with a quotation from a letter written by the Archpriest George Blackwell, as recorded in Henry More's history of the Society, 'wherein he giveth such prayses to the Jesuites in England as are truly high & wonderfull & shewes that they are so far from seeking to have superiority that they do most charitably, and at great expence, assist and comfort the clergy ... extolling their virtuous lives & hopes the Cardinall will punish those envious persons who goe about to blemish their reputations'.[88] This, of course, could be interpreted as a standard Jesuit line, maintaining that the controversy was the product not of principled disagreement but instead of faction whipped up by the regime. However, Blundell was not so dismissive of the other major division during this period surrounding Thomas White.

Thomas White (alias Blacklow) was a controversial Catholic philosopher. One-time president of the English College in Lisbon, by the mid-1630s he had left the post to concentrate on writing. His emphasis on passive obedience to any government meant that his followers became 'Notorious for their willingness to sacrifice Jesuits and any papal temporal powers in return for religious toleration'.[89] White's work provided a particular focus for Blundell's notes as the disparaging of the Tridentine papacy promoted a national English Church, forcing a renewal of the divide between secular and regular clergy.[90] As with other material that Blundell disagreed with, he was not critical of all White's work, noting with approval his position on the nature of disputations.[91] This exception aside, Blundell's brief notes on White, under the title 'Blacklous', were scathing in their criticism.[92] Unfortunately Blundell referred to an entry in another of his notebooks that cannot be identified, where he claimed that one could find 'the condemnation of all his Bookes'.[93] None the less, an analysis of his surviving commonplaces provides a good indication of the areas of White's work that caused him most offence.

It appears that, with the exception of *Monumetham Excantatus*, most of Blundell's information about White came not from the original sources but from citations in George Leyburn's *Encyclical Answer*.[94] Naturally for an individual with such close connections to regular clergy, White's criticisms were not esteemed by Blundell whose commonplaces recorded simply that 'He is bitter against the Jesuites'.[95] Blundell also took issue with his arguments for passive obedience, made in *Grounds of Obedience and Government*.[96] Using Leyburn's account, Blundell recorded a number of White's points that offended him including a non-specific reference to 'a most horrid one' and the argument that 'If a magistrate be inocent and wrongfully dispossessed, he is obleeged absolutly to renounce all right and clayme to Government: and if he does not, he is worsse then an Infidell'.[97] Written after Cromwell's ascension to power, White's *Grounds* called for individuals to accept Cromwell's *de facto* position, a distasteful notion to any ardent Royalist.[98] Not content with recording only Leyburn's criticism of White's work, Blundell also included his own musings on White's morality, noting that a number of priests had been entrusted to the supervision of White, 'but he applyeth the money to his privat ends'.[99] The brief section on this topic was concluded, in two separate entries, with a smug note that 'It is a great matter of much edification to see the great sylence of Mr Blacklo's party since the censure of his works [by the Pope]'.[100]

IV

The final area of Blundell's notes on religion to be considered concerns his musings on the differences between the Protestant and Catholic churches. The comparatively slight emphasis that he gave to religious differences reflected his view that the primary motives for acceptance of 'Luther's heresy' were political.[101] His notes suggest an awareness that there were some problems in the pre-Reformation church, most notably the granting of indulgences, seen in his brief entry on the life of Pope Boniface IX 'who lived Anno 1400 [and] gave great scandal by granting Generall Indulgence to freely, wherby he got money with which to enrich his kindred'.[102] However, in his notes on Pallavicino's history of the Council of Trent he recorded that Luther and later Protestant theologians received support from 'sundry ... princes & powerful men' in Germany and elsewhere 'For many of them seized on great quantityes of Land which belong'd to the church'.[103] He claimed that the Reformation had nothing to do with religious issues and was merely a result of 'policy of state' interfering with 'points of religion'.[104]

In his commonplace books Blundell was keen to reduce the religious differences between Protestants and Catholics. A number of entries refer to Protestants who had highlighted the sound religious nature of Catholicism, such as the record that James I had stated that 'I acknowledge the church of Rome to be our mother church'.[105] Blundell also drew attention to similarities in scripture. Certainly, on a number of occasions he alluded to differences, recording, for example, that the 'Booke of Job is far differently translated by Chatholicks and protestants allmost in every lyne'.[106] However, he put many of the differences down to problems in translation, noting that 'Mat 19 v5. The Protestants translate *they twaine* of the two. I note it to shew how soone a vulgar language doth change'.[107] To support his argument that these differences were the result of incorrect Protestant translations Blundell compared two Protestant Bibles, recording how he compared 'Fulks text (which he printeth in his answer to the Rhemist) with the byble printed at London for Wm Bentley 1646. They do frequently differ much.'[108] Instead Blundell's notes concentrated on the similarities. In a note from Isaac Basier's scathing history of the Presbyterians, Blundell recorded that John Calvin 'seemeth to approve of the English prayer Booke'.[109] Elsewhere he quoted the Protestant Peter Heylyn, claiming that his work showed that 'the Common prayer [was] little differing from the Latin Service'.[110] The only major religious difference between Protestants and Catholics that Blundell alluded to appeared in his notes on John Sergeant's *Sure-Footing*, in which he speculated that one of the primary differences was that Catholicism encouraged its followers to stick stringently to the laws, punishing only those who deviated from them. Protestants, conversely, 'punish those under them for following too close to that Rule which themselves recommended & applauded as the whole & sole Basis of their Reformation'.[111]

For Blundell the theological differences between Protestantism and Catholicism were surmountable and he was eager to discuss how this might be facilitated. From Richard Baxter's *Grotian Religion*, a text that Blundell was highly critical of, he recorded that 'ther was a designe (& favoured by K Ch: 1) to reconcile the English church to Rome &c'.[112] He found evidence that such a venture could work in a brief note taken from John Ray's *Observations*, which claimed that 'The towns of Glaris and Appenzel ... consist of Catholicks and Protestants which use the same churches for their several services'.[113] His motivation for highlighting the similarities in Protestant and Catholic scripture were indicated in his comment that 'If the doctrin ther delivered be sound, it cuts off a great part of our difficulty in dealing with Hereticks, by making the poynts of faith to be fewer much than they are commonly esteemed to be'.[114] Thus, he was concerned that Protestants need not be excluded fully by the Catholic Church because of their religious beliefs. Indeed, in a note on Thomas Browne's *Religio Medici*, Blundell claimed that Browne's view that heathens could not get salvation was 'very severe'.[115] However though prepared to overlook some of the religious differences between Catholics and Protestants, Blundell's views on what he saw as the political aspirations of Protestantism were a major concern that resulted in him rewriting the histories of both groups.

V

Like many of his contemporaries, Blundell approached history with a personal use in mind.[116] In his appropriation of religious and political histories, he sought to demonstrate the loyalty and virtue of Catholics and the subversive nature of Protestantism. This was where his adversarial readings were most marked, because of his belief in the overriding importance of history.

He emphasised the 'usefullness of history' in interpreting religion, claiming that one could be considered a Divine only if conversant with past events.[117] His notes include a number of philosophical reflections on the nature of history, such as Francis Bacon's comment that 'As *Statues* & pictures are dumb Historyes, so Historyes are speaking pictures'.[118] However, as we have already seen, Blundell was particularly concerned that much historical writing had been twisted by author bias, noting that 'Historyes of the present tyme are alwaies partiall'.[119] For this reason he tried to redress what he perceived as the imbalance of religious histories written during this period. Throughout his commonplace books he engaged with historical writing in an aggressive manner, distorting the meaning of authors' arguments, manipulating their material to counter their own position and writing diatribes against particular texts with which he disagreed. These efforts suggest that he believed the misrepresentation of English Catholic history was the main factor influencing their current position.

As was the case in his correspondence, in his reading and note-taking Blundell was anxious to portray English Catholics as a homogeneous group of passive victims. This involved the recording of occasions in the texts he read of 'persecution', and extended to a selective reading of history to demonstrate his point.[120] For instance, Blundell included a section of notes on the reign of Queen Mary based on Heylyn's history of the English Church, in which Bishop Bonner is described as that 'bloody Butcher' and Mary's reign as being 'polluted with the blood of so many Martyrs, unfortunate by the frequent insurrections, and made inglorious by the loss of the town of Calais ... only commendable in the brevity or shortness of it'.[121] However, Blundell ignored these hostile remarks to record that the total number of martyrs made during her reign amounted to *only* 277, noting, for instance, that 'In the Diocese of York none were brought to the stake but one at Chester; & many other places of England were as free'.[122] Blundell also twisted Heylyn's record that the only Protestant group to reject the English Protestants during Mary's reign were Lutherans; instead it was recorded as 'See p80 how very much the English Protestants were abhominated by the Lutherans. The Rigid Lutherans called those that suffered in England the Divells Martyrs.'[123] The way in which this was presented suggests that Blundell was trying to show that Mary was not the only person involved in the persecution of English Protestants, removing her as the sole focus for criticism and also suggesting that they deserved the treatment they received at her hands.

In a similar manner Blundell rewrote the history of the Catholic Inquisition. In his note from the anonymous Catholic text *The Politicians Catechisme*, in which the penal laws that English Catholics were subject to were compared with the Inquisition, Blundell commented on the legality and virtue of the Inquisition in comparison to what he viewed as the corrupt penal laws in

England. As he recorded, 'The Inquisition medleth not with those that never were Catholicks ... The Inquisition condems no Heretick to death but only declares their Heresy'.[124] He closed his brief notes on the Inquisition by quoting Andrew Marvell, an author usually considered an anti-Catholic.[125] In concluding with Marvell's words, 'The Inquisition hath lost its edg in the popish countryes, ther is little appearance it should be set up in England', it was suggested that not only was the Inquisition nothing to do with English Catholics, but it was also relegated to the distant past.[126] Blundell's commonplaces on this topic are exemplified in his statement that Catholics 'hate persecution'.[127]

The commonplace books also contain significant material on the history of Catholicism in England in more recent times. Writing on the Armada in his notes from Francis Obsourne's *Memoirs*, Blundell recorded that, during the Spanish attempt on England in 1588, 'ther was not one man here that appeared for the Spaniard. The very Papists themselves being no lesse unwilling then the Rest, to see their Native Country in Subjection.'[128] Elsewhere, Blundell included two folios of notes on the Gunpowder Plot. We have already seen that in his treatise 'A Short Discourse' he presented the plot as being perpetrated by a collection of extremists whose aims and objectives were not held by other contemporary Catholics.[129] However, there is a brief indication in the Adversaria that his attitude may not have been as straightforward as he presented in his public works. In a discussion of the reign of James I, Blundell was far more critical of his policies, noting that while King of Scotland and during the first two years of his reign in England he had treated Catholics in a particularly harsh manner, and 'It was the opinion of the Court that after the Pouder plot, the king was more tender of the preservation of Papists; They obteyning by feare what no pity nor policy could procure'.[130] Thus, while Blundell may or may not have disapproved of the methods that the plotters used, he was happy to reap the rewards. In the same way his commonplace books indicate that his losses during the Civil War, while great, did not have the impact on him that his letters suggest. In a cryptic entry he recorded how 'my Greatest losse and greefe ... was no lesse then of my whole Estate, by incurring Delinquency, and the mutilation of the strongest Limne in my Body, by a Musquet Shot', though he concluded that 'it hath proved in the end (as far as human prudence can yet conjecture) the greatest temporal fortune that ever befell me; and that for many reasons partly knowne to others, but principally to myself'.[131] Though the precise meaning of this is unclear, we have already seen that by 1658 the total of Blundell's money and goods exceeded his debts by £208 and that the claims of victimhood scattered throughout his letters were often motivated by an aim to secure the sympathy of the recipients.[132] None the less, Blundell's insistence that Catholics were defined by passive victimhood permeates his commonplace books, and is most evident in his treatment of the history of the Irish Catholics and the 1641 Rebellion.

Both the Historica and the Adversaria demonstrate a near-obsessive interest in the Irish. Blundell's notes include regular comments on what he read about the character of the Irish, including the claims that 'Ther is little found in praise of the Irish: much in dispraies of their maners', that they had a particular love of justice, that the Irish 'are born logicians', its people 'most barbarous' and a number of entries stating 'that next the Spaniard it is the laziest Generation'.[133] Alongside these notes can often be found the latest information that Blundell could find about the country, including estimates on the customs figures for given years and lists of the names of individuals who in 1660 were responsible for putting in execution the Explanatory Act.[134] The concern that Blundell had with Irish affairs was no doubt motivated by a number of factors, not least that his daughter had married into the Irish Butler family and that the overwhelming majority of Ireland was Catholic. This interest led to Blundell interpreting material concerning the country and its people in a particular way.

Throughout Restoration England there was a deep unease about Ireland, which became a focus for Protestant anxiety. Horrific stories of the Irish Rebellion of 1641 were reprinted during periods of particular anti-Catholic feeling, emphasising the dreadful atrocities of the Irish, who became synonymous with Catholics in general.[135] In his notes on Ireland, Blundell recorded that 'The Crueltyes of Irish against the English are in everybodyes mouth, and set forth in Printed Pageants sold at London'.[136] Throughout his reading and note-taking he sought to correct this, as seen in the section immediately proceeding this comment, which Blundell headed 'Some Crueltyes on the Contrary part are these that follow'.[137] Here we find accounts related to him by friends, including the chilling relation of the Protestant minister from the Wirral who 'killed with his own hands one Sonday morning 53 of his owne Parishoners most or all of them ... Weomen and children', the repentant English soldier who witnessed one of his own 'take an Infant upon his Pyke and tosse it up in the Ayre', or the Captain who tried to intervene without success when those under his command unclothed a young woman and 'afterwards dash't out her braynes'.[138] That such a disproportionate amount of information concerning Ireland was relayed by his associates reflected the scarcity of such material in printed sources and, no doubt, this was a regular topic of conversation for Blundell and his friends.

Blundell also took accounts from available printed sources. From the anonymous Catholic text *The Politicians Catechisme*, he noted that 'Few of the Populous Country of Fingale left a lyve all perished by fyre or sword being an innocent people and haveing nothing Irishlyke in them but Catholicke Religion'.[139] Furthermore, on the advice of his friend Richard Bellings, who wrote an unpublished manuscript on the Irish Rebellion, Blundell turned to a recently printed pamphlet to help reconcile what he saw as the unfair criticism of the Irish, recording in the Historica that 'as for the particular outragious Actions, those which concern the Vindicating the Irish by way of retaliation could not be expressed more Emphatically & faithfully then by that small book intitled a Collection of some murthers & massacres committed against the Irish in Ireland'.[140] Published in 1662, the *Collection* was an anonymous Catholic pamphlet sceptical of the widely accepted account of the Irish Rebellion. T. C. Barnard argues that such texts did not have the desired effect and 'these early attempts to impugn the authenticity of the figures and details, coming as they did mainly (but not exclusively) from Catholic writers, merely strengthened Protestant belief that the published histories ... were of "unquestionable truth"'.[141] Unsurprisingly Blundell was receptive to the arguments of the text, providing a page by page summary of the atrocities alleged to have been carried out by English Protestants on the Catholic population. In this list, Blundell gave a direct quote from the author, which dismissed all Protestant accounts as 'There were not so many Protestants of the Brittich Nation living in Ireland in the begining of the Rebellion as have beene printed to be murthered'.[142]

In the mid-1670s, Blundell's reading about Ireland took on new urgency and was put to practical use. For a number of years he had maintained friendships with two scholars: the Irish Catholic Richard Bellings and the Protestant physician Edmund Borlase. To Blundell's surprise each began work on a history of Ireland and both turned to him for support at roughly the same time. To Bellings Blundell happily supplied a list of relevant references, as well as a summary of Isaac Basier's *The History of the English & Scotch Presbytery*.[143] At the same time Blundell read a draft of Borlase's history. The list of comments that he made does not survive, what does is the corresponding letter in which Blundell tried to excuse the number of criticisms, which he was concerned might lead to accusations of favouring the Irish, noting 'I do not meane by this to favour the Rebellion of the Irish or to give any colour but Bloody to their barbarous murders'.[144] Later in the same year he sent Borlase a list of books written by Catholics, or sympathetic to them, the addition of which he felt would benefit the work.[145] In a letter sent to Bellings shortly after, Blundell noted that he had 'discoursed 3 dayes since with a Learned & ingenious person who I take to be a friend to me but not altogether so to the Catholick part of your Nation'.[146] In the letter he outlined his motives for giving Borlase the references: '(in case he use them fairely) [they] may somewhat alay the spirit which posseth his party'.[147] This exchange demonstrates the practical application of Blundell's reading and the extent to which his interpretation was often informed by a desire to protect his co-religionists from criticism. It was not until much later in his life that notes survive detailing how Blundell engaged with a text arguing contrary to his position on this subject.

In the last decade of his life Blundell read Richard Cox's *Hibernia Anglicana*, in two separate parts as it was originally published. His notes on the text straddle both his commonplace books, with the first volume being engaged with in the Adversaria and the second in the Historica. In these controversial works Cox developed an interpretation of Irish history in which he celebrated the 'self-evident superiority of English over Irish culture' in Ireland, maintaining that the 'only hope for Irish papists lay in "total conversion and conformity to the laws, language, habits, manners, and religion of England"'.[148] For Blundell, Cox's arguments about Irish Catholics caused considerable distress. None the less, for the first volume of Cox's history, which covered the period until the end of Elizabeth's reign, he was content to make notes on the geography and early history of Ireland, with little intercession, noting how infighting amongst the Irish caused much bloodshed and the English annexation of the country was a massive venture. Blundell interjected with his own thoughts only to highlight the story 'of a horrid injustice committed by the English against a great Irish man called Hugh Roe' who was hung by an English official after an inheritance dispute.[149] It was in his work on Cox's second volume that his notes became most animated.

Blundell's entries on Cox's second volume rapidly move from summary to diatribe, as he claimed that Cox was 'a bitter enemy to the Papists' and that 'Hee seems to have much reason mixed with great prejudice all along'.[150] Unable to contain himself, Blundell opened with an adversarial reading in which he countered Cox's argument by cross-referencing to the first volume, noting that though the author claimed that the rebellions of the Irish were because 'they would not obey the Protestant King, it is most clear by the whole series of the first book which he published concerning Ireland from the time of the Conquest made by King Henry the 2d, that the people of that Country mantained a Nationall quarrell against every (or almost every) Catholick King of England'.[151] Therefore any proclivity to rebellion was part of the national Irish heritage, as opposed to their religious beliefs. Blundell went on to note Cox's argument that the Irish were divided, accepting that some 'did shamefull things', which he juxtaposed with a note from one of Cox's transcriptions of a letter from Ormond, in which he stated '*that the Nobility & greater part of the Gentry continued faithfull to his Majesty, obedient to his Authority & worthy of his favour*'.[152]

The core of Blundell's criticism of Cox concerned his harsh stance against the Irish Catholics while ignoring the activities of the Scots, a factor that Blundell noted of work on the Irish Rebellion in general.[153] Recording how the Irish had been forced to adhere to an English liturgy 'which they understand no more then they do the masse', that attempts at toleration had been blocked by Protestant Bishops of Ireland stating that 'The Religion of the Papists is superstitious', and that 'the parliament provoked the Irish & made them desperat', Blundell believed that the Irish had been driven to rebellion.[154] On the other hand the Scots had been treated with complete respect throughout the century preceding the troubles. Indeed, Blundell noted that 'Tho' the Irish cannot excuse the Rebellion and much less the murthers comitted by them; yet they have many things to say which may render the first more excusable then the Rebellion of the Scots', concluding his work on Cox with the statement 'whilst every thing don by the Irish (who were extreamly faulty) is most rigorously represented, the Scots & the English comitted some percadilios the first of them selling for money their indulgent King to the later who cut off his head'.[155] Furthermore, in a comment on the behaviour of James II, Blundell manipulated the contents of Cox's work on a further level, recording how in a letter written by Charles I as transcribed in Cox's appendix, Charles 'justifyes that he had a power to free the Catholicks from penaltyes imposed upon the exercise of their religion. Which I note, by reason that King James the 2d has been chiefly charged & opposed for Exercising of such a power'.[156]

Blundell's commonplaces also regularly emphasised that Catholics were naturally inclined to loyalty to monarchy and found the notion of rebellion morally repugnant. In a brief note on Catholics and loyalty Blundell stated that 'Catholicks deny the Oath yet keep their Allegience to the King Others take the oath & fail in Allegiance'.[157] To support this assertion he recorded Anthony Weldon's comment, included to sully James's reputation by associating him with Catholics, that when James I came to the throne the Earl of Northumberland offered to bring him forty thousand Catholics to support him, which Blundell used as evidence for the support that English Catholics gave to monarchy.[158] A further example of Catholic loyalty was given in Blundell's notes on the Ormond family, in which he took from Cox's *Hibernia Anglicana*, against the general grain of the text, the conclusion that James Butler Earl of Ormond was 'most true to the Crown & was therfore sorely perplext & traversed by the Rebells of all Religions'.[159] While the notion that Catholics were by nature loyal to monarchy was equally evident in his correspondence, his commonplace books identify a further motivation for avoiding rebellion. In his notes on Edward Coleman's trial, Blundell accepted the claim that if Catholics ever tried to bring in their religion by destroying the king 'they shal find that the papists will therby bring destruction upon them selves so that not a man of them would escape', recording how 'This he seems to have spoken to good Purpos: & what simple Catholick doth not see that for this reason alone (besydes the horridness of the fact itself) any such designe is madness'.[160]

Blundell's reading of the Catholic Thomas Blount's *Boscobel* was a focus for his notes on Catholic loyalty.[161] In his initial notes on the text Blundell recorded how 'Mr Blounts booke ... relateth right elegantly & exactly the escape of King Charles from Worcester Battle'.[162] The main thrust was to record that Catholics were responsible for the preservation of the King, despite the fact that there was 'the reward of 1000*l* for those that should discover the King, & certain death on the other syde for those that conceyled him', a factor Blundell noted was all the more remarkable when one considered that the recusants who protected him were under serious financial pressure because of the penal laws.[163] In a separate entry in the Adversaria Blundell noted that 'Catholicks were many of them the sole instruments of his safety'.[164] He returned to the topic again having read in a news book that 'a little Booke named Boscobel ... hath dyvers errors and mistakes in it, & therfore not to be admitted as a tru and perfect narative of his sacred Majestyes deliverance'.[165] Blundell claimed that the advertisement was a result of 'hot heads' who were jealous 'that Catholicks should be looked upon as the Kings chief preservers next to God'.[166] He then presented a defence for *Boscobel* noting that its account was confirmed in both Richard Baker's *Chronicle* and George Bates's *Elenchus Motuum* 'wher you may read sondry more delightfull things concerning the Kings travails in the West of England than Mr Blunt (who writ Boscobel) was able to relate, who wanted tru intelligence of the same'.[167]

Only on one occasion did Blundell feel compelled to write in defence of Catholics who had rebelled against a monarch. The activities of Catholics against the monarchy during the French Wars of Religion posed a particular sticking point. His notes on the topic were taken mainly from the Catholic Arrigo Caterino Davila's history of the French wars, which was overwhelmingly sympathetic to the French Catholics.[168] Although, as we will see, Blundell's notes were mainly concerned with French Protestants, he included some interesting asides on the behaviour of French Catholics. His position on the creation of the Catholic League was ambivalent, noting that 'I take this covenant to be little better then the Scots against our late King of England, saving that it had the pretence of Defending the Catholicks cause'.[169] However, later in his notes on this topic he recorded that he could not comment on whether those Catholics who formed the League against the Protestant Henry IV were justified in their actions, citing his reason as 'They had never ownd him for their King & ... it had been ever essential to the Constitution of the French Government that the king should take an oath to defend the Catholick faith before the subjects were to swear allegiance to him'.[170] This rather weak defence of the French Catholics was elaborated on in his argument that the Pope had offered French Catholics military support, which they initially refused and 'more stifly do adhere to the King [Henry IV]'.[171] Only after four further single sides of folio recording how poorly Catholics were treated did Blundell concede that they seriously considered rebellion.[172] As with his account of the Irish Rebellion, while Blundell may have criticised aspects of Catholic behaviour, he ended on a comparison with Protestant actions, reflecting that 'I doubt whether the Protestants of any kingdom would shew the like obedience in such case to a Chatholick King' and that Catholics submitted to Henry IV 'allthough there were rationall fears that that Kings Conversion was fained'.[173] The converse of this argument centred on Protestants, upon whom Blundell projected the blame for those activities from which he had excused Catholics.

VI

Blundell frequently noted the importance of religion in keeping both the monarchy and the state safe and strong.[174] However, his commonplaces regularly emphasised that Protestantism obstructed this. He included a number of entries that highlighted a Protestant inclination to brutality, seen in his notes from Pallavicino's history of the Council of Trent which recorded that during the early stages of the Reformation Protestants plundered Catholic towns with 'more barbarity shew'd therin then they could have expected from the Turks'.[175] He also identified Protestantism with rebellion, at one stage recording that 'All parts of Europe (except England) which pretended reformation, did effect it by Rebellion; This I think may be proved even by Protestant Authors'.[176] His supporting examples included a general allusion to 'Heylins Cosmografy upon the respective countryes that admitted or caused the change of Religion' and specific page referenced notes from Heylyn's *Ecclesia Restaurata*, in which Blundell recorded the numbers put to death during Henry VIII's reign and the 'shameful Act made by Edward 6th to restraine the Bishops Power'.[177] For Blundell the Protestant inclination to rebellion was an issue of immediate relevance, for it was to Protestants that he ascribed full responsibility for the English Civil War.

Though Blundell noted that social standing had some part to play in Civil War allegiance, recording that the Royalist forces 'were maneged in England on the Kings behalf chiefly by the Gentry, as I heard the Lord Gerard Brandon truely affirm', he overwhelmingly perceived it as a war of religion.[178] Referring to the Civil Wars as 'the rebellious wars of the Puritans against King Charles the first', Blundell asserted that not only did Protestants fight against Charles but he was 'beheaded before his owne Pallace by sentence of a high Court of Justice, elected by a Protestant or a Puritan Parliament'.[179] For Blundell, Charles had fought the war 'in defence of his New Church, against his schismatical subjects'.[180] His focus in these sections was not just the past activities of Protestants but also the dangers of forgiving Parliamentarians without punishment, which left Blundell fearful for both his personal safety and the future of monarchy. To emphasise the damage lack of retribution could cause, Blundell turned to examples from ancient history. From Suetonius he noted that while Caesar was wise to accept that those who remained neutral in war were not his enemies, his failure to punish those who fought against him set 'a bad example to other conquerors, for many of those whome he pardoned procured his death'.[181] This point was also made in his notes from

Bede, wherein Blundell recorded that Sigbert the King of the East Saxons was murdered by his brothers 'for no other reason ... but ... his over much clemency in pardoning his Enemyes & forgiving all offences don'.[182] Blundell highlighted his frustration with the post-Restoration regime through a comparison with his historical reading, noting that 'Bede complayned that the Brittons whoe succeeded those that had beene destroyed, in their former lamentable warrs, not remembering well those miseryes fell in to a retchlesse course of lyfe. It seemeth to be the condition of England AD 1660.'[183] Such observations about Protestants can be seen also in Blundell's histories of more recent events, particularly in his notes on the French Wars of Religion.

Blundell's most detailed notes on Protestant history were made in his entries on Davila's history of the French Civil Wars.[184] Over twenty-eight folios of the Historica he summarised the entire text, making general notes for each section of the volume. Blundell also noted that he read both the English translation and, later, the French version.[185] In his brief notes on the latter, from which Blundell stated he took 'confusedly & by snatches', he provided only a few extra points that he missed from the English version, the primary motive apparently being to improve his language skills as opposed to checking for inaccuracies. His notes on Davila also included seven further folios under the title 'Some observations of my own concerning this History of France'.[186] We have already seen that Blundell made some brief notes on the topic of the Catholic League from this text; however, his main concerns were a re-evaluation of the position of the Huguenots and the establishment of a parallel between the French and English Civil Wars.

The notes that Blundell took from Davila centred on a number of main points. From the outset the religious dimension of the French wars was emphasised, and in his personal reflections Blundell ascribed each side specific characteristics. For example, Louis I de Bourbon, Prince de Condé, was noted as 'a fyry Calvenist', while his adversary the Duke of Montmorency was noted as being 'wholy for the church of Rome a wise and Resolute man'.[187] The attribute that was overwhelmingly given to the Huguenots was their penchant for rebellion. Throughout Blundell's notes, the Huguenots are represented as 'Male contents' and 'sacrilegious & bloudy'. He claimed that they were responsible for 'many Vilanous acts against the Churches and Catholick people' long before the Civil Wars broke out and that 'The bloody seditions of Hugonetts were great & frequent'.[188] Any Catholic action was represented as purely defensive, the most illustrative example being that of Henry III, who Blundell noted was 'wholy avers to war', yet after years of provocation reluctantly realised it 'was tyme to betake him selfe to war in a resolute way'.[189] The brutality of the Huguenots was juxtaposed with the efforts of Catholics to give them all they wanted. Blundell frequently recorded that they had been offered complete toleration, with the conditions often being 'extreamly bad for the church & the Crown', both being anxious for peace.[190] Even in his concluding note for 1572, the year of the St Bartholomew's Day Massacre, Blundell's entry reads that 'The King of France deales very gently with the Hugonots'.[191] While he recorded that during the St Bartholomew's Day Massacre more than forty thousand were 'most cruelly Massacred', he was quick to note that Huguenots were not the only victims and 'Besydes thes were many Catholicks slain in that bloudy confusion'.[192] He repeatedly drew attention to Catholick deaths emphasising that during a battle in 1587 despite the fact that the Huguenots were 'totally routed ... 3500 *Catholicks* left dead upon the place'.[193] That the Huguenots suffered more was simply due to the fact that the Catholics were better fighters, Blundell noting, for instance, from the French edition of Davila that 'The Catholicks gained a cleare victory of the Huguenots AD 1569 with the loss of about 400 men they killed 10000'.[194] Blundell concluded his notes on one section of Davila's work with the statement, 'I do observe that allthough the Huguenots were allmost ever upon the loosing hand, yet such was their zeal or fury that no maner of loss could keep them from farther rebellions'.[195]

In his section 'some observations of my own concerning this history of France', Blundell expanded on much of the material presented in his summary. However, his first concern was to establish the accuracy of the account. He speculated that the fact that Davila had fought for the French monarchy may have had an impact on his account, noting that 'It is hard for such a man not to be partiall & therfore I question what he somtymes layes to the charge of the house of Guise'.[196] Despite this, he overwhelmingly concurred with Davila's arguments, even in relation to the house of Guise, concluding that 'the proceedings of those *Lords* seem to be unlawful and scandalous'.[197] Blundell's personal reflections on the text largely overlapped with Davila's work. He wrote that 'The French Nation seems to be prone to sedition and war, and the Nobility over Numerous, & potent', and gave a personal warning about the dangers of religious wars, recording that 'we may judge that no animosity is more violent than wher religion is pretended to be the cause'.[198] However, the bulk of his notes were concerned with where blame for the Civil Wars lay. Blundell held that the whole conflict was the result of Protestant machinations. Having noted that Catholics were free from nearly all criticism, he recorded that 'It is likwise observed by the Story that the Calvenists were implacably rebellious'.[199] To support this he reported that they swapped sides and appeared loyal whenever they were weak, taking up arms as soon as they repaired their strength. Though this was never directly stated, his notes imply that French Catholics had no other choice but to remove the Huguenots from their midst as they were so untrustworthy. Certainly, he did not conclude by mourning the numbers lost, but instead marvelled at the survival of Catholicism, recording that 'it is wonderfull that Religion was not quite lost in those long confusions, when so many parts of Europe had lost it so lately'.[200] However, Blundell did not end his notes by merely blaming Protestants for an event in the past, he continued by demonstrating how this was relevant to interpreting contemporary issues.

Davila's work received widespread attention in early modern England, frequently being appropriated in new ways to suit readers' needs. During and after the English Civil Wars, it received particular attention from Royalists, who 'found in his account of the French wars compelling similarities with their own recent past'.[201] However, Blundell's reading of Davila did not follow a pattern adopted by all Royalists. As Paul Seaward notes of Davila's work, 'it provided a reading of the politics of rebellion that emphasized their roots in factional interest and personal ambition, dismissing the claims of the rebels to be fighting on behalf of religion and liberty'.[202] Blundell's approach was the opposite of that adopted by the Protestant Royalists of whom Seaward speaks. While Blundell accepted that in France the nobility were both numerous and over-mighty, he saw the causes of the war as being firmly located within religious conflict.[203] As we have seen, both his summary and his personal reflections on Davila's work emphasised that the French wars were the fault of zealous Huguenots who wanted religious dominance. This overlapped with Blundell's view of the causes of the English Civil War, though he did not only draw comparisons. His notes on Davila also suggest possible lessons that could be taken from the French wars. In a brief entry comparing the wars Blundell's anxieties are instantly identifiable, where he claimed 'It is wonderfull to consider how little [blood] hath been spilt in England & how much in France. Yet their Kings do to easily pardon Rebellions, and make few *or no* Examples of publick justice'.[204] He was adamant that Henry IV was mistaken in not punishing both the Protestants and Catholics who fought against him, concluding his comparison with the statement 'So that we have little reason in England to complain of the Favors shewn to those who were once King Charles his Enemyes'.[205] In a cautionary note he recorded how the actions of both were 'more like to make knaves to becom honest, then to keepe honest men from becoming knaves', suggesting that they would lose the support of those who had always remained loyal.[206] The dangers of this behaviour are seen clearly in relation to the Kings of France, in Blundell's note that they 'appeare to have lost all credit & allmost to have lost themselves by their Excessive dissimulations'.[207]

VII

Although they are more difficult to classify for the purposes of this book, Blundell's commonplace books also contain lengthy musings on Quakers – a further group who he believed were compromising the image of English

Catholics. The notes appear sporadically in his entries on baptism and are also allocated a number of specific sections under the title 'Quakers'.[208] His interest in the group appears to have stemmed from his contact with a number of followers. For instance, in the footnote to a brief entry which recorded a recipe to fix shoes, Blundell stated 'I had this from a shoemaker in Chester. A Quaker'.[209] Elsewhere he noted that 'One John Blaket ... a great man among the Quakers' told him that he did not use water to baptise, a factor confirmed by 'my Neighbour Johnson the Quaker' who also told him that Quakers were pacifists.[210] Furthermore, Blundell briefly summarised the Quaker John Perrot's 'sufferings' whilst in Rome, from which he noted Perrot's conclusion that 'I have read the suffering of Job and the slaughters of many of the martyers, but yet this can I say in God, that such were my suffering dayes in Rome ... that no soul that lived immediatly in his Grace ever suffered the lyke'.[211] Part of Blundell's motivation for making such comprehensive notes on the Quakers was to counter these claims of 'sufferings', which were interfering with Blundell's deeply held conviction that Catholics were the most persecuted of religious groups within England.

The commonplaces on Quakerism are overwhelmingly hostile. Blundell's position was outlined in the direct quotation he lifted from John Owen's *Epistle to the Author of the Animadversions upon Fiat Lux*, where he noted that they 'have nothing of Christianity but only the morall part, which in deed and truth is but honest paganisme'.[212] Blundell's notes on Quakers suggest that specific areas of Quaker practice and behaviour caused him upset. Blundell attacked Quaker political and social views as well as their religious stance. In a single entry he recorded with distaste the Quaker view of monarchy, noting simply that 'Quakers do speake disrespectfully of the King'.[213] His notes also contained further material on social hierarchy, specifically concerning the role of women within the movement. Modern-day writing on the Quakers has shown that they not only had a preaching ministry open to women but were particularly distinctive because of 'the consistency and coherence of their positive teaching about women's nature and about female ministry'.[214] This was a particular bugbear for Blundell, and his notes on Quakers include a number of Bible references, such as 1 Corinthians 14:35, which he noted as 'women forbiden to speake in the church', and 1 Timothy 2:12, 'suffer not a woman to teach'.[215] As we will see, these comments fall into part of a wider dialogue in Blundell's commonplace books about the role of women in society, though from the outset it is clear that he believed that female agency had little place in religion. A further issue for Blundell concerned the Quaker position on baptism. Blundell's notes reiterate time and again the importance of baptism, his attitude being suggested by a small note under his record that Richard Johnson told him Quakers do not use water to baptise, which he juxtaposed against John 3:5, 'Unless a man be born againe of water and the spirit;

he cannot enter into the kingdom of God'.[216] Finally, as we have already seen, Blundell was uncertain as to what the Bible's overall message on conflict was, and, having been told by a Quaker that all Friends denounced violence, he noted 'Christ bad them buy swords Luk 22.36 to what end?'[217] The crucial point of these notes was to demonstrate that, unlike Catholics, Quakers were correctly punished for subverting Christianity.

VIII

Blundell's commonplace books offer a unique insight into his perspective on religion and religious history. Although his notes on transubstantiation, purgatory and the virtues of a religious life attest to his Catholic beliefs, his entries also disputed the validity of accounts of contemporary miracles and saints' lives, and drew attention to contradictions in the Bible. Furthermore, while meticulous lists of providential intervention against persecutors of Catholicism indicate that Blundell accepted that God maintained an active presence in the world, he frequently questioned certain accounts in a manner that offended many of his contemporary co-religionists. None the less, as in his correspondence, Blundell adhered strictly to the view that English Catholics were passive victims of a corrupt Protestant state. So powerful was this belief that it prompted him to engage aggressively with both Protestant and Catholic works of history. It is in Blundell's attitude to theology and religious history that we see an underlying tension in his identity. On the one hand, Blundell's freethinking approach to the world conflicted with the type of Catholic that he aspired to be, seen in his reluctant identification of himself as a 'cold Christian', while on the other his aggressive engagement with contemporary works of history shows that he was no passive victim.[218]

NOTES

1 Adversaria, fols 78, 83, 110, 125, 127–b, 142b, 149b–50, 211b, 215b.

2 Adversaria, fol. 297b.

3 Historica, fols 204–8b; Adversaria, fol. 257; A. Arnauld and P. Nicole, *La Perpetuite de la Foy de L'Eglise Catholique Touchant L'Eucharistie* (Paris, 1666).

4 Adversaria, fols 97, 218; J. Taylor, *The Great Exemplar of Sanctity and Holy Life According to the Christian Institution* (1657), p. 331. For a discussion of early modern Catholicism and virginity see M. E. Wiesner-Hanks, *Christianity and Sexuality in the Early Modern World: Regulating Desire, Reforming Practice* (London: Routledge, 2000), pp. 107, 158.

5 Adversaria, fols 210b, 228. For Hacket's bizarre career see A. Walsham, '"Frantick Hacket": prophecy, sorcery, insanity, and the Elizabethan Puritan movement', *Historical Journal*, 41 (1998), pp. 27–66.

6 Adversaria, fols 125–b, 136–b; J. Mumford, *The Question of Questions* (1658), see pp. 411–14 for example.

7 Adversaria, fol. 7.

8 N. Johnstone, *The Devil and Demonism in Early Modern England* (Cambridge: Cambridge University Press, 2006), p. 94.

9 Historica, fol. 10.

10 Historica, fol. 9.

11 Historica, fol. 69.

12 See, for example: Adversaria, fols 43b, 44–5b, 56b.

13 Historica, fol. 152b.

14 Adversaria, fol. 32b.

15 Adversaria, fols 37b–9, 41b.

16 Adversaria, fol. 356.

17 Adversaria, fols 361–3, 366–7.

18 Adversaria, fol. 273.

19 Historica, fol. 138.

20 Adversaria, fol. 149b.

21 J. Deploige, 'Bertulf or Galbert? Considerations regarding a sample of historical and psychoanalytical criticism of medieval dreams', *Psychoanalytische Perspectieven*, 20 (2002), p. 236; R. Starn, 'Truths in the archives', *Common Knowledge*, 8 (2002), p. 398.

22 Starn, 'Truths in the archives', p. 396.

23 Adversaria, fol. 423; Mabillon, *Traité des Études Monastiques*.

24 Adversaria, fol. 358b.

25 Adversaria, fol. 381b.

26 Adversaria, fols 111–11b, 134–b, 167b, 191, 216, 232, 258–b, 273–b, 292.

27 Adversaria, fol. 292; Bureau d'adresse et de Rencontre, *General Collection of Discourses*, p. 109.

28 Adversaria, fol. 111b; H. Grotius, *Two Discourses, I. Of God, and his Providence. II. Of Christ, his Miracles and Doctrine* (1653).

29 Historica, fol. 47b.

30 Adversaria, fol. 66.

31 Adversaria, fol. 134b.

32 Adversaria, fol. 258.

33 Adversaria, fol. 258.

34 Adversaria, fol. 273b.

35 Adversaria, fol. 232.

36 Adversaria, fol. 111.

37 P. Brown, *Augustine of Hippo: A Biography* (London: Faber and Faber, 1967), pp. 415–18.

38 Adversaria, fol. 258; R. Baker, *A Chronicle of the Kings of England from the Time of the Romans Government, unto the Death of King James* (1674), p. 282.

39 Adversaria, fol. 258b.

40 Adversaria, fols 111–b, 167b.

41 Adversaria, fol. 191.

42 A. Walsham, 'Miracles in post-Reformation England', in K. Cooper and J. Gregory (eds), *Signs, Wonders, Miracles: Representations of Divine Power in the Life of the Church*, Studies in Church History, 41 (Woodbridge: Boydell and Brewer, 2005), p. 273; A. Walsham, 'Miracles and the Counter-Reformation mission to England', *Historical Journal*, 46 (2003), pp. 782, 785–6.

43 Walsham, 'Miracles and the Counter-Reformation', p. 785.

44 Walsham, 'Miracles and the Counter-Reformation', p. 781; Walsham, 'Miracles in post-Reformation England', p. 281,

45 Walsham, 'Miracles and the Counter-Reformation', p. 786.

46 Walsham, 'Miracles in post-Reformation England', p. 278.

47 A. Walsham, *Providence in Early Modern England* (Oxford: Oxford University Press, 1999), p. 2; Walsham, 'Miracles in post-Reformation England', pp. 286–8; Walsham, 'Miracles and the Counter-Reformation', pp. 791–3.

48 W. Johnston, 'The Anglican apocalypse in Restoration England', *Journal of Ecclesiastical History*, 55 (2004), p. 468.

49 W. Johnston, 'Revelation and the Revolution of 1688–1689', *Historical Journal*, 48 (2005), pp. 351–89, at p. 389; Johnston, 'Anglican apocalypse', pp. 467–501.

50 Walsham, 'Miracles and the Counter-Reformation', p. 793.

51 Historica, fols 44, 62, 123; M. Alford, *Fides Regia Britannica sive Annales Ecclesiae Britannicae* (Liege, 1663), IV, pp. 74–5; F. Godwin, *A Catalogue of the Bishops of England, Since the First Planting of Christian Religion in this Island* (1615), p. 77.

52 Historica, fol. 90; Adversaria, fol. 60b; Caussin, *The Holy Court*, III, pp. 38–44.

53 Historica, fols 90, 126b; T. S., *The Adventures of (Mr. T. S.) an English Merchant Taken Prisoner by the Turks of Argiers* (1670), p. 238.

54 Adversaria, fol. 320b.

55 F. E. Dolan, 'Ashes and "the archive": the London Fire of 1666, partisanship, and proof', *Journal of Medieval and Early Modern Studies*, 31 (2001), pp. 379–408.

56 Historica, fols 31b, 61b.

57 Historica, fol. 31b; Great Hodge Podge, fol. 55b. Ian Atherton notes that Scudamore was restoring Dore and it is unlikely that he would have removed the altar in the first place: I. Atherton, *Ambition and Failure in Stuart England: The Career of John, First Viscount Scudamore* (Manchester: Manchester University Press, 1999), pp. 60, 64–5.

58 Historica, fol. 56.

59 Historica, fol. 56.

60 Historica, fol. 32.

61 Historica, fol. 48b.

62 Historica, fol. 48b; St Bede, *The History of the Church of Englande* (1565), pp. 81–2, 85–6.

63 Adversaria, fols 14–15, 32b, 36b–7, 44, 49b, 56, 62, 75–b, 85–b, 94b–5, 96–b, 112–b, 135–b, 188b–9, 230b–1, 296b, quotation at fol. 85. For a discussion of the way contem-

poraries could ascribe the Bible, like other texts, with different meanings at different times, see K. Sharpe, 'Reading revelations: prophecy, hermeneutics and politics in early modern Britain', in K. Sharpe and S. N. Zwicker (eds), *Reading, Society and Politics in Early Modern England* (Cambridge: Cambridge University Press, 2003), pp. 122–63.

64 Adversaria, fol. 62.

65 Adversaria, fol. 96.

66 Adversaria, fol. 188b.

67 Adversaria, fol. 96.

68 Adversaria, fols 96, 188b–9.

69 Adversaria, fol. 321.

70 Adversaria, fol. 230b.

71 Adversaria, fol. 62. This point was also made by Blundell in the margins of the family Douai Bible held at Crosby Hall: English College of Doway, *The Holie Bible*, II, p. 722.

72 Adversaria, fol. 62.

73 Adversaria, fols 56, 273b.

74 Adversaria, fol. 149.

75 Adversaria, fols 230b–1.

76 Adversaria, fol. 273.

77 See, for example C. T. Burris, E. Harmon-Jones and W. R. Tarpley, '"By faith alone": religious agitation and cognitive dissonance', *Basic and Applied Social Psychology*, 19 (1997), pp. 17–31.

78 Seaver, *Wallington's World*, pp. 143–81.

79 See, for example: William Blundell to Colonel R. L., 1656; William Blundell to Unnamed Recipient, 19 November 1681, in Letter Book One, fols 26, 117b.

80 Walsham, *Church Papists*, pp. 2, 22–49; Questier, 'Clerical recruitment', p. 86.

81 Adversaria, fol. 101.

82 Historica, fol. 91.

83 The Latin title reads 'Paenitentia Sera': Historica, fol. 91.

84 Adversaria, fol. 113; P. Heylyn, *Cosmographie in Four Books Containing the Chorographie and Historie of the Whole World* (1657), p. 116. For other instances in which Blundell praised the Jesuits see: Adversaria, fols 53, 143, 154b–5b, 182–b, 212–b; Historica, fols 33b–4, 49–b, 57, 79–b.

85 Adversaria, fol. 96b.

86 Only one of Blundell's surviving letters alludes to the issues raised by the Archpriest Controversy. In a letter to one H. Long, Blundell stated 'I have too curiously wished somtymes that I might know the sense of the difference, and (religiously I think) desyred we might at length have a Bishop of our own. Yet still with a tacit submission to those superiour decrees.' The extent to which this letter revealed Blundell's true feelings, or whether it merely pandered to the leanings of the recipient who supported the secular cause is not clear. Throughout his life Blundell's patronage was overwhelmingly given to regular clergy: William Blundell to H. Long, 26 March 1675, in Draft Letter Book, II, fol. 37.

87 Adversaria, fol. 14b.

88 Adversaria, fol. 204b; H. More, *Historia Missionis Anglicanae Societatis Jesu* (Douai, 1660); F. Edwards (ed.), *The Elizabethan Jesuits:* Historia Missionis Anglicanae Societatis Jesu *(1660) of Henry More* (London: Phillimore, 1981), pp. 195–8.

89 B. Southgate, 'White [Blacklo], Thomas (1592/3–1676)', in *ODNB*; B. Southgate, *'Covetous of Truth': The Life and Work of Thomas White, 1593–1676* (Dordrecht: Kluwer Academic Publishers, 1993); B. Southgate, '"White's disciple": John Sergeant and Blackloism', *Recusant History*, 24 (1999), pp. 431–6; B. Southgate, 'Blackloism and tradition: from theological uncertainty to historiographical doubt', *Journal of the History of Ideas*, 61 (2000), pp. 97–114.

90 J. R. Collins, 'Thomas Hobbes and the Blackloist Conspiracy of 1649', *Historical Journal*, 45 (2002), p. 311.

91 Adversaria, fol. 77b.

92 Adversaria, fols 77b, 151b–2.

93 Adversaria, fol. 77b.

94 'it is ceited (with other the lykestuffe) in Dr Leybourns Encyclical Answer &c': Adversaria, fol. 77b; G. Leyburn, *Dr. Leyburns Encyclicall Answer to an Encyclicall Epistle Sent to our Brethren of England* (1661). For Blundell's notes on *Monumetham Excantatus*, see: Adversaria, fol. 77; T. White, *Monumetham Excantatus sive Animadversiones in Libellum Famosum Inscriptum de Anglicani Cleri Retinenda in Apostolicam Sedem Observantia* (Rouen, 1660).

95 Adversaria, fol. 77b.

96 T. White, *The Grounds of Obedience and Government* (1655).

97 Adversaria, fol. 77b.

98 White, *Grounds of Obedience.*

99 Adversaria, fol. 77b.

100 Adversaria, fols 77b, 152.

101 Historica, fol. 149b.

102 Adversaria, fol. 170b.

103 Historica, fol. 145b.

104 Historica, fol. 150.

105 Adversaria, fol. 127b.

106 Adversaria, fol. 85b.

107 Adversaria, fol. 95.

108 Adversaria, fol. 135b. Blundell was not alone in noting the instability of Protestant translations of the Bible, a factor that David Katz has argued was 'a powerful argument in the Roman Catholic polemical arsenal, since it implied a pervasive lack of authority': D. S. Katz, *God's Last Words: Reading the English Bible from Reformation to Fundamentalism* (London: Yale University Press, 2004), p. 44.

109 Adversaria, fol. 92; I. Basier, *The History of the English & Scotch Presbytery* (1660), p. 125.

110 Adversaria, fol. 100b; P. Heylyn, *Ecclesia Restaurata, or, The History of the Reformation of the Church of England* (1661), p. 126.

111 Adversaria, fol. 127b.

112 See Blundell's claim that Baxter's *Grotian Religion* was 'a notable knavish bitter discourse against the old Protestants of England': Adversaria, fol. 147b; R. Baxter, *The Grotian Religion Discovered* (1658), p. 105. For a discussion of Baxter's work see W. Lamont (ed.), *Richard Baxter: A Holy Commonwealth* (Cambridge: Cambridge University Press, 1994), pp. ix–xxi.

113 Adversaria, fol. 253b; Ray, *Observations Topographical, Moral, & Physiological*, p. 419.

114 Adversaria, fol. 82.

115 Adversaria, fol. 128b; T. Browne, *Religio Medici* (1642), p. 103.

116 Woolf, *Reading History*, pp. 79–80.

117 Adversaria, fol. 358b.

118 Historica, fol. 55b; T. Matthew, *A Collection of Letters* (1659), p. 27.

119 Adversaria, fol. 132.

120 For instances in which Blundell recorded the persecution of Catholics from all periods of history see: Adversaria, fols 9b, 10b–11, 13b, 32, 100, 124b, 155–b, 162b, 172b, 202b, 266b–7, 306, 321b, 324b, 325b.

121 Heylyn, *Ecclesia Restaurata*, pp. 80–1.

122 Historica, fol. 60b; Heylyn, *Ecclesia Restaurata*, pp. 80, 84.

123 Historica, fol. 60b; Heylyn, *Ecclesia Restaurata*, p. 80.

124 Historica, fol. 79; N. N., *The Politicians Catechisme for his Instruction in Divine Faith and Morall Honesty* (1658), pp. 152–5.

125 Blundell noted that Marvell's *Rehearsal Transpros'd* 'pleads hard for the ... presbiterians', and modern-day scholars have shown that it based many of its arguments for religious toleration on those made by leading contemporary Independents: Historica, fol. 79b; M. Dzelzainis and A. Patterson, 'Rehearsal Transpros'd: introduction', in A. Patterson (ed.), *The Prose Works of Andrew Marvell* (London: Yale University Press, 2003), I, pp. 3–22.

126 Historica, fol. 79b; A. Marvell, *The Rehersal Transpros'd; or, Animadversions Upon a Late Book, Entituled, A Preface Shewing what Grounds there are of Fears and Jealousies of Popery* (1672), p. 131. Blundell was not the only Catholic to manipulate Marvell's arguments to support Catholic goals. Roger Palmer, Earl of Castlemaine, 'drew repeatedly on R[ehersal] T[ranspros'd] ... as a suitably Protestant stick with which to beat his Anglican opponents': Dzelzainis and Patterson, 'Rehearsal Transpros'd: introduction', p. 21.

127 Adversaria, fol. 118b.

128 Adversaria, fol. 14b.

129 Blue Book, fols 13b–14b.

130 Adversaria, fol. 10b.

131 Adversaria, fol. 31b.

132 Small Account Book, fols 63, 84b.

133 Adversaria, fols 7, 211, 285, 298, 327b.

134 Adversaria, fols 126b, 184.

135 Discussed in E. H. Shagan, 'Constructing discord: ideology, propaganda, and English

responses to the Irish Rebellion of 1641', *Journal of British Studies*, 36 (1997), pp. 4–34; T. C. Barnard, 'The uses of 23 October 1641 and Irish Protestant celebrations', *English Historical Review*, 106 (1991), pp. 889–920.

136 Historica, fol. 51b.

137 Historica, fol. 51b.

138 Historica, fols 51b–2.

139 Historica, fol. 52; N. N., *Politicians Catechisme*, pp. 155–8.

140 Historica, fol. 96. Richard Bellings's manuscript text survives in the library of Trinity College, Dublin, and in the British Library. It was transcribed and printed in the nineteenth century: J. T. Gilbert (ed.), *History of the Irish Confederation and the War in Ireland, 1641–1643 Containing a Narrative of Affairs of Ireland ... by Richard Bellings* (Dublin, 1882–91).

141 T. C. Barnard, 'Crises of identity among Irish Protestants 1641–1685', *Past and Present*, 127 (1990), p. 50.

142 Historica, fols 58–9; R. S., *A Collection of Some of the Murthers and Massacres*, pp. 7–8.

143 William Blundell to Richard Bellings, 7 November 1674, in Draft Letter Book, II, fols 29–30b.

144 William Blundell to Edmund Borlase, 20 January 1675, in Draft Letter Book, II, fol. 35.

145 William Blundell to Edmund Borlase, 15 July 1675, in Draft Letter Book, II, fols 41b–2.

146 William Blundell to Richard Bellings, 31 July 1675, in Draft Letter Book, II, fol. 44b.

147 William Blundell to Richard Bellings, 31 July 1675, in Draft Letter Book, II, fol. 45.

148 J. Smyth, '"Like amphibious animals": Irish Protestants, ancient Britons, 1691–1707', *Historical Journal*, 36 (1993), p. 790.

149 Adversaria, fols 326b–7b; Cox, *Hibernia Anglicana*, I, p. 399.

150 Historica, fol. 141.

151 Historica, fol. 141.

152 Historica, fol. 142; Cox, *Hibernia Anglicana*, III, p. 34.

153 Historica, fol. 96.

154 Historica, fols 96, 142b; Adversaria, fol. 101.

155 Historica, fols 142b–3.

156 Historica, fol. 141b; Cox, *Hibernia Anglicana*, V, pp. 119–20.

157 Adversaria, fol. 267.

158 Adversaria, fol. 267; A. Weldon, *The Court and Character of King James Whereunto is now Added The Court of King Charles* (1651), p. 224.

159 Historica, fol. 117b; Cox, *Hibernia Anglicana*, III, pp. 1–72.

160 Adversaria, fol. 265b; Anon, *The Tryal of Edward Coleman* (1678), p. 94. Blundell's use of the term 'papist' reflects that he is speaking from another's perspective. The way in which Blundell used this term was similar to how Nehemiah Wallington used the pejorative term 'Puritan', which was 'normally only used when quoting those hostile to the godly who employed such expressions about them': Seaver, *Wallington's World*, p. 143.

161 T. Blount, *Boscobel, or, The Compleat History of His Sacred Majesties Most Miraculous Preservation After the Battle of Worcester 3 Sept. 1651* (1662).

162 Historica, fol. 30b.

163 Historica, fol. 31.

164 Adversaria, fol. 32.

165 Historica, fol. 87b.

166 Historica, fol. 87b.

167 Historica, fol. 87b; G. Bate, *Elenchus Motuum Nuperorum in Anglia, or, A Short Historical Account of the Rise and Progress of the Late Troubles in England* (1685), II, pp. 125–50; Baker, *A Chronicle of the Kings of England*, pp. 625–8.

168 Davila, *Historie of the Civil Warres.*

169 Historica, fol. 101.

170 Historica, fols 112b–13.

171 Historica, fols 106–b.

172 Historica, fol. 108.

173 Historica, fol. 113.

174 Adversaria, fol. 16.

175 Historica, fol. 148; Pallavicino, *Istoria del Concilio di Trento.*

176 Historica, fol. 59b.

177 Historica, fols 59b, 78b; Heylyn, *Cosmographie*; Heylyn, *Ecclesia Restaurata*, pp. 15, 51.

178 Adversaria, fol. 114b.

179 Historica, fol. 28; Adversaria, fols 232b, 252b–3.

180 Adversaria, fol. 9b.

181 Historica, fol. 16b; Suetonius, *The Historie of Twelve Caesars, Emperours of Rome* (1606), pp. 33–6.

182 Historica, fol. 47; Bede, *History of the Church of Englande*, pp. 98–9.

183 Adversaria, fol. 67b; Bede, *History of the Church of Englande*, p. 29.

184 Davila, *Historie of the Civil Warres.*

185 E. C. Davila, *Historia Delle Guerre Civili di Francia* (Paris, 1644); Historica, fol. 113b.

186 Historica, fol. 111.

187 Historica, fol. 98.

188 Historica, fols 97b–8b, 114.

189 Historica, fols 101–b.

190 Historica, fol. 101.

191 Historica, fol. 100b.

192 Historica, fol. 100.

193 Historica, fol. 102b.

194 Historica, fol. 114.

195 Historica, fol. 100b.

196 Historica, fol. 111b.

197 Historica, fol. 111b.

198 Historica, fols 111, 112b.

199 Historica, fol. 112b.

200 Historica, fol. 112b.

201 P. Seaward, 'Clarendon, Tacitism, and the Civil Wars of Europe', *Huntington Library Quarterly*, 68 (2005), pp. 295–6. After it was translated into English in 1647, Charles I ordered a further translation with a continuation, which was not printed until 1678: J. H. M. Salmon, *The French Religious Wars in English Political Thought* (Oxford: Clarendon Press, 1959), p. 100.

202 Seaward, 'Clarendon, Tacitism, and the Civil Wars', p. 299.

203 Historica, fol. 111.

204 Historica, fol. 111.

205 Historica, fol. 112.

206 Historica, fol. 112.

207 Historica, fol. 111.

208 Adversaria, fols 88b, 89b–90, 127b–8, 151–b.

209 Adversaria, fol. 101.

210 Adversaria, fol. 151.

211 Adversaria, fol. 89b; J. Perrot, *Battering Rams Against Rome; or, The Battel of John the Follower of the Lamb, Fought with the Pope and his Priests, Whilst he was a Prisoner in the Inquisition-Prison of Rome* (1661), p. 130.

212 Adversaria, fol. 127b; J. Owen, *An Epistle to the Authour of the Animadversions Upon Fiat Lux in Excuse and Justification of Fiat Lux Against the Said Animadversions* (Douai, 1663), p. 42.

213 Adversaria, fol. 90.

214 C. Trevett, *Women and Quakerism in the 17th Century* (York: Ebor Press, 1991), p. 13.

215 Adversaria, fol. 128.

216 Adversaria, fol. 151.

217 Adversaria, fol. 127b.

218 Adversaria, fol. 273.

Chapter 5

A Catholic approach to the world

Blundell's commonplaces on contemporary issues of social and scientific importance suggest that there was an underlying tension in his worldview. Although his notes indicate that he was profoundly influenced by the work of Francis Bacon, Blundell's commitment to Catholicism often prohibited him from fully accepting Bacon's approach to the world. Torn between these two at times contradictory viewpoints, Blundell's commonplaces show that his worldview constituted an uneasy fusing of the central tenets from both. Following the broad groupings of notes that Blundell made in his commonplace books, this chapter considers his comments on four main areas: the social order and gentility, the place of women in society, other cultures and, finally, his approach to the physical world. Here we see most clearly how his intellectual struggle with aspects of his religious identity informed his practical engagement with the world.

I

Throughout his commonplace books Blundell had a preoccupation with the social order. That the manuscripts in which they were written were never intended for publication makes his entries particularly interesting. Contemporary printed material on the social order was released into the public domain, and as such 'portrayed society as it ought to be, providing a prescription for an ideal harmony in social relations'.[1] None the less, Blundell's private commonplaces are preoccupied with many of the same concerns as printed material. Like his contemporaries he viewed society as being highly stratified and was mainly concerned with those individuals who formed the 'political nation'.[2] The rare entries that discuss those below the standing of gentleman suggest an anxiety that his commonplaces sought to dispel. This is not to say that Blundell did not accept that social mobility was a reality. In a brief entry in the

Adversaria he recorded a direct quotation from Caussin's *The Holy Court* that 'The property of a Reasonable Creature is to work for an end, otherwaies it is a Brutish action'.[3] It would appear that he held that the aim of each individual was to climb the various rungs of the social order, seen in his speculation on the relativity of wealth, where he stated 'A Beggar would think him self a Prince, if he were sodainly made the master of a few Akers of Land and a little house. A poore husbandman that enjoyeth as much as that, finding his owne wants, hath not a greater ambition then to arryve to the fortune of a yeoman. A yeoman would gladly be a Gentleman, & a Gentleman a Lord.'[4] Blundell noted how the various categories of the social order had expanded over the last century.[5] However, while he accepted that social mobility was a reality, he also maintained that, as the lower orders progressed, so the requirements for being considered noble altered.[6]

Throughout the early modern period there was increasing ambiguity about the place of certain occupational and social groups in the social order. The majority of contemporary observers paid most attention to the various delineations within the gentry, though below that there was a degree of confusion.[7] Blundell was no exception and his notes display a particular lack of clarity about the classification of two groups: the clergy and merchants. He recorded on two separate occasions that 'I remember I read in Watsons Quolibets that the place of a Priest ought, in the world, to be before a squire, and allso (as I remember) before a knight'.[8] Blundell summarised William Watson's remarks on the practical consequences of this uncertainty, recording an account of how an English priest pulled a gentleman by the sleeve so he could take his place 'allthough the Gentleman could spend £800 per annum'.[9] The connections between money and status can be seen most clearly in Blundell's comment on mercantile groups in England. In a brief entry on the topic, following his engagement with Edward Chamberlayne's *Angliae Notitia* that maintained tenurial status alone as indicative of one's standing in the social order, Blundell recorded, '*Angliae Notita* is severe against Merchants, as being below Gentlemen; I mean such merchants or Trades men as serve apprenticeship'.[10] Blundell juxtaposed the statement with a note from his travel reading, recording that 'Heylin ... saith that the merchants of Italy are for most part Gentlemen of Noblehouses: that they are the wealthyest merchants in Christendom'.[11] Though this juxtaposition does not indicate whether Blundell was happy for merchants to be regarded as gentry, he was clearly exercised by definitions of gentility.

Like many of his contemporaries Blundell regarded a multiplicity of criteria as inherent in any conception of gentility.[12] He frequently alluded to the importance of wealth and lineage in social standing, recording, for instance, that 'Camden reckoneth wealth as one (sole) cause which maketh a Gentleman', while in the Great Hodge Podge he displayed a deep interest in the history of his family and meticulously updated records concerning his pedigree.[13] However, wealth and lineage were only part of his definition, and the overwhelming emphasis of his entries focused on other attributes. He viewed the primary element of gentility as being a state of nobility and a commitment to honour that was ever present in the individual's character. This accorded with the broad consensus in early modern England that gentility was defined by cultural criteria.[14] As Blundell recorded in an entry based on his own experience, 'The French have a saying that the King can make a man a Count, a Marques or a Duke, but not a Gentleman'.[15] He turned to the Bible to support his viewpoint, noting that James 2:2 stated that 'A man in fine apparrell and with a Gold ring not to be preferred before a poore man'.[16] Blundell instead highlighted the importance of an active life. The emphasis on the virtue of an active life for gentleman had its origins in Stoic works that emphasised its value over that of a life of contemplation, a position supported in a range of Bacon's writings, most notably *Of the Advancement of Learning*, a text regularly cited in Blundell's commonplace books.[17] However, there was general agreement amongst contemporaries that an active life axiomatically entailed the holding of public office, which raised a particular problem for Blundell: how could he retain his honour whilst excluded from public office as a result of his recusancy?[18]

Blundell was not alone in trying to circumnavigate this problem. Richard Cust shows that the Catholics Thomas Shirley and Henry Hastings emphasised the importance of lineage, instead of public office.[19] However, while Blundell frequently spoke of his pedigree, an attachment to the concepts of an active life precluded complete reliance on this approach. Instead, Blundell's commonplaces suggest that he sought to change the mark of gentility from public office to a far broader, and therefore accessible, conception of public service. In his notes on this topic, Blundell emphasised the importance of a more generic approach to the advancement of society, quoting directly from Caussin's *The Holy Court* that the very rich 'have power in your hands, to discharge the dutyes of all the World'.[20] This concept of public service involved setting an example to society, particularly as the lower orders were wont to imitate them; as Blundell noted from Clement Ellis's *The Gentile Sinner*, 'Speaking of the true Gentleman – all his words & all his actions ... are so many calls to virtue & goodness'.[21] Blundell highlighted the importance of avoiding idleness at all costs and he compiled commonplaces about the education of children that emphasised the dangers of idleness, noting that Charlemagne encouraged his daughters to sew or spin to keep them active.[22] He also emphasised the importance of charity as a means to support society and frequently reflected on methods to identify deserving poor.[23] There are a number of informal parallels between the approach to politics that Blundell adopted to navigate around the penal laws that prevented him from holding public office, and contemporary female attitudes to politics. Women were more concerned with demanding a political voice, as opposed to political rights, because 'women during the seventeenth century had at once a broad and more inclusive understanding of politics than we possess today'.[24] Lois Schwoerer argues that while most women did not compete for and exercise political power in conventional terms they played an active role within the 'political culture' of early modern England, a definition which 'shifts the focus away from elite political structures (without denying their importance) and permits the inclusion of women from all classes (as well as more men)'.[25] Blundell believed that the emphasis on a more accessible interpretation of public service was validated by the composition of the Royalist forces, which, in his estimation, had been managed entirely by gentry, both Catholic and Protestant.[26] However, he was well aware that there was a widening gulf between the 'true gentleman' whose actions accorded with his broad interpretation of public service and those who may have held public office but behaved in a manner hardly befitting what he conceived as nobility.

In a series of notes scattered throughout the Adversaria entitled 'Nobiles parum Nobiles' ('Nobles without nobility') Blundell listed what he viewed as the manifold evils of his own social group.[27] In a rhetorical question, he juxtaposed the sins described in Ezekiel 16:49 with those of the gentry, stating 'It seemes that plenty Idlenes, Pride & uncharitablenes were the great sinns of Sodom. Are they not so of our English Gentry?'[28] Elsewhere, in a direct quotation from the anonymous Catholic text *The Politicians Catechisme*, Blundell noted that there was not 'a more contemptible generation of men then the English Nobility at this Present'.[29] That Blundell was motivated to record such derogatory citations reflected his belief that the majority of the English gentry were not living up to the noble role that their position in society demanded of them. Their talent for idleness and loathing of charity were causing a wider breakdown of societal values, prompting Blundell to record Richard Allestree's charge against the '*scandalous visciousness of the Gentry*'.[30] In his notes on travel writing it was argued that this situation was not unique to the English, but could also be found in China where, despite the fact that labourers often lived to be a hundred years old, the nobility commonly did not survive into their fifties, the difference in life expectancy proceeding 'from their debaucheries with the female sex and their immoderate eating, in which they prescribe no bounds to themselves'.[31] His fears about the gentry were not only prompted by a tendency to selfishness that he observed in many of his group but also emanated from a breakdown of respect between different levels of the gentry. Blundell's most penetrating insight on this topic came from word of mouth, relayed to him by an unspecified Lord. He recorded that two gentlemen who were known to him, one a knight and the other 'in some respects, much his superiour', were great friends who shared 'a rusticall freedom', which broke down the hierarchy of the social order with disastrous consequences. 'The one [the knight] desyred the other to give him some Wallnuts which he had in his hand, upon which that other thrust a walnut up into his own taile, and ther layd it on the table; his friend tooke it and offerred to crak it with his teeth but complayned it was bitter and stinking; at which that Other Laughed and sayd ther was reason for it, for he had put it into his arse.' The account concluded by stating that in revenge the other gentleman 'thrust the end of a Tobacko pipe (not long after) up into his own Fundament'.[32] Although the story may appear whimsical, that it was relayed in a section which compiled accounts of misdemeanour amongst the gentry places it as one part of a broader critique. Blundell's notes on this topic, as this account indicates, went on to directly criticise the sexual shenanigans that he believed many members of the gentry were engaged in.

Blundell's notes include little about sex, and, in the rare occasions that it is alluded to, it is with a sense of distaste. This was particularly the case with an account of public masturbation. Throughout the seventeenth century both male and female masturbation was considered a taboo, ignored in sections on adolescence in the child-rearing handbooks of the sixteenth and seventeenth centuries. It was not until the late 1680s and beyond that an increasing fear of masturbation led contemporary commentators to emphasise the fatal health and moral consequences of such physical self-indulgence.[33] Lawrence Stone has speculated that male masturbation was deliberately ignored as contemporary medical understanding highlighted the benefits of occasional removal of excess bodily fluids, whether through the letting of blood or masturbation.[34] While private engagement in such activity may have been ignored, public exhibition was unlikely to ever receive broad toleration. The wording of Blundell's notes from his reading of travel literature, in which he claimed that the Chinese do not have a name for their 'secret obscene parts' and the Jews do not touch their 'secret part, yea even when they make water', suggests that he believed the penis was part of the body that should be kept out of public sight at all costs.[35] In a note on the misbehaviour of the gentry, Blundell recorded that one 'Sr Ch Dyd: in that notorious debauchment in the Balconey at London did there publickly frig him self before the people'. While the act itself may not have been to Blundell's taste, it was the status of the individual involved that caused him most distress, and he concluded his account 'Quere if Sr Ch: be not a member of Parliament. I think he is.'[36] In a similar manner Blundell also relayed a contemporary account of sexual violence, which he noted on two separate occasions. Opening the account not with a description of the incident, Blundell instead bemoaned that 'It is sad to hear (as I have don Lately) that a very great person (no less than an Earle) should call his own Lady out of bed, and make her drink healths in her smock, with him self and his foot-men. But this is not the greatest injury he dos her.'[37] That the account opens with astonishment at the perpetrator's position in the social order suggests that Blundell's revulsion was motivated equally by the individual's failure to accord with the behaviour expected of one at his level, as by the act itself. At a later date Blundell outlined the assault in more detail, noting that the 'Earle Rivers ... made his wif to Rise out of her bed in her smock and to stand ther in her smock ... whilst he and his servants did drink and that they threw drink into her breasts or boosoms. That he had clapt her sorely &c for all which shee had left him.'[38] This breakdown in 'sexual honour' amongst the gentry did not just raise questions about the place of the gentry within the social order but, by discrediting the system, threatened patriarchy.[39] This has been convincingly argued by Cynthia Herrup in her work on the trial of Mervin Touchet, second Earl of Castlehaven, who was found guilty and executed for the assisted rape of his wife and acts of sodomy. Herrup maintains that Castlehaven's trial and execution was not primarily the result of his involvement in the alleged sexual assaults, but instead because of his transgressions against the patriarchal order, which not only destroyed his household but represented a direct threat to social hierarchy.[40]

Paralleling Blundell's notes on 'sexual honour' was a broader concern with honour *per se*, evident in his attempt to refute the perceived links between honour and duelling. In his entries entitled 'duellem', which were accorded large sections in both commonplace books, Blundell provided extensive notes from textual sources and information from friends along with his own thoughts on duelling.[41] The thrust of these sections was to highlight the absurdity of the practice, arguing that the underlying conceptions that informed duelling were wrong, as seen in his conclusion to one section that 'Duells are the maddest acts in the World'.[42] Blundell's attack had a number of elements. His entries open by noting a list of honourable gentlemen who had refused duels, including an unreferenced note that Caesar had turned down a duel from Mark Antony and that Kenelm Digby, 'a Person very famous for valour and other great parts', had turned down an invitation from a young courtier.[43] He also recorded that subsequent monarchs had disapproved of the practice, noting with praise the 1660 proclamation against duelling introduced by Charles II.[44] Building on these notes, Blundell sought to show that duelling was the antithesis of a traditional English conception of honour.

According to Blundell duelling was a modern innovation that had no basis in history or the concepts of nobility recognised by ancient families. As he noted, 'I do not remember that eyther the Romans, Graetians, or any other warlick Nation before our tymes, did eyther hold or practice the moderne lewd principles maintained by many Christians, concerning duels'.[45] His comments, both in his personal speculation and in records of conversations he had with individuals, on 'the endlesse use of Duels' on the continent, also imply that he did not view the practice as being English and therefore it was an alien concept being projected on to English notions of nobility.[46] Finally, Blundell maintained that involvement in a duel was an act against God, arguing in his own reflections that any individual who initiated a duel lived in 'fear of Hell and a halter'. He supported this with a direct quote from *The Gentleman's Calling*, where there are 'many good things against Duells', including the argument that 'To initiate a Duellist his first challeng must be against God himself'.[47] For Blundell, those who would fight a duel over a slight on their honour were often the least honourable of people, a factor born out in the only example of such a practice that he could find in ancient history, when he compared duellists with gladiators, though any study would reveal 'what base men were used in that'.[48] Blundell quoted from Nathanial Ingelo's *Bentivolio and Urania*, a religious romance first published during the Restoration, that while duellists 'looke upon it as an ungentile thing to suffer wrong, they never scruple the doing of it, though that be a 100 tymes more base'.[49] Conversely, those who obstructed duelling were, in Blundell's eyes, true men of honour, a belief that led to one of his only positive comments on the Parliamentarian forces. In a note of a conversation that Blundell had with one Colonel Daniel in 1665, he recorded how Daniel told him that during his service for Parliament he never knew of any on that side who fought in a duel, with the exception of a corporal and a drummer. The corporal killed the drummer and was subsequently hanged. Recording that two regiments were assembled to execute justice on the corporal, Blundell stated that 'I hope it will not be denyed but that these armyes consisted of valiant men'.[50]

Blundell viewed the persistence of duelling as being the result of a range of factors. In a broad sense he maintained that duelling reflected misconceptions of honour and cowardice, or, in a phrase he lifted from Caussin's *The Holy Court*, 'the mistaken gallantry of the world'.[51] He turned to a number of incidents to demonstrate that duels represented 'false honour' and the issuers of the challenge had no conception of what honour was.[52] The most striking example was that of one Mr Fielding 'a forward Duellist', who Blundell noted had previously killed a coachman for refusing to pick him up, yet 'did most shamefully misbehave himself (I mean lik a coward) in one of our great Battles in the Late Dutch War at sea'.[53] Here Blundell twisted the notion of cowardice that had been perpetuated by duellists, maintaining that even the most accomplished dueller had failed to understand what true honour was. This position was supported in Blundell's reading of *Bentivolio and Urania*, from which he concluded that duellists 'stand so upon a false notion of Reputation ... that is they undervalue the estimation of God & the opinion of wise men, because they are unwilling that a few fooles should take them for Cowards'.[54] He was particularly concerned that such mistaken views of honour were being transferred to children by deluded parents, recording with horror how he had failed to engage a local boy in conversation after years of effort, though by chance he had mentioned duelling, whereupon Blundell noted 'you canot beleeve by how far he was transported with this discourse ... he gave me a spontaneous account of the most remarqueable actions of that nature in the County where he lived, and seemed able to give a list both of the sword men & the cowards'.[55] Blundell held parents responsible for such behaviour, noting elsewhere an account of a conversation he had with a 'person of great virtu' who spent many hours at prayer, yet described a duel in which his son had been involved with 'a kynd of glory in his sons supposed gallantry. So much doth false honour deceive even vertuous men.'[56] A close reading of Blundell's commonplaces indicates a final reason for the continued presence of duelling: women. In a personal reflection that parallels the story of Adam and Eve, and the image of woman as temptress, Blundell noted that one of the main reasons for the continued survival of the practice was that 'The Weomen (or young Girles) do urge on the men, by crying that down for Cowardize, which God & the Lawes comand'.[57] While this comment may, in part, recognise that women had a pivotal position in the gossip networks in which honour was upheld, as we will see, this deliberate juxtaposition of women with the forces of both law and religion is one that underlay many of Blundell's comments on women.[58]

Blundell offered a unique solution to duelling. Although he criticised the underlying conceptions of honour and virtue that informed the practice, he offered an alternative for those false conceptions of honour and valour to be retained. Blundell argued that, when challenged to partake in a duel, individuals should decline and instead offer to embark with the protagonist on 'some most noble and dangerous Enterprise, warranted & lawfull power in their Countryes service & that they may give a noble testimony to the world what true valour is'.[59] This was a theme that Blundell picked up again in a remarkable entry in the Adversaria entitled 'Here followes an answer to a chalenge which I had framed for a friend in or about the year 1666 or 67 being resolved then to have seconded him in so fayr and just a way', though, as Blundell recorded, the dispute was eventually resolved without recourse to violence. In the letter the individual categorically refuses to partake in a duel and offers to publicise the fact, stating that 'I shall own to all the world that I dare not be damn'd'. In place of a duel he proposes that he and the challenger should embark on a dangerous adventure in the Navy to prove their valour.[60] Whether Blundell conceived the offer as being serious or not is open for debate, and he may simply have viewed it as a method to flush out cowardly individuals who claimed to have been motivated by honour. However, it accorded with Blundell's view that a true gentleman would set an example to the rest of society. His alternative to the duel highlighted his conviction that duellists were individuals bereft of honour, and offers a positive outlet akin to his belief in the value of an active life for gentry in place of the duel.[61] That Blundell spent so much effort on behalf of his anonymous friend accords with Robert Shoemaker's view that during the early modern period the role of seconds was increasingly to defuse a duel before it started, as opposed to becoming antagonists in the process.[62] Finally, the entry that Blundell drafted for his friend shows how Blundell's reading practices often had a practical end. In this instance, his notes on duelling informed advice he was providing a friend and may have helped save him from engaging in such a deadly activity.

Blundell's attitude to duelling reflected broader contemporary attitudes to the practice. J. A. Sharpe claims that during the seventeenth century it was common for juries to give participants who killed their opponents nominal punishments, as long as the duel had been fought in a proper manner.[63] This does not mean that there was universal acceptance of duelling; recent studies have shown quite the opposite. Attitudes to violence gradually changed over the seventeenth century and an increasing aversion to the practice of duelling can be identified, which has led Shoemaker to observe 'a paradox: although duels were apparently fought to defend reputations, they were increasingly fought in private'.[64] In the early modern period duelling peaked during the early part of James I's reign and again during the reign of Charles II, which led both monarchs to make efforts to suppress the practice.[65] However, it may be that Blundell also had a vested interest in dismissing duelling as representing a false conception of honour. As Cust remarks, the 'man of honour was seen as someone constantly on his mettle, responding to potential challenges to his reputation, or to that of his family, if necessary, with the sanction of violence'.[66] Blundell could not respond to such challenges as he was unable to bear arms because of his recusancy.[67] His letters frequently complained that 'I was troubled a little some months agoe to see my trusty old sword taken from me which had been my companion when I lost my Limbs my Lands my Liberty for acting against the Rebels, in the Kings behalf', the insult being made worse by the the fact that the officer who took the weapon had fought for Parliament during the Civil War.[68] Thus, it may be that Blundell was partly motivated to attack duelling with such vigour because it was a demonstration of honour from which he was effectively excluded.

Blundell's commonplaces on the social order and his criteria for gentility provide not only a commentary on others but a reflection of his own interpretation of his position and duties as a gentleman. Throughout his life he pursued the active life advocated by Bacon, but interpreted through his own prism of a broader concept of public service. As we have seen, in his letter books and notebooks Blundell listed in detail his involvement in local, national and international affairs, with an emphasis on how he had fought for the monarchy and what he believed was the true Christian church.[69] Furthermore, in Little Crosby Blundell employed a distinctively paternal approach to estate management, where he protected the welfare of his tenants. The reward that he expected to receive for this was the loyalty and obedience of those he supported. This prescriptive attitude to the place of individuals in society was dictated not only by genteel standing but also by gender.

II

Blundell's commonplace books contain a miscellany of information about women, including notes on didactic material about gendered roles, such as Richard Allestree's *The Lady's Calling*, and historical and theological material which offered Blundell an insight into this topic.[70] Entries on women appear throughout the volumes under topical headings, such as the note on women and adultery, which appears under the title 'Adulterium'.[71] As is the case with much of the surviving Blundell material, a superficial reading can fail to identify nuances within his arguments. His commonplaces initially suggest a 'liberal' attitude to women. He frequently recorded that 'It is wonderfull how much this sex hath conduced to the increase of the Christian faith', supporting his argument with notes from history, such as Bede's example of Bertha the Christian wife of King Ethelbert whose example prompted the King's conversion, or the note from M. Alford's *Annales* that Clotilda brought the Christian faith into France.[72] He also highlighted instances when women had played an active and successful role within politics, recording in his own comments on Catherine de' Medici that 'Her courage & skill in Government was very great ... I have rarely read of any *man* who hath undergone so great a weight of Cares as this Queen Catherin'.[73] This unusual admiration of Catherine de' Medici was apparently a response to her brutal hounding of Protestants, Blundell turning a blind eye to the methods when he believed the cause was right. Elsewhere he commented on the practical abilities of women, noting almost verbatim from *An Accurate Description of the Netherlands* that it was common for women there to manage both household and business accounts, and that 'where the Wife's have the direction of the purs and trade, the husband seldom proves bankerupt'.[74] In one instance Blundell even challenged the contents of didactic literature on gendered roles, taking issue with the argument in Allestree's *Ladies Calling* that it is accounted 'ill breeding' for a man to go abroad with his own wife, in the statement 'I suppose those who brought up these rules are not to seeke what use to make of them'.[75]

Initially it would also appear that Blundell's theoretical perspective on the place of women in society extended to the manner in which he treated the female members of his family. His wife, daughters and sisters were literate. They made a number of, albeit brief, entries in his letter books, while Blundell's wife and one of his daughters signed the title page of the family copy of *An Epitome of Ortelius*.[76] As we have already seen, Blundell's wives, sisters and daughters played an active part in protecting the family estate during the Civil

War: his wife managed the estate while he was in exile and later his sisters lent him money to repurchase it. However, we should be wary of accepting Blundell's behaviour as indicative of his true values, or his commonplaces as indicative of a fixed personal perspective. Blundell's position on a range of contentious issues changed over time and in relation to his perceived audience. Furthermore, as Elizabeth Foyster has argued, contemporary comments on the position of women within society invariably represented an 'ideal model of gender relations rather than a reflection of its reality'.[77] Instead, recent work on women's history has shown that male comments about women often tell us more about the author's own conception of manhood.[78]

Blundell's commonplaces suggest that he was conscious of the physical differences between men and women. The defining physical aspects of womanhood, menstruation and childbirth, have been the subject of a number of studies, which have emphasised their ability to define gender boundaries during the early modern period.[79] Blundell's main issue with the female body was the point at which a man and woman could engage in sex after childbirth, the lack of any significant age gap between his children indicating that this was a matter of immediate personal concern. From two disparate sources Blundell drew information on this matter. From Bede's history he recorded St Gregory's instruction that a husband and wife could not lie together until the child was weaned, noting later from Richard Bloom's description of America that the natives of New York followed this practice strictly.[80] Blundell also noticed some subjective differences between male and female. In one entry he recorded that women were prone to idleness, a factor referred to later in the Adversaria which was juxtaposed with a note from his 'Scaligeriana' text, where he recorded how in Bearn, France, 'the wives as soon as they are delivered of a child goe to the plow & the Husbands betake them selves to their beds'.[81] Elsewhere he recorded that women were obsessed with consumption, claiming that although at one time clothing was passed between the generations for decades and women knew nothing more of London than its name, 'Now they know the streets as well as the Porters of the Town: & they pay not for their Gownes & silk stockings till there be half a dozen on the schore'.[82] For Blundell the tendency of women to accumulate could be controlled. However, he was deeply concerned with the consequence of failure to moderate female excesses, prompting him to emphasise the importance of placing them within strict boundaries controlled by men.

In a brief citation from *The Politician's Catechisme* Blundell noted that it was widely believed that 'the English Nation is more inclined to be advised by weomen than any other'.[83] Whether or not Blundell was in agreement with this statement is not revealed, however the view that English women were given too much freedom is manifest throughout his commonplaces. We have already seen that one of his chief complaints about the Quakers was what he viewed as the sacrilegious inclusion of women in services.[84] Furthermore, while the female members of Blundell's family had, at various times, held important positions within the household, he was conscious that this should be only within boundaries determined by the senior male in the family. He argued that women should have no authority to take over management of an estate or business because a man's actions were damaging it. In a personal reflection he juxtaposed women taking management from inept husbands, with what he viewed as the unlawful and unholy Reformation, noting that 'Women may pretend a title to governe because men have governed so ill, as plausibly as some have reformed the church upon the lyke pretenses'.[85] In this telling statement, women who overstepped boundaries prescribed by men are compared with the ungodly, irreligious forces of Protestantism, with male dominance representing the forces of law and true, Catholic religion. Blundell also believed that excessive freedom for females was promoting licentiousness. He recorded his dismay at seeing women behaving in an inappropriate manner around members of the other sex 'as impudent as syrens', noting from *The Holy Court* Caussin's rhetorical question, 'how can you account a gadding hos-wife, a dancing Reveler an idle wanton to be modest?'[86] The clearest example of Blundell's concern over the freedom of women surrounded female literacy. While Blundell was keen to educate the female members of his family, he was distressed that some women not only learnt to read but 'yet they have dared to censure in publicke the gravest divines, and whole religious orders in Gods Church', concluding that female criticism of works was invariably incorrect and that such opinions should be censored.[87] These fears did not concern only the improper behaviour of women but also the emasculation of their male counterparts.

Patricia Crawford has argued that since 'it was believed that women could turn into men by masturbation, or men degenerate into women, anxieties about gendered identities are not surprising'.[88] A preoccupation with protecting the male gendered identity from a subversive female influence underlies many of Blundell's notes on women. This was evident in his observation of female activity in all spheres of life, even those where they traditionally had a level of autonomy. In his own comments Blundell recorded his fears that the extent of female influence over simple household chores such as milking, washing and making cheese, was allowing them to exert control over men, in some cases even forcing them into marriages early. Recording that in Flanders and Holland men have complete control over all aspects of household management, he reflected that 'in England, seeing men are the best cookes Bruers Bakers & Midwives why should it be held a shame to milk &c: The want of this causeth many men to marry fondly or to do worse, seeing they cannot ... keep hous without a woman'.[89] Outside the home Blundell's anxiety about female activity increased, a factor that was no doubt influenced by the widely held view that male honour was determined equally by the behaviour of their wives as by their own.[90] We have already seen that he believed one of the major reasons for the continued practice of duelling was that women and girls urged on men, questioning their honour and emasculating them if they failed to partake in a duel.[91] This fear can be seen also in Blundell's notes on adultery.

In a series of notes grouped together by Blundell under the title 'Adulterium' Blundell recorded a deep concern over female inclination to adulterous behaviour, apparently believing, like many contemporaries, that adultery was a crime against both the husband and society.[92] He lingered less on observing the physical encounter and more on how female sexuality could be controlled and cuckolded men prevented from being relegated to a lesser status.[93] Like many of his male contemporaries Blundell was keen to stop the threat to patriarchal society that the adulteress posed. A number of methods were noted in his commonplaces. From Paul Rycaut's history of the Ottoman Empire Blundell recorded that 'Among the Turks a man is not said to be a cuckold or any wayes disgraced in case his wife play false', instead the 'horns' were reserved for her father, brother and other male family members.[94] Although this method removed the husband from blame, it still did not draw enough attention to the woman, the emphasis remaining, unsatisfactorily for Blundell, on men. Instead he listed methods in which the woman could be made to pay directly for her actions. Throughout the early modern period contemporaries employed social shaming rituals to punish women who threatened the patriarchal order; the variety of such charivari was immense.[95] Although more conventional punishments, such as the ducking stool, do not appear in Blundell's notes, he offered a variety of chilling alternatives including one in which the adulteress was forced to drink 'a certain water & thereupon her thigh to rot', or the example taken from Juan Luis Vives, that 'Bawdes in Spain are punished by being set naked in the hot sun anointed with honey which drawes to it an exceeding number of Bees, Flyes and Wasps'.[96] Blundell's attitude to those women who operated outside the boundaries of patriarchal society was seemingly summed up in his version of Ecclesiasticus 22:4, that 'Shee that is bold shameth father and husband'.[97]

The emphasis on the manifold virtues of marriage that runs throughout Blundell's commonplace books emphasises the importance of what he saw as the primary tool for managing the excesses of female behaviour.[98] Blundell was not atypical in this belief, and during the early modern period marriage 'functioned as a guarantor of gender difference' with women losing their individual role in society and being recognised instead by their marital status.[99] For Blundell, a successful marriage involved a careful balance of control by the male party, evident in his juxtaposition of two quotations from Proverbs: 'He that is a foole serve the Wife. Proverbs 11.29. A ring of gold in a swines snowt a fair woman and a Foole. Proverbs 11.22'.[100] As these entries show, Blundell's view of women was that on the one hand a controlled woman could represent accord, for the husband, the family and society, though without clear boundaries female agency threatened to topple the patriarchal order, and along with it law and religion. This was a view which crossed the confessional divide, and Blundell was not unique in viewing women as being at once objects of beauty, symbols of harmony and sources of constant fear.[101]

III

Blundell's observations on society also include ethnographic notes on other cultures. These appear throughout both commonplace books in relation to particular issues, such as different approaches to providing charity, or under specific headings which consider the behaviours and beliefs of particular religious groups (such as 'Judei') or nations (such as 'Holandi').[102] Blundell used a broad range of sources to construct his ethnographic commonplaces. The main focus was the texts he engaged with, which included many noted contemporary works of travel writing, such as Henry Blount's *Voyage into the Levant*, the anonymous *Adventures of (Mr T. S.) an English Merchant taken Prisoner by the Turks of Algiers* and Peter Heylyn's *Cosmographie*.[103] These were supplemented with two other categories of information. In his notes on Europe he regularly included material drawn from his own experience, describing, for instance, how he had seen Jews in Amsterdam in their synagogue and witnessed the Dutch workhouses.[104] He also interviewed travellers with first-hand experience and natives of different countries. During his stay in London in the late 1680s, Blundell deliberately sought out individuals with connections to China. In a brief entry in the Historica he recorded that in 1687 and 1688 he had regular conversations 'in Latin with a natural Chinese whom I did sundry times meet with by reason that he went to the Latin school at the Savoy. He told me that he was a Native of Pekim (or Pekin) and that he had been about 8 years absent from China.'[105] During the same period he also interviewed one Father Couplet, the author of a broadside on the population of China, who told Blundell that he had been a Jesuit missionary there for twenty years and 'he was waiting for an opportunity to pass once again to *his beloved China*'.[106] Elsewhere Blundell noted that while in Dieppe in 1660 he had chance to interview 'a young Polander ... Stanislaud de Raciberko Morstin', with whom he discussed a range of issues from language to philosophy.[107] The three types of source Blundell used were amalgamated in his commonplaces, and his entries demonstrate that he was at once both a reader and writer of travel literature, as well as yielding important insights into the manner in which Blundell approached both the world and his place within it.

In his essay 'Of Travel', Bacon outlined principles that should inform travel writing.[108] The logical conclusion of his work was that travel should be used to advance knowledge through rational inquiry.[109] Bacon challenged his readers to travel in an objective manner, marked by a rationalist engagement with the cultures discovered, concluding that one should not seek to assert superiority, but instead collect 'some Flowers', which the traveller can subsume into 'the Customs of his own Country'.[110] Bacon's work on travel clearly had an impact on the approach evident in Blundell's ethnographic commonplaces. Blundell frequently quoted the essay 'Of Travel', most notably recording Bacon's wonder that comparatively few accounts of land travel had been published in contrast to the many accounts of sea travel, though 'nothing is to be seene but sky and sea'.[111] Initially it appears that Blundell strictly adhered to Bacon's prescriptions, and that his only goal in engaging with this material was to empathise with and understand the cultures he studied on their own terms, most evident in his recognition that all cultures seem bizarre to the outsider: 'We can laugh when we hear how the Indian Widows cast themselves upon the burning piles of their dead Husbands; and they can laugh at our custom of fighting Duels; yet neither they nor we can discern our own follyes'.[112] However, as we will see, a nuanced reading of this material demonstrates another, more subtle purpose.

The breadth of topics covered in Blundell's travel commonplaces is wide. Like many of his contemporaries he viewed the nation as a physical space.[113] He frequently made entries on the geography of different nations, such as his note that China 'is as big as France, Spaine, Itally, Germany, Low countries, great Brittaine and all the Isles belonging to it'.[114] This approach was evident in his notes on England, where he recorded from Chamberlayne's *Anglia Notitia* that 'It contains about 30000000 Acres, about the thousandth part of the Globe & 333 part of the habitable Earth, almost ten tymes as big as the United Netherlands'.[115] His interest in the physical aspects of the spaces he studied can also be seen in his comments on architecture, among which we find his astonishment that 'All buildings in Japan are made of wood'.[116] Alongside this interest in space was a concern with the wildlife of particular areas, which included comments on the numbers of fish in the Caspian Sea and the 'wonderfull number of Bees & of Bears in the forests of Lithunia'.[117] However, the focus of Blundell's interest in different nations was the people and cultures that the intrepid traveller might discover.

Blundell frequently remarked on the national characteristics that travel writers used to define groups, such as his note that the French are constantly rushing.[118] This extended to notes on national diets, including his comment from Simon de La Loubere's history of Siam, that 'in their Bazars or Markets they do sell Insects boil'd or rosted'.[119] As was the case with much early modern travel writing, an obvious preoccupation of Blundell's commonplaces was the physical appearance of the different peoples he studied.[120] In his summary of Avril's *Travels* he provided a large section on the physical features of the Tartar people, including notes on their height, posture and usual attire, as well as recording that they 'are all swarthy, but more inclineing to Olive colour then black. Their face usually broad, falling in below and jutting above; their eyes small, but sparkleing & full of fire; their noses short & very flat with little hair upon their lip or chin.'[121] His entry on the 'natural Chinese' he met in London in 1688 follows a similar pattern, the bulk of which focuses on the physical characteristics that Blundell personally observed while speaking with the man. He recorded that 'His stature was low and his complexion very swarthy. His nose was very flat and his eyes, by reason that his face, in that part, was also flat, stood outward somwhat odly and were bery brown: yet his countenance was pleasing & smileing.'[122] Like Bacon, Blundell did not correlate types of behaviour with physiognomy.[123] Instead he stood in wonder at the myriad differences and similarities that both linked and separated different peoples.[124]

One of the defining features of Blundell's approach to different nations was a propensity to note positive aspects in the cultures he studied. In this sense his notes initially appear to accord with the arguments of many modern-day scholars, who, challenging the conclusions of Edward Said's *Orientalism* for the late eighteenth and nineteenth centuries, have maintained that early modern English writers did not always 'automatically assume the cultural, economic, or even religious superiority of Christianity'.[125] In his notes from Avril's *Travels* Blundell was awed at the strength of Muscovy Russia's trade in fish, speculating that it was so strong that 'it seems to me that almost all our trade for Sturgeon comes from thence'.[126] He praised the soldiers of the Ottoman Empire not only for their gallantry on the battlefield but also for their honourable behaviour off it. With the activities of Parliamentarian troops during the English Civil War fresh in his memory, Blundell recorded from Rycaut's history of the Ottoman Empire that their armies pay for the goods and lodging that they use with cash and that 'there are no complaints by Mothers of the rape of their Virgin daughters, no violences or robberies offered on the Inhabitants'.[127] He also noted that when St Francis 'went to the Great Turk to convert him ... with what great respect he was entertained by him'.[128] Elsewhere he alluded to the 'incomparable moral virtues of the Japanese' and noted that China 'is known by every body to have exceeded for many ages all other Countryes, in ... all these things which the world esteems to be great'.[129] Blundell even adversarially engaged with Avril's work on Muscovy Russia to draw out positive aspects of the culture. Noting that Avril maintained 'the great aversion which the Moscovian Scizmaticks, that are the Greek Church, bear to the Church of Rome', Blundell proceeded immediately by recording the 'great charity & kindness shew'd to him [Avril] & his companion by the Archbishop of Astrakan' who went out of his way to ensure their safe passage.[130] He appears to have held Avril as ungrateful for the generosity he received, believing his comments were motivated by a desire to demonstrate his religious superiority over the Muscovites.

That Blundell frequently found positive aspects in the cultures he read about reflected his engagement with the Baconian approach to travel writing; large sections of his notes suggest that he read to *learn* from the cultures that he discovered in his reading. In his entries on the Dutch, Blundell found a system of managing the poor that suited this purpose. Blundell was committed to providing charity for those in need, which formed part of a broader approach to public service that he deemed as an essential component of gentility. However, evidence from both his commonplace books and his correspondence indicates a concern that the undeserving poor should be chastised and punished.[131] In his summary of *An Accurate Description of the Netherlands* he noted that, while there were hospitals and hostels for widows and children, individuals who refused to work 'are set in a tubb wherein if they do not pump the water will swell over their heads' and praised 'Another house for whores to be kept at work'. This distinction between deserving and 'idle' poor in Amsterdam was one that Blundell believed could be applied with positive results in England, and he noted that 'I my self who note these things from my Author, did, in the year 1660 stand in great admiration at the charity, order & magnificance of a number of these houses [for the poor]'.[132] The most pertinent of Blundell's observations that he believed could be emulated with positive effect in England concerned the place of religion in society. As we have seen, Blundell was wary of the damage that letting unworthy individuals engage in religious debate could do to society.[133] From his viewpoint this had been the catalyst for the Reformation and subsequent wars of religion, the cause of various sects appearing in the mid-seventeenth century, and had eventually resulted in the execution of a lawful monarch by his subjects. This was reinforced in Blundell's observations on the Ottoman Empire where he noted from Heylyn's *Cosmographie* that 'The Turks forbid all dispute on Religion ... a cause of their long continuance'.[134] This form of engagement with other cultures may have acted also as a substitute for Blundell's lack of any real public role. As a recusant Blundell could not hold office and therefore could not effect change in relation to the regime's treatment of the poor or the place of religion in society. It may be that his comments on these issues in other societies functioned as projects which allowed him a form of theoretical political engagement by proxy.

Blundell's interest in the role of religion in other cultures permeates his notes. He was particularly interested in the spread of Christianity and his commonplaces on travel writing often allude to the success of Jesuit missionaries in such remote lands as Japan and Russia.[135] The relation of the number of conversions in different nations may have helped assure him that the Catholic Church was increasing, but he was also particularly concerned to make observations on the religious beliefs of other cultures. A number of these observations were made without criticism and often slanted in a positive manner. We have already seen how Blundell critically engaged with Avril's *Travels* to draw out positive elements of the Greek Orthodox Church.[136] This was supplemented with additional material taken from the *Relation of the Siege of Candia*, from which he noted that their priests are 'exceedingly respected by the people'.[137] Comments on Islam followed suite. Blundell noted from Avril's *Travels* 'the Turks great devotion in praying devoutly, at the least 3 or 4 times a day' and from Rycaut's history of the Ottoman Empire that '*so large benevolence is (there) given to places destinate to Gods service that as some compute one thirds of the Lands of the whole Empire are allotted and set out to a holy use*'.[138] A particular concern with the Jews is also evident. From a range of textual sources, supplemented with his own experience of the Jewish community in Amsterdam, Blundell noted that the Jews were 'the most skilful people in the world' in their study of the Old Testament, made estimates of the number of Jews living in the areas that he read about, and included material about their history from Biblical times to contemporary.[139] It is tempting to ascribe Blundell's interest in the Jews to an affinity with their persecution; as Janell Metzger argues, Jews were 'the original recusants' and Blundell no doubt found parallels in the way the two groups had been treated.[140] However, the way in which these notes were constructed suggests another, more calculated, purpose.

Although Blundell was influenced by the approach to different cultures outlined by Bacon, when it came to the study of religion it appears that he had a vested interest. The focus of Blundell's writing on these groups was apparently to compare them with Catholicism, both in the ways they intersected and in how they diverged. He selectively read many of the sources used in these sections to argue that other religious groups were similar to Catholicism, but for a few 'chief error[s]', further contributing to the historical credibility that Blundell tried to argue for Catholicism, as well as suggesting that Catholicism was the original and correct interpretation of both Christianity and religion in general.[141] For instance, in his notes on the Greek Orthodox Church he highlighted the similarities with Catholicism, noting from Sandys's *Europae Speculum* that 'Those of the Greek Church do concurre *with Rome* in the opinion of Transubstantiation, & generally in the sacrifize and whole body of the Masse' as well as accepting the importance of the saints, auricular confession and purgatory. In this note from Sandys, Blundell completely ignored other material presented on the same page excerpted, where it was argued that the Greek Church fell 'betweene the Romanists and Protestants' and that many aspects of their practice and belief were mirrored in Protestantism.[142] Blundell noted only that their 'chief error seems to be concerning the Holy-ghost', though he failed to elaborate further.[143] Elsewhere he recorded having read the French text *La Créance de l'Église*, which he claimed 'does chiefly endeavour and to prove (as it does most abundantly) that the Greek Schismaticks since the 11th age of the Church even to this present seventeenth, have mantaind the Doctrin of transubstantiation'.[144] This approach was also evident in his treatment of non-Christian religious groups.

In a brief note taken from Avril's *Travels* Blundell alluded to Buddhism, recording in his own words that they 'are Idolaters and do acknowledg for their Patriarck the Dalai-Lama ... It is wonderfull to hear what reverence is given to this Imposter Dalae by all this Idolatrous people ... They do believe he never dies and an imposture is used to give credit to that opinion.'[145] However, rather than dismissing the Dalai Lama altogether, Blundell recorded Avril's argument that 'this Dalae-Lama is the same with the famous Preste-Jean'.[146] Prester John was a mythical character in Christian folklore, prominent from the twelfth century onwards, whom contemporaries claimed was the ruler of a powerful Christian empire in the East and would one day join co-religionists in the west in the battle against the Ottoman Empire.[147] In resurrecting this notion, Blundell was implying that, while the foundations of Buddhism were idolatrous, they were based on a subverted notion of Catholicism. In a similar manner, while Blundell may have had an interest in Jews, he viewed them as failed Catholics, consistently noting that they did not adopt many of the 'correct' practices of Catholicism. Interestingly Blundell made no reference to the fact the Jews did not recognise Jesus as the Son of God, instead recording that 'They kneele not at their Church service; and are otherwaies exceeding irreverent'.[148] In his notes from Sandys's *Europae Speculum* Blundell recorded that 'Their Chief Scandals in Christian Religion' surrounded their failure to accept transubstantiation and the reverence that is given to images.[149] Therefore, while Blundell was clearly influenced by the approach to other cultures outlined by Bacon, he failed to adopt it in its entirety, and, as was the case with his approach to English Protestants, when discussing other religions he sought to demonstrate the supremacy of Catholicism.

Recent research on travel writing has shown that, when reading and writing travel literature, contemporaries embarked on a journey of self-discovery as well as an exploration of the other.[150] Work on Protestants has emphasised that a central component of the emerging sense of an English and, later, British identity during the late seventeenth and eighteenth centuries was the juxtaposition of a nascent culture of Britishness with a politically, ideologically and religiously different country on the continent, usually France.[151] There are numerous examples of contemporaries using travel to assert what Mary Fuller has referred to as 'cultural superiority'.[152] This is evident in Gerald MacLean's study of William Biddulph, an English clergyman whose account of nearly a decade spent in the Ottoman Empire, first published in 1609, 'largely reinforced prejudices that he had brought with him, but at the same time they reflect the different degrees to which he felt foreign customs threatened Protestant belief'. Thus, in an account littered with bigotry, not only did Biddulph regularly draw on hearsay to inform his work but his writings are rife with the 'compulsive correcting of other people's errors'.[153] In the same way, Blundell was unable to avoid asserting 'cultural superiority' and like the Protestant William Biddulph he eventually labelled all practices that deviated from his own as erroneous corruptions of the belief system that he upheld. Thus, Blundell's approach to other cultures was endemic amongst his contemporaries, wherever they stood in relation to the confessional divide. However, as a Catholic in a Protestant country it seems likely that Blundell's need to do so may have been all the greater. By emphasising the supremacy of his own faith compared with others, Blundell no doubt reinforced his resolve at the times when it cost him most dearly to adhere to Catholicism.

IV

The area of Blundell's notes that was most clearly influenced by Bacon was his interpretation of science writing and natural wonders. Erica Fudge has described Bacon as the 'Father' of the new science movement of the early modern period, while the Baconian approach was 'the basis for much of the most substantial scientific work' that Charles Webster detailed in his study of science in the mid-seventeenth century.[154] This was a factor recognised by Blundell, who constructed elaborate defences in his commonplace books of both the new science movement, epitomised in the approaches to the world adopted by the Royal Society, and Bacon's specific interpretation of natural philosophy. In a brief entry in the Historica, Blundell collated references from learned individuals who had praised Bacon, which included a non-specific reference from Ben Jonson, alongside notes from James Howell and the Catholic convert Toby Matthews.[155] Blundell's entries imply that natural philosophy was the most rigorous and complex of all disciplines, recording from the *General Collection of Discourses of the Virtuosi of France* that while 'any man or woman of competent age' can be taught all there is to know about logic, geography, moral philosophy and metaphysics by a great teacher in a matter of hours, '*for Natural philosophy he required ten times as much*'.[156] In his notes on Rapin's *Oeuvres Diverses* Blundell was highly critical of Rapin's arguments against the new science movement, recording that 'I can no wayes approve of his 19th chapter where he endeavours to prove that the ancient Philosophy is much better then the new'.[157] Reading against the grain of the text, Blundell claimed that Rapin's arguments were 'a great deal too weak, as depending too much on generalityes (& being some of them also untrue) to prove his assertion'.[158] The crux of Blundell's argument was to pick out contradictions in Rapin's work, notably that Rapin praised the new inventions of the Royal Society, which Blundell viewed as a validation of the new science approach.[159]

Furthermore, Blundell argued that the new science approach had altered perceptions of science and philosophy, claiming that it is clear from Rapin's own arguments that 'Bacon renewed in England the love of Philosophy'.[160] Blundell's commonplaces suggest a profound belief that his was an age of discovery and progress, arguing that the work of Bacon and his contemporaries had contributed to the fact 'that the sixty years last past have produced more discoveryes therin then a thousand years before'.[161]

In positing such an argument Blundell embroiled himself in a debate that was rife throughout early modern England concerning whether the ancients or moderns held supremacy. As Joseph Levine states, 'Apparently, everyone was profoundly concerned about the authority of classical antiquity, and everyone had to fix a position with respect to it before taking the plunge into modern life; and apparently, there was no subject, from art and literature to philosophy and science, from religion to politics, that was exempt from its concerns'.[162] While the centrality of this debate to the lives of contemporaries has long been recognised, links with modernity have traditionally been associated with Protestantism. In terms of religion this connection may seem obvious; however, even in regard to scientific advances many contemporaries and historians have highlighted the Puritan origins of modern science, often ignoring the input from other religious groups.[163] As Charles Webster remarks of the contemporary Puritan outlook, 'The sparkling image of the agricultural and technological proficiency of the ancient Hebrew culture was contrasted with the subsequent backwardness of the Roman Empire and catholic Christendom'; it was left to the Puritans to rekindle progress.[164] Recent work has begun to remedy this. In his study of the French aristocrat Charles de Marguetel de Saint-Denis-le-Gast, who was forced into exile in England shortly after the Restoration until the end of his life in 1703, Levine draws attention to an influential Catholic who exhibited a marked penchant for the moderns from an early age. In his literary tastes he had a preference for such 'moderns' as Pierre Corneille, while he praised the work of Descartes and the French scientist Pierre Gassendi, noting that they had both discovered truths unknown to Aristotle.[165] Indeed, Blundell's remarks on Bacon and the 'moderns' highlights that the debate between the authority of ancient and modern was one that all contemporaries had to navigate and that one's position on the confessional divide did not automatically determine how a contemporary would engage with this issue.

Bacon's approach to scientific discovery was to collect evidence, interpret it and develop axioms.[166] He held that observers must avoid projecting their beliefs on to their sensory observations, and instead rely wholly on their 'instrument' to rid themselves of the damaging effects of their 'idols'.[167] Successful observations, which Bacon called 'primary histories', involved the observer ensuring that 'all superstitious stories ... and experiments of ceremonial magic should be altogether rejected'.[168] This had important consequences for the place of religion in such work, and as he noted in a letter to Toby Matthews, 'the world must not "reject truth in philosophy, because the author dissenteth in religion"'.[169] Blundell sought to emulate this approach. However, like Bacon, he did not altogether abandon more traditional views of the world.[170] For instance, we have already noted that Blundell believed that God intervened in day-to-day affairs and that providential acts resulted in painful endings for many of those who opposed Catholicism. None the less, Bacon's influence can be felt throughout Blundell's notes on science and the natural world.

Blundell's interests in scientific discovery were manifold. We have already noted the praise with which he lauded the inventions of his age, a factor which informed his meticulous entries on the workings of contemporary inventions, most notably a sophisticated music box built in London.[171] He copied brief sections on chemicals and light from Digby's *Powder of Sympathy* and noted that in *Micrographia* Robert Hooke 'holds no colours but black and white'.[172] Incorporated within Blundell's notes on scientific discovery were entries on mathematical problems. Despite noting what 'very little knowledge I have had in this kind of study', Blundell briefly considered methods for measuring angles and notes on probability, including nine single sides of folio on the probability of dice landing on certain numbers.[173] Most of Blundell's notes on scientific discovery were observations on the natural world. Blundell recorded a myriad of material on this topic, including information on behemoths, huge fish and eels that hunted whales, from such disparate sources as the verbal testimony of an ex-pirate turned Jesuit priest, weekly newsbooks and travel and historical literature.[174] Blundell also speculated on the existence of creatures such as the phoenix and the dragon, noting with regard to the latter that 'I do not know in what part of the world Dragons are now to be found, nor doe I know the shape or size. They are often mentioned by the prophets in holy writ.'[175] He was fascinated by the workings of the human body and his commonplaces regularly incorporate entries such as the account relayed by a friend that during the siege of Harwarden Castle a servant was 'shot in to her mouth and the bullet cam out of her Arse hole, and shee recovered the hurt ... But the bullet (you must know) cam many days after it was shot, through the common passage with her excrements.'[176] His notes on the natural world were concerned with three main topics: the weather, the earth and abnormalities in the natural order, and were grouped together in sections throughout the commonplace books under headings relating to the specific topic (as opposed to theme) at hand.[177]

Blundell had a deep interest in the weather. In his Small Account Book he and his daughter Clare Frances made and compared daily observations on the weather over a period of two months between November and December 1656.[178] The main concern of his commonplace books was extreme weather.

Under the title 'Gelu' (Chill), he quoted directly from a letter by one Michael Roth, which detailed the Thames being frozen over in January 1683.[179] From Nieremberg's *Treatise of the Difference Betwixt the Temporal and Eternal* he listed earthquakes, recording how the force of one was such that the sea 'swelled above the tops of howses in Alexandria and left ships upon the howses tops'.[180] He recorded a number of powerful storms, noting both contemporary and historical instances when hail 'as big as a mans head' had killed pigeons and destroyed fields of crops, and from Knolles's *General History of the Turks* that in 1625 hailstones of seven or eight ounces had fallen in Constantinople.[181] Interestingly, throughout these accounts Blundell never alluded to possible causes for such weather, nor did he predict further incidents. In his record of the earthquake in Alexandria, Blundell made no reference to the fact that the account was from a section on the apocalypse, and was used by Nieremberg as evidence of God's punishment for 'the vanity and deceit' of peoplekind, removing the account fully from the context in which it was originally related.[182] Instead his commonplaces on this topic are entirely concerned with describing the events in meticulous detail. The most revealing example of this occurred when Blundell was seventy-seven years old and Lancashire was victim to a violent hailstorm. He provided a summary of the incident spanning three single sides of folio which gave extensive notes on the damage it did to Crosby Hall, including the number of windows broken and animals killed by hailstones.[183] In a proto-scientific experiment, despite the hailstones melting rapidly Blundell 'caused more then 40 of the bigger sort to be gathered in a wooden dish. Those expecially and infinite many of the rest were most certainly larger somewhat in diameter then the bigger sort of henns eggs. I weighed some few which I found to exceed in weight above two ounces but none to weigh 2 ounce & a halfe.'[184] Blundell's meticulous collecting, weighing and measuring of the hailstones reflected aspects of the approach to the weather detailed in Robert Hooke's 'Method for Making a History of the Weather', printed in Thomas Sprat's *History of the Royal Society* in 1667.[185] Although Blundell never referred directly to Hooke's method, his commonplaces show that he read Sprat's *History*, suggesting that he probably engaged with Hooke's contribution on observing the weather.[186] During the late seventeenth and eighteenth centuries most observers were moving to similar 'objective' records of the weather, but this approach was by no means universally accepted. In his work on an anonymous weather diary of 1703, Jan Golinski shows how its author drew on 'the resources of analogy and metaphor, rather than instrumental measurements ... to describe the vicissitudes of atmosphere'.[187] Furthermore, central to seventeenth and eighteenth century approaches to meteorological phenomena was the debate over whether the weather was 'the result of natural causes or a product of direct divine intervention', with many holding that storms were 'a divine punishment for the depravities of modern life'.[188] That Blundell's lexicon of the weather was devoid of religious interpretation or analogy and metaphor was apparently a deliberate effort to eradicate his idols from his interpretation of the world.

The late seventeenth century, particularly the 1690s, was a period noted for 'theories of the earth'.[189] This is reflected in Blundell's notes and a number of commonplace entries concern such topics as estimations of the distance between the sun and the earth and entries on Descartes's argument that objects are lighter the further from earth they are.[190] While in a brief entry under the indicative title 'Atheisme', Blundell was quick to concur with the view of Thomas Burnet's *The Theory of the Earth*, which he noted was 'most notable against the Epicureans to prove that the world was made by God & not by a fortuitous concours of Attoms', the rest of his notes on this topic were distinctly secular in tone, aggressively rejecting scriptural interpretations of natural events.[191] By the early seventeenth century Galileo was one of a number of philosophers supporting the view that the earth was in constant motion, though this opinion was far from universally accepted at the time Blundell was writing and formed a preoccupation for his notes.[192] He recognised that the primary objections to the theory that the earth was in motion were taken from 'scripture and from ocular experience, which are two great testimonyes if we do not mistake them', but, as we will see, dismissed arguments based on these sources with an alacrity that bordered on aggression.[193] Blundell's notes suggest that he believed that the earth being in motion was almost self-evidently true, backing up the view with only two brief examples in which he argued that the occurrence of earthquakes was incontrovertible proof of the motion of the earth, and noted the view of *Britannica Baconica* that the motion of the earth was 'the cause of the flowing and ebbing of the sea' and the reason why the Thames flooded.[194] Instead he focused his attention on ridiculing scriptural interpretations of the earth. For instance, in a 'Scriptura Difficultis' section Blundell quoted Psalms 21:6, which he recorded as 'My heart is made as wax melting in the middest of my Belly', under which he wrote 'I do note this expression to oppose to those texts wherby some would prove that the Earth is fixt: and I do not see but they may as wel say that Davids heart was in his Belly'.[195] His belief that it was wrong to accept scriptural interpretations of the motion of the earth was starkly pronounced in his rhetorical question, 'I saw 4 angels standing upon the 4 corners of the Earth Apocalyps: c7 v1 hath it therefore corners?'[196] Blundell's notes are not unique for the position adopted, but the contempt with which he rejected scriptural interpretations provides an important insight into his worldview.

Blundell's critical approach to the world can also be seen in his notes on abnormalities in the natural order. Scattered throughout the commonplace books, these entries are found in notes on the country in which the abnormality originated, or in some cases were grouped together under titles indicating the monstrosity discussed.[197] Throughout the early modern period there was a fascination with individuals with severe disabilities or deformities. So-called monster literature, which detailed the distinguishing features of such individuals, was widely popular, and the efforts of entrepreneurial publishers meant that its content was accessible to all levels of society.[198] Katherine Park and Lorraine Daston have shown that during the sixteenth and seventeenth centuries monster literature evolved in light of philosophic and scientific advances. While their arguments have been criticised for suggesting that this shift was a rapid, linear transition, during the early modern period contemporaries increasingly rejected providential interpretations of monsters, instead highlighting the intrinsic wonder of the monstrous elements discussed and offering natural causes in place of supernatural.[199] Bacon provided an important step in 'the gradual process of naturalization begun in the wonder books'.[200] In his *Novum Organum* he praised the study of such monsters, arguing that 'he who has learnt ... [nature's] deviations, will be able more accurately to describe her [normal] paths'.[201] The central tenets of Bacon's approach to monstrous births and wonders of nature, which encouraged observers to avoid projecting 'idols' of the mind on to their observations of the world, were studiously adopted by Blundell in his notes on this area.[202]

While Blundell dismissed as doubtful Augustine's musings that there existed 'whole Nations, as it were, of monsters', his commonplace entries on this topic spanned a wide range of monster related interests.[203] Blundell recorded Howell's claim that women of North Holland excrete a form of afterbirth which 'is a thing lyke a Batt ... The midwife throws it into the fyre, and holds a sheet before it, least it should fly awaye'.[204] He noted the account of a forty-two-year-old woman who gave birth to 365 children in one sitting, 'the od one wher of was a Hermophradite, the rest both sexes equally divided', all of which died after being baptised.[205] He also had a particular interest in recording abnormally tall people. He personally took 'the Mesure of Mrs Jane Mere a Lancashyre mayd AD 1664 she was 2 yards 3 inches high in low shoes' and while in London in the same year he paid 6*d* to meet one John Dodes and that 'All I could do standing flat on my heels was to reach with the point of my long finger to the very top or midle part of his head'.[206] These observations were supplemented with notes from texts he read, such as 'Stowes Abridgment speakes of a Dutch man at London in 1581 whose stature was 7 foote 7 inches'.[207] Blundell's thirst for monster literature is not only documented in his commonplace books.

In 1668 Blundell's *A Letter Writ to a Friend: Being a Description of a Horn, which Grows in the Back Part of the Head of an Ancient Woman ... Living at Saughal* was printed, and it now constitutes the only contemporary printed work written by Blundell that survives.[208] In the broadsheet, which contains just over 650 words, Blundell noted that one Mary Davies, a widow of seventy-one years of age 'shewed me growing fast upon the back part of her head, a perfect Horn, not unlike in colour to the horn of a Sheep ... I found it from the Root to one end of the Tip ... to be half a foot in length, bating out half an inch'. He continued by providing details on the colour and texture of the horn, along with notes on Davies's medical history.[209] Blundell's description highlights a condition well documented in medical literature. Human horns, known to the medical profession as *cornu cutaneum* or cutaneous horns, are compacted keratin that forms in the shape of a horn. They are 'exceedingly rare in humans' and can develop in a variety of locations on the body and grow to lengths of more than 25 cm.[210] Blundell's account of Davies was corroborated in a 1676 anonymous pamphlet entitled *A Brief Narrative of a Strange and Wonderful Old Woman that Hath a Pair of Horns Growing Upon her Head* and again in Charles Leigh's observations on the natural history of Lancashire and Cheshire printed in 1700.[211]

Early modern accounts of cutaneous horns overwhelmingly offered the reader an explanation for their growth. The earliest case of a cutaneous horn to be described in full, that of Margaret Gryffifth in 1588, was thought to have been caused by 'that in her youth, her husband had suspected her of "some light behaviour" and chided her severely. She had denied with as much vehemence and rejoined that if she had given her husband the horn, she wished that a horn would grow from her own forehead'.[212] In 1646 a seventy-year-old Dutch woman who had a long cutaneous horn speculated that it was divine judgement for her arguments with her prodigal son.[213] As wonder works became popular, so interpretations of the causes of cutaneous horns altered. Leigh's explanation was based not on divine forces but instead on the power of maternal imagination. Recording a picture of a horned woman he once observed at Whalley Abbey in Lancashire, Leigh speculated that 'whence came this *Lusus Naturae*, or Praeternatural accident, is, I think, a *Phoenomenon* not to be accounted for, unless at the time of Coition some such Monstrous Idea might then be imprinted on the *Foetus*'.[214] Leigh noted the example of a child born with the figures of leaves, boughs and cherries in the palms of its hand, which was the result of the mother dreaming 'she was with Child of a Cherry-Tree, which made such a wonderful Impression on the Foetus' but claimed he could not give further examples, as to do so 'wou'd too much swell this Chapter to recite them'.[215] Margrit Shildrick argues that this reasoning behind monstrous births does not highlight the power of the female body but its 'inherent weakness' and reflects the female's inability to separate appearance from reality.[216] However, increasingly authors were offering more secular perspectives for such occurrences, such as that found in the *Brief Narrative* concerning Mary Davies's horn, which the author claimed was 'occasioned by wearing a straight Hat'.[217]

Both in his commonplace entries on monsters and in his broadsheet, Blundell made no attempt to identify possible causes for such deformities, whether the growth of a horn or the birth of 365 babies which died after being baptised. Instead he followed Bacon's method closely, noting particular details about the respective monsters without speculating on their cause. Only on two occasions did his commonplace entries deviate from the 'objective' approach to natural philosophy outlined by Bacon, when Blundell provided a brief entry taken from Digby's *Powder of Sympathy* detailing 'strange storyes' of the power of maternal imagination, and a quotation from Ephraim Pagit's *Heresiography* that Anne Hutchinson 'a troublesome Antinomian Sectary in New England' was delivered of thirty monstrous births at one sitting '*much about the number of her monstrous opinions*'.[218] However, with both entries Blundell referenced their content with no indication that he agreed with their arguments. His observations deliberately emulated the approach outlined by Bacon and further indicate that Blundell's life cannot be dismissed as having been defined entirely by his recusancy.

V

Blundell's social and ethnographic commonplaces along with his notes on science writing suggest the same tension in his engagement with the practical world as was the case with his approach to the religious. Blundell's worldview was not dictated solely by an acceptance of Catholicism but instead by a tenuous balance of factors incorporating, amongst others, his religious beliefs, a commitment to the values of patriarchal society and support for the approach to the world advocated by the new science movement. A study of Blundell's ethnographic notes shows that the make-up of his identity was untidy and reveals the complexity of how individuals construct a sense of self. While Blundell made efforts to learn from the world around him, seeking to accept it on its own terms, he could not avoid viewing it through the prism of his own belief systems and in many cases failed to fully discharge his idols. In the same manner his observations on social hierarchy and female activity did not portray a fixed reality but instead his interpretation, from which he could not separate his own anxieties. Blundell's worldview fused elements from different areas of his life. Neither distinctly Catholic, fully representative of broad gentry concerns, nor in complete accordance with the approach outlined by Bacon, Blundell's approach to the world was idiosyncratic and incorporated strands that were apparently contradictory. The way in which these competing aspects were interwoven in Blundell's commonplace books suggests that the format could play a central role in the construction of a sense of self, supporting Sharpe's view that they were 'a place where the early modern self emerged from contemplation'.[219]

NOTES

1 K. Wrightson, *English Society 1580–1680* (London: Hutchinson, 1982), p. 19; K. Wrightson, 'The social order of early modern England: three approaches', in L. Bonfield, R. M. Smith and K. Wrightson (eds), *The World we Have Gained: Histories of Population and Social Structure* (Oxford: Basil Blackwell, 1986), p. 182.

2 D. Cressy, 'Describing the social order of Elizabethan and Stuart England', *Literature and History*, 3 (1976), p. 31; Wrightson, 'Social order', p. 182; H. R. French, 'The search for the "middle sort of people" in England, 1600–1800', *Historical Journal*, 43 (2000), p. 278.

3 Adversaria, fol. 31; Caussin, *The Holy Court*, I, p. 78.

4 Adversaria, fol. 9.

5 Adversaria, fols 40b, 51–b, 67b.

6 Adversaria, fol. 21.

7 Wrightson, *English Society*, p. 20; French, 'The search for the "middle sort of people"', p. 278; Cressy, 'Describing the social order', passim; F. Heal and C. Holmes, *The Gentry in England and Wales, 1500–1700* (Basingstoke: Macmillan, 1994), pp. 7–9.

8 Adversaria, fols 51–b; W. Watson, *A Decacordon of Ten Quodlibeticall Questions Concerning Religion and State* (1602), p. 119.

9 Adversaria, fol. 51b; Watson, *A Decacordon*, p. 117.

10 Adversaria, fol. 85; E. Chamberlayne, *Angliae Notitia, or, The Present State of England* (1672), p. 320; Cressy, 'Describing the social order', p. 31.

11 Adversaria, fol. 85; Heylyn, *Cosmographie*, p. 67.

12 Wrightson, *English Society*, pp. 20–2; Wrightson, 'Social order', p. 180; Heal and Holmes, *The Gentry in England and Wales*, pp. 6–19.

13 Great Hodge Podge, fols 89b–90, 184; Adversaria, fol. 139b. Although Blundell did not specify which Camden text he used for this statement, it was probably his *Remains* which include numerous comments on the social order: W. Camden, *Remains concerning Britain* (1674).

14 Cressy, 'Describing the social order', passim.

15 Adversaria, fol. 139b.

16 Adversaria, fol. 114.

17 R. Cust (ed.), *The Papers of Sir Richard Grosvenor, 1st Bart. (1585–1645)*, Record Society of Lancashire and Cheshire, 134 (1996), p. xxvi. Bacon's emphasis on the importance of an active life is discussed in: M. Peltonen, 'Politics and science: Francis Bacon and the true greatness of state', *Historical Journal*, 35 (1992), p. 288; M. Peltonen, 'Francis Bacon, the Earl of Northampton, and the Jacobean anti-duelling campaign', *Historical Journal*, 44 (2001), pp. 13–14; Bacon, *Of the Advancement and Proficience of Learning*. Blundell used the *Advancement of Learning* for a variety of purposes, in this context having read Bacon's comments on riches, Blundell speculated that 'Rich men are slaves some to pleasure some to profit', emphasising instead other aspects which he believed should inform one's approach to life, particularly Bacon's emphasis on the importance of charitable behaviour: Adversaria, fols 40b, 115; Bacon, *Of the Advancement and Proficience of Learning*, p. 302.

18 Thomas Beaumont, for example, placed significant emphasis on service in office in the construction of honour: R. Cust, 'Honour and politics in early Stuart England: the case of Beaumont v. Hastings', *Past and Present*, 149 (1995), p. 70.

19 R. Cust, 'Catholicism, antiquarianism and gentry honour: the writings of Sir Thomas Shirley', *Midland History*, 23 (1998), pp. 46–8; Cust, 'Honour and politics in early Stuart England', p. 74.

20 Adversaria, fol. 40b; Caussin, *The Holy Court*, I, p. 17.

21 Adversaria, fols 21, 53b; C. Ellis, *The Gentile Sinner, or, England's Brave Gentleman* (1661), p. 124.

22 Adversaria, fol. 51.

23 Adversaria, fols 39b, 165b–6, 218–b, 276b, 294b.

24 H. L. Smith, 'Introduction: women, intellect, and politics: their intersection in seventeenth-century England', in H. L. Smith (ed.), *Women Writers and the Early Modern British Political Tradition* (Cambridge: Cambridge University Press, 1998), p. 4.

25 L. G. Schwoerer, 'Women's public political voice in England: 1640–1740', in Smith (ed.), *Women Writers and the Early Modern British Political Tradition*, p. 58.

26 Adversaria, fol. 114b.

27 Adversaria, fols 55, 60b, 67b, 114, 139b, 180, 260b.

28 Adversaria, fol. 60b.

29 Adversaria, fol. 67b; N. N., *The Politicians Catechisme*, p. 77.

30 Adversaria, fol. 180; R. Allestree, *The Gentlemans Calling* (1660), p. 136.

31 Adversaria, fol. 260b.

32 Adversaria, fol. 180.

33 M. Stolberg, 'The crime of Onan and the laws of nature: religious and medical discourses on masturbation in the late seventeenth and early eighteenth centuries', *Paedagogica Historica*, 39 (2003), pp. 701–17; T. W. Lacqueur, *Solitary Sex: A Cultural History of Masturbation* (New York: Zone Books, 2003), pp. 185–245.

34 L. Stone, *The Family, Sex and Marriage in England 1500–1800* (London: Penguin, 1979), p. 319.

35 Adversaria, fols 15, 219.

36 Adversaria, fol. 180b. Neither the *History of Parliament* volumes or the *ODNB* mention anyone whose name accords with Blundell's description, suggesting either the name Blundell provided was incorrect or the debauchment was not as notorious as he suggested: B. Henning (ed.), *History of Parliament: The House of Commons, 1660–90*, 3 vols (London: Secker and Warburg, 1983).

37 Adversaria, fol. 180.

38 Adversaria, fol. 180b. I have been unable to locate further accounts of this incident. The date at which Blundell received the story suggests that the Earl Rivers being referred to was Thomas Savage, third Earl Rivers (1628–1694), who was married to Elizabeth Scrope, the illegitimate daughter of Emanuel Scrope the Earl of Sunderland: M. James, 'Scrope, Emanuel, Earl of Sunderland (1584–1630)', rev., in *ODNB*. Interestingly, Savage's son, Richard the fourth Earl Rivers (1654–1712), was at the centre of another

divorce scandal later in the century when he fathered two children with Anne Gerard, the countess of Macclesfield who was at the time separated from her husband Charles Gerard: L. Stone, *Road to Divorce: England 1530–1987* (Oxford: Oxford University Press, 1990), p. 317; A. Sherbo, 'Brett, Anne [other married name Anne Gerard, Countess of Macclesfield] (1667/8–1753), in *ODNB*.

39 E. Foyster, *Manhood in Early Modern England: Honour, Sex and Marriage* (London: Longman, 1999), p. 8.

40 C. B. Herrup, *A House in Gross Disorder: Sex, Law, and the 2nd Earl of Castlehaven* (Oxford: Oxford University Press, 1999).

41 Historica, fols 26–7, 49b–50, 83b–4; Adversaria, fols 20b, 41, 48b, 163–b, 177–b, 182b, 199–200b, 203–b, 314–b.

42 Adversaria, fol. 182b.

43 Historica, fol. 26; Adversaria, fols 41, 48b.

44 Historica, fol. 27.

45 Adversaria, fol. 177.

46 Historica, fol. 49b; Adversaria, fols 4b, 200.

47 Adversaria, fol. 177; Allestree, *Gentlemans Calling*, p. 141.

48 Historica, fol. 83b.

49 Adversaria, fol. 163; N. Ingelo, *Bentivolio and Urania* (1660), p. 40.

50 Adversaria, fols 163–b.

51 Adversaria, fol. 41; Caussin, *The Holy Court*, I, pp. 25–9.

52 Adversaria, fol. 177b.

53 Historica, fol. 83b.

54 Adversaria, fol. 163; Ingelo, *Bentivolio and Urania*, p. 40.

55 Adversaria, fols 203–b.

56 Adversaria, fol. 177b.

57 Adversaria, fol. 203.

58 Cust, 'Honour and politics in early Stuart England', p. 89.

59 Adversaria, fol. 177.

60 Adversaria, fols 314–b.

61 Peltonen, 'Francis Bacon', p. 14.

62 R. B. Shoemaker, 'The taming of the duel: masculinity, honour and ritual violence in London, 1660–1800', *Historical Journal*, 45 (2002), p. 535.

63 J. A. Sharpe, *Early Modern England: A Social History 1550–1760* (London: Arnold, 1997), p. 175.

64 Shoemaker, 'The taming of the duel', p. 537. For many, disapproval of duelling was informed by the controversy between Francis Bacon and Henry Howard, the Earl of Northampton, following James I's efforts to place stringent controls on its practice: Peltonen, 'Francis Bacon', pp. 14–27.

65 Shoemaker, 'The taming of the duel', p. 527; M. Peltonen, *The Duel in Early Modern*

England: Civility, Politeness and Honour (Cambridge: Cambridge University Press, 2003), p. 2.

66 Cust, 'Honour and politics in early Stuart England', p. 74. See also Shapin, *A Social History of Truth*, pp. 107–14.

67 Quintrell, 'The practice and problems of recusant disarming', pp. 205–22. This was a problem that all Catholics faced, as Cust notes of the Catholic George Shirley, who was disarmed because of his recusancy: 'a notoriously sensitive issue, because the right to bear arms was one of the distinguishing marks of a gentleman and was generally only removed from those considered a threat to the state': Cust, 'Catholicism, antiquarianism and gentry honour', p.46.

68 William Blundell to John North, 4 April 1679; William Blundell to Viscount Mountgarret, 22 October 1679, in Draft Letter Book, III, fols 39b, 54b–5. See also LCRO, DDBl 24/16, Draft letter from William Blundell complaining of soldiers of Thomas Fairfax, 1647.

69 See, for example: William Blundell to Richard Langhorne, 14 May 1673, in Letter Book One, fol. 101b.

70 R. Allestree, *The Ladies Calling* (1677). Cited at: Adversaria, fols 84, 162b, 167b, 175b, 190b, 193, 218.

71 Adversaria, fol. 295.

72 Historica, fol. 45–b, 89b; Alford, *Fides Regia Britannica*, p. 109; Bede, *The History of the Church of Englande*, pp. 30–2.

73 Historica, fol. 104.

74 Historica, fol. 198; English Gentleman, *An Accurate Description of the United Netherlands, and of the Most Considerable Parts of Germany, Sweden, & Denmark* (1691), p. 25.

75 Adversaria, fol. 175b; Allestree, *The Ladies Calling*, p. 188.

76 I am grateful to Philip Burton for supplying me with photographs of this text. The volume used is part of his personal collection: Ortelius, *An Epitome of Ortelius*.

77 Foyster, *Manhood in Early Modern England*, p. 2.

78 P. Mack, 'Women and gender in early modern England', *Journal of Modern History*, 73 (2001), p. 380.

79 Of particular note is Patricia Crawford's work on menstruation in which she argues that 'Social roles and relations between the sexes are sustained by ideas and beliefs about menstruation': P. Crawford, *Blood, Bodies and Families in Early Modern England* (Harlow: Pearson, 2004), pp. 19–53, quotation at p. 19.

80 Adversaria, fols 175b, 219; Bede, *The History of the Church of Englande*, p. 36; R. Blome, *A Description of the Island of Jamaica with the Other Isles and Territories in America, to which the English are Related* (1672), p. 171.

81 Adversaria, fols 46, 253b.

82 Adversaria, fol. 204. This association of women with luxury reflected broader contemporary trends that continued throughout the seventeenth century: L. Levy Peck, *Consuming Splendor: Society and Culture in Seventeenth-Century England* (Cambridge: Cambridge University Press, 2005), pp. 21–2, 61–71, 353–5.

83 Adversaria, fol. 5; N. N., *The Politicians Catechisme*, p. 189.

84 Adversaria, fol. 128.

85 Adversaria, fol. 50b.

86 Adversaria, fol. 50b; Caussin, *The Holy Court*, I, pp. 207–12.

87 Adversaria, fol. 47.

88 Crawford, *Blood, Bodies and Families*, p. 7. Laura Gowing notes that there was also a practical element to such fears, as 'single, sexually active women posed a threat to parish economies': L. Gowing, 'Ordering the body: illegitimacy and female authority in seventeenth-century England', in M. J. Braddick and J. Walter (eds), *Negotiating Power in Early Modern Society: Order, Hierarchy and Subordination in Britain and Ireland* (Cambridge: Cambridge University Press, 2001), p. 45.

89 Adversaria, fol. 165.

90 Foyster, *Manhood in Early Modern England*, p. 2; L. Gowing, *Domestic Dangers: Women, Words, and Sex in Early Modern London* (Oxford: Oxford University Press, 1996), pp. 106–7, 112–19.

91 Adversaria, fol. 203.

92 See: D. M. Turner, *Fashioning Adultery: Gender, Sex and Civility in England, 1660–1740* (Cambridge: Cambridge University Press, 2002), pp. 6, 194.

93 Foyster claims that the concern that women should not be able to reduce men to 'subordinate masculinities' was widespread. Foyster, *Manhood in Early Modern England*, p. 5.

94 Adversaria, fol. 295; P. Rycaut, *The History of the Present State of the Ottoman Empire* (1675), p. 271.

95 D. E. Underdown, 'The taming of the scold: the enforcement of patriarchal authority in early modern England', in A. Fletcher and J. Stevenson (eds), *Order and Disorder in Early Modern England* (Cambridge: Cambridge University Press, 1985), pp. 123–5. See Turner, *Fashioning Adultery*, pp. 143–71 for a discussion of adultery in the church courts.

96 Adversaria, fol. 174b; St Augustine and J. Luis Vives, *Saint Augustine, Of the Citie of God with the Learned Comments of Io. Lodouicus Vives* (1620), pp. 422–3.

97 Adversaria, fol. 47.

98 Adversaria, fols 97, 218.

99 Mack, 'Women and gender', pp. 387, 389.

100 Adversaria, fol. 42b.

101 Crawford, *Blood, Bodies and Families*, p. 7.

102 Historica, fols 25b, 197b.

103 H. Blount, *A Voyage into the Levant* (1650), cited Adversaria, fol. 184b. T. S., *The Adventures of (Mr. T. S.)*, cited Adversaria, fol. 184b; Historica, fols 57b, 90, 126b. Heylyn, *Cosmographie*, cited Adversaria, fols 14, 37, 51b, 53, 54, 85, 87b, 102b, 103, 113, 127, 128b, 139, 140b, 142b, 150b, 196, 206, 208b, 217–b, 227b, 229, 232, 233, 236b–7; Historica, fols 28b, 30, 37b, 40, 41, 52–b, 59b, 65b, 68b–9, 79b, 120b–1, 123b–4, 126, 129b, 135b.

104 Historica, fols 25b, 197b. Blundell wrote a travel diary while in Scotland in 1657 in which he meticulously noted his observations from the trip: Small Account Book, fols 52b–8b; Baker, 'An unpublished account'.

105 Historica, fol. 139b.

106 The broadside, which cannot be located, is discussed in Historica, fol. 140.

107 Adversaria, fols 145b–6.

108 F. Bacon, *The Essays, or, Counsels, Civil & Moral, of Sir Francis Bacon* (1663), pp. 96–101.

109 G. M. MacLean, *The Rise of Oriental Travel: English Visitors to the Ottoman Empire, 1580–1720* (Basingstoke: Macmillan, 2004), p. 134.

110 Bacon, *The Essays*, p. 101.

111 Adversaria, fol. 153b; Bacon, *The Essays*, p. 97.

112 Adversaria, fol. 182b.

113 B. Klein, 'Imaginary journeys: Spenser, Drayton, and the poetics of national space', in A. Gordon and B. Klein (eds), *Literature, Mapping and the Politics of Space in Early Modern England* (Cambridge: Cambridge University Press, 2001), pp. 204–23.

114 Adversaria, fol. 15.

115 Adversaria, fol. 201; Chamberlayne, *Anglia Notitia*, pp. 2–3.

116 Historica, fol. 88.

117 Historica, fols 164, 173–b.

118 Historica, fol. 143b.

119 Adversaria, fol. 359b; S. de La Loubère, *A New Historical Relation of the Kingdom of Siam* (1693), p. 37.

120 W. MacGaffey, 'Dialogues of the deaf: Europeans on the Atlantic Coast of Africa', in S. B. Schwartz (ed.), *Implicit Understandings: Observing, Reporting and Reflections on the Encounters Between Europeans and Other Peoples in the Early Modern Era* (Cambridge: Cambridge University Press, 1994), p. 262.

121 Historica, fols 167–b; Avril, *Travels into Divers Parts of Europe*, pp. 164–5.

122 Historica, fol. 140.

123 J. Schiesari, 'The face of domestication: physiognomy, gender politics, and humanism's others', in M. Hendricks and P. Parker (eds), *Women, 'Race,' and Writing in the Early Modern Period* (London: Routledge, 1994), p. 57; K. F. Hall, *Things of Darkness: Economies of Race and Gender in Early Modern England* (Ithaca: Cornell University Press, 1996), p. 6.

124 Blundell's preoccupation with physiognomy was not exclusive to his notes on travel. In his writing on Descartes Blundell included a detailed description of his appearance including material on his beard, height and paunch: Historica, fols 189–b.

125 R. Markley, 'Riches, power, trade and religion: the Far East and the English imagination, 1600–1720', *Renaissance Studies*, 17 (2003), pp. 494–5; MacLean, *Rise of Oriental Travel*, p. xiii; M. G. Aune, 'Early modern European travel writing after orientalism', *Journal for Early Modern Cultural Studies*, 5 (2005), pp. 122–8, 134; E. W. Said, *Orientalism* (Harmondsworth: Penguin, 1991).

126 Historica, fol. 140; Avril, *Travels into Divers Parts of Europe and Asia*, p. 73.

127 Historica, fols 57–b; Adversaria, fols 120–b, 294; Rycaut, *History of the Present State of the Ottoman Empire*, pp. 357–72.

128 Historica, fol. 70b.

129 Historica, fols 88, 178; Adversaria, fols 15, 89, 165, 175.

130 Historica, fol. 165b; Avril, *Travels into Divers Parts of Europe and Asia*, p. 109.

131 Adversaria, fols 39b, 165b–6, 218–b, 276b, 294b.

132 Historica, fol. 197b; English Gentleman, *An Accurate Description of the United Netherlands*, pp. 23–5.

133 Adversaria, fol. 195.

134 Adversaria, fol. 37; Heylyn, *Cosmographie*, p. 779.

135 Historica, fols 10b, 88, 163–4; Adversaria, fols 15, 379–b.

136 Historica, fol. 165b; Avril, *Travels into Divers Parts of Europe and Asia*, p. 109.

137 Adversaria, fol. 58; Volontaire, *A Relation of the Siege of Candia* (1670), p. 45.

138 Adversaria, fol. 292b; Historica, fol. 162b; Avril, *Travels into Divers Parts of Europe and Asia*, p. 44; Rycaut, *History of the Present State of the Ottoman Empire*, pp. 201–6.

139 Historica, fols 25–b, 40, 41, 126; Adversaria, fols 119, 219, 278b, 304b.

140 M. Janell Metzger, '"Now by my hood, a Gentile and no Jew": Jessica, The Merchant of Venice, and the discourse of early modern English identity', *PMLA*, 113 (1998), p. 54.

141 Adversaria, fol. 296.

142 Historica, fols 25–b; E. Sandys, *Europae Speculum. Or, A View or Survey of the State of Religion in the Westerne Parts of the World* (1638), p. 335. See also: Historica, fol. 165b.

143 Adversaria, fol. 296.

144 Historica, fol. 201; A. de Paris, *La Créance de l'Église Grecque Touchant la Transsubstantation* (Paris, 1672).

145 Historica, fols 166b–7.

146 Historica, fol. 167; Avril, *Travels into Divers Parts of Europe and Asia*, p. 161.

147 S. Phillips, 'The outer world of the European middle ages', in Schwartz (ed.), *Implicit Understandings*, p. 26; MacGaffey, 'Dialogues of the deaf', p. 252.

148 Historica, fol. 25.

149 Historica, fol. 25; Sandys, *Europea Speculum*, p. 330.

150 This is the subject of Brian Dolan's study of late eighteenth century travel: B. Dolan, *Exploring European Frontiers: British Travellers in the Age of Enlightenment* (Basingstoke: Macmillan, 2000), p. 3

151 Dolan, *Exploring European Frontiers*, p. 3; Metzger, '"Now by my hood, a Gentile and no Jew"', p. 55.

152 M. C. Fuller, 'Making something of it: questions of value in the early English travel collection', *Journal of Early Modern History*, 10 (2006), p. 36. This debate was put forward in Edward Said's *Orientalism*, where he argued that for westerners during the eighteenth and nineteenth centuries the terms 'oriental' and 'occidental' were diametrically opposed, with 'oriental' denoting the opposite of its advanced western counterpart: Said, *Orientalism*, passim.

153 MacLean, *Rise of Oriental Travel*, pp. 84–99, quotation at p. 96.

154 E. Fudge, 'Calling beasts by their true names: Bacon, the new science and the beast in

man', in E. Fudge, R. Gilbert and S. Wiseman (eds), *At the Borders of the Human: Beasts, Bodies and Natural Philosophy in the Early Modern Period* (Basingstoke: Palgrave, 2002), p. 91; C. Webster, *The Great Instauration: Science, Medicine and Reform 1626–1660* (London: Duckworth, 1975), p. 515.

155 Historica, fol. 38b; Matthew, *A Collection of Letters*, preface; Howell *Epistolae Ho-elianae*, IV, pp. 107–8.

156 Adversaria, fols 277b, 386; Bureau d'adresse et de Rencontre, *A General Collection of Discourses*, p. 4.

157 Adversaria, fols 334–b; Rapin, *Oeuvres Diverses.*

158 Adversaria, fol. 334b.

159 Adversaria, fols 334–6.

160 Adversaria, fol. 336b.

161 Adversaria, fols 334–7b.

162 J. M. Levine, *Between the Ancients and the Moderns: Baroque Culture in Restoration England* (London: Yale University Press, 1999), p. viii.

163 Discussed in: M. Hunter, 'Scientific change: its setting and stimuli'. in B. Coward (ed.), *A Companion to Stuart Britain* (Oxford: Blackwell, 2003), pp. 214–29; Webster, *The Great Instauration*, pp. xiii–xvi, 496–7.

164 Webster, *The Great Instauration*, p. 327.

165 Levine, *Between the Ancients and the Moderns*, pp. 113–58, especially pp. 113–19, 140–1.

166 C. Condren, 'The paradoxes of recontextualisation in early modern intellectual history', *Historical Journal*, 37 (1994), p. 226.

167 As discussed in J. Martin, *Francis Bacon, the State and the Reform of Natural Philosophy* (Cambridge: Cambridge University Press, 1992), p. 151.

168 Cited in Martin, *Francis Bacon*, p. 153.

169 Cited in M. Peltonen, 'Bacon, Francis, Viscount St Alban (1561–1626)', in *ODNB*.

170 Bacon, for instance, continued to believe in divine intervention. However, it appears that this belief differed somewhat from Blundell's. Rather than viewing God as constantly embroiling himself in the world to deliver vengeance on wrongdoers, as Blundell did, in the *Advancement of Learning* Bacon admired divine creation in the same way that contemporary wonder works did, noting that 'knowledge appeareth to be a plant of God's own planting, so it may seem that the spreading and flourishing, or at least the bearing and fructifying of this plant, by a providence of God, nay not only by a general providence but by a special prophecy, was appointed to this autumn of the world': cited and discussed in B. Vickers, 'Francis Bacon and the progress of knowledge', *Journal of the History of Ideas*, 53 (1992), pp. 495–6. See also Hunter, 'Scientific Change', p. 224.

171 Adversaria, fols 111, 397–8.

172 Adversaria, fol. 70b–3b; K. Digby, *A Late Discourse Made in a Solemn Assembly of Nobles and Learned Men at Montpellier in France ... Touching the Cure of Wounds by the Powder of Sympathy* (1664), p. 75; R. Hooke, *Micrographia: or Some Physiological Descriptions of Minute Bodies Made by Magnifying Glass* (1667).

173 Historica, fols 85–b; Adversaria, fols 17, 21b, 157–b, 186b, 316–20. This was an interest shared by William Blundell junior, in whose papers survives a section entitled 'Some perticular rules concerning arethmatick and first of addition': Letters of Blundell Junior, fols 4–b.

174 Historica, fols 29, 70–b, 168b.

175 Adversaria, fols 8, 305.

176 Historica, fol. 38.

177 For example, Blundell's notes on weather were generally separated into types of weather (such as 'Gelu' (Chill), Historica, fol. 137) as opposed to being grouped together indiscriminately under the title 'weather'.

178 Small Account Book, fols 87b–92.

179 Historica, fol. 137.

180 Historica, fols 68–b; Nieremberg, *A Treatise of the Difference*, p. 190.

181 Historica, fols 10, 61–b, 84; R. Knolles, *The Generall Historie of the Turkes from the First Beginning of that Nation to the Rising of the Othoman Familie* (1638), p. 1464.

182 Nieremberg, *A Treatise of the Difference*, p. 185.

183 Adversaria, fols 356–7b.

184 Adversaria, fol. 356b.

185 T. Sprat, *The History of the Royal-Society of London for the Improving of Natural Knowledge* (1667), pp. 173–9.

186 Sprat's *History* is referenced at: Adversaria, fols 106, 111, 178, 188b.

187 J. Golinski, '"Exquisite atmography": theories of the world and experiences of the weather in a diary of 1703', *British Journal for the History of Science*, 34 (2001), pp. 150, 152, 155, 161.

188 Golinski, 'Exquisite atmography', p. 161.

189 Golinski, 'Exquisite atmography', p. 160.

190 Adversaria, fols 141b, 388–9.

191 Adversaria, fol. 293b; T. Burnet, *The Theory of the Earth* (1691), pp. 289–310.

192 K. Hutchinson, 'Sunspots, Galileo, and the orbit of the earth', *ISIS*, 81 (1990), p. 68.

193 Adversaria, fol. 141.

194 Adversaria, fol. 141; Childrey, *Britannia Baconica*, p. 55.

195 Adversaria, fol. 36b.

196 Adversaria, fol. 141.

197 For instance, Blundell discussed the heights of peculiarly tell people under the heading 'statura hominum': Historica, fols 45, 73b, 125b.

198 K. Park and L. Daston, 'Unnatural conceptions: the study of monsters in sixteenth- and seventeenth-century France and England', *Past and Present*, 92 (1981), p. 22; P. Semonin, 'Monsters in the marketplace: the exhibition of human oddities in early modern England', in R. Garland Thomson (ed.), *Freakery: Cultural Spectacles of the Extraordinary Body* (London: New York University Press, 1996), pp. 69–81.

199 K. M. Brammall, 'Monstrous metamorphosis: nature, morality, and the rhetoric of monstrosity in Tudor England', *Sixteenth Century Journal*, 27 (1996), p. 5; Park and Daston, 'Unnatural conceptions', pp. 23, 26; Semonin, 'Monsters in the marketplace', pp. 71–5.

200 Park and Daston, 'Unnatural conceptions', pp. 35–41, 43.

201 Cited in P. K. Wilson, 'Eighteenth-century "monsters" and nineteenth-century "freaks": reading the maternally marked child', *Literature and Medicine*, 21 (2002), p. 6. See also: Semonin, 'Monsters in the marketplace', p. 71.

202 Brammall, 'Monstrous metamorphosis', p. 5; Park and Daston 'Unnatural conceptions', pp. 45, 48; Martin, *Francis Bacon*, p. 151.

203 Historica, fol. 135b; Augustine and Vives, *Saint Augustine, Of the Citie of God*, pp. 548–9.

204 Historica, fol. 36b; Howell, *Epistolae Ho-elianae*, II, p. 15.

205 Historica, fol. 30; Howell, *Epistolae Ho-elianae*, II, p. 14.

206 Historica, fols 45, 73b.

207 Historica, fol. 125b; J. Stow, *The Abridgement of the English Chronicle* (1618), p. 337.

208 Blundell, *A Letter Writ to a Friend.*

209 Blundell, *A Letter Writ to a Friend.*

210 M. Michal, M. Bisceglia, A. Di Mattia, L. Requena, J. C. Fanburg-Smith, P. Mukensnabl, O. Hes and F. Cada, 'Gigantic cutaneous horns of the scalp: lesions with a gross similarity to the horns of animals: a report of four cases', *American Journal of Surgical Pathology*, 26 (2002), p. 789.

211 Anon., *A Brief Narrative of A Strange and Wonderful Old Woman that Hath a Pair of Horns Growing Upon Her Head* (1676), p. 4; C. Leigh, *The Natural History of Lancashire, Cheshire, and the Peak, in Derbyshire* (1700), II, pp. 3–4. While it is possible that these two accounts were based on Blundell's broadsheet, the *Brief Narrative* was written after Davies travelled to London, gave precise details of her location in the city suggesting that others went to view her, and stated that the anonymous author had seen Davies her or himself. She did not appear in print again until 1791, when she was one of the case studies in Everard Home's seminal paper on cutaneous horns: J. Bondeson, 'Everard Home, John Hunter, and cutaneous horns', *American Journal of Dermatopathology*, 23 (2001), p. 366.

212 Bondeson, 'Everard Home', p. 362.

213 Bondeson, 'Everard Home', p. 364.

214 Leigh, *The Natural History*, II, p. 3.

215 Leigh, *The Natural History*, II, p. 4.

216 M. Shildrick, 'Maternal imagination: reconceiving first impressions', *Rethinking History*, 4 (2000), p. 249.

217 Anon., *Brief Narrative*, p. 6.

218 Historica, fols 34b, 46, 60b; Digby, *Late Discourse*, pp. 104, 109; E. Pagitt, *Heresiography, or, A Description and History of the Hereticks and Sectaries Sprang Up in these Latter Times* (1662), p. 133.

219 Sharpe, *Reading Revolutions*, pp. 281, 339.

Conclusion

The surviving papers of William Blundell provide a unique window into the activities and worldview of a seventeenth-century English Catholic. Through an examination of this material, this book has shown that the carefully choreographed pose of a politically quiescent yet unquestioningly committed Catholic, with which Blundell sought to delude his contemporaries, disguised the innovative ways in which he exerted agency and the convolution of his belief structure. Although Blundell was clearly an apt political operator with a talent for survival, his papers show that his actions, his beliefs and the environment in which he lived were frequently at odds with one another. What is striking about Blundell is the skill with which he avoided possible conflict between these different areas of his life. Not only did he create a series of survival mechanisms which enabled him to evade the full effects of the penal laws but he used his commonplace books as a forum in which to hide, from others and possibly himself, the extent of his reservations about Protestantism in general and the activities of the Protestant regimes under which he lived, as well as his scepticism about particular aspects of Catholicism. This book has shown that Blundell was far more complex than the two-dimensional character of 'the Cavalier' that early historians eagerly presented to the world. Certainly this formed one aspect of his persona but other, at times contradictory, elements held an equally important place.[1]

Blundell was never a passive victim. Throughout his life he determinedly sought out methods to avoid the penal laws. His first line of defence was discretion, and the extent of his involvement in Catholic activities was never discovered by Protestant authorities. This was facilitated by the close family circle in which Blundell operated, an arena where he found both elementary protection as well as opportunities to promote the Catholic interest. A cursory glance at Blundell's children provides a stark illustration of this, with seven of the ten children who survived into adulthood entering religious orders. Like many contemporary Catholics, Blundell supplemented these aspects of his defence with the so-called 'Catholic connection' and he eagerly developed a nexus of Catholic contemporaries throughout the British Isles.[2] However, his extensive links with Catholics did not make him part of a hermetically sealed Catholic community. According with recent work that has emphasised the fluid nature of divisions between Protestants and Catholics in early modern England, Blundell regularly interacted with Protestants.[3] Not only do

Blundell's papers show that he engaged with many Protestants on a regular basis, but many went out of their way to shield him from the laws that had been put in place to protect them from alleged Catholic treachery. These aspects of Blundell's behaviour may initially appear introspective; however, as Kaushik has argued, 'in the politicized context in which they were conducted, [such activities] served as a form of *defensive* resistance'.[4]

Blundell's resistance was not just reactive to the policies of the successive Protestant regimes under which he lived. He continued the work of his forefathers in ensuring that Little Crosby was a Catholic haven. His estate sheltered a Catholic burial ground which served priests and poor Catholics from the locality and beyond. He also manipulated the leasehold system on his land to ensure that Catholic tenants paid considerably less to renew leases, effectively excluding Protestants from the area and allowing Blundell to exert significant control over his tenants in exchange for the preferential rates that he charged. The spheres within which Blundell operated were not restricted to his locality. He maintained regular contact with friends in Ireland to whom he supplied the latest news, as well as charitable gifts: links which became more immediate after his daughter Emilia married Richard Butler, heir to the Mountgarret estates. Likewise, his links to religious orders on the continent developed new significance as his children entered religious houses. Blundell frequently corresponded with St Omer and the different houses of the Poor Clares that his daughters joined, though he developed a particular relationship with the Poor Clares of Rouen, for whom he acted as an agent, disseminating correspondence, brokering portions for the daughters of local families and collecting and distributing money on their behalf. However, these activities were not as selfless as he proclaimed. Not only did his work as an agent for the Poor Clares allow Blundell to control a patronage network lending money out to individuals at preferential rates but recognition of the vital work that he did for the order aided his negotiations to keep his daughters' annuities as low as possible. Finally, Blundell addressed issues concerning Catholics in a printed pamphlet and letters disseminated amongst members of his networks. In turn his arguments helped inform the works of Roger L'Estrange and were recycled in a letter written by Roger Bradshaigh to the Earl of Derby demanding that Catholics be allowed to enlist in the militia.[5] In light of these actions Blundell's claim that he and other Catholics were 'his Majesties most faithful subjects' might be questioned.[6] However, through Blundell's writing it is apparent that he saw no contradiction between his actions and these claims. His loyalty was to the person of the monarch, not what he viewed as the misguided policies of the Protestant regimes under which he lived. This meant that Blundell could partake in blatantly illegal activity, while remaining fiercely loyal to the monarchy.

Blundell's reading and commonplacing practices offered a further forum in which he navigated the restrictions placed upon him because of his recusancy. Like many of his contemporaries Blundell used his commonplace books as reference tools to help him manage the mass of information that he acquired through his reading. The inclusion of commentaries on contemporary politics, social issues and religion, matters that his social standing should have allowed him to negotiate in public had it not been for his recusancy, shows that his commonplaces allowed him to engage with the same issues in a limited forum, offering him a proxy public life. As was increasingly the case in the early modern period, Blundell's approach to commonplacing deviated from the stringent, precise methods suggested by some of his contemporaries.[7] Rather than following any single approach, Blundell used only the processes which he thought would work for him. His engagement with the materials he recorded was equally selective. Throughout the commonplace books Blundell was discriminating in his note-taking, sometimes taking particular messages from a source that deviated significantly from the overall grain of its argument. He frequently included critiques of the works that he disagreed with, at times demonstrating flagrant disregard for both the arguments and the author. In this sense his commonplace books illustrate that Blundell crossed an important line in his commonplacing practice, and it is *his* authorship that is stamped over each of the entries that populate these works. At no stage was Blundell a passive receptacle of the information that he read. His reconstruction of the material that he recorded is a further example of his agency in spite of the restrictions placed upon him, and it is within this arena that we are given the clearest insight into Blundell's worldview.

Blundell's commonplace books demonstrate the complexity of his religious beliefs. While many of his entries indicate a commitment to the Catholic faith, he used his commonplace books as a forum in which to air his doubts concerning aspects of Catholicism, including contradictions within the Bible and his scepticism about particular miracle stories. While the sincerity of his Catholic professions should not necessarily be questioned, it is clear that Blundell's faith was not as strong as he aspired and, in allowing him to air his issues with particular aspects of Catholicism, the commonplace books functioned as a form of confessional. More in keeping with the professions in his correspondence was his aggressive defence of the political aspirations of Catholicism. Here he adversarially engaged with historical works to show both that Catholics were unconditionally loyal to the regimes under which they lived and that they were the victims of brutal Protestant repression, while Protestants were a subversive presence responsible for the major incidents of civil unrest in the early modern period. In no other surviving papers are Blundell's doubts about particular aspects of his faith explored or his harsh line on Protestant malcontents fully discussed, and his commonplace entries offer a unique window into his private values. Furthermore, a number of his comments suggest that at times Blundell's religious beliefs were dictated partially by utility. While he refused to accept a number of modern-day miracles, he eagerly sought out incidents of providential intervention against Protestants. Such accounts helped reinforce his faith during difficult times, the recounting of which was no doubt an important element of his survival strategies. It is striking how quick Blundell was to dismiss evidence to the contrary, failing to reflect on the full extent of how the financial and physical injuries that he sustained during the Civil War, for instance, contradicted his claims that God intervened on behalf of Catholics.[8] This may have been a major factor in Blundell's cryptic claim in the commonplace books that the Civil War had, in fact, been 'the greatest temporal fortune that ever befell me; and that for many reasons partly knowne to others, but principally to myself'.[9] By reducing the negative impact of the Civil War, Blundell may have been seeking to illustrate God's support of his actions.

Finally, we have considered the impact that tensions in Blundell's identity had on his approach to the world. Despite his protestations to the contrary, he created a series of nuanced arguments that maintained that other religions represented a subverted form of Catholicism, further supporting his view that Catholicism was the one true representation of God's will. This ultimate assertion of 'cultural superiority' over the subjects of his study may have been expedient, if subconsciously so, in that it added credibility to the religion he was periodically punished for adhering to.[10] His concerns with the social order and conceptions of nobility were, to some extent, held by all gentlemen who wished to pursue an active life. However, Blundell reinterpreted this material to make these ideals relevant to him, moving from a conception of an active life that involved public office, to a broader interpretation that highlighted the virtues of a concept of public service accessible to him. In turn Blundell also criticised conceptions of honour that were inaccessible to him, most notably in the entries which referred to incidents when office-holding members of the nobility had behaved in a manner which was, according to Blundell, not befitting of their position. Blundell's attitude to women was apparently dictated less by his religious beliefs, and more by his gender and the belief that patriarchy should be upheld at all costs. Despite initially appearing to be open to female agency, he harboured a profound fear of unrestricted female activity and viewed women as a constant danger to the social order. Blundell's approach to science was equally devoid of a specifically Catholic stance. He aggressively dismissed a number of Biblical interpretations of the natural order, preferring instead to adhere stringently to the approach to the world outlined by Francis Bacon. The, at times, competing aspects of Blundell's worldview further highlight the complex nature of his identity. He was at once a recusant, a member of the gentry and a male, all of which contributed to and coexisted in his worldview.

In light of this book it seems apparent that historians have been overly keen to take at face value the claims of seventeenth-century Catholics that they were passive victims who voluntarily made a distinction between religion and politics. Certainly, at times Catholics were victims, but claims of *passive* victimhood could also be used as a means of avoiding unwanted attention from the regime, or exaggerated by those seeking to fashion an identity that portrayed them as martyrs for the Catholic cause. William Blundell was one such Catholic, and his continued political activity, whether directly, or indirectly through his networks or reading, reminds us that the exclusion of English Catholics from the political histories of early modern England is an artificial and anachronistic division.

NOTES

1 See Blundell (ed.), *Cavalier: Letters*.

2 Hibbard, 'Early Stuart Catholicism', pp. 2–3.

3 Milton, 'A qualified intolerance', pp. 85–115.

4 Kaushik, 'Resistance, loyalty and recusant politics', p. 41.

5 L'Estrange, *Toleration Discuss'd*; NLS, Acc. 9769, Crawford Muniments, Personal Papers 42/2/5, Draft Reply of Sir Roger Bradshaigh.

6 Blue Book, fol. 6.

7 Moss, *Printed Commonplace Books*, passim.

8 On only one occasion did Blundell briefly consider the impact that his perceived victimisation had on his view that God intervened on behalf of the true, Catholic faith: Historica, fol. 48b.

9 Adversaria, fol. 31b.

10 Fuller, 'Making something of it', p. 36.

Appendix

Map of Little Crosby and surrounding area

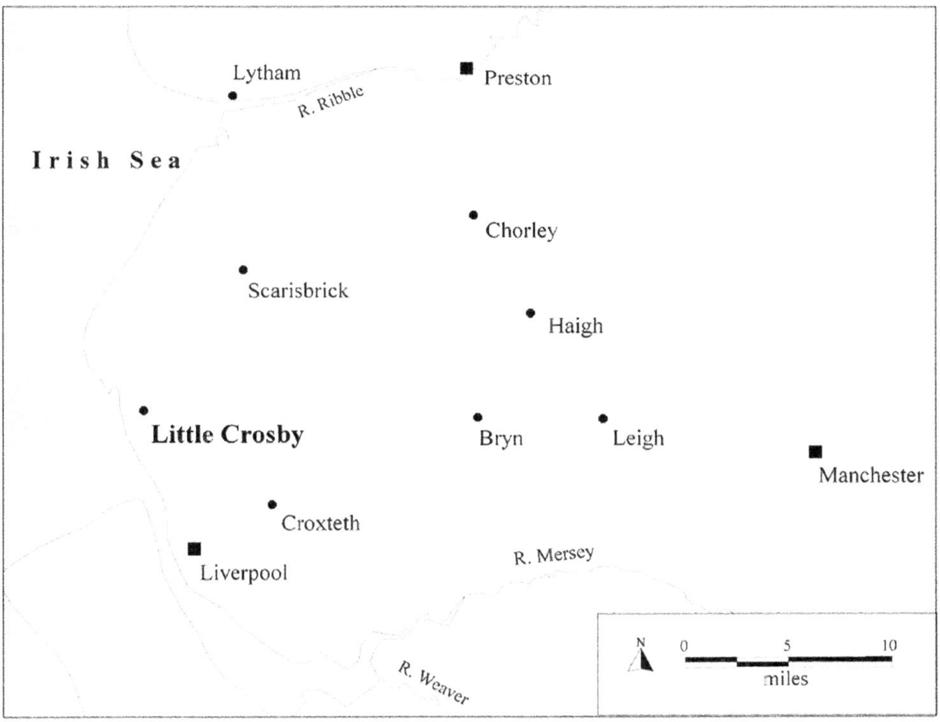

Select bibliography

MANUSCRIPT PRIMARY SOURCES

Bodleian Library, Oxford

Carte MSS. 181, Nairne Papers.

Cheshire and Chester Archives, Chester

EDC 5, Consistory Court Papers.

Douai Abbey Archives, Woolhampton

MS 38, Thomas Blundell, The Catholic Doctrine of Transubstantiation, 1687–1688.
MS 54, Thomas Blundell, De Virtutibus Theologicus & Tractatus De Paenitentia, 1687.

Folger Shakespeare Library, Washington DC

V.a.260, Miscellaneous commonplace book.
V.a.399, Miscellaneous commonplace book.
V.a.439, Miscellaneous commonplace book.
V.b.93, Commonplace book of John Evans.

Huntington Library, California

Mss HM 15369, Certain collections of the right Hon. Elizabeth late Countess of Huntingdon.

Lancashire County Record Office

Main sources on which this book is based:
DDBl acc. 6121, Box 1, Harkirk burial register.
DDBl acc. 6121, Box 2, 1672–1693 letter book.
DDBl acc. 6121, Box 2, Blue Book.
DDBl acc. 6121, Box 2, Copies of letters to William Blundell the Cavalier 1665–1679.
DDBl acc. 6121, Box 2, Hodge Podge the Third.
DDBl acc. 6121, Box 3, Account of the Jacobite Trial, 1694, copied by Nicholas Blundell.
DDBl acc. 6121, Box 3, Cavalier's Small Account Book 1646–1675.

DDBl acc. 6121, Box 3, Transcription of *The Affairs of the Portuguese in India.*
DDBl acc. 6121, Box 3, Transcription of 'The Touchstone of Truth'.
DDBl acc. 6121, Box 3, William Blundell the Cavalier's letter book 1681–90.
DDBl acc. 6121, Box 4, Adversaria.
DDBl acc. 6121, Box 4, Great Hodge Podge.
DDBl acc. 6121, Box 4, Historica.
DDBl acc. 6121, Box 6, Extracts from religious books, 1677.
DDBl acc. 6121, Box 6, Letters and accounts of William Blundell the son of the Cavalier.
DDBl acc. 6147, Box 1, Loose leaf transcripts by William Blundell.
Other material at Lancashire County Record Office:
DDBl 1–55, Blundell Papers.
DDKe/8/1–37, Kenyon Papers, Lancashire Jacobite Plot.
QSP/468/4, Quarter Sessions Papers, 1677.
QSP/718/10, Quarter Sessions Papers, 1692.
QSP/811/1, Quarter Sessions Papers, 1697.

Manchester Central Library

L1/48/6/1, Letter book of Roger Bradshaigh of Haigh.

Manx National Heritage Library, Douglas, Isle of Man

MS 741C, Manuscript history of the Isle of Man, 1650.

National Library of Scotland, Edinburgh

Acc. 9769, Crawford Muniments, Personal Papers 42/2/5, Draft reply of Sir Roger Bradshaigh, 1st Bart, to Charles Stanley, 8th Earl of Derby, 1666.

Northamptonshire Record Office

NRO, FH3000–FH4653, Finch Hatton Papers.

Nottingham University Library

Portland Papers, PwA2460, Verse entitled 'A letter to Dyer ... upon the Lancashire Plot'.
Portland Papers, PwA2706, Victual Office to Godart van Ginkel, 1st Earl of Athlone, 11 February 1695.

Poor Clares of Rouen Archives, Darlington

Chronicles of the Poor Clares, Rouen I 1644–1701.
Miscellaneous Rouen manuscripts: notebook describing foundation.
Miscellaneous Rouen manuscripts: extracts of death notices.

Sheffield Archives

Bagshaw Collection, C365, William Blundell to Rowland Eyre.
Bagshaw Collection, C2705, Postnuptial Settlement between William Blundell the son and Mary Eyre now his wife, 12 April 1668.

Staffordshire Record Office

D240, Aston Papers.
D590, Giffard Papers.

The National Archives

SP23, Papers of the Committee for Compounding.

Wigan Record Office

D/DSt. M1/1–20, M2/1–25, M3/1–34, Standish Hall plot papers.
D/DAn9/7, Anderton Papers, Jacobite cipher.

PRINTED PRIMARY SOURCES

Place of publication London unless otherwise stated

Alford, M., *Fides Regia Britannica sive Annales Ecclesiae Britannicae* (Liege, 1663).
Allestree, R., *The Gentlemans Calling* (1660).
Allestree, R., *The Ladies Calling* (1677).
Anon., *A Brief Narrative of A Strange and Wonderful Old Woman that Hath a Pair of Horns Growing Upon Her Head* (1676).
Anon., *The Case of Divers Roman Catholics as it was Lately Stated to a Person Eminent in the Law and Thought not Unfit to be made Publicke* (1662).
Anon., *The Tryal of Edward Coleman* (1678).
Arnauld, A. and P. Nicole, *La Perpetuite de la Foy de L'Eglise Catholique Touchant L'Eucharistie* (Paris, 1666).
Augustine, St and J. Luis Vives, *Saint Augustine, Of the Citie of God with the Learned Comments of Io. Lodouicus Vives* (1620).
Avril, P., *Travels into Divers Parts of Europe and Asia, Undertaken by the French King's Order to Discover a New Way by Land into China* (1693).
Bacon, F., *The Historie of the Raigne of King Henry the Seventh* (1622).
Bacon, F., *Of the Advancement and Proficience of Learning or the Partitions of Sciences* (1640).
Bacon, F., *The Essays, or, Counsels, Civil & Moral, of Sir Francis Bacon* (1663).
Baillet, A., *The Life of Monsieur Des Cartes Containing the History of his Philosophy and Works* (1693).
Baker, R., *A Chronicle of the Kings of England from the Time of the Romans Government, unto the Death of King James* (1674).
Basier, I., *The History of the English & Scotch Presbytery* (1660).

Bate, G., *Elenchus Motuum Nuperorum in Anglia, or, A Short Historical Account of the Rise and Progress of the Late Troubles in England* (1685).
Baxter, R., *The Grotian Religion Discovered* (1658).
Bede, St, *The History of the Church of Englande* (1565).
Blome, R., *A Description of the Island of Jamaica with the Other Isles and Territories in America, to which the English are Related* (1672).
Blount, H., *A Voyage into the Levant* (1650).
Blount, T., *Boscobel, or, The Compleat History of His Sacred Majesties Most Miraculous Preservation After the Battle of Worcester 3 Sept. 1651* (1662).
Blundell, W., *A Letter Writ to a Friend: Being a Description of a Horn, which Grows in the Back Part of the Head of an Ancient Woman ... Living at Saughal* (1668).
Borlase, E., *Latham Spaw in Lancashire with some Remarkable Cases and Cures Effected by it; Together with a Further Account of it* (1672).
Borlase, E., *The History of the Execrable Irish Rebellion Trac'd from many Preceding Acts, to the Grand Eruption, the 23 of October, 1641, and then Pursued to the Act of Settlement, 1662* (1680).
Bramhall, J., *The Victory of Truth for the Peace of the Church to the King of Great Britain to Invite him to Embrace the Roman-Catholick Faith* (1653).
Brevint, D., *Missale Romanum, or, The Depth and Mystery of the Roman Mass* (1684).
Browne, T., *Religio Medici* (1642).
Bureau d'adresse et de Rencontre, *A General Collection of Discourses of the Virtuosi of France* (1664).
Burnet, T., *The Theory of the Earth* (1691).
Camden, W., *Britain, or A Chorographicall Description of the most Flourishing Kingdomes, England, Scotland, and Ireland, and the Ilands Adjoyning* (1610).
Camden, W., *Remains concerning Britain* (1674).
Caussin, N., *The Holy Court in Three Tomes* (1634).
Chamberlayne, E., *Angliae Notitia, or, The Present State of England* (1672).
Childrey, J., *Britannia Baconica, or the Natural Varieties of England, Scotland and Wales* (1661).
Cicero, M. T., *A Very Necessary and Profitable Entraunce to the Speakyng and Writyng of the Latin Tongue* (1575).
Cox, R., *Hibernia Anglicana, or, The History of Ireland from the Conquest Thereof by the English to this Present Time* (1692).
Davila, A. C., *The Historie of the Civill Warres of France* (1647).
Davila, E. C., *Historia Delle Guerre Civili di Francia* (Paris, 1644).
Digby, K., *A Late Discourse Made in a Solemn Assembly of Nobles and Learned Men at Montpellier in France ... Touching the Cure of Wounds by the Powder of Sympathy* (1664).
Drexel, J., *Aurifodina Artium et Scientiarum Omnium* (Antwerp, 1638).
Drexel, J., *The Considerations of Drexelius Upon Eternity* (1663).
Ellis, C., *The Gentile Sinner, or, England's Brave Gentleman* (1661).
English College of Doway, *The Holie Bible Faithfully Translated into English out of the Authentical Latin*, 2 vols (1609).
English Gentleman, *An Accurate Description of the United Netherlands, and of the Most Considerable Parts of Germany, Sweden, & Denmark* (1691).
Ferguson, R., *A Letter to Mr. Secretary Trenchard* (1694).

Godwin, F., *A Catalogue of the Bishops of England, Since the First Planting of Christian Religion in this Island* (1615).
Grotius, H., *Two Discourses, I. Of God, and his Providence. II. Of Christ, his Miracles and Doctrine* (1653).
Heylyn, P., *Cosmographie in Four Books Containing the Chorographie and Historie of the Whole World* (1657).
Heylyn, P., *Ecclesia Restaurata, or, The History of the Reformation of the Church of England* (1661).
Hooke, R., *Micrographia: or Some Physiological Descriptions of Minute Bodies Made by Magnifying Glass* (1667).
Howell, J., *Epistolae Ho-elianae Familiar Letters Domestic and Forren* (1650).
Ingelo, N., *Bentivolio and Urania* (1660).
James I, *Basilikon Doron. Or His Majesties Instructions to his Dearest Sonne, Henrie the Prince* (1603).
Kingston, R., *A True History of the Several Designs and Conspiracies Against his Majesties Sacred Person and Government; as they were Continually Carry'd on from 1688 till 1697* (1698).
Knolles, R., *The Generall Historie of the Turkes from the First Beginning of that Nation to the Rising of the Othoman Familie* (1638).
Leigh, C., *The Natural History of Lancashire, Cheshire, and the Peak, in Derbyshire* (1700).
L'Estrange, H., *The Alliance of Divine Offices, Exhibiting all the Liturgies of the Church of England Since the Reformation as also the late Scotch Service-Book, with all their Respective Variations* (1659).
L'Estrange, R., *Toleration Discuss'd* (1663).
L'Estrange, R., *L'Estrange No Papist* (1681).
Leyburn, G., *Dr. Leyburns Encyclicall Answer to an Encyclicall Epistle Sent to our Brethren of England* (1661).
Loubère, S. de La, *A New Historical Relation of the Kingdom of Siam* (1693).
Loveday, R., *Loveday's Letters, Domestick and Forreign* (1662).
Mabillon, J., *Traité des Études Monastiques, Divisé en Trois Parties* (Paris, 1691).
Marvell, A., *The Rehersal Transpros'd; or, Animadversions Upon a Late Book, Entituled, A Preface Shewing what Grounds there are of Fears and Jealousies of Popery* (1672).
Matthew, T., *A Collection of Letters* (1659).
May, T., *A Breviary of the History of the Parliament of England* (1680).
Montaigne, M. de, *The Essayes or Morall, Politike and Millitarie Discourses of Lo: Michaell de Montaigne* (1603).
More, H., *Historia Missionis Anglicanae Societatis Jesu* (Douai, 1660).
Mumford, J., *The Question of Questions* (1658).
N., N., *The Politicians Catechisme for his Instruction in Divine Faith and Morall Honesty* (1658).
Nieremberg, J. E., *A Treatise of the Difference Betwixt the Temporal and Eternal* (1672).
Ortelius, A., *An Epitome of Ortelius his Theater of the World* (1601).
Owen, J., *An Epistle to the Authour of the Animadversions upon Fiat Lux in Excuse and Justification of Fiat Lux Against the Said Animadversions* (Douai, 1663).
Pagitt, E., *Heresiography, or, A Description and History of the Hereticks and Sectaries Sprang Up in these Latter Times* (1662).

Pallavicino, P. S., *Istoria del Concilio di Trento* (Rome, 1657).
Paris, A. de, *La Créance de l'Église Grecque Touchant la Transsubstantation* (Paris, 1672).
Perrot, J., *Battering Rams Against Rome; or, The Battel of John the Follower of the Lamb, Fought with the Pope and his Priests, Whilst he was a Prisoner in the Inquisition-Prison of Rome* (1661).
Plutarch, *The Lives of the Noble Grecians and Romains* (1631).
Prynne, W., *A Seasonable, Legal, and Historical Vindication of the Good Old Fundamental Liberties, Franchises, Rights, Properties, Laws, Government of all English Freemen* (1657).
Rapin, R., *Oeuvres Diverses* (Amsterdam, 1686).
Ray, J., *Observations Topographical, Moral, & Physiological Made in a Journey Through Part of the Low-Countries, Germany, Italy, and France* (1673).
Rycaut, P., *The History of the Present State of the Ottoman Empire* (1675).
S., G., *Anglorum Speculum, or The Worthies of England, in Church and State* (1684).
S., R., *A Collection of some of the Murthers and Massacres Committed on the Irish in Ireland since the 23d of October 1641* (1662).
S., T., *The Adventures of (Mr. T. S.) an English Merchant Taken Prisoner by the Turks of Argiers* (1670).
Sacheverell, W., *An Account of the Isle of Man, its Inhabitants, Language, Soil, Remarkable Qualities* (1702).
Sandys, E., *Europae Speculum. Or, A View or Survey of the State of Religion in the Westerne Parts of the World* (1638).
Seacome, J., *Memoirs Concerning a Genealogical and Historical Account of the Ancient and Honourable House of Stanley, From the Conquest to the Death of Late Earl of Derby, In the Year James 1735; As also a full Description of the Isle of Man, &c* (Liverpool, 1741).
Sergeant, J., *Sure-footing in Christianity, or Rational Discourses on the Rule of Faith* (1665).
Sprat, T., *The History of the Royal-Society of London for the Improving of Natural Knowledge* (1667).
Stow, J., *The Abridgement of the English Chronicle* (1618).
Strada, F., *De Bello Belgico The History of the Low-Countrey Warres* (1650).
Suetonius, *The Historie of Twelve Caesars, Emperours of Rome* (1606).
Swall, A., *New Proposals for Printing by Subscription, Cambdens Britannia* (1693).
Swall, A., *Proposals for Printing by Subscription, Cambdens Britannia* (1693).
Taylor, J., *The Great Exemplar of Sanctity and Holy Life According to the Christian Institution* (1657).
The Post Boy.
The Present State of Europe: or, the Historical and Political Monthly Mercury.
Volontaire, *A Relation of the Siege of Candia* (1670).
Wadding, L., *The History of the Angelicall Virgin Glorious S. Clare* (1635).
Wagstaffe, R., *A Letter out of Lancashire to a Friend in London, Giving some Account of the late Tryals there* (1694).
Watson, W., *A Decacordon of Ten Quodlibeticall Questions Concerning Religion and State* (1602).
Weldon, A., *The Court and Character of King James Whereunto Is now Added The Court of King Charles* (1651).
White, T., *The Grounds of Obedience and Government* (1655).
White, T., *Monumetham Excantatus sive Animadversiones in Libellum Famosum Inscriptum*

de Anglicani Cleri Retinenda in Apostolicam Sedem Observantia (Rouen, 1660).
Wicquefort, A. van, *L'Ambassadeur et ses Fonctions* (The Hague, 1681).

LATER EDITIONS

Addy, J., J. Harrop and P. McNiven (eds), *The Diary of Henry Prescott, LL.B., Deputy Registrar of Chester Diocese*, 3 vols, Record Society of Lancashire and Cheshire, 127, 132, 133 (1987, 1994, 1997).

Beamont, W. (ed.), *The Jacobite Trials at Manchester in 1694*, Chetham Society, 1st Series, 28 (1853).

Berland, K., J. K. Gilliam and K. A. Lockridge (eds), *The Commonplace Book of William Byrd II of Westover* (London: University of North Carolina Press, 2001).

Blundell, M. (ed.), *Cavalier: Letters of William Blundell to his Friends, 1620–1698* (London: Longman & Co., 1933).

Burnet, G., *Bishop Burnet's History of his own Time* (London: Henry G. Bohn, 1850).

Cobbett, W. (ed.), *Parliamentary History of England from the Norman Conquest in 1066 to the Year 1803*, 36 vols (London: R. Bagshaw, 1806–20).

Cust, R. (ed.), *The Papers of Sir Richard Grosvenor, 1st Bart. (1585–1645)*, Record Society of Lancashire and Cheshire, 134 (1996).

Edwards, F. (ed.), *The Elizabethan Jesuits:* Historia Missionis Anglicanae Societatis Jesu *(1660) of Henry More* (London: Phillimore, 1981).

Everett Green, M. A. (ed.), *Calendar of the Proceedings of the Committee for Compounding, &c., 1643–1660*, 5 vols (London: HMSO, 1892).

Firth, C. H. and R. S. Rait (eds), *Acts and Ordinances of the Interregnum 1642–1660*, 3 vols (London: HMC, 1911).

Gibson, T. E. (ed.), *Crosby Records: A Cavalier's Note Book* (London: Longmans, Green & Co., 1880).

Gibson, T. E. (ed.), *Crosby Records: A Chapter of Lancashire Recusancy*, Chetham Society, New Series, 12 (1887).

Gilbert, J. T. (ed.), *History of the Irish Confederation and the War in Ireland, 1641–1643 Containing a Narrative of Affairs of Ireland ... by Richard Bellings* (Dublin, 1882–91).

Goss, A. (ed.), *II – The Trials at Manchester in 1694*, Chetham Society, 1st Series, 61 (1864).

Harrison, W. (ed.), *A History of the Isle of Man. Written by William Blundell, Esq. of Crosby, Co. Lancaster 1648–1656*, 2 vols, Publications of the Manx Society, 25, 27 (1876, 1877).

Historical Manuscripts Commission, *The Manuscripts of Lord Kenyon*, HMC 14th Report, Appendix Part IV (London: HMC, 1894).

Lamont, W. (ed.), *Richard Baxter: A Holy Commonwealth* (Cambridge: Cambridge University Press, 1994).

Latham, R. and W. Matthews (eds), *The Diary of Samuel Pepy*, 11 vols (London: Harper Collins Publishers, 2000).

SECONDARY SOURCES

Albers, J., 'Seeds of Contention: Society, Politics and the Church of England in Lancashire, 1689–1790' (DPhil thesis, Yale University, 1988).

Atherton, I., 'The itch grown a disease: manuscript transmission of news in the seventeenth century', in J. Raymond (ed.), *News, Newspapers and Society in Early Modern Britain* (London: Frank Cass, 1999), pp. 39–65.

Aveling, H., 'The Catholic recusants of the West Riding of Yorkshire 1558–1790', *Proceedings of the Leeds Philosophical and Literary Society*, 10 (1963), pp. 191–306.

Aveling, H., 'The marriages of Catholic recusants, 1559–1642', *Journal of Ecclesiastical History*, 14 (1963), pp. 68–83.

Aveling, H., *Northern Catholics: The Catholic Recusants of the North Riding of Yorkshire 1558–1790* (London: Geoffrey Chapman, 1966).

Aveling, J. C. H., *Catholic Recusancy in the City of York 1558–1791*, Catholic Record Society Monograph Series, 2 (London: Catholic Record Society, 1970).

Aveling, J. C. H., *The Handle and the Axe: The Catholic Recusants in England from Reformation to Emancipation* (London: Blond and Briggs, 1976).

Baker, G., 'The Political and Cultural Worlds of William Blundell (1620–1698), A Seventeenth-Century English Catholic Gentleman' (PhD Thesis, Keele University, 2007).

Baker, G., 'William Blundell and late seventeenth century English Catholicism', *Northern History*, 45 (2008), pp. 259–77.

Baker, G., 'An unpublished account of an English Catholic's tour to Edinburgh in 1657', *Scottish Historical Review* (Forthcoming).

Barclay, A., 'The rise of Edward Colman', *Historical Journal*, 42 (1999), pp. 109–31.

Barclay, A., 'James II's "Catholic" Court', *1650–1850 Ideas, Aesthetics, and Inquiries in the Early Modern Period*, 8 (2003), pp. 161–71.

Barnard, T. C., 'Crises of identity among Irish Protestants 1641–1685', *Past and Present*, 127 (1990), pp. 39–83.

Barnard, T. C., 'The uses of 23 October 1641 and Irish Protestant celebrations', *English Historical Review*, 106 (1991), pp. 889–920.

Barry, J., 'Literacy and literature in popular culture: reading and writing in historical perspective', in T. Harris (ed.), *Popular Culture in England, c.1500–1800* (London: Macmillan, 1995), pp. 69–94.

Beal, P., 'Shall I die?', *Times Literary Supplement* (3 January 1986), p. 13.

Beal, P., 'Notions in garrison: the seventeenth-century commonplace book', in W. Speed Hill (ed.), *New Ways of Looking at Old Texts: Papers of the Renaissance English Text Society, 1985–1991* (New York: Renaissance English Text Society, 1993), pp. 131–47.

Beales, A. C. F., *Education Under Penalty: English Catholic Education from the Reformation to the Fall of James II* (London: Athlone Press, 1963).

Bennett, M., 'Roman Catholic Royalist officers in the north midlands, 1642–1646', *Journal of Military and Strategic Studies*, 6 (2003), pp. 1–15.

Blackwood, B. G., 'The Lancashire cavaliers and their tenants', *Transactions of the Historic Society of Lancashire and Cheshire*, 117 (1965), pp. 17–32.

Blackwood, B. G., *The Lancashire Gentry and the Great Rebellion, 1640–60*, Chetham Society, 3rd Series, 25 (1978).

Blair, A., 'Humanist methods in natural philosophy: the commonplace book', *Journal of the History of Ideas*, 53 (1992), pp. 541–51.

Blair, A., 'Reading strategies for coping with information overload ca.1550–1700', *Journal of the History of Ideas*, 64 (2003), pp. 11–28.

Blair, A., 'Note taking as an art of transmission', *Critical Inquiry*, 31 (2004), pp. 85–107.

Blair, A. and A. Grafton, 'Reassessing humanism and science', *Journal of the History of Ideas*, 53 (1992), pp. 535–40.

Bossy, J., 'The English Catholic community 1603–1625', in A. G. R. Smith (ed.), *The Reign of James VI and I* (London: Macmillan, 1973), pp. 369–87.

Bossy, J., *The English Catholic Community, 1570–1850* (London: Darton, Longman and Todd, 1975).

Bossy, J., 'English Catholics after 1688', in O. P. Grell, J. I. Israel and N. Tyacke (eds), *From Persecution to Toleration: The Glorious Revolution and Religion in England* (Oxford: Clarendon, 1991), pp. 369–87.

Bowden, C. M. K., 'The Abbess and Mrs. Brown: Lady Mary Knatchbull and Royalist politics in Flanders in the late 1650s', *Recusant History*, 24 (1998), pp. 288–308.

Brayman Hackel, H., *Reading Material in Early Modern England: Print, Gender, and Literacy* (Cambridge: Cambridge University Press, 2005).

Burke, V. E., 'Ann Bowyer's commonplace book (Bodleian Library Ashmole MS 51): reading and writing among the "middling sort"', *Early Modern Literary Studies*, 6.3 (2001), 1.1–28.

Caine, P. W., 'William Blundell and his Manx history', *Isle of Man Natural History and Antiquarian Society Proceedings*, New Series, 5 (1946–1950), pp. 128–35.

Callow, J., 'The last of the Shireburnes: the art of death and life in recusant Lancashire, 1660–1754', *Recusant History*, 26 (2003), pp. 589–615.

Cerdeira, C., 'Early modern English medical wills, book ownership, and book culture', *Canadian Bulletin of Medical History*, 12 (1995), pp. 427–39.

Chartier, R., 'Leisure and sociability: reading aloud in early modern Europe', in S. Zimmerman and R. Weissman (eds), *Urban Life in the Renaissance* (London: Associated University Presses, 1989), pp. 103–20.

Clancy, T. H., 'A content analysis of English Catholic books, 1615–1714', *Catholic Historical Review*, 86 (2000), pp. 258–72.

Clark, P., 'The ownership of books in England, 1560–1640: the example of some Kentish townsfolk', in L. Stone (ed.), *Schooling and Society: Studies in the History of Education* (London: Johns Hopkins University Press, 1976), pp. 95–114.

Clifton, R., 'Fear of popery', in C. Russell (ed.), *The Origins of the English Civil War* (Basingstoke: Macmillan, 1973), pp. 144–67.

Collins, J. R., 'Thomas Hobbes and the Blackloist Conspiracy of 1649', *Historical Journal*, 45 (2002), pp. 305–31.

Coward, B., *The Stanleys Lords Stanley and Earl of Derby 1385–1672*, Chetham Society, 3rd Series, 30 (1983).

Cust, R., 'News and politics in early seventeenth-century England', *Past and Present*, 112 (1986), pp. 60–90.

Cust, R., 'Honour and politics in early Stuart England: the case of Beaumont v. Hastings', *Past and Present*, 149 (1995), pp. 57–94.

Cust, R., 'Catholicism, antiquarianism and gentry honour: the writings of Sir Thomas

Shirley', *Midland History*, 23 (1998), pp. 40–70.

Dacome, L., 'Noting the mind: commonplace books and the pursuit of the self in eighteenth-century Britain', *Journal of the History of Ideas*, 65 (2004), pp. 603–25.

Dolan, F. E., 'Ashes and "the archive": the London Fire of 1666, partisanship, and proof', *Journal of Medieval and Early Modern Studies*, 31 (2001), pp. 379–408.

Duffy, E., *The Stripping of the Altars: Traditional Religion in England 1400–1580* (London: Yale University Press, 1992).

Fincham, K. and P. Lake, 'The ecclesiastical policy of King James I', *Journal of British Studies*, 24 (1985), pp. 169–207.

Finkelstein, D. and A. McCleery, *An Introduction to Book History* (London: Routledge, 2005).

Foley, H., *Records of the English Province of the Society of Jesus: Historic Facts Illustrative of the Labours and Sufferings of its Members in the Sixteenth and Seventeenth Centuries*, 7 vols (London: Burns and Oates, 1883).

Forster, A. M., 'The Chronicles of the Poor Clares of Rouen – II', *Recusant History*, 18 (1986–87), pp. 149–91.

Fox, A., 'Remembering the past in early modern England: oral and written tradition', *Transactions of the Royal Historical Society*, 6th Series, 9 (1999), pp. 233–56.

Fox, A. and D. Woolf, 'Introduction', in A. Fox and D. Woolf (eds) *The Spoken Word: Oral Culture in Britain 1500–1850* (Manchester: Manchester University Press, 2002), pp. 1–51.

Galgano, M. J., 'Restoration Recusancy in the Northwest of England: A Social History, 1658–1673' (DPhil thesis, Vanderbilt University, 1971).

Ginzburg, C., *The Cheese and the Worms: The Cosmos of a Sixteenth-Century Miller*, trans. J. Tedeschi and A. Tedeschi (London: Penguin, 1992).

Glickman, G., 'John Caryll and the Context of English Catholic Jacobitism 1679–1712' (MPhil thesis, Cambridge University, 2002).

Glickman, G., 'Politics, Culture and Ideology in the English Catholic Community 1688–1727' (DPhil thesis, Cambridge University, 2006).

Gritt, A. J., 'Aspects of Agrarian Change in South-west Lancashire, c.1650–1850' (DPhil thesis, University of Central Lancashire, 2000).

Gritt, A. J., 'The operation of lifeleasehold in south-west Lancashire, 1649–97', *Agricultural History Review*, 53 (2005), pp. 1–23.

Guilday, P., *The English Catholic Refugees on the Continent 1558–1795* (London: Longmans, Green and Co., 1914).

Haigh, C., *Reformation and Resistance in Tudor Lancashire* (Cambridge: Cambridge University Press, 1975).

Haigh, C., 'The fall of a church or the rise of a sect? Post-Reformation Catholicism in England', *Historical Journal*, 21 (1978), pp. 181–6.

Haigh, C. (ed.), *The English Reformation Revised* (Cambridge: Cambridge University Press, 1987).

Haigh, C., *English Reformations: Religion, Politics, and Society Under the Stuarts* (Oxford: Clarendon Press, 1993).

Haigh, C., 'Catholicism in early modern England: Bossy and beyond', *Historical Journal*, 45 (2002), pp. 481–94.

Hawkes, A. J., *Sir Roger Bradshaigh of Haigh, Knight and Baronet 1628–1684 With Notes*

of his Immediate Forbears, Supplement to the *Transactions of the Lancashire and Cheshire Antiquarian Society* (Manchester: Lancashire and Cheshire Antiquarian Society, 1945).
Hibbard, C. M., 'Early Stuart Catholicism: revisions and re-revisions', *Journal of Modern History*, 52 (1980), pp. 1–34.
Hibbard, C., *Charles I and the Popish Plot* (Chapel Hill: University of North Carolina Press, 1983).
Hobson, A., '"The King's most loyal subjects": the relationship between Anglican loyalists and Roman Catholics in the reign of Charles II', *Royal Stuart Review* (1996), pp. 6–15.
Hopkins, P. A., 'The commission for superstitious lands of the 1690s', *Recusant History*, 15 (1980), pp. 265–82.
Hopkins, P. A., 'Aspects of Jacobite Conspiracy in England in the Reign of William III' (PhD thesis, Cambridge University, 1981).
Hopkins, P., 'Sham plots and real plots in the 1690s', in E. Cruickshanks (ed.), *Ideology and Conspiracy: Aspects of Jacobitism, 1689–1759* (Edinburgh: Donald, 1982), pp. 89–110.
Hopper, A. J., '"The popish army of the north": anti-Catholicism and Parliamentarian allegiance in Civil War Yorkshire, 1642–46', *Recusant History*, 25 (2000), pp. 12–28.
Hughes, A., *Gangraena and the Struggle for the English Revolution* (Oxford: Oxford University Press, 2004).
Israel, J., 'William III and toleration', in O. P. Grell, J. I. Israel and N. Tyacke (eds), *From Persecution to Toleration: The Glorious Revolution and Religion in England* (Oxford: Clarendon Press, 1991), pp. 129–70.
Jardine, L. and A. Grafton, '"Studied for action": how Gabriel Harvey read his Livy', *Past and Present*, 129 (1990), pp. 30–78.
Katz, D. S., *God's Last Words: Reading the English Bible from Reformation to Fundamentalism* (London: Yale University Press, 2004).
Kaushik, S., 'Resistance, loyalty and recusant politics: Sir Thomas Tresham and the Elizabethan state', *Midland History*, 21 (1996), pp. 37–72.
Keeble, N. H., *The Literary Culture of Nonconformity in Later Seventeenth-Century England* (Athens: University of Georgia Press, 1987).
Keeble, N. H., *The Restoration: England in the 1660s* (Oxford: Blackwell, 2002).
Kenny, N., 'Books in space and time: bibliomania and early modern histories of learning and "literature" in France', *MLQ: Modern Language Quarterly*, 61 (2000), pp. 253–86.
Kenyon, J., *The Popish Plot* (London: Phoenix Press, 2000).
Lake, P., 'Anti-popery: the structure of a prejudice', in R. Cust and A. Hughes (eds), *Conflict in Early Stuart England: Studies in Religion and Politics 1603–1642* (Harlow: Longman, 1989), pp. 72–106.
Lake, P. and M. Questier, 'Prisons, priests and people', in N. Tyacke (ed.), *England's Long Reformation 1500–1800* (London: UCL Press, 2000), pp. 195–233.
Lake, P. with M. C. Questier, *The Anti-Christ's Lewd Hat: Protestants, Papists and Players in Post-Reformation England* (London: Yale University Press, 2002).
Larminie, V., *Wealth, Kinship and Culture: The Seventeenth Century Newdigates of Arbury and their World*, Royal Historical Society Studies in History, 72 (Woodbridge: Boydell, 1995).

Lindley, K. J., 'The lay Catholics of England in the reign of Charles I', *Journal of Ecclesiastical History*, 22 (1971), pp. 199–221.

Lindley, K. J., 'The part played by the Catholics', in B. Manning (ed.), *Politics, Religion and the English Civil War* (London: Arnold, 1973), pp. 126–76.

Lockridge, K., 'Individual literacy in commonplace books', *Interchange*, 34 (2003), pp. 337–40.

Lonsdale, E. L., 'John Lunt and the Lancashire Plot, 1694', *Transactions of the Historic Society of Lancashire and Cheshire*, 115 (1964), pp. 91–106.

Loomie, A. J., 'Oliver Cromwell's policy toward the English Catholics: the appraisal by diplomats, 1654–1658', *Catholic Historical Review*, 90 (2004), pp. 29–44.

Love, H., *Scribal Publication in Seventeenth-Century England* (Oxford: Clarendon Press, 1993).

Love, H., *English Clandestine Satire 1660–1702* (Oxford: Oxford University Press, 2004).

McCoog, T. M., 'Richard Langhorne and the Popish Plot', *Recusant History*, 19 (1988), pp. 499–508.

Mack, P., *Elizabethan Rhetoric: Theory and Practice* (Cambridge: Cambridge University Press, 2002).

Miller, J., *Popery and Politics in England, 1660–1688* (Cambridge: Cambridge University Press, 1973).

Miller, J., 'The correspondence of Edward Coleman, 1674–78', *Recusant History*, 14 (1977), pp. 261–75.

Miller, J., *James II: A Study in Kingship* (London: Methuen, 1989).

Milton, A., *Catholic and Reformed: The Roman and Protestant Churches in English Protestant Thought, 1600–1640* (Cambridge: Cambridge University Press, 1995).

Milton, A., 'A qualified intolerance: the limits and ambiguities of early Stuart anti-Catholicism', in A. F. Marotti (ed.), *Catholicism and Anti-Catholicism in Early Modern English Texts* (Basingstoke: Macmillan, 1999), pp. 85–115.

Monod, P. K., *Jacobitism and the English People, 1688–1788* (Cambridge: Cambridge University Press, 1993).

Moss, A., *Printed Commonplace Books and the Structuring of Renaissance Thought* (Oxford: Clarendon Press, 1996).

Moss, A., 'The *Politica* of Justus Lipsius and the commonplace-book'. *Journal of the History of Ideas*, 59 (1998), pp. 421–36.

Mullett, M., '"A recepticle for papists and an assilum": Catholicism and disorder in late seventeenth-century Wigan', *Catholic Historical Review*, 73 (1987), pp. 391–407.

Newman, P. R., 'Catholic Royalist activists in the north, 1642–46', *Recusant History*, 14 (1977), pp. 26–38.

Newman, P. R., 'Catholic Royalists of northern England 1642–1645', *Northern History*, 15 (1979), pp. 88–95.

Newman, P. R., *Old Service: Royalist Regimental Colonels and the Civil War, 1642–1646* (Manchester: Manchester University Press, 1993).

Porteus, T. C., 'New light on the Lancashire Jacobite Plot, 1692–4', *Transactions of the Lancashire and Cheshire Antiquarian Society*, 50 (1934–35), pp. 1–64.

Questier, M. C., 'Clerical recruitment, conversion and Rome c.1580–1625', in C. Cross (ed.), *Patronage and Recruitment in the Tudor and Early Stuart Church* (York: Borthwick Institute of Historical Research, 1996), pp. 76–94.

Questier, M. C., 'Crypto-Catholicism, anti-Calvinism and conversion at the Jacobean court: the enigma of Benjamin Carier', *Journal of Ecclesiastical History*, 47 (1996), pp. 45–64.

Questier, M. C., *Conversion, Politics and Religion in England, 1580–1625* (Cambridge: Cambridge University Press, 1996).

Questier, M. C., 'Loyalty, religion and state power in early modern England: English Romanism and the Jacobean Oath of Allegiance', *Historical Journal*, 40 (1997), pp. 311–29.

Questier, M. C., 'Conformity, Catholicism and the law', in P. Lake and M. C. Questier (eds), *Conformity and Orthodoxy in the English Church, c.1560–1660* (Woodbridge: Boydell, 2000), pp. 237–61.

Questier, M. C., 'What happened to English Catholicism after the English Reformation?', *History*, 85 (2000), pp. 28–47.

Questier, M. C., *Catholicism and Community in Early Modern England: Politics, Aristocratic Patronage and Religion, c.1550–1640* (Cambridge: Cambridge University Press, 2006).

Questier, M. C. and S. Healy, '"What's in a name?": A papist's perception of Puritanism and conformity in the early seventeenth century', in A. F. Marotti (ed.), *Catholicism and Anti-Catholicism in Early Modern English Texts* (Basingstoke: Macmillan, 1999), pp. 131–53.

Quintrell, B. W., 'The practice and problems of recusant disarming, 1585–1641', *Recusant History*, 17 (1985), pp. 208–22.

Rosamond, M., 'A Derbyshire family in the seventeenth century: the Eyres of Hassop and their forfeited estates', *Recusant History*, 8 (1965), pp. 12–77.

Rowlands, M. B. (ed.), *Catholics of Parish and Town 1558–1778*, Catholic Record Society Monograph Series, 6 (London: Catholic Record Society, 1999).

Scarisbrick, J. J., *The Reformation and the English People* (Oxford: Blackwell, 1984).

Scott, G., 'A Benedictine conspirator: Henry Joseph Johnston (c.1656–1723)', *Recusant History*, 20 (1994), pp. 58–74.

Scott, J., 'England's troubles: exhuming the Popish Plot', in T. Harris, P. Seaward and M. Goldie (eds), *The Politics of Religion in Restoration England* (Oxford: Basil Blackwell, 1990), pp. 108–27.

Seaver, P. S., *Wallington's World: A Puritan Artisan in Seventeenth-Century London* (Stanford: Stanford University Press, 1985).

Sena, M., 'William Blundell and the networks of Catholic dissent in Post-Reformation England', in A. Shepard and P. Withington (eds), *Communities in Early Modern England: Networks, Place, Rhetoric* (Manchester: Manchester University Press, 2000), pp. 54–75.

Shagan, E. H., 'Constructing discord: ideology, propaganda, and English responses to the Irish Rebellion of 1641', *Journal of British Studies*, 36 (1997), pp. 4–34.

Shagan, E. H., 'Introduction: English Catholic history in context', in E. H. Shagan (ed.), *Catholics and the 'Protestant Nation': Religious Politics and Identity in Early Modern England* (Manchester: Manchester University Press, 2005), pp. 1–21.

Sharpe, K., *Reading Revolutions: The Politics of Reading in Early Modern England* (London: Yale University Press, 2000).

Sharpe, K., 'Reading revelations: prophecy, hermeneutics and politics in early modern Britain', in K. Sharpe and S. N. Zwicker (eds), *Reading, Society and Politics in Early*

Modern England (Cambridge: Cambridge University Press, 2003), pp. 122–63.
Shell, A., *Catholicism, Controversy and the English Literary Imagination, 1558–1660* (Cambridge: Cambridge University Press, 1999).
Shell, A., '"Furor juvenilis": Post-Reformation English Catholicism and exemplary youthful behaviour', in E. H. Shagan (ed.), *Catholics and the 'Protestant Nation': Religious Politics and Identity in Early Modern England* (Manchester: Manchester University Press, 2005), pp. 186–206.
Shell, A., *Oral Culture and Catholicism in Early Modern England* (Cambridge: Cambridge University Press, 2008).
Smyth, J., '"Like amphibious animals": Irish Protestants, ancient Britons, 1691–1707', *Historical Journal*, 36 (1993), pp. 785–97.
Southgate, B., *'Covetous of Truth': The Life and Work of Thomas White, 1593–1676* (Dordrecht: Kluwer Academic Publishers, 1993).
Southgate, B., '"White's disciple": John Sergeant and Blackloism', *Recusant History*, 24 (1999), pp. 431–6.
Southgate, B., 'Blackloism and tradition: from theological uncertainty to historiographical doubt', *Journal of the History of Ideas*, 61 (2000), pp. 97–112.
Spurr, J., *The Restoration Church of England, 1646–1689* (London: Yale University Press, 1991).
Spurr, J., 'Religion in Restoration England', in L. K. J. Glassey (ed.), *The Reigns of Charles II and James VII & II, 1660–1689* (Basingstoke: Macmillan, 1997), pp. 90–124.
Szechi, D., 'Defending the true faith: Kirk, state, and Catholic missioners in Scotland, 1653–1755', *Catholic Historical Review*, 82 (1996), pp. 397–411.
Szechi, D., 'A blueprint for tyranny? Sir Edward Hales and the Catholic Jacobite response to the Revolution of 1688', *English Historical Review*, 116 (2001), pp. 342–67.
Thomas, M. W., 'Reading and writing the renaissance commonplace book: a question of authorship', *Cardozo Arts and Entertainment Journal*, 10 (1992), pp. 665–79.
Tyrer, F., 'An Account of the Recusancy of the Blundell of Crosby Family and the Inhabitants of the Township of Little Crosby in Lancashire', 3 vols (Unpublished work held at Lancashire County Record Office, 1955).
Walker, C., 'Prayer, patronage, and political conspiracy: English nuns and the Restoration', *Historical Journal*, 43 (2000), pp. 1–23.
Walker, C., *Gender and Politics in Early Modern Europe: English Converts in France and the Low Countries* (Basingstoke: Palgrave Macmillan, 2003).
Walsham, A., *Church Papists: Catholicism, Conformity and Confessional Polemic in Early Modern England* (Woodbridge: Boydell Press, 1999).
Walsham, A., *Providence in Early Modern England* (Oxford: Oxford University Press, 1999).
Walsham, A., '"Domme preachers?" Post-Reformation English Catholicism and the culture of print', *Past and Present*, 168 (2000), pp. 72–123.
Walsham, A., 'Miracles and the Counter-Reformation mission to England', *Historical Journal*, 46 (2003), pp. 779–815.
Walsham, A., 'Miracles in post-Reformation England', in K. Cooper and J. Gregory (eds), *Signs, Wonders, Miracles: Representations of Divine Power in the Life of the Church*, Studies in Church History, 41 (Woodbridge: Boydell and Brewer, 2005), pp. 273–306.

Weiser, B., 'Owning the King's story: the escape from Worcester', *Seventeenth Century*, 14 (1999), pp. 43–62.
Williams, J. A., 'English Catholicism under Charles II: the legal position', *Recusant History*, 7 (1963), pp. 123–43.
Williams, J. A., 'Sources for recusant history (1559–1791) in English official archives', *Recusant History*, 16 (1983), pp. 331–443.
Woolf, D. R., 'Little Crosby and the horizons of early modern historical culture', in D. R. Kelley and D. Harris Sacks (eds), *The Historical Imagination in Early Modern Britain: History, Rhetoric, and Fiction, 1500–1800* (Cambridge: Cambridge University Press, 1997), pp. 93–132.
Woolf, D. R., *Reading History in Early Modern England* (Cambridge: Cambridge University Press, 2000).
Woolf, D., *The Social Circulation of the Past: English Historical Culture 1500–1730* (Oxford: Oxford University Press, 2003).
Wormald, J., 'Gunpowder, treason and Scots', *Journal of British Studies*, 24 (1985), pp. 141–68.
Wright, A. D., 'Catholic history, north and south', *Northern History*, 14 (1978), pp. 126–51.
Yeo, R., 'Managing knowledge in early modern Europe: essay review of Peter Burke, *A Social History of Knowledge: Gutenberg to Diderot*', *Minerva*, 40 (2002), pp. 301–14.
Yeo, R., 'A solution to the multitude of books: Ephraim Chambers's *Cyclopedia* (1728) as "the best book in the universe"', *Journal of the History of Ideas*, 64 (2003), pp. 61–72.
Yeo, R., 'John Locke's "new method" of commonplacing: managing memory and information', *Eighteenth-Century Thought*, 2 (2004), pp. 1–38.
Zwicker, S., 'The reader revealed', in S. Baron (ed.), *The Reader Revealed* (London: University of Washington Press, 2001), pp. 11–17.

Index

Literary works can be found under authors' names.

CPSIA information can be obtained at www.ICGtesting.com
Printed in the USA
BVOW06s0005010715

406879BV00006B/34/P